Women, the arts and globalization

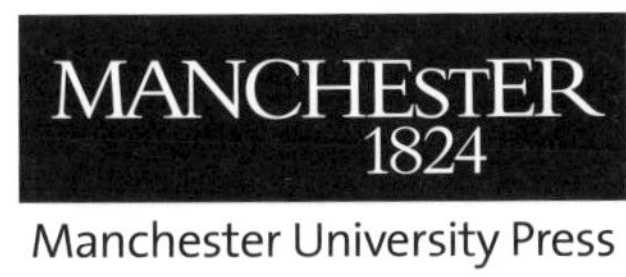

Manchester University Press

rethinking
art's histories

SERIES EDITORS
Amelia G. Jones, Marsha Meskimmon

Rethinking Art's Histories aims to open out art history from its most basic structures by foregrounding work that challenges the conventional periodisation and geographical subfields of traditional art history, and addressing a wide range of visual cultural forms from the early modern period to the present.

These books will acknowledge the impact of recent scholarship on our understanding of the complex temporalities and cartographies that have emerged through centuries of world-wide trade, political colonisation and the diasporic movement of people and ideas across national and continental borders.

Also available in the series

Art, museums and touch Fiona Candlin

The 'do-it-yourself' artwork: Participation from fluxus to relational aesthetics Anna Dezeuze (ed.)

After the event: New perspectives in art history
Charles Merewether and John Potts (eds)

Vertiginous mirrors: The animation of the visual image and early modern travel Rose Marie San Juan

Screen/space: The projected image in contemporary art Tamara Trodd (ed.)

Timed out: Art and the transnational Caribbean Leon Wainwright

Women, the arts and globalization

Eccentric experience

Edited by
Marsha Meskimmon and Dorothy Rowe

Manchester University Press

Manchester and New York
distributed in the United States exclusively by Palgrave Macmillan

Published by Manchester University Press
Oxford Road, Manchester M13 9NR, UK
and Room 400, 175 Fifth Avenue, New York, NY 10010, USA
www.manchesteruniversitypress.co.uk

Distributed in the United States exclusively by
Palgrave Macmillan, 175 Fifth Avenue, New York,
NY 10010, USA

Distributed in Canada exclusively by
UBC Press, University of British Columbia, 2029 West Mall,
Vancouver, BC, Canada V6T 1Z2

British Library Cataloguing-in-Publication Data
A catalogue record for this book is available from the British Library

Library of Congress Cataloging-in-Publication Data applied for

ISBN 978 0 7190 8875 9 *hardback*

First published 2013

Typeset in Minion with Myriad display by
Koinonia, Manchester
Printed in Great Britain by
TJ International Ltd, Padstow

Contents

List of illustrations

The authors and editors have made every possible attempt to obtain copyright permissions for all of the images included in this book. If for any reason there has been an oversight or omission please accept our apologies and contact the publisher.

For Davy (b. 2006) and Jasmine (b. 2011),
with whom this journey opened and closed,
as they begin their own adventures.

Editorial introduction: Ec/centric affinities: locations, aesthetics, experiences

Marsha Meskimmon and Dorothy Rowe

Contemporary art is embedded within the very structures that characterize globalization – from the transnational circulation of artworks as commodities to the cross-cultural exchange of images, objects and ideas. Contemporary artists traverse the same routes as empowered, metropolitan elites and the economic migrants left in their wake, and, arguably, the territories described by these global circuits are always already gendered. The specificity of women's encounters with globalization thus tend to be marginalized, or subsumed within, masculine-normative accounts in the literature.[1]

Attending to women's particular engagements with globalization is to explore their *ec/centric experiences* as a means by which to survey the dynamics of transnational migration, circulation and exchange from *beyond the centre* – from the edges and borders – of mainstream narratives. Such attention involves disarticulating eccentricity from its negative associations with deviation and abnormality and understanding it instead as a term that implies both 'not agreeing' and relating to something 'that has its axis, its point of support … otherwise than centrally placed'.[2]

As the present collection of writings demonstrates, contemporary women's art practices provide one such angled view of the myriad effects of globalization on visual and material culture at the locus of situated, sexed subjectivity. This angled, sometimes edgy, viewpoint does not posit an artificial 'outside' to globalization, but rather enables embodied and embedded subjects to articulate their specificity in and through resonant, *eccentric affinities*, even within structures that ordinarily favour homogeneity. Emphasizing both the angled, 'ec-centric', position of women within globalization and the connections that can be drawn between them (their 'affinities') is a consistent strategy within this anthology. Affinities concern likeness, attraction and communities of interest or sympathy; there is, in affinity, no absolute resolution of difference, reduction to consonance or to 'the same', but rather there is an acknowledgement of the importance – politically, intellectually and creatively – of connection and dialogue. The positions this book explores are multivalent, multilayered and multifaceted, but their edges and angles can coincide and connect, rather than repel, as they engage us in the worlds they make.

Focusing on the idea of eccentric affinities, the present volume takes *location* seriously, underestimating its importance neither in the mutual constitution of places and subjects, nor in the articulation of complex and multifaceted identities. Significantly, the chapters that make up this anthology never assume location to be singular and, in very different ways, each demonstrates the intellectual and creative potential offered by engaging with multiple *locations* – conceptual, methodological and, of course, geopolitical.

Operating within highly contested academic and political terrain, *Women, the Arts and Globalization: Eccentric Experience* treads its conceptual location carefully. There are various terms deployed within the chapters of this volume that seek to describe the complex encounters between women, the arts and the processes of globalization that each explores. The volume as whole, therefore, neither eschews difficult terms such as *postcolonial*, *diasporic*, *migratory*, *transnational*, *transcultural* and *globalization*, nor does it merely accede to simplistic or over-determined readings that assume these terms to be *a priori* categories of meaning. Instead, each chapter mobilizes its terms within the frame of its own specific encounter; the volume as a whole thus acts as a *conversational location*, where meanings are in process and dialogic, rather than fixed and determinate. The eccentric frame of the volume enables the terms to suggest a charged middle-ground, an intersectional 'in-between' occupied by women and the arts, that signifies difference, the occluded other and the space of identities performed in and through repetition, reiteration and revision.

The significance of movement and mutable meanings-in-process to both postcolonial and feminist theory marks one of the key eccentric affinities of this anthology. Many of the locational terms that are significant within the chapters in the collection are associated with literal and figurative border-crossings, not least 'transnational' and 'diasporic'. In electing to use these terms here, we acknowledge their mobility or, as Deborah Cherry so aptly argues with regard to the term 'diasporic' in her chapter in this volume, that it is a travelling concept; it travels 'across disciplines, times and cultures'. Etymologically derived from *dia* (through) and *speirein* (to sow or scatter), the term has most frequently been associated with the movement, displacement and resettling of Jewish people from Israel. Yet, as Nicholas Mirzoeff noted, the emphasis on the diasporic in the writings of a wide range of cultural commentators from the 1990s onwards led to a reconsideration of the boundaries, definitions and uses of the term as applied to other global cultures within the context of postcolonial criticism and theory.[3]

Significantly, focusing on conceptual mobility emphasizes the processes that constitute migratory agency, rather than positing a definition of migration or diasporas *per se*. This dialogic approach opens this volume to the ebbs and flows of globalization, itself understood less as a fixed entity and more as multilayered and multivalent processes of circulation and exchange. As Arjun Appadurai has observed, 'in the postnational world ... diaspora runs with and not against, the grain of identity, movement and reproduction'.[4] The concepts of mobility and transience underpinning *Women, the Arts and Globalization*, are particularly appropriate to describe the fluidity of contemporary social and cultural life in the West. Thus, we would agree that transnational and cross-cultural encounters between different exiles, migrants and diasporas characterize the contemporary world in which former binaries of centre and periphery have been replaced 'by a global pattern of flows and resistances' and the significance of eccentric experience.[5]

Exploring these processes of circulation and exchange bring the *macro* into vital connection with the *micro*: global activities impact at the level of the local; the personal is political. For feminists, this is hardly a novel insight, but interrogating eccentric, migratory identities and the experience of globalization in light of feminist theory refocuses our attention onto the dynamic encounter between the 'personal' and the 'political' where subjects are marked by multiple differences. There is a vital connection between politics and aesthetics in the work brought together by this volume. It is clear that women artists and scholars concerned with interrogating the significance of gender and sexual difference in the geopolitical contexts of globalization are not afraid to make explicit their political and ethical imperatives. One of the more marked 'eccentric affinities' within *Women, the Arts and Globalization* is, in fact, the question of the legacy of feminist activist and socially committed practice. Far from declaring this a 'post-feminist' age, the work in this anthology reaffirms the importance of the arts to the production of gendered cultural identity and civil society – to the formation of global citizenship through justice and equality that can recognize difference.

Articulating the distinctive and located subject positions that women occupy as global citizens, denizens or migrants, the works explored in this anthology remind us that intersectional agency emerges through the productive interaction between individuals and society – through the micro- and macro-encounters of intersubjectivity. This, in turn, commits us to engaging with processes of subjectification that are effected in and through making art: rather than assuming that art *represents* subjects or *expresses* identity, we are concerned with women's art practices as a location through which subjects-in-process make and re-make the world.

The epistemological challenges of feminist theory – specifically, the proposition that all knowledge is produced from a perspective and is *located*, and, more powerfully, that 'knowledges are practices' – led to a number of critical editing decisions concerning the disciplinary and methodological framework of *Women, the Arts and Globalization*.[6] We are aware that as editors we are implicated within the very arguments concerning discipline and method that this volume raises in its varied explorations of women's art and globalization. That is, we are as involved in the making of the connected, global futures we envisage as the authors of the chapters of this volume whose work has challenged, engaged and moved us.

One critical decision was to encourage the inclusion of very different *kinds* of texts within the anthology, rather than to homogenize them with simplistic editorial mechanisms, such as a specified word length or 'house style'. We have sought to enable a multilayered textu(r)ality, or polyphonic conversation, to be located within the volume as a whole, by enabling auto/biography and distinctive 'disciplinary' voices to emerge. Hence, the work indebted to social science or political theory reads differently from the work more aligned with art theory and interpretation; some chapters take a dialogic, interview form, countering a singular authorial/narrative voice, whilst others use a micro-level mode of 'close reading' to demonstrate the power of particular works of art to provide new understandings of transnational and transcultural, gendered aesthetics. We would argue that coherence is not homogeneity; the selected texts speak to our theme not because of a forced unity of content, form or perspective but because of an absolute commitment to acknowledge the *location* of the writing – in or through a personal examination of migration, gender and identity, in or through a practical, affective engagement with art and, as we discuss at greater length later in this introduction, in or through the UK as a primary nexus in the global economy.

The book's structure is not strictly conventional, in art historical terms, but it is a rigorous rethinking of some of the territories most associated with art's histories, theories and practices. No longer a discipline confined to the realms of self-referential iconographic interpretation and fine-art connoisseurship, contemporary art history has been enriched by the possibilities of cultural, aesthetic, social and ethical interpretations of works of art enabled by recognizing affinities with other disciplines and engaging their methodological tools and perspectives to new ends. As editors we have deliberately maintained the diversity of our contributors' approaches to, conversations with, and interpretations or critiques of women's art practices, and these disciplinary crossings again implicate the volume in a critical encounter with *location*.

Academic research by humanities scholars and social scientists sits alongside practice-led research by artists and transcriptions of 'interviews' (conversations/dialogues) with practitioners that demonstrate how art is or becomes the substance of intellectual enquiry in its own right. Some texts argue for paradigm shifts in disciplines, fields or methodologies; others provide first-hand accounts of making art as a border-crossing activity that opens quite particular research questions in its material engagement with subjects and society. From a disciplinary perspective, then, *Women, the Arts and Globalization* is located at the interstices of conventional fields, ranging from social science, ethnography, political theory and public policy studies, to feminist critical theory, visual culture, cultural studies, art history and practice-led research in the arts. Yet, despite the deliberate inclusion of multivalent voices as appropriate to the heterogeneity of the subject matter, self-reflexive subjectivity and elements of auto/biography remain pertinent to all of the contributions. A shared concept of the contingency of subjective identities and how they impact on the possibilities for active agency and potential change within transnational and global contexts informs the 'eccentric' locations from which all of our contributors 'speak'.

Geographically, *Women, the Arts and Globalization* brings transnational feminist theory and criticism together with women's art practices in a discussion of the legacy and trajectory of aesthetics, gender and identity from a specifically anglo-global perspective. We are not alone in selecting a single geocultural focal point through which to concentrate a complex set of discussions on the phenomenon of globalization – and not alone in recognizing the significance of the Anglophone context within the macro-politics of transcultural exchange and circulation. For example, a specific focus on the UK as the perspective from which issues of the global and transnational might be reflected upon is one that has informed the work of leading cultural theorist Paul Gilroy since the late 1980s.[7] For Gilroy, and others such as Stuart Hall and Kobena Mercer, Britain's post-imperial reconfiguration since the end of Empire has offered peculiarly fertile ground for a micro-cosmic analysis of the effects of postcolonialism on the contested concept of the nation-state. Gilroy has consistently analysed the contribution that its diasporic subjects make to a renewed culture of conviviality in Britain, highlighting both the losses and gains required to balance the political demands of an effective multiculturalism against the forces of reactionary nationalism and entrenched conservatism.[8]

Mica Nava argued a similar case for the UK as a locus through which to explore what she called 'visceral cosmopolitanism', an embodied openness to difference and 'others' that belied the conservatism of British political responses to decolonization and immigration in the middle and late twentieth century.[9] Significantly, in her work, Nava countered the assumption that the most prominent effect of mass immigration on British culture was negative – the rise of racist nationalism and conservative, exclusionary immigration policies. Rather, she looked to the cultural sphere and to local exchanges between specific groups of people throughout the country, and found overwhelming evidence that an equally significant impact had been the establishment of a positive and lasting legacy of cross-cultural exchange.

The work discussed briefly above enables us to posit two key elements of our argument here – that the UK's *centrality* (its 'centricity') within the processes and structures that commonly define globalization is both an awkward legacy of the disintegration of the British Empire *and* a fascinating location from which to interrogate the parameters of the concept itself. Hence, our attention in this volume to the complex articulation of sexual difference within the sphere of the 'anglo-global' enables an important, and *doubly eccentric*, counter-argument to be made against the prevailing idea that globalization must necessarily homogenize experience. The generic geopolitics of the transnational corporate complex cannot wholly colonize culture, annex the arts or stifle subtly inflected identities. The UK location from which women's eccentric experiences are self-consciously constructed in and through art practices thus offers a particular perspective on a much larger kaleidoscope of global possibilities for the futures of women's diasporic, migratory and transnational art practices.

If location is pivotal to understanding how embodied subjects navigate the complex terrain of transnational geographies and the transcultural generation of meaning, it is equally significant in reconceiving contemporary aesthetics. Art's role as a pivot or springboard for critical explorations of political, social and ethical ideas has a long history within Western cultural tradition and discourse. The expanding field of migratory aesthetics and transnational art sees art at the forefront of debates concerning transnational identities and the social effects of globalization on the construction of identities and identifications of both the individual and the nation. Clearly, homogeneous definitions of migratory aesthetics are deliberately eschewed here in favour of exposing the multiple voices and diverse methodologies more apt to the varieties of contemporary art practices and cultural debates that concern us.

In keeping with those perspectives, our use of the notion of aesthetics moves beyond the confines of the 'philosophy of art' to engage the challenges offered by knowledges produced through our embodied encounters with/in the world. The chapters in this anthology demonstrate a clear commitment to acknowledging the significance of embodiment to feminist art practices and politics, and are also noteworthy for their emphasis upon the body and a concept of *experience*. In this emphasis, however, they are neither naïve nor essentialist; the call to the body does not reinforce a dualism that would equate woman with body and remove the possibility of subjecthood, nor does the evocation of experience suggest an uncritical assumption of the truth or transparency of 'biography'.

Quite the contrary. In turning toward corporeality and embodiment, we understand 'the body' to be a crucial social fiction, one that precedes individual subjects and constitutes them even as their continual reiteration of an 'identity' redefines its contours. In tandem with this, our experiences of the world are always situated and partial as well as affective. In this volume, we do not assume that knowledges are, or even can be, disembodied or formed without the residues of affective experience; rather, we move toward what has been called an 'affective turn',[10] explicitly not a discourse of personal 'feeling', but a way of accounting for art's ability to act politically or, arguably, have agency.

This is an understanding of art as an active constituent of meaning production, rather than a mute 'mirror' onto the world. Following this logic, the texts and images that make up *Women, the Arts and Globalization* are focused on the ways in which art constructs locations, articulates subjects and engenders critical thought in participant-spectators, not how it 'represents' a pre-given 'real'. We would argue that the work within the present volume demonstrates the active role that the arts play in the formation of complex subject-positions that move across and within conventional cultural and geopolitical boundaries to make possible a range of 'diasporic futures'.[11]

The realm of possibility is intrinsically linked to imagination and, in that link, tends to be viewed pejoratively as impotent fiction in terms of its political or ethical efficacy. What is the point of discussing women's art when women's economic and social exclusion in a globalized world demands our attention and action? We would argue that there is every reason to explore the locations that enable us to imagine the world otherwise, make possible the futures that we need to bring to bear on a world marked by social injustice and inequity, precisely because the status quo is not sufficient to the task. Engaging the powerful 'fictions' through which subjects are interpellated and conceptual structures such as 'the nation', citizenship, justice and equity are determined is not a disengaged or politically ineffective activity. Critical thought and agency for change are effected first at the level of the subject who is moved to respond; the micro-economies of affect are a necessary corollary to the macro-economies of political change.

The chapters

Mobility, difference and the possibilities for transformation characterize the premises of the chapters collected together in this volume. There is a deliberate editorial resistance to homogeneity in the diversity of the voices collected, and a number of very different approaches to the politics of representation in the individual contributions. Whilst many chapters demonstrate how the artists discussed continue to regard their work as engaging with the important political projects begun in the 1980s and 1990s to make visible and celebrate otherwise ignored aspects of women's lives, others privilege a more open-ended and affective form of politics in their work in which participatory practices inform their mode of address and interaction with the viewer.

In the opening chapter, Angela Dimitrakaki asks how feminist art history can contribute to the making of feminism relevant to present social conditions produced as a result of globalization, and how it can contribute to the transformation of these conditions. Globalization is understood here as a particular phase in the development of capitalism, a series of expansive imperial projects whereby capitalist relations of production and the demands of the market economy achieve planetary domination. Globalization is conceived as 'the management of heterogeneity for profit' and, because it is defined by flows of people linked to some aspect of the economy, the author suggests that globalization upsets former paradigms of diaspora and notions of identity. For Dimitrakaki, the negative aspects of globalized experience for women are the mass experiences of economic oppression that result in new forms of female sexualized labour, and readers are reminded that the mobility and transnational aspects of migration undoubtedly enjoyed by the economically enfranchized are also the cause for the re-emergence of the signifying power of the female prostitute in the new millennium – the subject of much contemporary video art. Citing the work of Michael Hardt and Antonio Negri, Dimitrakaki suggests that 'global citizenship' should be the 'first political demand' of the multitude since it would transform the lives of millions of women worldwide on an even greater scale than the right to vote did within national contexts during the twentieth century. She observes that the conditions of transnationalism currently in bed with global capitalism need to be disarticulated by the multitude in a politics of resistance with strategies learned from feminism. By highlighting the emergence of a body of work by contemporary artists who take transnational migration and prostitution as their predominant subject matter, the chapter also concerns itself with the future of feminist art history as a politically relevant discipline.

Continuing an investigation of the effects of globalization on migrant female workers, Maggie O'Neill explores the 'visual turn' in the social sciences. She considers the possibilities for a new sociology of art and reports on the results of how arts-based research can impact on the lives of new migrants arriving in the UK and potentially change social and cultural policies and praxis. O'Neill considers specific case studies illuminating on a micro-level some of the more broadly conceived ambitions set out by Dimitrakaki in chapter one. The transformative role of art and the methodological approaches selected for working with particular artists in order to conduct ethnographic research with refugees and asylum seekers are considered in this chapter. Tellingly, O'Neill stresses three major themes to have emerged from the empirical work: 'first, the importance of stories and storytelling, biography and narrative; second, the importance of re-presenting life stories in visual/artistic form; third, the importance of working with people as subjects through participatory methodologies'. What is of particular interest here, and is something that emerges from all of the contributions to the book, are the ways in which specifically personal experiences tend to inflect academic discourses of migratory experience such that they differ from many other modes of scholarly enquiry into the visual arts.

The third chapter develops this further in an edited dialogue ('interview') between art critic and curator Tracey Warr and artist Misha Myers, focused on Myers' use of a participatory method of engaged art-making to develop a mode of migratory aesthetics. Using what she eloquently describes as 'performative mapping', Myers invites groups of new settlers in the UK (refugees, asylum-seekers, economic migrants, expatriates) to wayfind through walking and talking, telling stories and navigating spaces, which brings the present locations they inhabit daily as migrants together with places they remember from the past in the countries they have left behind. These cartographic palimpsests are 'moving' in every sense – as Warr aptly says in her dialogue with Myers, they are 'fluid, expansive' and, we would add here, affective. Continuing this theme in their discussion, Myers makes two further points that reinforce the significance of an affective dimension within a practice-led methodology. First, she stresses that her fellow wayfinders are not 'participants' in the conventional sense of either spectators or community members associated with 'participatory' arts; rather, she distinguishes them through the term 'percipient', stressing their embodied, sensory knowledge and experience of the work in its making. Second, Myers is clear that conversation is critical to the practice. Her work is not complete before the conversations between all percipients take place, before their active engagement with the project performs the maps.

Women, the Arts and Globalization is as a whole indebted to the strong sense of conversation that such claims entail and our editorial decision to include a number of dialogues/interviews within the volume was a deliberate strategy designed to encourage readers to encounter the volume as a polyphonic conversation between multiple voices and ideas: a speaking-from (here *and* there) and a speaking-with (ourselves *and* others). This is not simply a matter of semantics. In addition to encouraging multidisciplinary methodologies to emerge with their own distinctive voices in the opening chapters, the volume's later chapters explore the tone and timbre of the 'close read' and the resonance of 'first-person' accounts, written individually or in dialogue. We would argue that considering the intersection between migratory aesthetics and sexed subjectivity produces a shift in perspective away from 'disembodied' critique toward the acknowledgement of intersubjectivity, situation and the dual play of response-ability and responsibility.[12] These are very different locations from which to articulate art's critical potential for women who work across political, cultural, religious and linguistic boundaries.

We underscore this insight throughout the anthology by including critical first-person accounts of practice-led interventions into the field (chapters three, four, five, nine and eleven). In chapter four, Lena Simic offers insights into the connections between institutional hierarchies and the work of women artists who, to use her tactical label, are 'Foreigners'. She does this by setting her own work, the *Magdalena Makeup* Live Art Event, unsentimentally within the cultural politics of UK arts funding policy and the academic art world. Arguing that the Arts Council's policies on 'diversity' have, in fact, informed the thinking that excludes and commodifies the artist/Foreigner as an interesting diversion within mainstream art institutions, Simic performs herself as Foreigner, as 'Magdalena Makeup', a migrant young woman from Dubrovnik, living in Liverpool, inviting audiences to see her as an eroticized commodity, crossing boundaries and causing disturbance. In a live art event, her two 'homes' (Dubrovnik and Liverpool) become destinations for 'Magdalena Makeup' postcards to be sent by audiences. In a performance resonant of Dimitrakaki's critique from chapter one, these ephemeral tokens – viewed, handled, posted or discarded – stand in for the exchangeable Eastern European woman migrant after the demise of the Communist bloc.

The fifth chapter is a dialogue between two academic feminist filmmakers concerned with the politics of diaspora. Focusing on Florence Ayisi's award-winning documentaries, Mo White raises important questions with Ayisi around the representation of African women in contemporary cinema. Drawing on her own status as a Cameroonian émigré coming into Britain, Ayisi is especially aware of the stereotyped understanding of gender roles and power relations as they are played out between the developed and the developing world. In works such as *Sisters in Law: Stories from a Cameroon Court* (2005) and *Zanzibar Soccer Queens* (2008), Ayisi's nuanced portraits of the lives of contemporary African women reject simplistic stereotypes and suggest that gender politics in a global world may not divide easily along the lines of nation-states, 'East' and 'West', or 'developed' and 'developing'. Significantly, Ayisi and White develop their dialogue around the complexity of materializing such sophisticated notions of identity through filmic form, rather than making any assumptions concerning film's ability to 'represent' underlying truths. In this way, their conversation reminds us of the affective economies of filmic mediation and the importance of our embodied and located encounters with cinema to the construction identity.

In chapter six, Marion Arnold further seeks to expand the boundaries of what scholarly considerations of the African diaspora might be, shifting the lens away from the Anglo-American transatlantic slave trade and/or the twentieth-century Jamaican Commonwealth 'Windrush' axis toward a consideration of internal migrations within the African continent itself and more specifically the visual culture of the southern African diaspora of contemporary women artists. In her alternate geography of the anglo-global, Arnold mobilizes the meaning of 'diaspora' from being one of 'forced dispersal' to being one of the intersection of individual and social circumstances, suggesting that choice (personal agency) and compulsion (imposed action) cannot be neatly separated in analyses of the reasons for general dispersal or relocation. She also considers what 'the diasporic condition' might mean, suggesting that it is both the experience and subsequent narration of processes of disruption, dispersal, relocation and adaptation to new experiences of place and domicile, shaped by individual and collective memory and current lived experiences. The diasporic condition is identified by Arnold as neither 'here' nor 'there' but in between, and is predicated on the search for a reconciliation of identities as inflected by past, present, ethnicity, gender, religion, language and generation. A particularly pertinent feature of this chapter is its collision of academic analysis and personal experience: a scholarly chapter framed by a visual narrative that is personal to the author/artist. As such it offers an interesting complement to the dialogic interviews between academics and artists within this volume.

Dialogue, transgression, de-territorialization, contingent subjectivity and self-reflexivity emerge as key strategies of diaspora aesthetics, combined in later chapters with a specific focus on the role of history, memory and postcolonial subjectivity from an anglo-global perspective. For instance, in chapter seven, Deborah Cherry offers a poignant analysis of diasporan aesthetics as mobilized in the art of Maud Sulter, arguing for an approach that moves from the sociological focus that characterizes many accounts of diasporic arts in Britain towards a focus on art as practice and its potential address to its audiences. For Cherry, like Arnold, diasporas are shown to co-exist, overlap and intersect globally, and diasporic art is characterized by a wide range of practices, forms and media. Diasporan aesthetics are also understood to be constantly in flux, shaped by local and global conditions and dialectic relations between art and audience. As she is an artist of Scots-Ghanian descent, Sulter's work references a wide range of cultural, geographic and historical sources: relationships between Europe and Africa, the slave trade and its legacies, histories of nationalism and colonialism, and the re-visibility and continued presence of black women in European culture.

Concerns of a similar though differently conceived nature also inflect Rosemary Betterton's consideration of the production, reception and controversy surrounding Marc Quinn's sculpture of *Alison Lapper Pregnant* unveiled to the public on the Fourth Plinth in the London's Trafalgar Square in September 2005. Betterton's chapter focuses specifically on the nature of Britishness in the contemporary era of globalization and government-led retrenchment of nationalist ideologies of 'belonging' that increasingly define difference as a threat. She foregrounds the symbolic status of Trafalgar Square as a site of tension between imperial narratives and the politics of dissent, and argues that *Alison Lapper Pregnant* acts as a lightning rod for competing claims by different national citizens to gendered, racialized and dis/abled selfhood. In a shift of emphasis from all of the other contributions in the volume, Betterton's chapter eschews a focus on migratory aesthetics addressing instead the possibilities of futures through the analysis of a specific spatialized politics (Trafalgar Square) and its transformation via Quinn's sculpture of a differently abled body of a pregnant woman and its mixed critical reception.

The focus on the historical construction of sexed subjectivity and diasporic identity continues throughout the ninth chapter, in which Jane Beckett interviews Lubaina Himid. Himid was a pioneer of the UK's Black Arts Movement in the 1980s and one of a number of women artists associated with it who were unflinching in their commitment to exploring the complex politics that reside at the nexus between 'race' and gender. Himid's installations interrogate the histories and practices of art that have fostered the exclusion of black women as subjects, whilst utilizing their bodies as objects. In this text, Beckett draws out the historical, aesthetic and ethical dimensions of Himid's work through her attentive conversation with the artist. Himid acknowledges that creating aesthetic dialogues between the past and the present, the personal and the political, are critical to her practice, as is her commitment to demonstrating the importance of the African diaspora to contemporary British culture. As Beckett says, Himid is 'visualising history' and in so doing she seeks to engage the viewer in an ethical response to history, asking us to acknowledge and thus bear the weight of the inequities of the past.

The focus on women's bodies at the heart of historical discourses of nationalism and politics is highlighted in Michele Waugh's consideration of Paula Rego's *Abortion Series* (1999) in chapter ten. As Waugh explains, Rego's position as a Portuguese artist living and working in the UK is key to an understanding of her work as a contribution to discourses of inter-cultural exchange. Waugh also observes that part of the affect of Rego's painting lies in part in its specific position of inter-culturalism, rather than in a depoliticized multiculturalism: Rego retains her distinct Portuguese roots within the context of her UK life and work and as such resists homogeneity in her practice. Rather, she uses her position in the UK to enable her to critique aspects of the treatment of women in her home country, where abortion remains a criminal offence and contraception is not permitted under the terms of national Catholicism. Although the *Abortion Series* is inspired by political events in Portugal it raises issues of women's right to choose on a global stage, and the work is analysed as an example or flashpoint for the collision of politics and subjectivity on a wider scale.

In the final chapter of the anthology, Dorothy Rowe is in dialogue with performance and video artist Oreet Ashery, whose work also locates the complexities of globalization at a point of collision between politics and subjectivity or, more specifically, where the body politic collides with the bodies of subjects inscribed through gender, 'race' and ethnicity. Using her own body, Ashery assumes alter egos through costume – probably the best known being

'Marcus Fisher' (an orthodox Jewish man). As 'Marcus' (and others), Ashery tests the limits of our visual identification of sexual difference and ethnic identity; by taking her alter egos into public spaces and situations that define social norms of behaviour through the regulation of gender, 'race', religion and/or ethnicity, she risks censure (even violence) as she undoes the sharply defined parameters of excluded difference, using eccentric performance to challenge political, social and gendered taboos. The films of the performances are in turns funny and frightening, ambivalent and apprehensive. As her work shifts the frame of diasporic identity through destabilizing gender and cultural identity, Ashery suggests directions for the future that might not be premised upon sharp or fixed distinctions between selves and others. These might be a route toward global citizenship, transnational belonging or diasporic futures open to difference.

While the emphasis on 'futures' in the anthology is deliberate, it is not (pre-)determined. The content of many of the writings and dialogues within this volume are based around explorations of artworks and projects from the past – often, a colonial past. However, they also point to new directions and possibilities for the future. This will be a future that negates neither the material consequences of the past nor the inequities of the present, yet is not wholly constrained by them. It is important to stress the concept of the 'new' in relation to the futures that are envisaged, and even materialized, by *Women, the Arts and Globalization.*

Simply, there is no teleological route to a future that can acknowledge and embrace difference; such a future is simply the ticking of the clock, the passage of time that brings with it the ever-same and not the radically different. Women artists and their artworks test the limits of the ever-same: well-rehearsed theories of globalization, and trans- and multicultural identities are relocated and revised by the active interventions of women making art. Hence, the ways in which women negotiate the postcolonial terrain of diaspora, migration and transnational exchange to articulate their specific position as sexed subjects challenge us to look again at the operations of global metropolitan networks of capital and power. In this sense, *Women, the Arts and Globalization: Eccentric Experience* both acknowledges and seeks to develop current work in the field by expanding the theoretical and methodological tools needed to move debates concerning diaspora, migration and identity forward, rather than fixing them in the historical past. In this way, it aspires toward the futures, as yet unknown, to which it speaks.

Notes

1 For example Michael Hardt and Antonio Negri's seminal volume on Empire refers generically to 'feminist movements' only once in its four hundred pages; see Hardt

and Negri, *Empire* (Cambridge, MA: Harvard University Press, 2001), p. 274. Also, see note 8 below concerning the extraordinary blindness of Nicholas Bourriard's *Altermodern Tate Triennial* exhibition catalogue (London: Tate Publishing, 2009).

2 'Eccentric' as defined by the *Oxford English Dictionary*, available at www.oed.com; accessed 29 September 2011.

3 Nicholas Mirzoeff, 'Introduction: The Multiple Viewpoint: Diasporic Visual Cultures' in Mirzoeff (ed.), *Diasporas and Visual Culture: Representing Africans and Jews* (London and New York: Routledge, 2000), p. 4.

4 Arjun Appadurai, 'The Heart of Whiteness', *Callaloo* 16/4 (1993), 796–807, p. 803.

5 Mirzoeff, 'The Multiple Viewpoint', p. 4 with reference to Arjun Appadurai, *Modernity at Large: Cultural Dimensions of Globalization* (Minneapolis: University of Minnesota Press, 1996).

6 'Knowledge is an activity; it is a practice and not a contemplative reflection. It does things.' Elizabeth Grosz, *Space, Time and Perversion: Essays on the Politics of Bodies* (London and New York: Routledge, 1995), p. 37.

7 See for example Paul Gilroy, *There Ain't No Black in the Union Jack* (London: Unwin Hyman, 1987); *The Black Atlantic: Modernity and Double Consciousness* (Cambridge, MA: Harvard University Press, 1993); *Small Acts: Thoughts on the Politics of Black Cultures* (London: Serpent's Tail, 1993); and most recently *After Empire: Melancholia or Convivial Culture?* (New York and London: Routledge, 2004).

8 Nicholas Bourriard's concept of the 'altermodern' somewhat belatedly acknowledges that 'artistic styles and formats must henceforth be regarded from the viewpoint of diaspora, migration and exodus', a political project that has informed the cultural criticism of Stuart Hall, Paul Gilroy, Kobena Mercer, Rashaed Araeen and a host of other cultural commentators in Britain since at least the 1980s, if not earlier. The institutionalization of diaspora within the economics of the contemporary art scene jostles uneasily against the more nuanced political agendas active in the writings of Hall, Gilroy, Mercer and others who are disturbingly omitted from Bourriard's account. See Bourriard, *Altermodern Tate Triennial*.

9 Mica Nava, *Visceral Cosmopolitanism: Gender, Culture and the Normalisation of Difference* (Oxford and New York: Berg, 2007).

10 See for example Patricia Ticineto Clough and Jean Halley (eds), *The Affective Turn: Theorizing the Social* (Durham, NC, and London: Duke University Press, 2007).

11 We use the phrase 'diasporic futures' deliberately here to invoke the conference *Diasporic Futures: Women, the Arts and Globalization* held at the Victoria and Albert Museum in London in July 2006. Convened and organized by Meskimmon, Rowe and Professor Fran Lloyd (Kingston University, London), it was this conference that began the work toward this volume. While its present shape has transformed radically during the intervening years, enriched by ideas emerging from the field as well as a range of additional contributors, its origin in the dialogues begun during that event is important.

12 This homonymical play is taken from Kelly Oliver, *Witnessing: Beyond Recognition* (Minneapolis and London: University of Minnesota Press, 2001).

Gendering the multitude: feminist politics, globalization and art history

1

Angela Dimitrakaki

From 2006 to 2007: feminist art history without politics and 'The Year of Feminism'

In 2006 the annual Association of Art Historians conference in Britain included a session entitled 'Whither Feminism?'. This was hardly a rhetorical question. Noting the contrast between the pervasive anti- or post-feminism of most academic time zones and the fact that 'second-wave feminist methodology is now well established within the academy' while often marginalized 'as an inappropriate or an outmoded form of historical enquiry', the session organizers proceeded to explain with exceptional clarity what is currently at stake in the '"endangered" field of feminist art history': 'this radical past yet ambivalent present suggests a future for feminist art history that is devoid of *feminism as a political agenda*'.[1] Such a future for feminist art history should not be hastily dismissed as a logical impossibility, even if it might be hard to answer the question 'what is feminism, if not politics?'. The belief that feminism *is* politics by default may, paradoxically, contribute to feminism's de-politicization if used to justify a lack of attention to the historical conditions that shape political subjects and contestations.

The radicalness of feminist art history at its inception, around 1970, rested on the project of proposing, substantiating and addressing a *political subject* at the individual and collective level. This was enabled by second-wave feminism as a politics that exceeded the academy – a politics, in other words, that positioned academic practice within wider social developments in rather unambiguous terms. The transformative gesture of this first 'wave' of feminist art history *was* the redefinition and expansion of the notion of politics as such – a redefinition and expansion much resisted at the time by traditional enclaves of academic practice as well as by traditional carriers of political discourse. Apart from fostering new political subjects, this redefinition and expansion of politics entailed novel ways of applying methodologies in, and to, art history as well as a close attendance to the specificity of its 'own' historical moment in a more general sense. Remarkably, all this took place in an intellectual climate where the hegemony of postmodernism, suspicious of every effort to think of the totality of social relations, threatened to bring about the very containment of politics within the conceptual territory of the 'micro'.

And so feminist art history achieved many of its objectives. It put women artists on the map and certainly in history; it successfully argued about the significance of gender and sexual politics in the analysis of both art and the material and discursive contexts where art circulates; it radicalized the discipline of art history by making explicit the connection between the construction of gendered hierarchies in art and visual culture. It did not however achieve a major objective, identified in some quarters, to transform those structures that relentlessly deliver the art world to a capitalist market economy, supported by an extensive ring of institutions operating at the interface of the entertainment and the education industries. I say a capitalist market economy and not the art market because, as both Hal Foster and Miwon Kwon have asserted, the forms that art has been assuming for some time now, alongside changes in the museum and related display cultures (e.g. biennials), locate art increasingly in a wider *network* of markets (e.g. the market catering for art tourism *and* the art market).[2] Bearing then in mind that the successes and failures of feminist art history had everything to do with, first, its self-conscious positioning in terms of a political project and, second, the obstacles presented by concrete socio-economic processes, the usefulness or sustainability of a feminist art history devoid of politics is questionable at best.

At its worse, a feminist art history without, or outside, politics betrays a spirit of defeat as its animating force. This may sound absurd, even ludicrous, but is far from unthinkable. A feminist art history without politics is the image of feminist art history projected through its failures rather than its successes. It is an image that says: that's how far we could have gone and we can go no further. Suffice to consider the academization of Marxism alongside its retreat from the political life of the 1990s to see how defeat can become the springboard for new intellectual trends. In his *Specters of Marx* Derrida suggested that Marxism had not been immune to processes of de-politicization.[3] Argued in California in 1993, in the context of a conference titled 'Whither Marxism?', Derrida's position was that the 'spectre' of Marx – in other words, dead Marx – was acknowledged in the academy on the grounds that Marxism would no longer be perceived as, precisely, *a politics*. Instead, Marx would find his place next to the other great philosophers. Fifteen years on, the question 'Whither Feminism?', officially asked in the context of a major international conference, provided further clues about the crisis of political consciousness apparently plaguing emancipatory discourses rooted in an earlier capitalist, imperialist, patriarchal paradigm – one often neutralized as 'modernity' in art historical circles. The reasons for this crisis are too complex to trace here but, as far as the crisis of feminist art history is concerned, what is extraordinary is that it is accompanied by a revival of feminism in other parts of the art world.

Just two years after the 'Whither Feminism?' question had been publicly voiced, *Grey Room* published 'Feminist Time: A Conversation'. The participants included Rosalyn Deutsche, Aruna D'Souza, Miwon Kwon, Ulrike Müller, Mignon Nixon and Senam Okudzeto, and the short introduction argued convincingly that there were good reasons for dubbing 2007 the '"year of feminism" in art': the many conferences, special issues of journals and exhibitions on feminism past and present justified this designation. The conversation revolved around the themes of 'difference', 'globalism', 'war', 'generations', 'femininities and masculinities' and 'archives'. The participants made a number of interesting points (some of which will be addressed later in this essay) but overall they expressed a dissatisfaction with the institutional revival of feminism, with Kwon noting that 'enthusiasm for feminism also relates to the art market and the changed conditions of museum politics over the past decade or so. Exhibitions of art and feminism on the spectacular scale ... signal not only institutional legitimation (or containment) but also visibility in the marketplace.' Kwon then wonders: 'Is this a problem or a sign of accomplishment?'[4] Surely, there is no single answer to Kwon's question because feminism has been the terrain of *conflicting* ideological positions, even of conflicting interests, that no appeal to a universal 'sisterhood' has managed to suppress. Some feminists had imagined a radically transformed (art) world while others had simply demanded access to the existent, prestigious institutional contexts from which women had been excluded. The complexity of this division rests on the fact that hegemonic ideologies – and these typically support the status quo – do not remain the property of one class, group or ruling elite. On the contrary, their status as hegemonic depends on how they fare in struggles enacted in the broader social terrain, their ability to spill across the social body and give rise to more general desires: for example, women's general desire to be in the museum as cultural producers, to receive *this* form of recognition. Revisiting the history of feminism in the arts since the 1960s as also *the history of an ideological struggle* is only beginning – a point to which I shall return. For now, suffice to note that the deployment of the terms 'problem' and 'accomplishment' by Kwon suggests that the recent revival of feminism can be approached from two contrasted ideological positions.

In 2008 Amelia Jones contended that to the extent we now witness a feminist revival, this happens for two diametrically opposed reasons. Jones notes that 'the market ... is a key motivator behind the spate of exhibitions and magazine issues highlighting feminist art' *and* that, following an American and global 9/11, 'the recuperation of feminism in art discourse and institutions is ... about a desire to return to, and take wisdom from, the most successful political movement within the visual arts in the past 50 years'.[5] On the one hand, this observation raises considerably the stakes of a feminist art history for the present as it provides a space for thinking how these, at first sight, antithetical demands (*of* the market and *for* models of political action) belong nevertheless to the same historical moment and feed from the same pool of global geopolitics. We further see that both reasons Jones offers for the recent revival of interest in feminism – the art market and 'the violent and apocalyptic destruction of the USA's phallic monuments to its economic and political dominance in the world' – ultimately converge on the prioritization of an economic axis that operates globally.

The revival of feminism in the art world emerges then as a rather complex operation. To the extent that it is market-driven, it is easy to see this revival as evacuated, precisely, from feminism as politics. Such revival does not then undermine in the slightest the thesis according to which feminist art history is presently experiencing a crisis – the crisis engendered by the suppression of feminism as a political discourse. Far from it, this kind of feminist revival dovetails with a depoliticized, unthreatening, tamed feminism. And so the predicament of feminism in 2007 does not seem to be too different from feminism's predicament in 2006.

However, the citing of global geopolitics both in the *Grey Room* conversation and in Jones' article make evident the need, as much as the possibility, of reconfiguring the meaning of feminism *as* politics and *within* politics as currently shaped in relation to art and beyond. This reconfiguring is not legitimated by disciplinary developments within art history and art practice but by historical conditions that, one hopes, make it hard to imagine a stage of *oppositional* politics evacuated from feminism. The rest of this chapter will therefore attempt, first, to explain why feminist art history cannot afford to be divorced from politics as well as why politics today is inconceivable without feminism and, second, to articulate points of convergence between feminism and theorizations of oppositional politics that may hold some interest for an art history of the present.

Globalization and politics: a framework for feminist art history

The 'failure' of feminism to transform the art world cannot be comprehended beyond other horizons of failure (that of the left) against which the achievement of 'globalization' must be measured. In this analysis, 'globalization' refers to a phase in the development of capitalism whereby capitalist relations of production and capitalist markets achieve planetary domination, affecting life in its entirety – an 'accomplishment' felt with some urgency in art since the mid-1990s. Globalization constitutes a particular phase in the development of capitalism as a series of expansive, imperial projects. The English language is in a privileged position for beginning to understand the specific project that 'globalization' is (unlike, for example, French or Greek, where the terms 'mondialization' and 'pan-cosmiopiisi' [παγκοσμιοποίηση] respectively point to a rather abstract 'worlding'). 'Globalization' on the other hand points to a kind of space that a) originates in a scientific discovery (that the earth is a 'globe'), b) is finite and can be filled/covered (e.g., with capitalist relations), c) is not inherently dangerous – even if it were, this danger would be manageable (there is no edge off which to fall in an abyss). This does not make globalization a smooth space or, indeed, a smooth phase/time/synchronicity. Globalization is not necessarily at least about homogenization (or, for that matter, Americanization). Instead it can be, and has been, seen as the management of heterogeneity for financial profit. This is eminently illustrated through the HSBC ('the world's local bank') advertising campaign, adorning airport walls and therefore familiar to globe-trotting labourers and tourists alike, where investors are urged to take heed of local knowledge. When it comes to the art world, the contagious culture of biennials, commonly associated with globalization, has been seen as both a challenge to the US hegemony in an international art world *and* an adequate example of a 'westernizing' process serving the interests of both art tourism and a more integrated art market.[6]

But how is globalization constituted as a historical experience? A continuous stream of data and analysis lend the ground for politics in the first two decades of the twenty-first century both a material and an ideological specificity. Let us then take a closer look: it is a ground marked by the rise of what Naomi Klein has called 'fundamendalist capitalism', an extremely aggressive form of global capitalist expansion, predicated on the dogma of forcing policies that guarantee wealth for the few and misery for the many, on subjects (citizens and their multiplying 'others') that are held in a permanent state of shock so that the chances for resistance to the rule of capital are minimized.[7] It is a ground defined by theories of emergent revolutionary subjects where inclusivity plays a predominant role, as for example in Michael Hardt and Antonio Negri's nomination of the 'multitude'.[8] It is a ground where, as Crystal Bartolovich contends in her discussion of Hardt and Negri's theoretical project, 'class is not just a relation between capital and the multitude but also between the North and the South'.[9] It is a ground where the mention of political activism mostly brings to mind oppositional formations such as the European Social Forum or the World Social Forum, where feminism, when it appears, contributes to a struggle perceived as 'of wider relevance'. When it comes to everyday life, the complex space where politics currently resides is also where the rise of racial hatred in all quarters suggests that 'multiculturalism' has become defunct, that 'cultural diversity' no longer appears harmless and that 'cultural difference' is increasingly understood *politically* – rather, that is, than culturally. When it comes to higher education, where feminist art history is currently trying to justify its existence right when the market allegedly takes an interest in feminist art, it is a space where a corporatist logic sees that Western universities compete over the available 'clients' (students) in a transnational context. Tertiary education is a good example of how geographical privilege operates today as class privilege – one afforded, for instance, to European youth that can study for less at universities competing for a place at the top of international lists. At the same time, in national contexts, such as Britain, that are in a process of privatizing tertiary education, universities covet especially overseas students paying higher fees, when higher fees for domestic students both impede the social mobility witnessed since the 1960s and promote a culture of debt. Academics based in the UK operate in a context rife with contradiction. Under continual pressure to develop courses and programmes of study that attract as many 'clients' (students) as possible, they also face the threat of a shrinking education market, especially in the humanities, bound to exclude those most likely to forge links between critical thinking and social action. And so the survival or not of feminist art history *also* depends on its appeal to an international 'clientele' as well as on how the changing class profile of the student body will shape the university in the years to come. In this sense, the future of feminist art history as an academic subject is tied to a global market economy, also affecting local economies, in quite an obvious way. In other words, whichever future feminist art history is to have is not just dependent on a rethinking of its past.

When it comes to women, globalization has provided a big picture where no country in the world can claim that it has closed the so-called 'gender gap', a euphemism for practices of socio-economic discrimination largely operating against women while also ensuring that economic differences among women are widening.[10] But overall globalization, intimately connected with increased capital mobility, has made women poorer. It no longer takes a feminist researcher to assert that globalization has meant 'the feminization of poverty worldwide'.[11] Overall, women, as a sex, appear to be under attack, with 'violence against women' classified as a major cause of death (like illness, war and poverty).[12] If anything, 'globalization', referring to the planetary hegemony of capital and the ideological dominance of neo-liberalism, names the prevalent condition in which discrimination and violence against women occur today (without this meaning that discrimination is somehow uniform). Moreover, the waves of economic migrants and refugees identified with globalization are in the process of formulating volatile political conditions and urban practices that remain profoundly gendered as much as they complicate the ideological positions both left and right. The situation in some of Europe's 'gateways' is telling. As the European Union is putting pressure on such gateways (Spain, Italy, Greece) to keep all conceivable 'others' away, in a city with a population of five million like Athens, for instance, areas of the large city centre have now turned into ghettos where women are divided into two 'groups': the 'imported' or plainly trafficked prostitutes offering their affordable services to impoverished or unemployed, often illegal, immigrants, and the 'collateral damage': those who run the risk of being raped in streets notable for a brothel renaissance, often on the way to work (not prostitution) or forms of entertainment associated with a failing gentrification process (alternative bars, art events and trendy hotels). This transformation of urban space was completed in less than a decade and took Athens, a relatively crime-free city for its size until the late 1990s, by storm. The ideological outcome, as it were, of such a situation is, on the one hand, that freedom is increasingly identified by constituencies *other than feminist* (and in some cases fascistic) as women's right to be in public space without being attacked and, on the other, rampant racism and xenophobia.

We note then that globalization has created a range of gender and class relations and political cultures that are particularly hard to unravel. Defined primarily by flows of people linked to some aspect of the economy (from students to prostitutes to 'successful' or 'unsuccessful' economic immigrants), it upsets former paradigms of diaspora and notions of identity. In any event, this kind of big picture makes it in fact easier to imagine a situation where feminism becomes *indispensable* to the articulation of political practices in the early twenty-first century. The real issue then facing feminist art historians at present is: how can feminist art history contribute to making explicit feminism's relevance to the present social conditions? And how can it contribute to the transformation of these social conditions?

Mobility, consumption, expendability: nomadic and diasporic presents

In the mid-1990s John Roberts noted that the museum had undergone a profound transformation to adapt to an expanding service economy, as a result of which it was able to accommodate precisely those postmodern practices that sought to challenge its authority.[13] In 2000 Boris Groys made an astute and witty observation about the condition of the contemporary artist: unlike the dinosaur, the contemporary artist knows that, if successful, he or she will end up in the museum.[14] Museums, and exhibition cultures more generally, play their own role in expanding the remit of mobilities today on a global scale. The participants to the *Grey Room* conversation about feminism and art noted the indignation of artists whom the Elizabeth Sackler Center of Feminist Art in Brooklyn Museum in New York made mobile for the purposes of the exhibition *Global Feminisms*, when these artists realized their explicit use as service providers (exhibition guides).[15] Possibly the artists who felt offended by this gesture uphold a view of the museum as a space not fully enmeshed in the service economy. Beyond this, however, *Global Feminisms* represents a historically specific curatorial ideology (in the sense of not always being conscious of what it re/produces).

This ideology is evident in the voluminous exhibition catalogue. *Global Feminisms: New Directions in Contemporary Art*, edited by Maura Reilly and Linda Nochlin, bears a paradoxical title, both accurately describing and misrepresenting the book's content. On the one hand, the title reflects the book's open acknowledgement of the diverse, situated projects claimed as feminist, hence the essays cover a broad geographical spectrum ranging from India to the former Eastern Europe – part of it now appropriated by the 'Western' European Union. On the other hand, the title misrepresents the book's content, for the case made through the essays suggests precisely the *absence* of a coherent oppositional, transnational platform of engagement, let alone a cluster of social movements, that might be termed 'global feminisms' in the arts. (Notably, the current existence of a 'global feminism' is disputed by feminist sociologists as well.[16]) The paradox encountered in *Global Feminisms* is an outcome of yet another structural absence: that of a systematic analysis within art history (and, for the purposes of the present chapter, within feminist art history) of the term 'global' and certainly of 'globalization'. In light of this absence, the term 'global' implicitly appears to hold a singularly *geographical* meaning. But feminist art history has been dealing with geography for some time now. To give one example, Griselda Pollock's edited volume *Generations and Geographies in the Visual Arts* appeared in 1996, prefiguring the outward gaze of *Global Feminisms* by eleven years.[17] *Generations and Geographies in the Visual Arts* as much as *Global Feminisms* consolidate the rise of plural histories and contestations while they also assert that the convergence of feminism and art has not been an exclusively Western affair. This has been a necessary project, very much connected with a transformed feminist consciousness brought about by postcolonial critique and the economic collapse of totalitarian pseudo-communist regimes. But this turn to geography and its social art histories is *not* commensurate with an attendance to globalization as a set of socio-economic practices that compose the contemporary horizon for gendered subjects and the hierarchies that structure their interface.

Nevertheless, the phrase 'Feminism's global imperative' provides the heading for a section of Reilly's catalogue essay focusing on the critique of white Euro-American feminism effected by women (some of them feminists) rightly contending that not all women are oppressed in the same way. Volumes of feminist writing on art and beyond have been devoted to fleshing out the empirical truthfulness of this statement. Apart from a passing mention of lesbians, Reilly's examples focus exclusively on critical voices addressing race and geographical-national differences. Reilly considers repeatedly the move from 'international' to 'transnational', seeing the latter as a more apt term for describing the task of contemporary feminism: 'in general it was argued [in the 1990s] that the new feminist practice must address the concerns of women across the globe, transnationally, in their historical and particularized relationships to multiple patriarchies and economic hegemonies.'[18] The phrase 'multiple economic hegemonies' is puzzling, given the consolidation of *one* economic hegemony, that of global capital, in the 1990s, which had by then ushered even 'communist' China into a global market economy.

Continuing with a brief presentation of feminist art exhibitions in the first decade of the twenty-first century, Reilly then explains how '*Global Feminisms* employs a different curatorial strategy'. She writes: 'The exhibition presents an even wider geographical selection, arranged thematically, with a special emphasis on placing works in dialogic relation, underscoring "common differences" between women from various cultures, nations, religions, ethnicities and sexualities. In doing so, the co-implicated histories, cultures and stories between women can become part and parcel of a larger, dissonant (versus a linear or synchronic) narrative.'[19] There are several points of interest here. First, the assumption that a synchronic narrative *must* be contrasted to a 'larger, dissonant' one. We have to ask in what sense a synchronic narrative, namely 'globalization', would not be both large (indeed, as large as it gets) *and* dissonant, given that globalization sustains an interplay between homogeneity and heterogeneity, fostering both a relational juxtaposition of local differences while also pitching one culture against another in a competitive context where public and market space become interchangeable. The finitude of a knowable and manageable, if uneven, space that 'globalization' implies does not inform the curator's argument. A second point of interest is the critical omission of one particular category of 'difference' in the curatorial strategy put forward, a category that appears implicitly earlier on in Reilly's text through a reference to the nebulous concept of 'economic hegemonies'. The missing category is what we might call 'economic difference' among women, or simply 'class' (although 'class' is never reducible to *just* economic difference). The absence of this category of difference in the curatorial essay is important in at least two ways. First, because it renews the ties between a liberal feminism and multiculturalism as an inherently problematic concept that disregards the fact that cultures are hierarchically positioned in global space or even within a given locality. The nature of this hierarchy is complex precisely because the latter is sustained by economics rather than by free-floating cultural signifiers. To bring together women from 'various histories, cultures, nations, religions, ethnicities and sexualities' in an art exhibition means that we bring together women from backgrounds that remain *critically asymmetrical* within a global capitalist economy (articulated also locally). Secondly, and this is a key point when it comes to museum cultures, international exhibitions such as *Global Feminisms* tend to function as radically different economic spaces, in the sense that the critical asymmetries pointed to above get to be *temporarily* suspended. Artists from Africa, Eastern Europe and the US are supposed to be represented as 'equals' in a smooth, democratic context: the exhibition. That they are in fact competing for market attention in that same space is illustrative of the perversion that the notion of 'democracy' has undergone in neo-liberalism, which has, at least until recently, seen democracy as a necessary condition for a free market defined by competition among 'free' agents. *Global Feminisms* illustrates perfectly what happens when this expectation (of the exhibition as a democratic space) breaks down, since as noted in the *Grey Room* discussion, the exhibition's financial constraints fell 'with disparate impact on artists from poor countries', causing considerable anger at this unseemly manifestation of economic difference.[20] Such exhibitions may then have the paradoxical effect of both revealing *and* concealing the economic relations that produce globalization in its current form. Feminist exhibitions with a transnational agenda are not spared this mystifying effect, an ideological by-product of the international art show of our times. 'Feminism's global imperative' cannot therefore continue to be articulated in terms of a neutral provision of women's art, anthologized from diverse geographical contexts, even if there is a rudimentary acknowledgement of the latter's different histories (simply because today a curatorial position that would elide such histories would appear nonsensical). We see then that current display cultures and curatorial strategies pose major questions for a feminist art history engaged with globalization. The question of how display cultures and curatorial policies contribute to a) the transnational flows that produce 'globalization' and b) the ideologies that sustain a notion of (gendered) geography as separate from an economic axis is of paramount importance.

But if contemporary feminist art history is only beginning to pick the lost thread of economic relations, contemporary artists have not managed to ignore it. Let us just consider one example: the return of the prostitute in contemporary art, in the knowledge that the first wave of feminist art history saw in the prostitute the exploited, gendered body that provided the experimentation ground for the modern 'masterpiece'. It is the prostitute that becomes a telling relational metaphor both in Andrea Fraser's work *Untitled* (2003), where a male collector buys a video that documents his intercourse with the artist, as well as in Santiago Sierra's *160 cm Line Tattooed on 4 Persons* (2000), where four prostitutes were paid (more than what they would be paid for a single fellatio, the artist's website explains providing hard numbers) to receive a *visibly* permanent marking on their bodies.[21] Feminist art history already provides the conceptual framework for considering the fact that Fraser, a female artist, *becomes* the subject of her work while Sierra, a male artist, can afford to retain his authorizing distance from the body that he drafts, alongside other bodies (such as that of the economic immigrant), into meaning-making practices that reveal economic exchange as the overarching framework of human relations at present.[22]

But the prostitute of today differs in important ways from that of early modernism as one of the primary 'deconstructed' figures of feminist discourse. To mention an obvious difference, the trafficking of women and its unprecedented visibility occurs in global space. The transnational trafficking of women can be understood more in terms of 'circulation' (as in circulation of goods) and less in terms of 'mobility', in ways that create historically specific forms of expendable nomadism and diasporas. In 2003 the American TV series *The Wire* (Season 2) opened with an unforgettable scene, capturing the zeitgeist, defined as it is by the interplay between mobility and circulation: thirteen young women asphyxiated in a container – the oft-cited symbol of global trade – as wasted cargo in a port of the world's promised land – that is, America. The prostitute is also now frequently associated with a border economy – usually a border economy as the material encounter of a poor national space and a wealthy one. She is a border-dweller or a border-crossing migrant in a situation where it can be hard to distinguish between coercion and consent.[23] But often the space that frames globalization's prostitute opens up to the global routes of human trafficking where evidently coercive forms of labour that can amount to slavery and torture are tied to the literal consumption of women. Such an updating of the figure of the prostitute as a player of an economic border animates, for example, Ann-Sofi Sidén's *Warte Mal! Prostitution after the Velvet Revolution* (1999), an emotionally devastating chronicle of the artist's interaction with the motel culture of Dubi, a town at the border between the Czech Republic and Germany, and Ursula Biemann's *Remote Sensing* (2001), a more distanced, essayistic, acutely technological account of the clandestine journeys of smuggled, expendable, female bodies that clearly exceed conventional designations of working-class femininity, or *Black Sea Files* (2005), where prostitution is found to be a situated form of labour, organized within the broader economic cultures and population displacements that frame the construction of a pipeline bringing oil from the Caspian Sea to Europe and beyond.

The re-emergence of the signifying power of the (mostly, female) prostitute in art around 2000, when public awareness of globalization was gaining momentum, speaks volumes about the still prevalent role played by gender across the vast terrain of social practices making up the 'contemporary'. And although the possible meanings of this return require some analysis, what appears to be at stake here is a heightened connection between a certain gender and a globally expanded capitalist economy incorporating problematic notions of 'mobility' often mutating into 'circulation' – a connection to which feminist art history must attend as a political, rather than an ethical, project.

Beyond the generational deadlock: feminism's unhappy marriage with postmodernism and the hope for divorce

The preceding sketchy outline of a more general context of engagement suggests that the complex space where feminist art history necessarily has to operate today differs in important ways from that of the early 1970s. The *intensification* of certain practices, processes and conflicts has brought about changes that necessitate a critical shift in our understanding of the political, which in its simplest form would take us from the local to the global, or from the 'micro' to a new, contentious and analytically resistant 'macro'. Yet there is hardly anything self-evident about this move and its meaning for the field of feminist art history. Whereas the interdependence and interpenetration of diverse orders of space (material, institutional, national, ideological and so on) framing women's 'difference', in its articulation as oppression, made frequent appearances in the feminist work done in the 1970s and 1980s, the implications of this knowledge were somehow forestalled. In the anti-intellectualism that ensued after the slow deflation of second-wave movements – and which was especially evident in post-Thatcher Britain, where Brit-art's recipe for fast success was to keep it simple and spectacular – the ideologically dominant trends in art history and art practice appeared to have forgotten the holistic work that the examination of women's social conditions requires. Today it has become apparent that feminism in the arts has been locked into a binary, generational logic since the 1990s, when the ideological construct of post-feminism signalled the de-politicization or the 'end' of feminism in the assumption that new social conditions had made feminist politics plainly redundant. One of the most prominent women artists of today, Swiss Pipilotti Rist, has confessed that it bothers her that her work is so much associated with gender and says: 'Of course I am a feminist because every normal person is a feminist … I am grateful to feminism. But women did it once so I don't have to go back and do what they did.'[24] But which women did 'it', where and, crucially, how?

In a 2007 issue of *Frieze* entitled 'Feminism', geographer Saskia Sassen gives an interview where she explains how the class of so-called emancipated, professional women in the West (including feminist academics such as myself) relies on the cheap labour of imported women looking after the children and the household.[25] The erosion of the welfare state experienced in Britain, advancing to the haven of women's rights that Scandinavia once was hailed as, alongside longer working hours for white-collar workers of both sexes, are precisely outcomes of intensified capitalist relations now operating globally. Indeed, mainstream ideology at present, massively visible through the incredibly popular women's magazines, clearly accepts that 'women's double burden of childcare and employment is seen as a personal issue to be solved by better time-management. … This form of debate means that the link between the personal and the political is obscured.'[26]

Far then from describing Western, middle-class women's reality at present, statements such as Rist's reflect a rather different problem: the inability of feminism in the arts to move beyond the generational deadlock (of which the spurious ideological construct of post-feminism is but its institutionally endorsed, spectacular moment) and align a feminist politics with a contemporary moment delivered to us through the intricacies of global space and the (gendered) labour relations that sustain it. But to achieve this would require a critical attendance to a conception of history where the spatial axis is not forgotten in favour of the temporal (read: generational).

Feminism's generational issue is also addressed in *Grey Room*'s 'Feminist Time' discussion. Questioning the value of a generational perspective for addressing the expanded field of sexual politics today, Ulrike Müller made a comparison between the 1970s and the 2000s arguing that 'the 1970s are not only the starting point for many debates that shaped our current thinking and artistic strategies; they were also politically similar to the present: a war overseas and the worst American president ever. The 1970s isn't a glorious past. It was a terrible time. So, the question is: what can we glean from earlier feminisms for our current moment?'[27] This is an urgent question indeed, but what legitimates a summary of the first decade of the twenty-first century as similar to that of the 1970s is a particular American ideology that Müller's statement is mired in: the war is 'overseas' and there is a problem with the US presidency. That this particular American ideology is encountered in the words of an Austrian feminist based in the US and participating in its queer art scene affords yet another opportunity to observe the mobility of ideologies as tied to the trajectories of artistic diasporas at present.

A different probing of the issue of generations comes from current efforts to re-engage the economic axis with feminist analysis. Both Helen Molesworth and Marina Vishmidt have attempted a rethinking of earlier feminist interventions in terms of labour. In 'House Work and Art Work', Helen Molesworth revisits the former division between a 1970s and 1980s feminism, corresponding to an 'untheorized' essentialism and feminism's turn to theory respectively, by considering how landmark works by Judy Chicago, Mary Kelly, Martha Rosler and Mierle Laderman Ukeles, so far classified as 1970s or 1980s feminism, highlight and address the gender division of labour.[28] In 'Line Describing A Curb: Asymptotes about VALIE EXPORT, the New Urbanism and Contemporary Art', Marina Vishmidt considers how VALIE EXPORT's actions in the city posit the female body not 'as a discursive abstraction' but as 'an embodied contradiction in narratives of culture, gender and labour'.[29] Published in 2000 (Molesworth) and 2007 (Vishmidt), these two essays already share an emphasis on labour with political discourses on globalization. They upset any smooth classification of feminist art in terms of generational differences by picking up where feminist materialism left off and the postmodern fixation on difference emerged as hegemonic. If the concept of 'generation' is to have any meaning for a feminist art history of the present, it requires at least two qualifications: first, that a generation is seen as a site of ideological struggle in its own right (meaning that a hegemonic ideology cannot be attributed to a 'generation', imposing thus a false homogeneity); second, that generation does not refer to the age of a feminist but to forms of self-consciousness that remain attuned to demands generated by historical process (without this negating the principle of an ideological struggle in the present tense). But if the emphasis on the consumption of woman as sign represented a certain ideological hegemony and was *also* a historically necessary route, today feminism's marriage to postmodernism as a cultural dominant endangers precisely the extension of feminism as a political discourse and social praxis, and one can only hope for a speedy divorce.[30] The turn to the economic subject denotes a broader shift of focus in contemporary art, and revisiting feminist art through the rise of this new subjectivity can generate a more complex 'feminist continuum' than one could perhaps have imagined – one that permits us to see feminism's alignment with identity politics as *one instance* in a struggle informed by more diversified and historically evolving feminist narratives produced out of social antagonisms.[31]

Theory and the struggles of the present: capital's empire, feminism and art history

Identity, travel, class

In 2000 Nikos Papastergiadis concluded his study on migration and globalization (from which art was not absent) with a chapter entitled 'Clusters in the Diaspora', detecting a 'paradox at the centre of this [his] book: does greater mobility entail more freedom? Can we construct identity without referring to essential and exclusive characteristics?'[32] The questions were related to the book's extensive discussion of 'cultural translation'. A postmodern project associated with key concepts of a postcolonial lexicon (such as cultural diversity, cultural difference, multi-culturalism, hybridity), cultural translation implied that somehow the problem requiring a solution was how to make one culture intelligible to another. 'Cultural translation' persisted in the twenty-first century – for example, in Tate Britain's fourth triennial, entitled *Altermodern* and curated by Nicolas Bourriaud, who contended: 'altermodernity arises out of negotiations between agents from different cultures and geographical locations. Stripped of a centre, it can only be a polyglot. Altermodernity is characterised by cultural translation.'[33] Yet cultural translation appeared to be a means to an end: it was intended to enable mobility. And in Bourriaud's vision mobility is affirmed, glorified and metaphorized: the artist is found to be immersed in the 'journey-form'.

Journeys, cultures, movement – all these were in place long before Bourriaud's Altermodern and long before Papastergiadis' enquiry into mobility, diaspora and freedom. However, in 2000 the latter already draws a distinction between forms of migration and diasporas up until the 1970s and the specific condition of globalization. He writes: 'while globalization has inevitably sharpened and intensified the "contact zones" between different cultures, it has also largely done this *from the position of promoting a given economic imperative as the unstated ground* upon which all forms of culture must be subordinated'.[34] This statement has three immediate implications: first, that by extension all projects of cultural translation must also be subordinated to this unstated ground; second, that this unstated ground re-introduces the vilified in postmodernism concept of a totality; third, that unless such projects manage to turn the 'given economic imperative' (the globalization of capital) into the *stated* ground of what holds them together, and acknowledge this ground as the condition framing intercultural dialogues, there is little hope for the transformation of such dialogues into social praxis.

But there is a fourth and more upsetting implication at work here: to the extent that postmodernism displaced the economic subject in favour of a cultural subject (as Hal Foster has rightly claimed), art's turn to a new and perplexing economic subject as a symptom of globalization suggests that the conceptual apparatus of postmodernism, resting as it is on exchanges between 'culture' and 'difference', may be ineffectual when deployed for political purposes in the age of global capital.[35] It is this condition which makes a good case for a divorce of feminism and postmodernism, and it is this condition that currently upsets the established methodologies and theoretical alliances of feminist art history as we have known it. Then again, such a divorce must be welcome, since postmodernism's insistence on a fragmented social body and an endless multiplication of micro- or 'particular' constituencies (Asian women, post-Socialist women, Arab women, queer women, heterosexual women, African-American women, African women, white women, middle-class women, working class women, and so on ad infinitum) ultimately played a role in the dissolution of the women's movements. The problem was not of course the articulation of difference, a politically and conceptually vital step in a feminist continuum that posed as its initial subject of address all women, but that, as a result of the logic of fragmentation that dominated postmodernism, difference was not introduced in a dialectical tension with the totalizing tendencies of capitalism as a historically privileged mode of production (the concept of 'totality' was eschewed as irrelevant). If anything, in its articulation as a totality, globalization calls attention to the 'unstated ground' that today sustains, exacerbates or dissolves women's differences according to, in the last instance, a 'given economic imperative'. If this given economic imperative has created the 'feminization of poverty' on a planetary scale, we see how feminist politics becomes indeed a crucial presence in current oppositional formations.[36]

But to say that globalization is a totality hardly challenges its newness – even if we must remain acutely aware that historical process never works by providing a stable and easily identifiable 'new' (in the sense that whatever 'new' historical process generates, it incorporates and mobilizes elements from both its past and unforeseen future). To give one example, contemporary art sees an emphasis on the journey and travelling: Kwon speaks of itinerant artists in 1997, and in 2009 Bourriaud finds the artist immersed in 'the journey-form'.[37] All this movement no longer occurs as part of a Van Goghian dream of finding an 'outside': the intense search for alternative economies (alternative to capitalism) focuses on the possibility of *making* rather than discovering-potential outsides. Concepts such as 'diaspora' and 'nomadic existence' may still be relevant but hold little analytical value for discourses that break with the status quo, unless these concepts get to be explicitly connected with the mobility of labour or flight from conflict that return us infallibly to states of 'unrealized democracy' perpetrated by economic interests.[38] More importantly, it cannot be assumed that a transformative politics is immanent in the act of migrating and the proliferation of diasporas. As Bartolovich notes, 'it is easy to understand the desire of migrants to make a better life for themselves and their families, but migrancy is still an *individualist* bid for upward mobility, entirely assimilable to capitalism'.[39] More than that, transnational labour mobility has been necessary to capital's global expansion in many ways – for example, because 'multiple ethnic divisions among the workers function as an element of control in the labor process': although 'contingency, mobility and flexibility' arise within (rather than being imposed by) global capital, they are nevertheless the latter's 'real power'.[40] Crisis management is global capital's favourite exercise because crisis is endemic in the current world order – and this applies equally to the financial crisis and the 'disruptions' effected by immigration.

A key issue in contemporary theories of globalization on the left has therefore been the examination of how such forms of mobility enter a social body where difference is always scripted into hierarchies that can be exploited for profit. This issue is also considered in Hardt and Negri's *Empire*, published in 2000. The designation 'empire' captures both the vastness and authority of the managerial operations of capital today as much as it alludes to a historical process (that of imperialism) that has at least provisionally accomplished its mission (empire). Not only has terrestrial space been appropriated into a combination of productive and consuming geographies, but technology has permitted the literal *invention* of new space (cyberspace) to be occupied by new forms of productivity and the market. More than this, *Empire* has been an explicit attempt to think of *class* in the age of global capital.

Having already impacted on art history and curatorial practice, *Empire* has been seen to identify a new political subject for globalization, the multitude. For example, in *Documenta 11* Okwui Enwezor engaged this term but claimed it for a postcolonial discourse *after* postmodernism – a gesture repeated in the exhibition's reception within art history.[41] Yet, in Hardt and Negri's theory, the multitude is not reducible to a postcolonial subjectivity. Neither is it reducible to any kind of nomadic or diasporic subjectivity. The question for global capital's empire, as theorized by Hardt and Negri, is not 'to negate or attenuate these differences but rather to affirm them and arrange them in an effective apparatus of command'.[42] What Enwezor missed (and what is often missed) is that the multitude constitutes the new productive *class* in the global 'empire' of capital, 'a new regime of production', reconfiguring the traditional working class.[43] The claim *Empire* makes about the re-introduction of class in contemporary politics offers immense possibilities for a new materialist feminism in art history and beyond. But gendering the multitude is far from simple – a point to which I shall return.

In considering how Hardt and Negri's theorization of globalization can enter a dialogue with feminist art history as a political discourse, two things need to be clarified. First is the fact that Negri's ideas, associated with Autonomist Marxism and familiar to Marxists for decades, received widespread attention only after the eruption of the global anti-capitalist movement that, for many, had its inaugural moment in 1999, with the demonstrations in Seattle achieving iconic status. This is important because it reminds us both where political energies concentrate at present and also that ideas do not gain political momentum without some grass-roots element (as the case of 1970s feminism also suggests) – indeed not without history happening. To that end, it is telling that Allan Sekula, the artist who 'happened' to document the uprising in Seattle, is not associated with feminist art. Rather, his work resonates with Marxism's preoccupation with labour: Sekula has consistently documented labour relations in a global context.[44]

Second, Hardt and Negri's multitude as the political subjectivity and productive class of empire has been subjected to much criticism. Bartolovich insists that the multitude cannot correspond to a unified revolutionary consciousness because it remains divided (in the sense that the most extreme poverty suffered by a US citizen is not as extreme as that of the poverty experienced in the South, and so the US poor ultimately have something to defend).[45] Alex Callinicos has made a similar point in the context of a more extensive critique, arguing further that *Empire* is not removed enough from the staples of a postmodern conceptual apparatus idolizing migration and nomadism.[46] Marxist-feminist critics, including those associated with Autonomist Marxism, have stressed, among other things, *Empire*'s misrecognition of the role that women still play in the operation of the family (no matter how transformed by globalization) as the site of 'reproductive labour' (the labour that reproduces the labourer in his or her materiality).[47]

Such criticisms have generated ongoing debates that highlight aspects of globalization which a politically engaged feminist art history cannot afford to dismiss. The current popularity of this theory of globalization has everything to do with the fact that Hardt and Negri did not proceed to dis-identify with postmodernist political consciousness *tout court* but literally shifted the terrain by strategically combining some of its elements, especially those associated with postcolonial critique and poststructuralism, with key elements of Marxist thinking, seeing globalization as instituting specific relations of production.

Labour, migration, biopolitics

One of the main points made in *Empire* is that it is impossible to understand globalization unless one attends to contemporary forms of labour and labour relations. It is the multitude's labour that both produces the empire of capital and that holds the power to overcome it. Hardt and Negri's attention to migration and nomadism emanates from their effort to provide a theory of labour for globalization that can be mobilized towards the precipitation of the fall of global capital's empire, and there are several things worth noting in their analysis.[48]

First, globalization is identified with the hegemony of immaterial labour. But what is meant by this is not that material and menial labour has ceased to exist but that an informational logic now penetrates the organization of production, even if this production takes place in a potato field or in a factory making something as material as a dishwasher. The expansion of a service economy is both a constitutive element *and* a symptom of the hegemony of immaterial labour. Second, the migratory waves shaping globalization are connected to labour mobility, the control of that mobility and resistance to that control. Capital is seen to exercise a form of bio-power and so whatever configuration of migration, labour and gender exists today is subject to this rule.[49] The ascendance of immaterial labour has meant, for instance, that life and work are impossible to separate for large segments of the population worldwide and this translates into more work. Indeed, the prevalence of continuous travelling as work in contemporary modalities of art production exemplifies this principle.

That today migration (like gender) is not just an isolated element of one's subjectivity but that it takes over one's life, dictating how it is lived, is easier to see. Papastergiadis' suggestion to 'link the concept of citizenship to migration' (encountered also in the philosophy of Giorgio Agamben, which enjoys much visibility in art theory lately) acknowledges this biopolitical dimension of migration.[50] We know of course that this suggestion has remained unrealized. On the contrary, even formal transnational spaces such as the European Union permit the mobility of the labour force without granting the right to vote, propagating thus diminished forms of citizenship. What I, as a UK-based academic born in Greece, have in common with a Greece-based construction worker born in Poland is that we exchanged our right to labour mobility with our right to vote where we pay taxes – in other words with our right to full citizenship. We see then that political disenfranchisement associated with forms of mobility instituted, and even encouraged, by transnational formations may affect a far broader constituency than that encompassing 'illegal' immigrants, 'trafficked' immigrants, economic immigrants departing from conditions of unbearable poverty, or asylum seekers and political exiles, or any combination of the above. Indeed, an important difference between earlier and current forms of labour mobility (the prevalent form of mobility today, from the artist to the construction worker) is that the latter are more acutely and formally dissociated from democratic rights, which is why Hardt and Negri argue that 'global citizenship' must be the 'first political demand' of the multitude.[51] Meeting this demand would transform the lives of millions of women worldwide – much more that the right to vote did in national contexts. Understanding if and how art is connected with investigating and imagining the links between gender, democracy and labour mobility would hold great interest – not least because of art's current emphasis on practices of direct intervention rather than representation (on which more shortly).

Beyond this, the hegemony of immaterial labour in the production spaces of contemporary capital and the biopolitical dimension of labour hold significant repercussions for feminist politics and for feminist art history. On the one hand, Hardt and Negri identify a central form of immaterial labour as 'affective labour'. Associating it explicitly with 'women's work' and noting the research of socialist feminist scholars in clarifying how this work features in the capitalist mode of production, they stress affective labour's expansion into a global paradigm and state: 'affective labor is biopolitical production in that it directly produces social relationships and forms of life'.[52] Drawing on and reassessing important aspects in the work of Foucault, Deleuze and Guattari, Hardt and Negri strive to unravel the complex grip of capital on *everything that is*, stressing the impossibility of an 'outside' from where identity might emanate and struggle might originate. If affective labour is now fully introduced into the production cycles of contemporary capitalism, we can expect a re-opening of the debates around the nature of domestic labour, the work of the mother, and its role in an economy where public (work) and private (life) time are losing their once-upon-a-time sharp contours. The visibility of affective labour today constructs an expanded, rather than narrow, conception of 'economy' in its biopolitical dimension, bringing nevertheless to the fore the original attendance of this Greek word (*oikos* (n. home) + *nemo* (v. to distribute/divide)) to labour in relation to the domestic. The second political demand of the multitude, 'a social wage and a guaranteed income for all', opens a space for an alliance of household and maternal (or a future paternal) labour with other forms of affective and reproductive labour and, should it be met, it would no longer be tied to the risk (identified by materialist feminists) of pushing women further into the domestic sphere.[53] It is not therefore surprising that a re-viewing of Mary Kelly's *Post-Partum Document* (1973–79) and Mierle Laderman Ukeles' Maintainance Art in the 1960s and 1970s through the prism of labour occurs right when affective labour emerges as a key feature of capitalist production. Yet Hardt and Negri's theorization of affective labour remains to an extent gender-blind or at least appears to misrecognize the significance of gender for shaping such forms of labour and vice versa. Marion von Osten has stressed that more elastic working hours (often meaning very long working hours) and 'work from home', enabled by advanced technology, are quickly transforming (though not positively) women's relationship to domestic space – a relationship that was a priority on the feminist agenda of the 1970s.[54] A less obvious implication concerns art as a form affective labour, as work on the spectator or the 'participant'. In what ways does art as affective labour remain gendered? Can this positing of art in terms of affective labour help de-heroicize the figure of the artist or does art constitute a privileged form of affective labour (as opposed to that associated with the household)?

At the same time contemporary artists have also turned to how women are consumed materially in the factory floors of multinational corporations. Ursula Biemann's video essay *Performing the Border* (1999), a work associated with the 'documentary turn' in contemporary art, offers a complex image of the US–Mexico border, where multinational corporations hire young women with 'nimble fingers' and literally consume them up, as these women gradually lose their eyesight.[55] We can of course observe that the documentation of women's work in the industry also preoccupied 1970s feminism. Given art's documentary turn in recent years, which coincided with the consolidation of global capital and the need to move *from a politics of representation to a politics of knowledge*, we should expect that works such as the collaborative project-exhibition *Women & Work: A Document on the Division of Labour in Industry* (1975), conceived and executed by Margaret Harrison, Kay Hunt and Mary Kelly, will receive new visibility.[56] This is one of the least known projects of the women's art movement in Britain, which eventually prioritized in its radical enquiry the *production* of the gendered subject in an economy of signs and attended therefore to the construction and reproduction of a performative, psychic reality, best approached through psychoanalysis. Comparative readings of 1970s projects focusing on working-class women's labour and the labour of a gendered multitude might both highlight the specificity of the processes identified with globalization and contribute to a rethinking of earlier feminist art in terms of an ideological struggle, evident even in the work of one artist.

It is also interesting to see how travel as work is implicated in the transformation of the identity of the 'woman artist', a historical figure critically appropriated by feminist art history, and the newly visible figure of the equally gendered curator. On the one hand, travelling today informs both new migratory identities (for example, an artist moving from a post-Socialist country to the West) and nomadic mobilities (the ceaseless travelling around the globe to produce site-specific art or exhibitions) as well as what we might call *biopolitical artworks* – projects such as Sidén's *Warte Mal!* or Jenny Marketou's *Trans/local: Camp in My Tent* (1996–2001), where the artist travels to participate in the broader terrain of social relations and where the boundary between work and life is explicitly undermined.[57] On the other hand, there are important differences between the various ways that a contemporary woman artist engages the 'journey-form' today as opposed to how women artists travelled in a modernity defined by European imperialisms. A cross-reading of such practices might illuminate further the transformative potential of the subjectivities addressed by feminist art history.

Representation, knowledge, politics

Biopolitical art invokes the emphasis placed by feminist epistemology on experiential forms of knowledge to the extent that they exemplify women artists' desire to participate in the relocation of art within the material terrain of global space-time – a project, in lack of a better term, that upsets a particular 1990s view of globality resting primarily on the connectivity of the Internet and relying on advanced technology, which gave us cyber-feminism. Today the exodus of large numbers of artists from the studio, associated with the many strands of 'participation art' as well as the documentary turn in contemporary art, suggests that the artist is no longer *just* an engineer fixed in front of a computer screen but that she attempts at least to engage the materiality of capital as a social relation.[58] It is because of this that contemporary art's documentary turn in particular has been connected with Fredric Jameson's 'cognitive mapping', a term that has been seen by some feminists as expressing a centralizing, phallocentric logic and a subject that, in his standing apart, reclaims a mastery over space.[59] To the extent that such mastery is identified with male subjectivity, an examination of masculinity in globalization – for example, the male subjectivities that projects of crossing global space give rise to – is also due as a core project of a new feminist art history. On the other hand, the encounter between specific modalities within contemporary art's post-documentary practice and the productivity of the multitude complicates such an outright rejection of cognitive mapping. As I have argued elsewhere and although a lot remains to be said, the hybrid form of the video essay in particular presents specific opportunities for both addressing gender relations in the classed geographies of capital and for considering how materialist feminism can inform an emerging politics of knowledge.[60]

The shift from a politics of representation, associated with a critical postmodernism that was informed by feminist and postcolonial critique, to a politics of knowledge is, in the first instance, commensurate with a broader crisis of representation spreading from current forms of democracy (operating on the basis of elected representatives of the people) to art as social praxis. Ulrike Müller's statement that 'representation isn't a primary function of LTTR [a queer feminist collective]. Our politics are more attuned to performance and to creating spaces with and for each other' resonates with Ursula Biemann's observation about how to address women's labour in relocating it from 'reality' to 'representation': 'all you can do is perform it'.[61] The implicit at least inflection of such statements is that knowledge production is not inherently an operation of mastery condemned to always bring forth and exploit an 'other'. Knowledge production is a key outcome of the necessarily co-operative productivity of the multitude that capital has every interest in managing.[62] If today the efforts of art are concentrating on a politics of knowledge rather than representation, the politicization of knowledge recognizes the co-operative production of the multitude and the need to redress capitalism's own emphasis on the accumulation of knowledge and information. Whereas new terms (such as 'denizen') have been coined to make specific new subjects representable, we can see Hardt and Negri's multitude as an attempt to think of a space for politics where representation, and therefore *identity*, is not a pre-requisite.[63] This resistance to identity is what would complicate the effort to gender the multitude – unless of course this process of gendering the multitude mobilizes, and is firmly inscribed within, a politics of solidarity. Papastergiadis' suggestion for 'clusters', alternative forms of social existence defined by 'a process of assembly' and offering a possibility 'to think of forms of attraction and modes of co-existence which do not rely exclusively on shared characteristics', expresses the same desire to forge politics beyond identity.[64] The departure from identity is especially evident in theoretical propositions that aim, among other things, to sustain the energies of a transnational anti-capitalist movement. In his *Change the World without Taking Power*, one of the key texts for anti-capitalist struggle since the beginning of the twenty-first century, John Holloway points out that 'anti-power is ubiquitous' but that the way that information is disseminated through formal media networks makes it 'invisible', insisting that 'all rebellious movements are struggles against invisibility'. Interestingly, feminism is among Holloway's 'clearest' examples of a rebellious movement having to fight the invisibility of the problem that provided the very reason for its politics. He states: 'There is an important distinction to be made here. The problem of anti-power is not to emancipate an oppressed identity but to emancipate an oppressed non-identity, the ordinary, everyday, invisible no, the rumblings of subversion as we walk in the street, the silent volcano of sitting in a chair. By giving discontent an identity, 'We are women', 'We are indigenous', we are already imposing a new limitation upon it, we are already defining it'.[65] Hardt and Negri's theorization of the multitude in terms of an aggregation of 'singularities' points pretty much to the same direction when they argue that 'the multitude transposes the exclusive and limiting logic of identity-difference into the open and exclusive logic of singularity-commonality' and that 'the multitude's resistance to bondage – the struggle against the slavery of belonging to a nation, an identity, and a people, and thus the desertion from sovereignty and the limits it places on subjectivity – is entirely positive'.[66]

Importantly, neither Holloway nor Hardt and Negri advocate this departure from identity politics on the grounds of the latter's failure or institutional containment. Instead, the pressing issue is how to enable a theory of revolutionary action or, in more modest terms, a theory of *oppositional engagement of the energies of the multitude* that is articulated as a continuous, everyday, transformative process rather than requiring a violent break or revolt. Clearly, the lessons of feminist theory have not been wasted. Arguably, the multitude's explication as an aggregation of singularities was, to an extent, anticipated by Julia Kristeva's theorization of a future modality of feminism of singularities and multiple identifications in her 1979 essay 'Women's Time'.[67] But much work will be required to render visible the hidden connections that might enable a critical interaction between the complex legacy of feminism and the theories of revolutionary praxis of today.

However, what is certainly questionable at present is that feminism must reiterate its separate ground. Do we really 'need to ask what distinguishes feminist politics from other kind of politics' today, as argued by Aruna d'Souza in 'Feminist Time: A Conversation'?[68] We know that what distinguishes feminist politics from other kind of politics is feminism's attendance to the multiple forms of discrimination and oppression (material and immaterial) affecting women, whether born or made, as subjects inhabiting and always formed within specific social conditions. What the political subjectivity of the multitude introduces with considerable urgency is quite the opposite question: *what are the points of convergence between feminist politics and other politics?* And how can they be best deployed so as to achieve a large-scale transformation of the social? A politics of knowledge in art and the social spaces it currently crosses cannot but be a knowledge of each other's politics, which also implies an agonistic sociality where the 'other' can at least potentially be re-inscribed as an agent of an expanded, global *polis*.

The notion of 'alliance' plays a critical role in the politicization of feminist art history. In the recent past a postmodern spirit had permeated the elective use of this term, or indeed the *practice* of this term (of forming alliances) – a postmodern spirit underwritten by identity politics, their potential but also their limitations. There seemed to be a clear, and possibly historically necessary, demarcation of the boundaries of any given struggle and these boundaries proliferated. But identity politics is not today displaced by any theoretical schema (poststructuralism's and psychoanalysis's attendance to the inherent instability of identity) but by historical processes that permit the rise of a political consciousness beyond identity. We know that postmodernism's favoured 'open-endedness' and 'unfixity' of identity was subverted by the explosive geopolitics created by global capital. Visualizations of identity, such as wearing the veil or the mini skirt, are today inscribed into political and not merely cultural discourses. In many respects identity became problematic after it crossed from culture to *real-politik*, with America's 9/11 as a landmark date. One of the most engaging points made in recent analyses of social life is that opposition to the biopolitical reality defined by and through global capital is *by default* predicated on the mobilization of commonalities and one should not waste one's breath in making a big deal out of this. The multitude is only conceivable as an expressed commonality among those constituting a new productive class, and in many respects it emerges at the aftermath of an identity politics taken to an extreme, an aftermath that has left us with assemblies of 'human resources' united (whether they know so or not) in the production and use of empire's 'common' wealth.[69] If the efforts of a new feminist art history become concentrated on the articulation of a materialist paradigm that situates women's practices of resistance and women's diasporas of labour into contemporary biopolitical production, where artists and cultural workers in general are also placed, a significant step will have been taken in the direction of reviving feminist art history's potential as a politics.

Notes

1 Francesca Berry and Amy Mechowski were the organisers of the 'Whither Feminist Art History?' session, Association of Art Historians 32nd Annual Conference, 'Contents. Discontents. Malcontents', University of Leeds, 5–7 April 2006 (my emphasis).

2 See H. Foster, 'The Artist as Ethnographer' in H. Foster, *The Return of the Real* (Cambridge, MA: The MIT Press, 1996) and M. Kwon, *One Place after Another: Site-Specific Art and Locational Identity* (Cambridge, MA: The MIT Press, 2004).

3 J. Derrida, *Specters of Marx: The State of the Debt, the Work of Mourning and the New International* (London: Routledge, 1994). See also B. Magnus and S. Gullenberg (eds), *Whither Marxism? Global Crises in International Perspective* (London: Routledge, 1995).

4 M. Kwon, in 'Feminist Time: A Conversation', *Grey Room* 31 (2008), 32–67. Here p. 2.
5 A. Jones, '1970/2007: The Return of Feminist Art', *X-tra Contemporary Art Quarterly* 10/4 (Summer 2008), www.x-traonline.org/past_articles.php?articleID=184, accessed 28 June 2009.
6 For a reading of biennials as operating against US hegemony, see M. Brenson, 'The Curator's Moment' in Z. Kocur and S. Leung (eds), *Theory in Contemporary Art since 1985* (Chichester: Wiley-Blackwell, 2005). For a discussion of biennials in terms of homogenization see J. Stallabrass, *Art Incorporated* (New York and Oxford: Oxford University Press, 2004). Of relevance are J. Tang, 'Of Biennials and Biennialists: Venice, Documenta, Münster', *Theory, History & Society* 24/7–8 (2007), 247–60 and Chin-tao Wu, 'Biennials without Borders?', *New Left Review* 57 (May–June 2009), 107–15.
7 N. Klein, *The Shock Doctrine: The Rise of Disaster Capitalism* (London: Penguin, 2007), p. 18.
8 M. Hardt and A. Negri, *Empire* (Cambridge, MA and London: Harvard University Press, 2000). See also M. Hardt and A. Negri, *Multitude: War and Democracy in the Age of Empire* (London: Penguin, 2004); and M. Hardt and A. Negri, *Commonwealth* (Cambridge, MA and London: Harvard University Press, 2009). For an engaging discussion of the concept of the multitude and its history, see Malcolm Bull, 'The Limits of Multitude', *New Left Review* 35 (September–October 2005), 19–39.
9 C. Bartolovich, 'History without History: Critical Counterfactualism and Revolution', *New Formations* 59 (2006), special issue *After Iraq: Reframing Postcolonial Studies*, 63–80.
10 In 2006 the World Economic Forum asserted that: 'Even in light of heightened international awareness of gender issues, it is a disturbing reality that no country has yet managed to eliminate the gender gap.' World Economic Forum, 'Women's Empowerment: Measuring the Global Gender Gap', www.weforum.org/pdf/Global_Competitiveness_Reports/Reports/gender, accessed 8 March 2006.
11 David Harvey, *The Enigma of Capital and the Crises of Capitalism* (London: Profile Books, 2011), p. 15.
12 In November 2005 a report entitled 'Women in an Insecure World' was delivered to the United Nations, raising the issue of the 'missing women': at the time 200,000 million women were missing because of various forms of 'violence against women', including sex-based infanticide. www.dcaf.ch/women/pb_women_ex_sum.pdf, last accessed on 8 March 2006.
13 J. Roberts, 'The Museum and the Crisis of Critical Postmodernism', *Third Text* 41 (Winter 1997–98), 66–73.
14 B. Groys, 'On the New' in *Art Power* (Cambridge, MA: The MIT Press, 2008), p. 25. First published in *Research Journal of Anthropology and Aesthetics* 38 (Autumn 2000).
15 See 'Feminist Time: A Conversation', p. 44. Senam Okudzeto, a participant to this discussion, mentioned the performance of South African artist Tracey Rose, which openly commented on how the artist felt she was being treated in the show.

Okudzeto explained that 'while the museum made funds available for travel, artists received no fees or per diems and were required to give twenty-minute public talks in return. These demands may seem to apply to everyone equally, but they fall with disparate impact on artists from poor countries. The sting of Rose's intervention was diluted by dint of its being presented as a "performance" and therefore easily dismissed as a fictional construction commenting on the past. In fact it was a direct and angry response to immediate events.'

16 See Sylvia Walby, *The Future of Feminism* (London: Polity Press, 2011), p. 6.

17 G. Pollock (ed.), *Generations and Geographies in the Visual Arts: Feminist Readings* (London and New York: Routledge, 1996).

18 M. Reilly and L. Nochlin (eds), *Global Feminisms: New Directions in Contemporary Art* (London: Merrell, 2007), p. 31.

19 Ibid.

20 S. Okudzeto in 'Feminist Time: A Conversation', p. 44.

21 For a detailed discussion of Fraser's 'Untitled' and its significance for contemporary feminist criticism see Angela Dimitrakaki, 'Labour, Ethics, Sex and Capital: On Biopolitical Production in Contemporary Art', *n.paradoxa* 28 (July 2011), pp. 5–15. A brief description of Sierra's piece can be found on www.santiago-sierra.com/200014_1024.php, accessed 26 September 2011.

22 This division becomes complicated (though it is not undone) by works that focus on male homosexuality such as the videos of Dani Marti documenting the male artist offering moments of sexual intimacy to other men in exchange for these men's licence to the artist to produce the video document as such. See Kirsten Lloyd, 'The Ethics of Encounter', *Artpulse Magazine* 2/4 (Summer 2011), 26–8.

23 See Laura María Augustin, *Sex at the Margins: Migration, Labour Markets and the Rescue Industry* (London: Zed Books, 2007).

24 Rist quoted in P. Phelan, 'Opening Up Spaces within Spaces: The Expansive Art of Pipilotti Rist' in H.-U. Obrist, P. Phelan and E. Bronfen, *Pipilotti Rist* (London: Phaidon Press, 2001), p. 53. Rist practically repeats her objection when saying in a 1994 interview included in the same volume: 'I admit it bothers me that gender has become such a dominant factor in the perception of my work.' See 'I'm only half-aware of the world: Interview with Cristoph Doswald', p. 120.

25 R. Kapferer and S. Sassen, 'Women on the Move', *Frieze* 105 (March 2007), 38–42.

26 www.fawcettsociety.org.uk/index.asp?PageID=188 accessed 1 May 2008.

27 Ulrike Müller in 'Feminist Time: A Conversation', p. 36.

28 H. Molesworth, 'House Work, Art Work', *October* 92 (Spring 2000), 71–97.

29 M. Vishmidt, 'Line Describing A Curb: Asymptotes about VALIE EXPORT, the New Urbanism and Contemporary Art' in W. Bradley and C. Esche (eds), *Art and Social Change: A Critical Reader* (London: Tate Publishing in association with Afterall, 2007), p. 449.

30 I am paraphrasing Heidi Hartmann's famous essay 'The Unhappy Marriage of Marxism and Feminism: Towards a More Progressive Union', *Capital & Class* 3/2 (1979), pp. 1–33.

31 See A. Dimitrakaki, 'The Spectacle and Its Others: Labour, Conflict and Art in the Age of Global Capital' in J. Harris (ed.), *Globalization and Contemporary Art* (Chichester: Wiley-Blackwell, 2011).

32 N. Papastergiadis, *The Turbulence of Migration* (Cambridge: Polity Press, 2000), p. 202.

33 *Altermodern*, 4th Tate Triennial, Tate Britain, 3 February–26 April 2009. Bourriaud notes in the exhibition guide: 'If twentieth-century modernism has mainly been a western cultural phenomenon, altermodernity arises out of negotiations between agents from different cultures and geographical locations. Stripped of a centre, it can only be a polyglot. Altermodernity is characterised by cultural translation.'

34 Papastergiadis, *The Turbulence of Migration*, p. 205 (my emphasis).

35 See Foster, *The Return of the Real*, p. 171.

36 Valerie M. Moghadam argued in 2005 that 'the perception is growing around the globe that poverty is becoming increasingly feminized', citing research mainly from the 1990s onwards. See V. Moghadam, 'The "Feminization of Poverty" and Women's Human Rights', SHS Papers in Women's Studies/Gender Research series, Unesco 2005, http://portal.unesco.org/shs/en/ev.php-URL_ID=8282&URL_DO=DO_TOPIC&URL_SECTION=201.html accessed 18 July 2009.

37 Miwon Kwon, 'One Place after Another: Notes on Site Specificity', *OCTOBER* 80 (Spring 1997), pp. 85–110; Nicolas Bourriaud, 'Altermodern Manifesto/Post-modernism Is Dead' (2009), www.tate.org.uk/britain/exhibitions/altermodern/manifesto.shtm, accessed 5 November 2010.

38 I borrow this term from Okwui Enwezor et al. (eds), *Documenta 11_Platform 1: Democracy Unrealized* (Ostfildern: Hatje Kantz, 2002).

39 Bartolovich, 'History without History', p. 70 (emphasis in original).

40 Hardt and Negri, *Empire*, p. 200.

41 Okwui Enwezor, 'Black Box' in *Documenta 11_Platform 5: Exhibition* (Ostfildern: Hatje Kantz, 2002).

42 Hardt and Negri, *Empire*, p. 200. They also proceed to re-view key terms of postcolonial and sexual politics – such as 'hybridity' – within a contemporary logic of production and productivity. Hybridity, mobility and artificiality are characterized as 'the common productive experience of the multitude'. See Hardt and Negri, *Empire*, pp. 216–17.

43 Ibid., p. 205. Both in *Empire* and *Multitude* the authors stress in numerous places that the multitude describes a class. This is an indicative excerpt: 'This is a *new proletariat* and a *new industrial working class*. … 'proletariat' is the general concept that defines all those whose labor is exploited by capital, the entire cooperating multitude … The industrial working class represented only a partial moment in the history of the proletariat and its revolutions, in the period when capital was able to reduce value to measure … This wide landscape of biopolitical production allows us finally to recognize the full generality of the concept of the proletariat'. Hardt and Negri, *Empire*, p. 402.

44 Allan Sekula's photographic documentation of a day during the protests against the WTO-summit in Seattle entitled 'Waiting for Teargas (White Globe to Black)' (1999–2000) and were first published in A. Cockbur, J. St Clair and A. Sekula, *5 Days that Shook the World: Seattle and Beyond* (London and New York: Verso, 2000).

45 Bartolovich, 'History without History', p. 69.

46 A. Callinicos, 'Toni Negri in Perspective' in G. Balakrishnan (ed.), *Debating Empire* (London and New York: Verso, 2003), pp. 138–9.

47 Julie Torrant argues: 'It is not possible … to produce feelings of ease and well-being in children … if these children are not provided daily and consistently with the basic necessities of food, clothing, shelter, and so forth … Hardt and Negri's theory of "affective labor", through its displacement of "reproductive labor", works to foreground the family as an inter-personal space. This, in turn, denies that the family in capitalism is subordinated to the reproduction of wage-labor and thus denies that it is economically shaped and determined by the relations of wage-labor/capital.' See J. Torrant, 'Empire versus Imperialism and the Question of Family Labor', *The Red Critique: Marxist Theory and the Critique of the Contemporary* 5 (July/August 2002), www.redcritique.org/JulyAugust02/index.html, accessed on 19 July 2009. See also L. Quinby, 'Taking the Millenialist Pulse of Empire's Multitude: A Genealogical Feminist Analysis' in J. Dean and P. Passavant (eds), *The Empire's New Clothes: Reading Hardt and Negri* (London and New York: Routledge, 2003); and, more recently, Silvia Federici, 'Feminism and the Politics of the Commons', *The Commoner* (January 2011), www.commoner.org.uk/?p=113, accessed 26 September 2011. The above references are only indicative. I am grateful to Alberto Toscano for his help in locating feminist critiques of *Empire*.

48 'Biopolitical circulation focuses on and celebrates the substantial determinations of the activities of production, self-valorization, and freedom. Circulation is a global exodus, or really nomadism; and it is a corporeal exodus, or really miscegenation.' Hardt and Negri, *Empire*, p. 364.

49 See especially 'Virtualities' in ibid.

50 Hardt and Negri also engage Agamben's concept of 'naked life'. See Hardt and Negri ibid., p. 366.

51 Ibid., p. 400.

52 Hardt and Negri, *Multitude*, p. 110.

53 Hardt and Negri, *Empire*, p. 403. For an engaging and detailed discussion of these issues, drawing on feminist traditions, see Kathi Weeks, *The Problem with Work: Feminism, Marxism, Antiwork Politics and Postwork Imaginaries* (Durham, NC: Duke University Press, 2011).

54 See Marion von Osten, 'She's Gone Flexible …' in J. Billing, M. Lind and L. Nilsson (eds), *Taking the Matter into Common Hands: On Contemporary Art and Collaborative Practices* (London: Black Dog, 2007).

55 'These workers [at the maquilas] don't just pay with their time. There is another, more disturbing side to this contract. A good part of the equipment produced in the maquiladoras are optical technologies: medical and cyber optics, surveillance instruments, x-ray satellite technologies, micro- and telescoping, audio-visual media, identification, scanning, digitizing, controlling and simulating electronics. They all improve our optical range from entering the tiniest particles to peeking into deep space. One of the major hiring criteria is excellent eyesight in order to be able to perform precision tasks.' Ursula Biemann in I. Szeman, 'Remote Sensing: An Interview with Ursula Biemann', *Review of Education/Pedagogy/Cultural Studies* 24/1–2 (January–June 2002), 91–109. Here p. 99.

56 A useful description of this project can be found in J. Mastai (ed.), *Social Process/Collaborative Action: Mary Kelly 1970–1975* (Vancouver, ON: Charles H. Scott Gallery, Emily Carr Institute of Art and Design, 1997).

57 The issue of women artists and travel was addressed in my paper 'Beyond the Global Flaneuse: Travelling, Women and the Politics of Art as Labour', presented on 3 April 2008 at the session 'Dis-Locations: Movements and Migrations' convened by Rosemary Betterton and Dorothy Rowe in the context of 'Location: The Museum, the Academy and the Studio', 34th Annual AAH conference, Tate Britain and Tate Modern, London 2–4 April 2008.

58 There is a burgeoning bibliography on participation art. Starting with the practices that renowned feminist artist Suzanne Lacy brought together in S. Lacy (ed.), *Mapping the Terrain: New Genre Public Art* (Seattle, WA: Bay Press 1995); N. Bourriaud, *Relational Aesthetics* (Dijon: Les presses de reel, 2002 [1998]); and G. Kester, *Conversation Pieces: Community and Communication in Modern Art* (Berkeley, CA and London: University of California Press, 2004), 'participation art' broadly encompasses practices that require the active involvement of people to produce an 'artwork'.

59 See, for example, C. Guerra, 'Other Europes: The Video Essay's Collective Pedagogies' in M. Lind and H. Steyel (eds), *The Greenroom: Reconsidering the Documentary and Contemporary Art* (New York: Lukas & Sternberg, 2009); and T.J. Demos in U. Biemann (ed.), *Mission Reports: Artistic Practice on the Field, Video Essays 1998–2008* (Umeå: Bildmuseet/Arnolfini, 2008).

60 A. Dimitrakaki, 'Materialist Feminism for the Twenty-First Century: The Video Essays of Ursula Biemann', *Oxford Art Journal* 30/7 (2007), pp. 205–32.

61 Ulrike Müller makes this statement in the context of 'Feminist Time: A Conversation', p. 47; Biemann is quoted in Dimitrakaki, 'Materialist Feminism for the Twenty-First Century', p. 227.

62 Hardt and Negri go as far as to argue that 'the reactionary deliriums of fascism and Nazism were unleashed when capital discovered that social cooperation was no longer the result of the investment of capital but rather an autonomous power, the a priori of every act of production'. See Hardt and Negri, *Empire*, p. 366.

63 See T. Hammar, *Democracy and the Nation State: Aliens, Denizens and Citizens in a World of International Migration* (Aldershot: Avebury, 1990). On current institutions, representation and the people (a designation sharply differentiated from the multitude) see Hardt and Negri, *Empire*, p. 311.

64 Papastergiadis, *The Turbulence of Migration*, 2000, pp. 210–11.

65 J. Holloway, *Change the World without Taking Power: The Meaning of Revolution Today* (London and New York: Pluto Press, 2002), p. 56.

66 Hardt and Negri, *Multitude*, p. 255; and Hard and Negri, *Empire*, pp. 361–2.

67 See J. Kristeva, 'Women's Time', translated by Alice Jardine and Harry Blake, *Signs* 7/1 (Autumn 1981), 13–35. Here pp. 34–5. However, Kristeva refers to 'the *singularity* of each person' (emphasis in the original), whereas Hardt and Negri's mention of singularities may also refer to singular instances of co-operative action in the context of the multitude.

68 A. d'Souza in 'Feminist Time: A Conversation', p. 44.

69 On the issue of identity, see the discussion of identity politics in Hardt and Negri, *Commonwealth*; and Amelia Jones, *Seeing Differently: A History and Theory of Identification in the Visual Arts* (Abingdon: Routledge, 2012).

2 Women, art, migration and diaspora: the turn to art in the social sciences and the 'new' sociology of art?

Maggie O'Neill

> Arts have a frontier role in building knowledge. We have to come to terms with the dilemma of 'difference' without feeling threatened by the Other … Engaging the creative process through the Arts brings meaning to humanity[1]

Introduction and context

This paper builds upon and extends previous work by the author that explores the transformative role of art and the methodological approach of working with artists to conduct ethnographic research as critical theory in practice.[2] Working in the space between art and ethnography with performance artist Sara Giddens (1998–2000) led to a trilogy of works called *Not all the time, but mostly*. Our collaboration aimed to work at the borders of art and ethnography and together we worked with (heavily anonymized) ethnographic biographical interviews with sex workers that I undertook between 1990 and 1995. Inherently feminist and keen to push the boundaries between social research and performance art, Sara choreographed two live art performances based upon the narratives. These two performances focused on the physical and material bodies of sex workers – walking, being, sensing, feeling, and negotiating the mundane material and emotional realities of being a sex worker, a mother, a lover. The performance worked with both the body and the narrative voice, expressing the ordinariness of the women whilst also challenging stigmatizing discourses on the 'prostitute' and sex work. The first performance was filmed and distributed as a DVD, and an exhibition of images from the second performance travelled between the East and West Midlands, London and Bristol.

This work was instrumental in exploring methodologically the possibilities involved in having an artist and social science researcher work together to analyse and represent ethnographic interviews. In developing this approach I wanted to extend the process so that the artist and researcher were involved in the entire research process from inception, research and design to writing up and disseminating. A second project based on this methodology began in 1999 and focused upon forced migration working in partnership with a Bosnian refugee community and two artists, Bea Tobolewska and Maggy Milner. Our participatory action research and participatory arts work examined refugees' and asylum seekers' experiences of exile, displacement and belonging, and the transformative role of art and culture in the development of new arrival communities. This second phase of work was committed to participatory ways of working, was funded by the AHRC (Arts and Humanities Research Council) and sought to realize 'performative praxis' by impacting upon social and cultural policy and practice.

This chapter is based on this second phase of research and was funded by the AHRB (Arts and Humanities Research Board)/AHRC. Four projects make up this period of research, from 1999 to 2010.The first project was called *Global Refugees: Exile, Displacement and Belonging* (1999–2001). We worked with an Afghan community in London and Bosnian community in the East Midlands; biographical interviews were conducted, and creative writing workshops and visual representations of lived experience (*Exile, Displacement and Belonging*) were produced and exhibited in Nottingham and London in partnership with Exiled Writers Ink! and Nottingham City Arts. This work led to the second project, a *Research Exchange* (1999–2001) between Bea Tobolewska, who was then director of City Arts, Nottingham, a community arts organization and me, based in a university. Together with research partners (Refugee Action) we produced a cultural strategy for working with refugees and asylum seekers in the East Midlands that was supported by the then Arts Council East Midlands. Funding to hold a conference 'The Long Journey Home' and support for an arts initiative/organization of the same name was provided by the Arts Council as one outcome of this work. New arrival communities, refugees and asylum seekers, were written in to arts and cultural infrastructures. These two projects brought our attention to the need for more networking in the region between communities, especially newly emerging communities, researchers, artists and policy makers. *Making the Connections: Arts, Migration and Diaspora* (2006–08) was subsequently funded. Over a two-year period a series of seminars and workshops led by communities, universities, practitioners and policy makers took place that sought to create bridges and opportunities across the theory/practice/community divides. Finally, this collaborative and participatory research led to a Knowledge Transfer Fellowship project, *Transnational Communities: Towards a Sense of Belonging*, in partnership with four community arts organizations in the East Midlands region.[3] This project enabled the partners to do more focused in-depth work with four refugee communities and four community arts organizations, including the Long Journey Home artists in exile group, around processes involved in belonging, a more relational and complex process than the then government's concept of 'integration' as a 'two-way' process.

All four projects were underpinned by the principles of participatory action research and participatory arts that included a focus upon inclusion, participation and valuing all local voices, as well as being interventionist, action oriented and interpretive. The projects illustrate that in the collaborative process between refugee/asylum seeker/migrant, artist and social researcher, a 'thicker'[4] understanding of the lived experiences of migration, and processes of belonging and diaspora can emerge that challenges identity thinking,[5] and helps to produce a richer notion of social justice. Thus this brings an approach to knowledge production as collaboratively made, not found, which loosens the knowledge/power axis involved in knowledge production and 'expertness' and may feed into policy making through praxis.

The collaborative process (a co-production) is conducted not 'on' or 'for' but 'with' the individuals who are usually the stereotypical subjects of research. This process, defined as ethno-mimesis (the combination of ethnographic, often biographical research and arts-based representation) is committed to fostering an interpretive role that includes creating spaces for the marginalized/subaltern to speak for themselves through engagement in research that combines ethnography with arts-based work and the production of images/poetic/performance texts.

As we worked in partnership and participation with artists and migrants, three major themes emerged in our work: first, the importance of stories and storytelling, biography and narrative; second, the importance of re-presenting life stories in visual/artistic form; third, the importance of working with people as subjects through participatory methodologies – such as participatory action research and participatory arts. The arts have a major role in processes of social inclusion, and are vitally important in helping to create spaces for creativity, dialogue and inclusion.[6] Indeed, I have argued elsewhere that the space or hyphen between ethnography (sociology) and arts-based practice – photos/installations/textual practice-(mimesis) becomes a 'potential space' for transformative possibilities.[7]

This chapter maps out the theoretical context to this work, explores these three themes in relation to the experiences and narratives of women asylum seekers and refugees, and, finally, asks how art might engage the experiences of recent migrant communities in the UK (drawing upon the research trajectory documented above) to challenge stereotypes and identity thinking and envision social justice through a 'radical democratic imaginary'.[8] Moreover, it is suggested that this work is part of a broader 'turn to art' in the social sciences feeding into the development of the 'new sociology of art'.[9]

Theoretical and methodological context

Re-presenting ethnographic data (life story interviews, biographical work) of migrants both forced and free, in artistic form (via ethno-mimesis) enables understanding of the complexities and sensuousness of lived experience, emotionally, materially and culturally. Such work can also reach a wider population, beyond academic communities, facilitating understanding/interpretation and, maybe, action/praxis in relation to de-mythologizing certain stereotypes, attitudes and identity thinking relating to 'refugees' and 'asylum seekers'.[10]

Theoretically and methodologically the research engages an interpretive feminist account of women's life histories, rooted in immersion in the feeling worlds of participants and represented through fragments of women's narratives, image-based work and poetic texts. Methodologically, this approach, defined as 'ethno-mimesis' (a combination of social research and arts practice), is rooted, for me in four key concepts:

(i) the interrelation between feminist thought and practice/praxis involving a process of immersion in women's lives or communities, followed by interpretation, commentary and critical analysis;
(ii) doing interpretive ethnography as a way of understanding women's lived experiences, especially the development of critical standpoint epistemologies that may be re-presented or emerge in the arts-based work;
(iii) the importance of arts-based work especially participatory arts; and
(iv) doing cultural sociology[11] as performative praxis.

Performative praxis involves the generation of knowledge that is purposeful, change causing or transformative. Hence, for me, the turn to art in the social sciences is a welcome move.

Feminisms and cultural sociology share a methodological and epistemological focus upon a primarily phenomenological approach to understanding the processes and practices of our socio-cultural worlds, and the everyday lived experiences and meaning-making practices we engage in. My earlier work on feminist aesthetics looked to develop an understanding of the foundations in social life for a feminist aesthetics of modernism rooted in an analysis of the transformative, liberating potential of women's art.

In a recent work (2001, 2007, 2011) I argued that the self-reflexivity inherent in the ethnographic process, alongside the crisis in ethnography and the 'linguistic' and 'cultural turn' in socio-cultural theory has led to demands for experimentation in the representation of ethnographic data, especially in relation to gender and race.[12] Drawing upon the work of Adorno and Benjamin,[13] I suggested that re-presentations of ethnographic work can create multivocal, dialogical texts that can make visible emotional structures and inner experiences which may 'move' audiences through what can be described as 'sensuous knowing' or mimesis.[14] The 'subjective-reflexive' feeling[15] involved in the process of creating/producing arts-based work can also be change-causing for the producer and can be therapeutic/healing[16] for the artist and audience. The process involved in the practice of 'ethno-mimesis' is reflexive and phenomenological but it is also critical and looks to praxis, as in the filmic work of Trinh T. Minh-ha.[17]

The work of Trinh, in undoing the realist ethnography project, shows that there is no single overriding vision of the world but rather multiple realities, multiple standpoints, and multiple meanings. This reflexivity acknowledges that the 'real' world can still be recovered through ethnographic work, through a postmodern 'multinational, multicultural gaze that probes, yet goes beyond local markets while it remains anchored in the interactional experiences of the reflexive ethnographer'.[18] I suggest that what Denzin and Alasuutari[19] call 'hybrid texts' emerge as the outcome of research that is intrinsically relational and engages with forms of representation, be it visual, performative, or literary/poetic.

In the following section I present some examples of 'hybrid texts' produced in the context of collaboration between art and ethnography and conducted with Bosnian and Afghan refugees as well as more recent arrivals to the English East Midlands. However, I want to first contextualize this work by providing an account of the empirical research on the lived experiences of women refugees and asylum seekers.

Women seeking asylum: context to the research

What we know about the lives and experiences of women seeking asylum in the UK is based upon a relatively small amount of research. Nationally the top five countries with the highest number of principal female asylum applicants in 2005 were Zimbabwe (1,085), China (775), Democratic Republic of Congo (770) and Pakistan (640). The Home Office has ceased to disaggregate the statistics by gender. However, in 2009 the Refugee Action vulnerable women's project found that the majority of the women they worked with were from Sri Lanka, Eritrea, Democratic Republic of Congo, Ivory Coast and Somalia.[20] Available research shows that asylum policy in the West is gender biased and statistical data on women is limited.[21] Women refugees and asylum seekers suffer particular problems and inequalities as a consequence of gender-biased asylum policies, and there is a dearth of research on refugee women and their families.

The needs of women refugees, asylum seekers and their children are clearly a major gap and an important focus for improving asylum policy in a way that is based upon equitable and transparent policy making for women and their families and children (some of whom are left behind in their home country). The legal context provides important benchmarks for social policy.[22]

In 2002, research conducted in the UK by Refugee Action, *Is it Safe Here?* subsequently formed the basis for Refugee Action's campaign *Standing up for Women's Safety*. The research documents that 83 per cent of women interviewed feel so unsafe that they live under self-imposed curfew, locking themselves indoors after 7 o'clock at night. A third of those interviewed had been spat on or shouted at in the street. One in two women felt so depressed and anxious they were not able to sleep at night.

In research published by the Refugee Council in 2005, *Making Women Visible*, the same author, Dumper, stressed the need for a gender-sensitive system of protection based upon women's specific gender-based experiences of persecution, which may include conforming to social expectations, sexual violence, trafficking, forced marriage, honour killings and female genital mutilation. The research also documents the many barriers that make it difficult for a woman to pursue a claim for asylum in her own right. Women claim asylum in the UK in their own right, as well as through family reunion and as dependants.

The study found that as a consequence of the impact of current asylum policy women seeking protection in the UK experience poverty and destitution, as well as problems with dispersal, accommodation, health and maternity issues, detention and difficulties getting access to information. The research also highlighted that many women seeking asylum in the UK suffer gross forms of sexual abuse before arrival and raises the issue of the sexual abuse of women by individuals they come into contact with here in the UK. Trafficking is also an issue of concern. The research documents reports of women being taken away from accommodation centres by traffickers. Moreover, girls and young women are especially vulnerable to sexual exploitation and often feel very isolated. Issues of domestic violence are also highlighted.

In addition to the issues of destitution and poverty mentioned above, of concern was the denial to asylum seekers of the right to work, and the researchers also highlighted the need for more investigation in this area. Dumper highlights the need for greater involvement of women in refugee-led community organizations and more projects led by refugee women that include supporting the capacity of refugee women to develop their own services and support systems.

Research conducted in 2005 by O'Neill, Pitcher and Krah[23] further supports the research by Dumper for Refugee Action. Women spoke of their first experience of coming to the UK:

> when I came to this country, [it was a] completely different system. Different life. Not only the language. At the beginning it was really difficult.[24]

For some the arrival experience was compounded by the authority's disbelief of their claims and they felt humiliated and degraded by their experiences.

> My experiences were disgusting and horrible. I was detained for two days and with my pregnancy. The officers knew about my pregnancy because they saw my bulge stomach. I was stripped naked because they said they were looking for drugs maybe because of suspicion. … since then it affected my reasoning and consciousness.[25]

A sense of dislocation, not knowing the language and also culture shock added to feelings of fear and isolation.

> When I was coming from London and was given a house here, the only thing I was given was an agreement with lists of facilities. Because I knew nothing of anything concerning the location of the areas I was depressed.
>
> It is so lonely, like I stayed in the house for I think two months. Would just go and pick the money, do some shopping and come back in the house.
>
> I think if I can get some counselling, if I talk it out first, then I will feel more settled, a bit better. You know I think it is because I am not busy, I have been thinking about so much it [circumstances including isolation, poor housing situation and living on a limited budget] and it is getting on my nerves. And it is the thing that has even stopped me from breastfeeding my baby.[26]

Our interviews with a range of support agencies further supported the women's narratives.

> There've been a lot of emotional needs, because either it has been the case that the women have come to this country on their own, or they have actually suffered trauma where they have come from, and that's in terms of not having their own family support over here, or it could be that some of their children are here with them and some of them they have had to leave behind. (Project support worker)
>
> People come over with a lot of problems, psychological, physical, and mental. Some have been tortured or raped. They don't tend to come with coughs or colds, but more serious problems. (Medical professional)[27]

We were also told about the impact of 'removals' on the mental health of families as well as the impact upon the friends and support workers/services who had made connections and offered support to asylum seekers. In one of the group interviews those present talked about a lady (who had hepatitis) and her child who were deported.

> Her husband had died and she was not allowed to stay. What happened to her, is she dead, is her baby gone too? The returns are devastating. (Agency representative)[28]

Another agency representative had this to say:

> Another family were taken, deported – their flat was left with everything there – they were taken at 3 am. It is desperate, their plight, their relationships, the people that are left behind … If they are known in the community, maybe going to CIP [Community Integration Partnership] and are gaining skills but also they are cared for, loved, understood they are treated like human beings their dignity is upheld. To see the mothers and for the kids to see their mothers treated with dignity, to see that Mum is valued and so the child is valued. In schools they are anxious to know that kids are whipped away at 3am. (Agency representative)[29]

Language problems, financial hardship, the impact of dispersal, and destitution are all part of the experiences of women asylum seekers.

> One family had three moves in two months, they were desperate and experiencing great difficulties … this can cause problems with the case, information goes to the wrong address and it can take a while to get it back on track. (Agency representative)

> … a woman from Uganda with mental health issues, the woman could not attend court because of her distress and a doctor signed a note to say so as she feared her case might be rejected on the grounds of non compliance. The very next day she had a letter telling her she was being moved to Hull and she had to return back to here for the court hearing – she had recently given birth to a baby. (Agency representative)

> Destitution is the big thing with this group and there are so many gradations along that line. (Agency representative)[30]

The agency representative documented these gradations as:

(i) asylum seekers without support due to refusal or non-compliance, or not re-registering;
(ii) asylum seekers of no fixed abode due to refusal to accept their one choice of accommodation;
(iii) documentation that is submitted too late to the court hearing.

We were told of one case of evidence being submitted to the Home Office two months earlier to which the applicants were still awaiting a reply; in the meantime the person was homeless.

> If they say your case is over, you are moved out of the NASS [National Asylum Support Service] house, you don't have anywhere to go. Sometimes you are forced to go and stay with a friend. If you stay with that friend she may also have problems. You become like a destitute, going back to where you started. It is so difficult. (Asylum seeker)[31]

Sexual exploitation and vulnerability are also concerns.[32] Research by the Refugee Council Vulnerable Women's Project found that of the 153 women they worked with between 2006 and 2008:

> 76% had been raped, either in their country of origin or the UK; 15% had become pregnant as a result of being raped; 5% had had a child as a result of being raped; 35% had suffered some form of violence; 22% had been sexually abused; 9% had been threatened with rape or sexual abuse while in detention in their country of origin; 27% had physical injuries; 76% were experiencing trauma-related psychological distress; 20% had gynaecological problems as a result of their experiences.[33]

The key issues women raised in O'Neill, Pitcher and Krah's research[34] were basic needs such as: a roof/supported housing of a reasonable quality/money; communication and relational needs; education and training opportunities; childcare and support; counselling; access to health and sexual health services; and related issues such as sexual exploitation, violence and vulnerability.

What is clear from these research findings is that creating spaces for women to tell their stories is vital (especially in the context of a gender-insensitive asylum system, lack of female interviewers and interpreters, being wrongly detained and decision makers lacking the gender-based knowledge and skills to make appropriate decisions). Listening to women's stories and making recommendations to improve processes and practices of integration and holistic support, foster human dignity and counter the prejudice, humiliation and loss of dignity that many women experience (in the process of seeking a place of safety in the UK for themselves and their families) are crucial responses. Moreover, it is clear that that co-ordinated horizontal (grass-roots, face-to-face work by refugee-support organizations, and arts and cultural organizations) and vertical processes (local and regional policy making) of social inclusion are vital too, and these include arts and cultural organizations and infrastructures.

To summarize, what we know about women asylum seekers and refugees is that women experience particular sexual and social inequalities when seeking asylum and in the process of integration; they are relatively absent in the literature and research; they suffer from gender-biased asylum policies (despite the gender guidelines introduced by the Home Office); their voices go unheard in many policy debates; yet Dumper[35] reported in 2006 that nationally 43 per cent of those asylum applicants supported through NASS accommodation were female, and Refugee Action's research shows that about half of refugee women in the UK are the head of their household.[36]

Women cope with the dislocation of arrival; the loss of families, loved ones and children (some of whom they have had to leave behind); the impact of violence, rape and abuse; and the impact of dispersal – and yet, as we have found, are resilient and hopeful, and want to contribute, work and earn a living for themselves and their children.

How might arts-based research that incorporates ethnographic and artistic thinking represent women's stories? How might the outcomes of this research challenge tired and deeply problematic stereotypes, inform and educate the general population *and* potentially impact on the lives of new arrivals to the UK? The following section examines the transformative role of arts and culture in fostering integration and belonging for women refugees and asylum seekers.

Transnational lives: arts, migration, diaspora

> Cultural activity and creative expression are key to the formation of identity both at an individual and a community level – it is vital for refugees to be able to engage in creative acts by being participants in its creation. Such participation brings benefits to them as individuals, communities and can also contribute to social inclusion.[37]

Methodologies that incorporate the voices and images of refugees and asylum seekers through ethno-mimesis and participatory collaborative research can not only serve to raise awareness about the issues for women but might also produce critical texts that may help to mobilize change. Ethno-mimesis is founded upon principles of mutual recognition and seeks to speak in empathic ways with new arrivals through narrative and visual texts which counter valorizing discourses and the reduction of the Other (the stranger) to a cipher of the oppressed, marginalized or exploited.

Arts and culture are profoundly important in processes of inclusion, including the creative regeneration of identities, communities, and subjectivities. Additionally, arts and culture (in the broadest sense) are integral to socio-cultural regeneration and important in fostering cultural citizenship and social justice. Cultural citizenship is understood here as: the right to presence and visibility, not marginalization; the right to dignity and maintenance of lifestyle, not assimilation to the dominant culture; and the right to dignifying representation, not stigmatization.[38]

Cultural citizenship is a key factor in imagining 'social justice'. Of course, research has also shown how the arts are co-opted by governments and corporations for instrumental or 'pragmatic benefits', for example around social cohesion or to mobilize the arts in redevelopment and for regeneration purposes.[39]

Participatory action research (PAR) is a useful methodology for working with marginalized groups. It emerged from developmental politics and interpretations of the works of Marx (we need to understand the world and to change it) and Gramsci ('common sense' or 'critical knowledge' is produced through mutual recognition and collaboration).[40] It suggests that the sum of knowledge from researchers and community/group members provides a more accurate picture of the issue/reality they/we want to transform. Participatory action research involves a commitment to research that values: participation and partnership working that is based on common goals and shared ownership; inclusion, which involves enrolling participants as co-researchers; democracy, hearing all voices, not just the loudest; methodological innovation, such as arts-based 'creative consultation'; and ethical research, creating safe spaces for dialogue,[41] based on mutual recognition and respect. Hence, PAR is both a process and a practice directed toward social change *with* the participants. It is interventionist, action oriented and interpretive.[42]

Participatory arts (PA) help to make visible people's experiences and ideas for change. Their methods are understood to be reflective, transformative, sustainable and problem-solving, with an emphasis on process as well as production.[43] This kind of creative, cultural, participatory research and arts-based work is inherently linked to specific conceptions of social justice. A holistic conception of social justice[44] draws upon and extends the work of Iris Marion Young and Nancy Fraser, and includes the following aspects: distributive justice (economic – the absence of exploitation, economic marginalization and deprivation/destitution); associational justice (networks of support – enabling people to fully participate in decision making and governance); and cultural justice (the absence of cultural domination, non-recognition and disrespect).

In accordance with these precepts, PAR can foster mutual recognition, and contribute to public awareness, understanding and social justice for migrant groups, both forced and free.

In the current climate of anxiety and xenophobia stoked by some elements of the mass media, recession and the UK coalition government's retrenchment from welfare there is a vital need for our collaborations and research to foster social justice and challenge essentialist thinking in policy making and practice in relation to issues of asylum, migration and belonging. The creative work produced, presented, and discussed here did have some impact in the region (England's East Midlands).[45] Creative methodologies can help to express and re-imagine the complexity of loss, exile and dislocation, as well as re-construction, and renewal through a combination of narrativity and arts-based work. This is a dialectical, constellational and relational process, and one that looks to creativity and the social role of art as one means of re-imagining and renewing our social worlds – towards a vision of social justice that upholds human dignity and counters processes of humiliation, instrumental reason and identity thinking.

The following images and poetic texts were produced through the various projects described above and illustrate the process undertaken in the space between art and ethnography by asylum seekers/refugees working with artists and social researchers.

In *Global Refugees: Exile, Displacement and Belonging*[46] (1999–2002), alternative forms of representing and raising awareness of the lived experiences of 'refugees' from Bosnia and Afghanistan were developed. Life-story narratives were conducted and re-presented in a visual artistic form. There were four stages to the project: gathering socio-demographic information; conducting in-depth interviews and focus group interviews with Bosnian and Afghan participants; developing arts workshops to re-present life experiences in artistic form with the help of City Arts and Exiled Writers Ink!; and producing an exhibition, a symposium and a report in collaboration with the participants.

The image in Figure 2.1 was created to express thanks to a 'good neighbour' who helped the family stay alive when soldiers were looking for Muslims. The image was developed as an installation and digitally photographed with the support of artist Karen Fraser. The woman who made this image also writes how her neighbours saved her life by hiding her in this way. She baked the bread pictured in the image to thank them.

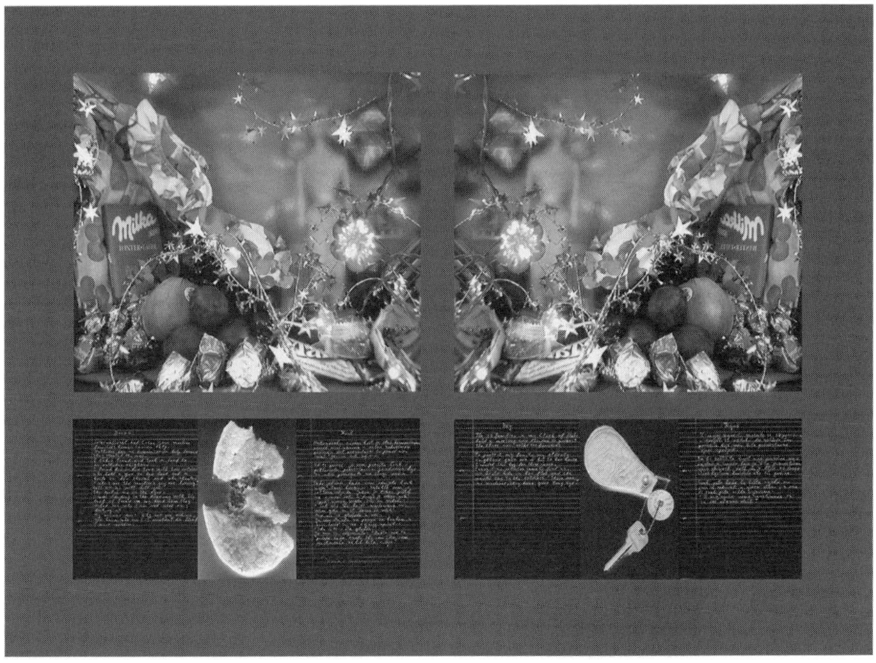

2.1 Karen Fraser with anonymous Bosnian refugee, *Good Neighbours*. From Global Refugees: Exile, Displacement and Belonging (1999–2001).

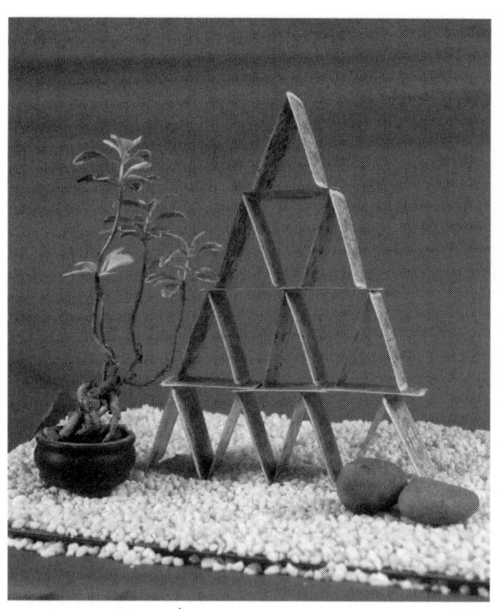

2.2 Maggie Milner and Vanessa (a Bosnian refugee), *My House I. Before, During and After the Bosnian War*. From Global Refugees: Exile, Displacement and Belonging (1999–2001).

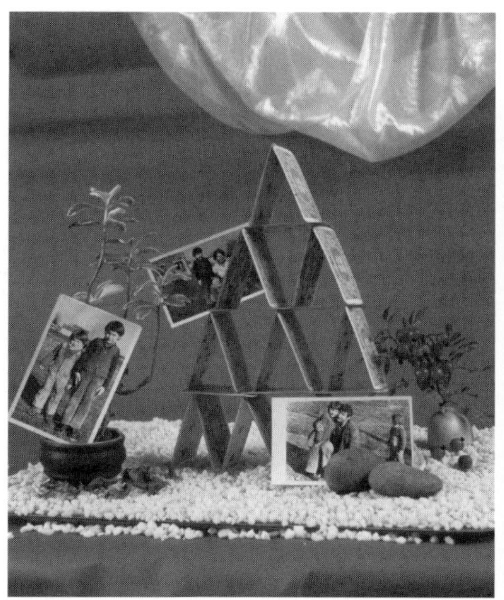

Maggie Milner and Vanessa (a Bosnian refugee), *My House II. Before, During and After the Bosnian War*. From Global Refugees: Exile, Displacement and Belonging (1999–2001).

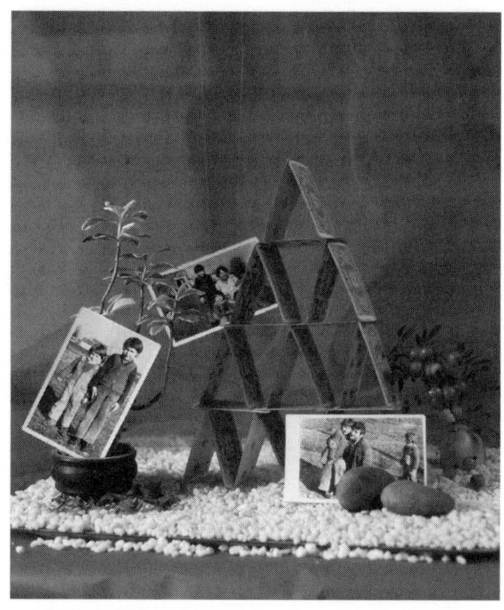

2.4 Maggie Milner and Vanessa (a Bosnian refugee), *My House III. Before, During and After the Bosnian War*. From Global Refugees: Exile, Displacement and Belonging (1999–2001).

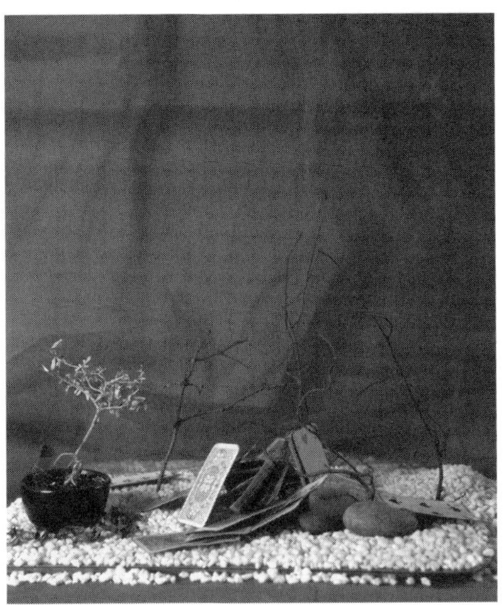

Maggie Milner and Vanessa (a Bosnian refugee), *My House IV. Before, During and* **2.5**
After the Bosnian War. From Global Refugees: Exile, Displacement and Belonging (1999–2001).

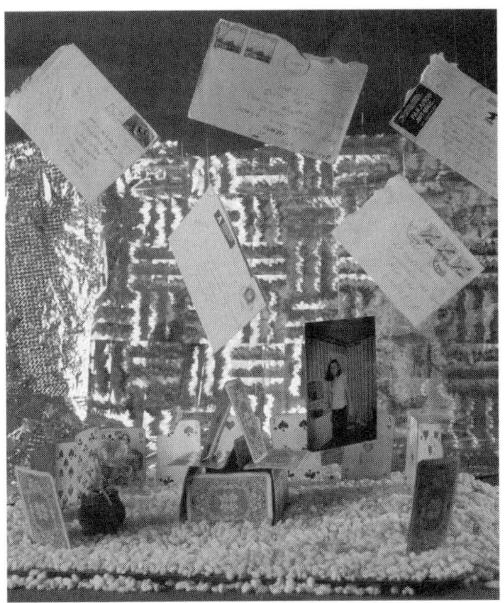

Maggie Milner and Vanessa (a Bosnian refugee), *My House V. Before, During and* **2.6**
After the Bosnian War. From Global Refugees: Exile, Displacement and Belonging (1999–2001).

Afghan participants worked with Exiled Writers Ink! in creative writing workshops to develop their biographical narratives. The texts that were produced resonate with loss and longing in relation to the sense of 'double consciousness' many feel in relation to memory and migration.

Arts, research process

The work that is produced by the participants, facilitated by artists, also bears the traces of the artists. The arts-based research workshops were initiated by the artists, researcher and participants sitting round a table looking at images, art books and examples of the artists' favourite works, some of this work on themes associate with migration and mobility, showing examples of what art might be.

Vanessa's still life photographs (Figures 2.2–2.6) bear the traces of Maggy Milner's own photographic work – the influence of the artist is present in Vanessa's use of her own artefacts, memory traces of her time in hiding, in exile and outside of citizenship. Maggy's work inspired Vanessa, and the collaborative process (starting with themes from the biographical narrative) between Maggy and Vanessa emerges in the relational work between them, mediated by Vanessa's story and the deeply evocative images and photographs she possessed and created of her life before, through and after the war.

The process of working with a researcher in the context of arts workshops with themes that had already emerged in the process of biographical research was new for the artists and was embraced as part of an interdisciplinary process. Issues of ethics and ethical considerations were discussed by the team. The research had been agreed by the university ethics committee and

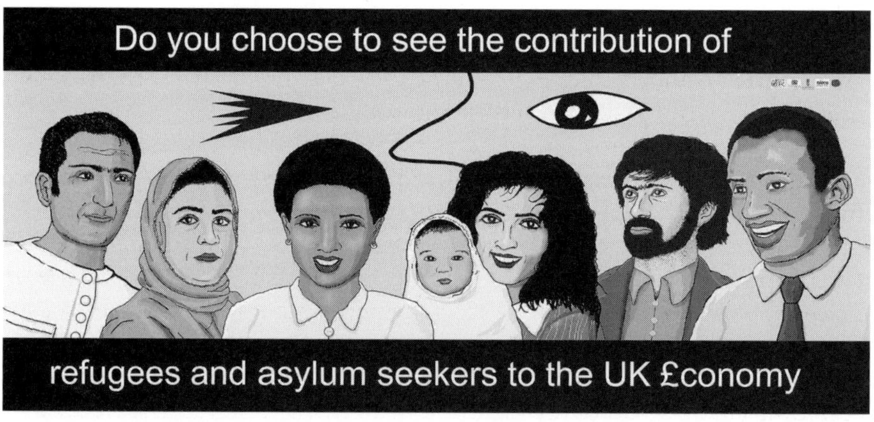

2.7 Sally Norman and Tove Dalenius (Soft Touch) with two asylum seekers: visual text representing experiences and aspirations of asylum seekers.

had been very carefully planned through processes of consultation with both community groups and arts organizations, with informed consent at the very core. In the arts workshops the artists were active listeners and enablers. In keeping with the principles of PAR/PA this relational approach enabled the participants to voice their thoughts and experiences, in a safe space, and to evaluate these as an ongoing process, in the dialogue with the artists and researcher as the work developed.

When the project was over two of the artists continued to work and develop their own arts practice in the field and continued to work within refugee communities and on the themes of war, exile and migration. The work of City Arts changed focus under the management of Bea Tobolewska: 'A focus is now aimed at supporting refugee artists (of which there are quite a few in the East Midlands) to utilise their skills and overcome blocks presented by language, lack of knowledge of the system, or lack of access to funding.'[47] With support from the regional arts council, funding was provided for the Long Journey Home conference, which in turn led to the emergence of a regional arts organization of the same name supporting artists in exile.

We can say that this project is situated amongst the tension between a modernist process of transformation through praxis and a postmodern project of hybridity, intertextuality and performative praxis. Hillis-Miller[48] argues against binaries (as in the reversibility of the politicizing of art into politics) and argues for new forms of consolidation and solidarity that can develop into processes of inclusion and belonging. For example, Exiled Writers' Ink! was set up by Jennifer Langer, herself the daughter of Jewish asylum seekers to the UK, and is a powerful example of the cultural contribution asylum seekers and refugees make to culture, cultural policy and the economy. This organization is a valuable and inspirational resource with contributions by and for refugee communities. The work described above illustrates the important role of the arts in processes of inclusion, developing new forms of consolidation and solidarity, and the combination of PAR and PA as ethno-mimesis is a useful process and practice to take on this issue.

Following these projects, work was commissioned to address issues of access to education, employment and training for new arrival communities, funded by Government Office East Midlands and Leicester Local Authority.[49] The research was conducted using arts-based research in partnership with Charnwood Arts in Loughborough and Soft Touch arts co-operative in Leicester. Focusing upon access to employment and training two artists, Sally Norman and Tove Dalenius, worked with me and with two asylum seekers to produce a visual text that would represent the experiences and aspirations regarding employment of the asylum seekers we interviewed (Figure 2.7).

The arts practice re-presents the diversity of asylum seekers and refugees and addresses the economic contribution of asylum seekers and refugees. The artists initially asked for volunteers (not refugees or asylum seekers for ethical reasons) to take part in a photograph for the poster, to 'stand in'. Overwhelmingly the response from people was

> negative … One person (who had never been an asylum seeker) said *'I would love to do it but my girlfriend said she would leave me if I agreed to it'*. In the end an artist was commissioned to draw people instead, a decision that will not have as great an impact on the poster, but a necessary one in the circumstances.[50]

This raised issues such as stigma and abjection in relation to the identification as asylum seekers and refugees, and was an important focus for re-imagining the welcome process for new arrivals, subsequent experiences including access to employment, and a sense of belonging. The billboard was sited outside the Shires Shopping Centre in Leicester for two weeks at the end of June (to coincide with National Refugee Week) and two posters were located inside the shopping centre.[51]

One outcome of the work describe above was a successful bid for funding to set up a regional network that addressed the need to forge connections between artists, refugees and asylum seekers, new communities, academics, policy makers and practitioners. The network 'Making the Connections: Arts, Migration and Diaspora' based on principles of participatory action research and participatory arts brought agencies together across the region to work together to address some of these issues. A series of nine workshops and an end of programme conference took place between April 2006 and July 2008. A follow-on project[52] was conducted to deliver a knowledge transfer project that would be a hub for research and practice in partnership between four refugee communities and four community arts organizations. The knowledge exchange, 'Towards a Sense of Belonging', focused upon home, place and belonging for asylum and refugee groups in the East Midlands.[53]

Towards a new sociology of art?

Returning to the three themes the chapter opened with – the importance of stories and storytelling, the importance of re-presenting life stories in visual/artistic form, and the importance of working with people as subjects through participatory methodologies – these themes and issues link very well to what is being called 'the new sociology of art'.[54]

The sociology of art's antecedents, for myself, are located in the work of Marx and the Frankfurt School, particularly Theodor Adorno and Walter Benjamin, alongside Howard Becker, John Berger, Janet Wolff, Robert Witkin, Tia DeNora and Pierre Bourdieu. De la Fuente makes a good case for the development of the 'new sociology of art' and the contingency of art making that includes 'framing questions about the aesthetic properties of art and artworks in a way that is compatible with social constructionism'.[55] First, he highlights the contestable character of art ('What does the word "art" mean to you?'[56]) in the context of the social sciences. Second, drawing upon a point made by Janet Wolff he argues that 'much of the sociology of art has not engaged in the kinds of questioning of power, representation and subjectivity, of the sort we find in cultural studies'.[57] Third, drawing upon papers by Willis and Inglis he suggests that 'a less dogmatic future is possible in social scientific analyses of art, if sociologists do to themselves what they have hitherto been doing to "art" and other academic disciplines, namely relativizing, historicizing, and laying bare tacit assumptions'.[58] Fourth, drawing upon DeNora's work on the sociology of music presented through her 'ethnographies of music in action' he shows how she 'advocates a music sociology in which there are no a priori categories and both "music" and the "social" are shown to be co-produced'.[59] Quoting directly from DeNora:

> For music sociology, the lesson is that … music is not simply 'shaped' by 'social forces' – such a view is not only sociologistic, it also misses music's active properties and thus diminishes the potential of music sociology by ignoring the question of music's discursive and material powers.[60]

For de la Fuente, DeNora's 'brand of music sociology epitomizes what is best about the new sociology of art: namely, a desire to speak about the aesthetic properties of art but to do so in a manner that is congruent with social constructionism and which avoids unnecessary "essentializing" of what we mean by art'.[61] Fifth, de la Fuente draws upon Molotch's 2003 sociology of consumer goods, *Where Stuff Comes From*:

> Art entails objects (or situations) that have the capacity to draw upon 'social-psychological associations' which are heavily compressed and give that object (or situation) an air of 'transcendence'. Art transcends mundane and routine perception, by compressing experience in the following manner: 'the magic of art is in the way complex social and psychological stimuli are made to conjoin, a kind of *lash up* of sensualities.[62]

He also directs our attention to institutional mechanisms, and the ways that social classes and groups advocate their versions of 'art'. Finally, drawing upon a collection that includes Becker, Menger and Kishenblatt-Gimblett, *Art: From Start to Finish*,[63] he argues that

> Art is social not because social variables affect it but because it is the product of collective work … which produces the result that is eventually taken to be the artwork itself. … The artwork is a result of a process that is co-produced, but not in conditions of its own choosing, rather within the context of choices

made 'shaped by all types of recalcitrant physical, social and economic realities, the attention to organizational constraints, collegial pressures, and career interests'.[64]

To this I would add the importance of relational dynamics,[65] and reflexivity in the production of art as knowledge; art is constitutive of sensuous knowing and it is made up (to paraphrase Janet Wolff) of the sedimentary 'stuff' of society.

The arts-based research presented in this chapter through ethno-mimetic texts provides examples of the ways in which art (and the social) is co-produced. The ethno-mimetic process lays this bare and also uncovers the relational, reflexive, co-productive aspects (the mimetic) – in tension with 'constructive rationality' – the organizational constraints and the forms and techniques of production. These aspects include the 'social and psychological associations' that are 'heavily compressed' in the art object, text or performance.[66]

The self-reflexivity in the ethnographic process and the visual and poetic representations of ethnographic work, emerge in the collaborative process between artist, refugee/asylum seeker and researcher. The representation and production of sensuous knowing through arts-based research (biography, narrativity and art) can raise awareness of the issues women face, educate, empower, and demand change through performative praxis. Returning to the four key concepts outlined in the introductory section as constitutive of ethno-mimesis – immersion, feminist theorizing, interpretation informed by women's standpoints and situations, and performative praxis – the turn to art can have powerful consequences for the social sciences and for a gender-specific analysis of the asylum–migration nexus.

Arts and cultural activities are an increasingly important part of urban regeneration in the UK and are effective routes to the development of policy.[67] The arts have a vital role in socio-cultural regeneration and are profoundly important in the creative regeneration of cultural identities, communities and individual subjectivities, particularly for groups who have been marginalized in the development of social and economic infrastructures. The arts have a vital role in promoting diversity, inclusivity and social justice in relation to women, migration and diaspora. Hence the 'turn to art' in the social sciences is an understandable move especially given the previous linguistic and cultural turns and the more recent development of performative social science that follows a similar trajectory.

Ethno-mimesis is an example of both the turn to culture and the turn to art, and sits well within the developing conceptualization of the 'new sociology of art'. Moreover, as I hope I have illustrated in this chapter – the combination of art and ethnography might engage and develop the experiences of women (asylum seekers/refugees/undocumented) and new arrival communities in the East Midlands to enhance their lives, feed into research and policy by challenging stereotypes and identity thinking and envisioning social justice through a 'radical democratic imaginary',[68] thus making useful intervention in art, politics and policy.

Notes

1 Rex Nettelford, keynote presentation to the 'The Arts and their Custodians Symposium' Northampton University, June 2007.
2 Maggie O'Neill and Bea Tobolewska, *Towards a Cultural Strategy for Working with Refugees and Asylum Seekers in the East Midlands*, Nottingham: City Arts and Staffordshire University, 2002; and Maggie O'Neill 'Participatory Methods and Critical Models: Arts, Migration and Diaspora' *Crossings: Journal of Media and Culture* 2 (2011), 13–37.
3 Charnwood Arts, Loughborough, www.charnwoodarts.com; Soft Touch, Leicester, www.soft-touch.org.uk/pages/frameset.htm; City Arts, Nottingham, www.city-arts.org.uk; and the Long Journey Home, a regional arts organization supporting artists in exile, www.longjourneyhome.org.uk.
4 Clifford Geertz, *The Interpretation of Cultures* (London: Hutchinson, 1973).
5 Such as the dominant knowledge/power axis embedded in current governance and media policy relating to forced migration, and the sexual, racial and social inequalities experienced by new arrivals.
6 H. Gould, *A Sense of Belonging* (London: Creative Exchange, 2005).
7 Maggie O'Neill, 'Transnational Refugees and the Transformative Role of Art?', *Forum for Qualitative Social Research* (May 2008), special issue: *Performative Social Science.*
8 Anna Marie Smith, *Laclau and Mouffe: The Radical Democratic Imaginary* (London and New York: Routledge, 1998).
9 E. de la Fuente, 'The "New Sociology of Art": Putting Art Back into Social Sciences', *Cultural Sociology* 1/3 (2007), 409–25.
10 See, for example, Sara Buchanan et al., *What's the Story? Results from Research into Media Coverage of Refugees and Asylum Seekers in the UK* (London: Article 19, 2003), www.article19.org.
11 This also applies to cultural criminology – see www.safetysoapbox.co.uk.
12 See Trinh T. Minh-ha, *Framer Framed: Film Scripts and Interviews* (London and New York: Routledge, 1992); and Sarah Pink, *The Future of Visual Anthropology: Engaging the Senses* (London and New York: Routledge, 2006) for examples.
13 Following Theodor Adorno, *Aesthetic Theory*, translated by R. Hullot-Kentor (Minneapolis: University of Minnesota Press, 1997), 'mimesis' does not simply mean naïve imitation, or mimicry, but rather feeling, sensuousness, spirit – a sensuous knowing. The concept of mimesis (as sensuous knowing) must be understood in tension with what Adorno calls 'constructive rationality': reason, instrumental rationality, the 'out there' sense of our being in the world. Michael Taussig, *Mimesis and Alterity: A Particular History of the Senses* (London and New York: Routledge, 1993), understands mimesis as 'both the faculty of imitation and the deployment of that faculty in sensuous knowing' (p. 68).

14 Taussig, *Mimesis and Alterity.*
15 Robert Witkin, *The Intelligence of Feeling* (London: Heinemann, 1974).
16 J. Bird, 'Towards Babel: Language and Translation in Art Therapy' in H. Burt (ed.) *Current Trends and New Research in Art Therapy: A Postmodern Approach* (Waterloo, ON: Wilfred Laurier University Press, 2008).
17 Trinh, *Framer Framed.*
18 Norman K. Denzin, *Interpretive Ethnography: Ethnographic Practices for the 21st Century* (Thousand Oaks, CA: Sage, 1997), p. 19.
19 Pertti Alasuutari, *An Invitation to Social Research* (Thousand Oaks, CA: Sage, 1998).
20 Refugee Council, *The Vulnerable Women's Project: Refugee and Asylum Seeking Women Affected by Rape or Sexual Violence* (London: Refugee Council, 2009).
21 For some excellent examples of research on and with women see: H. Crawley, *Refugee and Gender: Law and Processes* (London: Jordan Publishing, 2001); S. Castles et al., *Integration: Mapping the Field*, report of a project carried out by the University of Oxford Centre for Migration and Policy Research, and the Refugee Studies Centre contracted by the Home Office Immigration Research and Statistics Service (IRSS), London: Home Office Online Report 28 March 2002; H. Dumper, *Is It Safe Here? Refugee Women's Experiences in the UK* (London: Refugee Action, 2002); H. Dumper, *Making Women Visible* (London: Refugee Council, 2005); H. Dumper, *Women Refugees and Asylum Seekers in the UK* (London: ICAR Navigation Guide, 2006).
22 Crawley, *Refugee and Gender.*
23 M. O'Neill, J. Pitcher and M. Krah, 'What About Me? Report on the Findings of a Research Project on the Service Needs of Asylum Seeker/Refugee Women', *MARCHBID* (January 2007). The research was commissioned by Marchbid and focused upon on the needs of refugee women and their children in an area of the UK.
24 Ibid., p. 23.
25 Ibid.
26 Ibid.
27 Ibid.
28 Ibid.
29 Ibid., p. 24.
30 Ibid.
31 Ibid.
32 Refugee Council, *The Vulnerable Women's Project.*
33 Ibid., p. 9.
34 O'Neill, Pitcher and Krah, 'What About Me?'.
35 Dumper, *Women Refugees and Asylum Seekers.*
36 Refugee Council, *The Vulnerable Women's Project.*
37 R. Butter, 'Keynote', in M. O'Neill and P. Hubbard (eds), *Making the Connections: Arts, Migration and Diaspora Regional Network Launch Report* (Loughborough: Loughborough University, 2006), p. 11.
38 Defined by J. Pakulski, 'Cultural Citizenship', *Citizenship Studies* 1 (1977), 73–86.
39 J.W. Ruane (n.d.) *Mobilization of the Arts*, http://faculty.frostburg.edu/soci/rmoore/Article2.htm, accessed 23 October 2011; Howard Saul Becker, *Art Worlds* (Berkeley: University of California Press, 1982).

40 Maggie O'Neill, *Asylum, Migration and Community* (Bristol: Policy, 2010); O'Neill, 'Participatory Methods and Critical Models'.

41 The work of Professor Jenny Pearce, International Centre for Participation Studies, University of Bradford, in the creation of safe spaces for dialogue using PAR is an important role model for work in this area. www.brad.ac.uk/ peace/academic/ ProfessorJennyPearce.

42 For further information on PAR see O. Fals Borda, *Knowledge and People's Power* (New York: New Horizons Press, 1988); and *The Origins and Challenges of PAR*, David Kinsey Dialogue Series (Amherst, MA: University of Massachusetts, 1999).

43 M. Webster, *Finding Voices, Making Choices: Creativity for Social Change* (Nottingham: Educational Heretics Press, 1997).

44 Summarized by Alan Cribb and Sharon Gewertz, 'Towards a Sociology of Just Practices: An Analysis of Plural Conceptions of Justice' in Carol Vincent (ed.), *Social Justice, Education and Identity* (London and New York: Routledge, 2003).

45 For example, the regional arts council supported and funded recommendations in the regional cultural strategy and subsequently are supporting both the regional network and knowledge-transfer fellowship; partnership working is a clear outcome across both disciplinary and organizational borders; knowledge-transfer activity at the grass roots, training and development, employability, and the exchange of both knowledge and research, all are emerging for the knowledge-transfer activity, and their impacts are being felt.

46 Images presented here are taken from the exhibition booklet. With thanks to Bea Tobolewska, Maggy Milner, Jennifer Langer, Karen Fraser, Suhaila Ismhat, Anna Musgrave, Berang Kohdamani, Fahira Hasedic and all the research participants.

47 O'Neill and Tobolewska, *Towards a Cultural Strategy*, p. 154.

48 Joseph Hillis Miller, *Illustration* (Cambridge, MA: Harvard University Press, 1992).

49 For new arrivals' access to employment, training and social enterprise; see: Maggie O'Neill, F. Galli and F. Aldridge, *New Arrivals Research Report: Access to Training, Employment and Social Enterprise in Charnwood and Leicester*, commissioned by GOEM, Stoke-on-Trent: Staffordshire University and Loughborough: Charnwood Arts, 2004.

50 Sally Norman, 'Creative Consultation: Leicester Soft Touch and ASSET UK', in M. O'Neill and F. Galli, *New Arrivals Access to Training, Employment and Social Enterprise: Mapping the Horizontal and Vertical Dimensions of Social Inclusion in Leicester and Charnwood* (Nottingham: Government Office East Midlands and Staffordshire University, 2004), p. 132.

51 Images reproduced from O'Neill et al., *Research Report*. With thanks to Sally Norman, Tove Dalenius at Soft Touch arts co-operative and Assett UK, Fiona Galli and Fiona Aldridge.

52 Also funded by the AHRC.

53 For more information see O'Neill, 'Participatory Methods and Critical Models'; and L. Pearce and M. O'Neill, 'The Arts of Migration' *Crossings: Journal of Media and Culture* 2 (2011), 3–11.

54 De la Fuente, 'The "New Sociology of Art"'.

55 Ibid., p. 409.

56 Ibid., p. 414.

57 Ibid., p. 415.
58 Inglis cited in ibid.
59 De la Fuente, 'The "New Sociology of Art"'.
60 DeNora cited in ibid.
61 De la Fuente, 'The "New Sociology of Art"',.p. 418.
62 Ibid, p. 419.
63 Howard Saul Becker, Robert R. Faulkner and Barbara Kirshenblatt-Gimblett, *Art from Start to Finish: Jazz, Painting, Writing and Other Improvisations* (Chicago: University of Chicago Press, 2006).
64 De la Fuente, 'The "New Sociology of Art"',.pp. 420–1.
65 K. Jones, 'A Biographic Researcher in Pursuit of an Aesthetic: The Use of Arts-based (Re)presentations in "Performative" Dissemination of Life Stories', *Qualitative Sociology Review*, 2/1 (April 2006), 66–85.
66 De la Fuente, 'The "New Sociology of Art"', p. 421.
67 F. Matarasso, 'Many Voices: The Importance of Cultural Diversity in Democratic Society', unpublished lecture given at Vara Konserthus, Sweden 25 September 2006, http://homepage.mac.com/matarasso/FileSharing20.html, accessed on 30 November 2007; C. Landry and F. Bianchini, *The Creative City* (London: Demos with Comedia Publications, 1995); Jim McGuigan, *Culture and the Public Sphere* (London: Routledge, 1996); M. Webster, *Finding Voices*; D. Bell and M. Jayne (eds), *City of Quarters: Urban Villages in the Contemporary City* (London: Ashgate, 2004).
68 Smith, *Laclau and Mouffe*.

Finding a different way home 3

Artist Misha Myers, in interview with Tracey Warr, Devon, January 2009

Introduction and works

Four works by Misha Myers[1] are referred to in the interview: *way from home* (Plymouth, 2002–08), *Take me to a place* (Plymouth, 2004), *Yodel Rodeo* (Exeter, 2004) and *Hevva Hevva* (Penzance, 2006). Misha Myers was born in 1967 and has been living in the UK since 1997.

2002–08 *way from home*, is a dialogical performance process, workshop and digital artwork created in collaboration with refugees and asylum seekers across the UK in a process of walking, talking and mapping a remembered landscape of the past in the encountered landscapes of the present (Figure 3.1). The digital artwork developed from this project was published and commissioned by *Performance Research Journal*, supported by an AOL Innovations in the Community Award, and exhibited in the 'Art in the Age of Terrorism' exhibition at Millais Gallery (2004), and documented in a book of the same title.[2]

2004 *Take me to a place* is an audio tour of songs created and composed by inhabitants of Plymouth who were asylum seekers and refugees, together with theatre and social-work exchange students. The songs are based on walks taken to different places in the city, which the group perceived as 'friendly places', 'lucky places', 'lost places', 'border places', 'places of power', 'quiet places', 'avoided places' and 'places of strength'. The songs, of as many different styles as there were members of the group, guide the listener on a walk to some of these locations and were based on the group's diverse associations, perceptions and experiences of these places. A website including a downloadable and online version of the map of songs is online at www.homingplace.org.[3]

2004 *Yodel Rodeo*, a place-specific, multi-sited, promenade performance commissioned by Spacex Gallery and Relational for the Homelands Exhibition, involved the participation of a local line-dance team with accompanying installation in a vacant shop window in Exeter's city centre. An audience was guided on a walk along the remains of Exeter's Roman walls with line-dances and cowboy yodels and ballads with lyrics replaced with geographical and historical details specific to Exeter's past and present (Figures 3.2 and 3.3).[4]

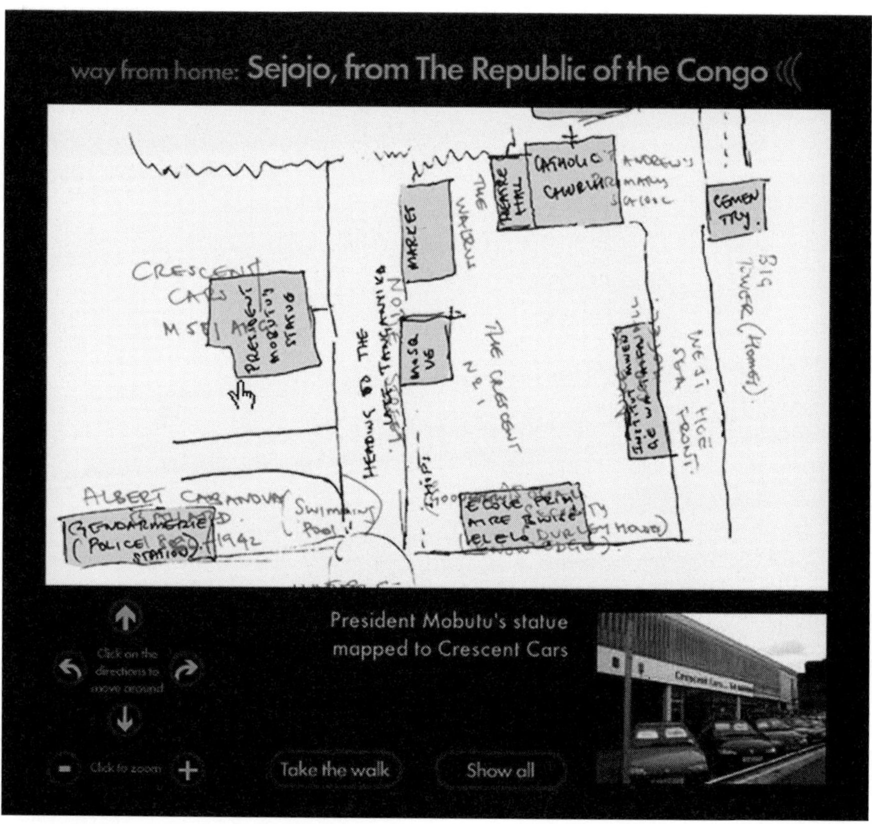

3.1 Misha Myers *way from home* (2004).

2006 *Hevva Hevva*, a place-specific performance work commissioned by Arts Surgery and Newlyn Art Gallery for the TRACT programme of site-specific performance, invited members of the public to record people and objects lost in a ledger of loss. At the edge of the sea beside Penzance's lido and in an intimate dialogue between the performer and individual audience member, their loss was called homeward in the language of semaphore and hue and cry used by the fishermen of the past Cornish pilchard industry (Figure 3.4).

Tracey Warr: Can we begin by talking about your work *way from home*, which started in 2002 and which is still going on. Can you describe what happened in that project and how it has evolved?

Misha Myers: That project is based around a set of instructions which I devised and that invite a participant to make a map of a journey from a place that they consider home to a special place that's nearby. They then take a

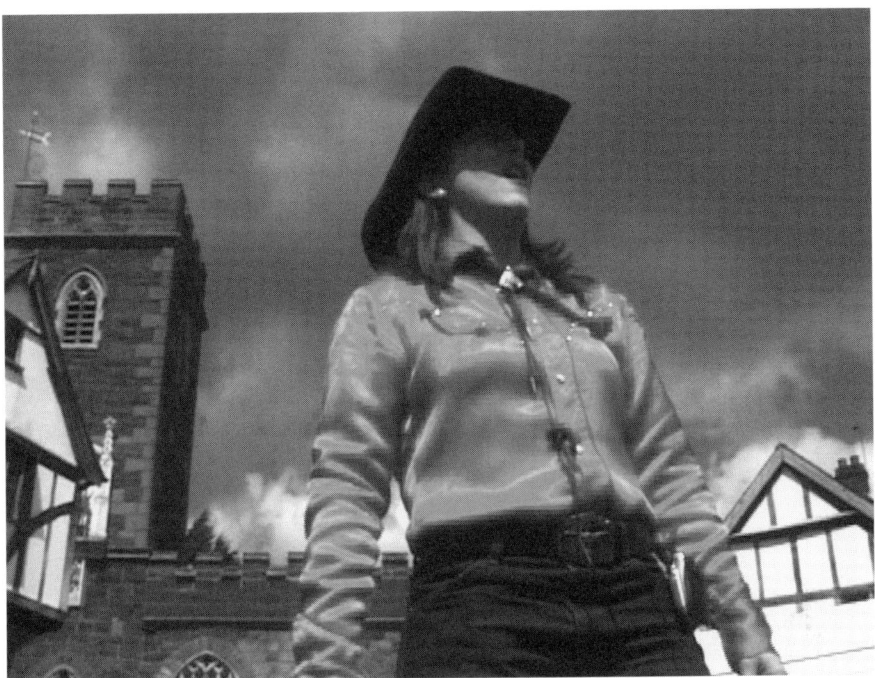

Misha Myers, *Yodel Rodeo* (2004). 3.2

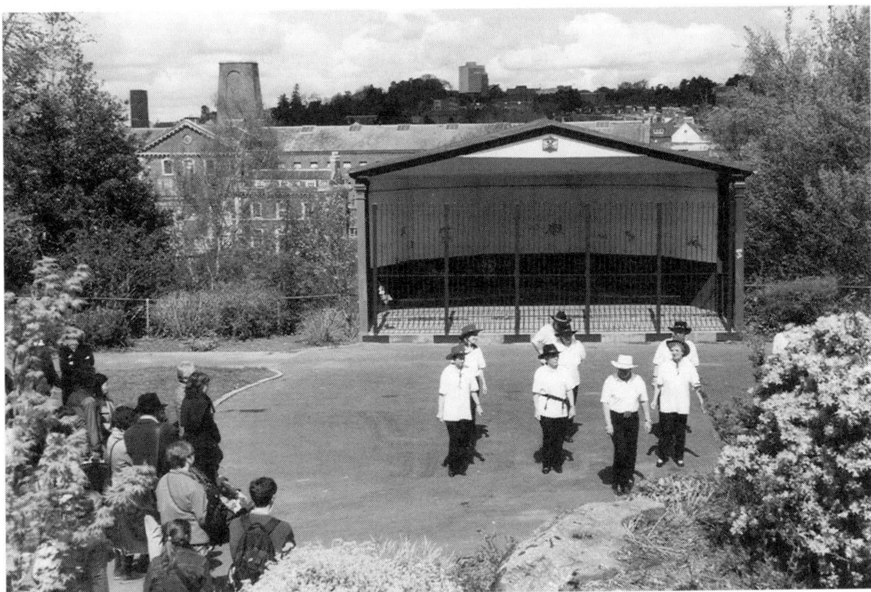

Misha Myers, *Yodel Rodeo* (2004). 3.3

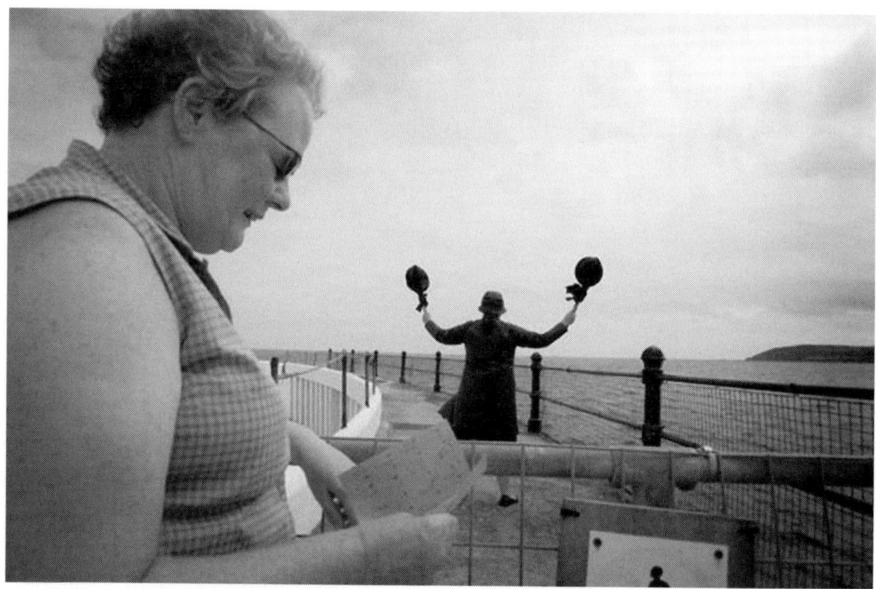

3.4 Misha Myers, *Hevva Hevva* (2006).

walk in a different place following this map and transposing the landmarks on the map onto this new place. This project developed through contact I made with inhabitants of Plymouth who are refugees and asylum seekers and with refugee support workers. In the build-up to the current war in Iraq, I invited support workers who were also refugees themselves to do this walk with me so that they were transposing their remembered homes onto Plymouth. The work later evolved into a digital artwork, which presented the maps and audio recordings of a selection of walks in an interactive interface [www.wayfrom-home.org].

TW: Could you give me an example of how one of the participants worked with the instructions and this process that you constructed?

MM: Everyone who has done the walks has reinterpreted the instructions in some way, which is what I'm really interested in – the way the instructions are propositional and invite a conversation. The first walk that I did was with a young Kurdish man on the day that the war in Iraq began. Ships were leaving the Plymouth Sound for Iraq and we were walking along the Hoe in Plymouth, where the military citadel is located. Following the route on his home map we passed Saddam's Palace, which became overlaid with the Plymouth Royal Citadel in an uncanny juxtaposition. In another walk with a man from the Congo the Social Security Office in Plymouth was transposed with his primary school. He made the associative link that these were both places of knowledge and learning for him – one in his present and the other in his past. He suggested that coming to a new country was like being a child again, having to learn all over how to live, and this office was a significant place of this kind of learning. So these juxtapositions, which might have personal resonances for the walker, become points of conversations where different experiences are spontaneously shared.

TW: So you have what you have described as a double exposure of place going on where one place is transposed onto another, the places of memories are overlaid onto the places of immediate experience, and that's a tactic that has occurred in several of your works isn't it? It happened in *Yodel Rodeo* as well, where you were overlaying the American south west onto Exeter.

MM: Yes. In that piece I guided a walk along the remains of the old Roman walls of Exeter by singing and yodelling traditional American cowboy ballads with the lyrics replaced with place names, past and present events, and details of histories and geographies of places in the landscape around and within the walls. A line-dance company from Exeter, the Montgomery Mavericks, accompanied me on the walk performing line-dance interludes along the way. In this performance the south west of England was transposed with the mythological Wild West landscape of the US. I'm interested in this experience of displacement, an experience I've had in the process of orientating myself to this new and strange country as a migrant, and through my work I've found that it's an experience that other migrants share. The memory of past familiar places are collaged to make the new place less strange and to create landmarks that are more easily identified with. This is what seemed particularly relevant to the refugees I initially began working with on the *way from home* project. They related to this way of identifying place through this double exposure or displacement of experience and mapping it onto things and renaming them. Of course, it's also a colonial tool or strategy of colonizing places to rename them. The names and landmarks of the prior or present occupants of an occupied territory are erased and replaced with the colonizer's familiar place names. This is written all over the American landscape by the Europeans. So in the context of working with refugees it was an alternative strategy of subverting that. The two coincide.

TW: There is a relationship in all of your work between the ephemeral and performative and the environment. So there is the ephemeral, performative use of voice and movement: songs in *Take me to a place*, line-dancing in *Yodel Rodeo* and walking in *way from home*, vocalization and movement in *Hevva Hevva* in conjunction with the environment that participants are immersed in. There's an interplay between them, a co-creation between the body and that environment, impacting on each other.

MM: In *Yodel Rodeo* I was initially interested in the sound of the voice as a way of experiencing, navigating and mapping space. My original idea was to perform at night when there would have been more echo, but the work shifted to include collaborations and sites that required a daytime performance. While there wasn't the same lonesome sound in the piece that I was initially interested in, a lonesomeness that mirrored how I was feeling at the time as a foreigner in the UK, there was still this sense of the voice navigating and mapping the city. I tried to sustain different yodels all along the walk, exploring the way my voice would meet particular architectural spaces or features of the cityscape. Sometimes there were resonant quiet places that felt easy and supportive on the voice and others presented the challenge to cut through the bustle. After three hours of this, I also felt the impact of the city on my voice, a kind of wounding. In *Hevva Hevva* I was calling out the directions of the semaphore as I was performing them. I was facing the sea at the edge of the Penzance lido. The lido amplified the sound, which created a strange sense of disembodiment and enlargement. With walking, like the singing, there's mutual impact. The walking leaves traces in the environment and the environment is felt in the body; sometimes there's the joy of gravity on a downward slope and other times there is the pain of a blistered toe or weary knees.

TW: With this performative mapping using voice and movement you end up with a form of mapping that is fluid and expansive rather than fixed and reductive. Rather than pinning something down in the way that a visual map functions with fixed co-ordinates, you develop a fluid map where there is a constant dynamic responsiveness between the space and the people moving through the space.

MM: I'm more interested in processes of wayfinding than maps or map-making. In wayfinding, as I see it, there is an embodied and sensorial process of responding to and negotiating with the immediate environment as it is in the present moment and in relationship to past knowledge of a particular route or landscape. The map is fixed in time while the landscape has necessarily changed. The wayfarer is in the flow of time and must negotiate those gaps between a mapped landscape that is in the past and the changed and changing landscape of the present. I'm interested in how that kind of lived knowledge of place is passed on through stories, a communicative act. That's what I see is happening in the *way from home* walks. I can't predict how someone will respond and where their map or their story will take us. That depends upon their own sensibilities, histories or whatever occurs in that time and place at that moment. In *Yodel Rodeo* there is a different structure. The line-dances and the songs were structuring time with a pre-determined route. But within that there were these gaps where people started to create their own narrative and to have their own experience, and the passers-by became a part of that. Some young people in a park yelled at me, 'Go back to America!' as we were passing by, for instance. All those things become part of the narrative. At one point in *Yodel Rodeo* one of the audience members said, 'Come along, pilgrims', joining into the fiction and creating their own version or take on it. They became a performer, as well. That's something I'm interested in, in all of my work: the participant is performing as much as I am and co-producing the work through their contribution to it. It's a dialogue.

TW: Yes, I was on that walk and I remember how at one point the line-dancers were dancing in their cowboy hats and boots across a raised footbridge over a major road junction and cars passing below started honking their horns and people in nearby flats were leaning out of their balconies looking at what was happening.

MM: Yes, that was a wonderful moment when someone drove by and yelled 'yee ha', and the circle of the conversation expanded to embrace the city.

TW: You've described your work as 'conversive wayfinding'.[5] Not only is the participant performative, ephemeral, moving, but also there's usually some element of the social, an exchange, at least two people walking and talking together, elements of improvisation and the unexpected from two or more points of view. It's always social. You don't send people off on their own on individual voyages of discovery.

MM: Yes, there's always conversation involved. There's a lot of interest and discourse around mapping in contemporary art. You were asking earlier about reductiveness and something that's fixed and that's something that maps can be, particularly the conventional cartographic map. It's about points and co-ordinates. But wayfinding is a more communicable encounter. There is often dialogue or sharing of stories, of directions so that navigation happens through an exchange. There's a position in the work about identity in this way, a way of looking at identity as a constant negotiation and exchange rather than a fixed position. It's always happening through dialogue. In documentation of the work I have also created instructions or situations that allow people to pick the work up and do something with it themselves. The locus of the work is in the conversive encounter.

TW: So a lot of the time what you are doing as an artist is initiating something?

MM: Yes, I offer a proposition that initiates a dialogue: asks a question that seeks multiple responses, not a fixed or predetermined answer. And sometimes the question itself gets questioned.

TW: You use the term 'percipient' rather than participant in discussing your work. Can you say something about that? What's the distinction for you?

MM: In its common usage the term percipient refers to a person who perceives the world through the senses. So the term suggests an active and embodied sense of knowing. So I'm applying that notion to a form of participation that is more active and involves the participant as a co-producer in the moment of performance, as opposed to a pre-determined or pre-directed and passive form of participation. This relates to the kind of engagement involved in processes of wayfinding. Sometimes in participation it may appear that there is an openness or the participant has agency in the work.[6] But power dynamics, cultural preferences, etc. might pre-determine or limit a response. When I said earlier that the question sometimes gets questioned, this is a moment where those limits imposed on the conversation get challenged. So, for me, the percipient is an active and critical engagement where the participant is really co-creating the work from their lived knowledge, world view and experience.

TW: Can we talk a bit more about the role of the artist in your work? In your works you are making what Umberto Eco called 'Open Works' where, unlike traditional compositional techniques, you are trying to shed as much authority and pre-determination as possible so that you can allow for agency as you have described on the part of your percipients and therefore there is co-creation and co-determination going on, and therefore that opens up questions around power.[7] As you suggested, it's very difficult, if not impossible, to know your own cultural proclivities. That was something that came up for you in *Take me to a place*, wasn't it? Where you had this initial design where you wanted people to use voice and not to use instruments. Could you talk about that a bit, about your retrospective recognition of your own cultural determinations there?

MM: Yes, in that piece a diverse group of people – inhabitants of Plymouth who were refugees, support workers, students from Dartington College of Arts where I teach, all worked together to compose a map of songs that guide a listener on a walk through Plymouth. These songs were written by the group collectively. I originally thought about the piece as a cappella singing because I thought it would be a way we could meet with different traditions and forms of singing. But in actual fact, the group of people who were first interested in participating included a group of Kurdish men who really wanted to play instruments and didn't conceive of singing without accompaniment. A lot of musicians turned up. But because I held on to this idea of a cappella they were not interested at all. I realized later that a cappella is a cultural form that I'm very comfortable with. I took my own cultural prejudices and preferences for granted. In that case, it was the overall structure of the piece and as we continued working I kept trying to find a way to undo it. In the end there were instruments involved. Others joined in, but that initial group never returned. That loss or failure of communication encouraged me to find methods that would open the question of the work out – invite reinvention and critique.

In *way from home* the question about home that initiates the dialogue immediately raises questions about what is meant by home. One thing I found interesting about that piece is that question elicits another question, i.e. 'What do you mean by home? Do you mean my house? Where I grew up? Where I live now?' An asylum seeker who participated and who was sleeping rough really felt that nowhere in the world was home and he drew a question mark as his sketch map. He ended up walking the question mark as his response to the work. So I'm always trying to see those aspects of the work that close down the potential for conversation, that impose limitations that make dialogue impossible.

TW: Is that something you just learn through experience, through trying things out?

MM: Yes, sometimes. But also through rigorous questioning of myself. I guess that's the craft of what I do. It is in trying to find that openness and sometimes it's elusive and it doesn't work out. Too much of the wrong kind of openness or too little of the right kind perhaps.

TW: So you're trying to find questions that are interesting and provocative enough, but are not leading questions.

MM: Yes, or offer the possibility for multiple responses. For instance, in the work, *Hevva Hevva*, that I made in Cornwall, in Penzance, I invited people to write in a ledger of losses about something they had lost that they wanted me to call in from sea in the old semaphore once used by pilchard fishermen. There was a very particular structure to that piece, but there were multiple responses to the sense of loss. People offered a whole spectrum of responses – their virginity, innocence, patience, a person who was close to them, a golf ball, a mobile phone, money, etc. In the multiplicity and collective response, the banal contributions were just as interesting as the more profound life-changing losses people recorded. There was room for humour and lightness, as well as seriousness and intimacy. I was looking for that range of experience. I want the work to ask what is relevant to participants, not assume what is relevant.

TW: So you feel that you need to begin your projects with a conversation?

MM: Yes, that's the challenging thing in the work. I want that dialogue about what is relevant to be the work itself. It's difficult within the structures of funding that exist.

TW: To say 'I'm going to do something and I don't know what it is'.

MM: Yes, I'm going do something and I don't know what its outcome will be. It's a speculative process. I've developed strategies for a process of research that is built as a piece of work itself. This conversation, these questions are performative and they are the artwork and then there's a stage two of that that becomes something else or there's a dissemination of that work that becomes something else. With *Hevva Hevva*, for instance, there is a stage two that hasn't happened yet. I would like to bring people to a dinner to talk about the future, the hard times and the good times looking forwards to the future for the communities of Cornwall. In *way from home* it started with a question, this instruction being about exploration and questions of home, and then it has become other things as I take it into other contexts and modes of working. For instance, the digital artwork, walks including public officials, workshops as part of Refugee Week, workshops that initiated the creation of art works by the participants and a participatory research project.

TW: That is a distinctive repeated pattern with your work isn't it? I think most of the works have several phases and layers, evolving and responsive forms. That means they are all quite a commitment! Are they all still going on or do they sometimes come to an end?

MM: I like the idea of multiple layers that keep unfolding and transforming over time; multiple layers of participation then continue to evolve out of the live event. The digital artwork of *way from home* is interactive in this way. It's an interface where the person experiencing it online can take that walk, follow those instructions, do it themselves and reflect on what occurs for them.

Also, for me, that long-term commitment is essential to the ethics of my approach. I try to work with sensitivity and a deeper understanding of a context that I'm working in. I don't want to just impose something and it can take time to develop that understanding or to develop collaborations with inhabitants or organizations of the context.[8] I like that *way from home* has continued to evolve, and I don't see an end point for that work. The works have a life that I guess will keep going as long as others and I have an interest in them. Or they provide seeds for new projects.

TW: Working in this way with people, you need time to build up trust and rapport through this conversation, this open work. I've often wondered with a lot of participatory projects, which are so prevalent now in contemporary art, about the aftermath for the participants. Not in the sense of governmental tick boxes about benefits and impacts but in other ways. You're still in touch with a lot of the participants from your projects, aren't you?

MM: Yes. It required a great deal of trust on the parts of the participants and was not easily earned. There was a kind of rapport that had to develop over a number of years and, out of that, friendships evolved. I wanted to make a contribution to that context. I'm interested in how the artist's role starts to transform here. I was invited to participate in city council policy meetings about asylum seekers to facilitate discussions on the arts, for example. One refugee support organization invited me to be on their board of governors and I was invited to consult on a welcome booklet for the city. So, like the multiple transforming forms of the work itself, the artist's role in this kind of socially engaged practice can also shift and become multiple. It includes a civic role and that takes a great deal of commitment and time. The friendships, the social aspect, were very important for many of the participants. They came to the work to make friends and become familiar with a place through becoming familiar with other people. Taking care of those relationships, monitoring the impacts of the work is important.

TW: It's interesting to hear you talking about taking care of relationships thinking about theories of Relational Art.[9] In a lot of participatory art projects relationships are formed but they are time limited, limited to the project.

Another way that you earned relationships was that you crucially contributed your own vulnerability about identity, place, displacement and being a migrant to the conversations?

MM: Yes the *way from home* and *Yodel Rodeo* were created simultaneously. *Yodel Rodeo* was very personal. It came from my experience as a migrant and my take on displacement. That's a very different experience. I'm not a refugee. I'm not an exile. I'm not a forced migrant. I'm a voluntary migrant and my condition of migration could be described as what Françoise Collin characterizes as the 'l'immigrée blanche' – the white immigrant.[10] I'm speaking my first language in the language of my adopted country. While that is a different experience to most of the refugees and asylum seekers I have been working with, there are also some similar experiences there that have provided moments for sharing perspectives. I wouldn't dare be so presumptuous to suggest these experiences are identical, as they are complex and shifting positions with very different rights to access, entitlement, power, etc. But sometimes those perspectives overlap and something can be exchanged. For example, we could reflect on the adopted culture as being foreign and through our own homesickness. In fact, *way from home* developed out of one of those homesick conversations with a few people at a refugee support organization where we were sitting around talking about smells we had experienced in Plymouth that reminded us of the place we called home. And sometimes assumptions were made about me by the people I was working with too.

TW: Yes wasn't there an occasion when some of the people you had been working with confessed that when they first met you their nickname for you was George W? Reductive stereotyping of national identity works all ways.

MM: Yes, but that act of stereotyping emerged from a different position of power. A refugee support worker from Iran I'd been working closely with on *way from home* told me that's how some of her clients referred to me when I first started working with the organization; that was their first impression. Apparently, they suspected I might be a CIA agent, an American hanging around and asking questions. She shared this with me at a point when we were evaluating the project and when there was enough trust in our relationship for her to wield and for me to receive criticism. At the same time it was quite a hard portrait to receive, it made sense to me and I appreciated the openness of this dialogue.

When I was working on *Yodel Rodeo* I was definitely concerned about how the work would be perceived in the context of the build-up to the war in Iraq. I'm definitely not a gun-toting American cowboy, but I'm from the Southern US and cowboy culture is part of the culture I grew up in and I've always been trying to come to terms with in my work.

TW: The layers of identity that got opened up in *Yodel Rodeo* were interesting. You were exaggerating your own persona as this stereotyped cowgirl, which is not just associated with being American. Every Western child associates with a childhood figure of the cowboy, so there's a kind of affection there as well as the national association. And then another layer was the Exeter-based line-dancers imitating a cultural phenomenon or the fictional version of it and then overlaying that onto Exeter.

MM: Yes, the group of line-dancers were from a neighbourhood in Exeter called Montgomery and they were called The Montgomery Mavericks. The leader was very much committed to the cowboy lifestyle. He was a truck driver. I found something really familiar in him. He was uncannily like the men in my family. I think he was drawn to the project and agreed to do it because he saw it as an expression of his own support for the British–American special friendship. He came to rehearsals wearing 'support the troops [in Iraq]' T-shirts. I was concerned that for him that was what this piece was about and for me it wasn't about that. I wondered if it could be both, all the things that all the participants wanted it to be.

TW: That raises an issue of whether you as an artist engaging in open work ever feel that something comes up in how your participants engage that you want to censor or edit. Are you aware of selecting things out?

MM: I lost a lot of sleep over the question of whether or not the line-dancers should be in the piece. But their participation felt so central to my methodology and to the piece being more than just about my own experience. In the end, when it came to the discussion about costume for the performance, we decided together that they would wear their company T-shirts with their group logo on it. So I tried to control it in a way that didn't feel like it was taking away or limiting their agency in the work. It's a difficult question. It comes back to the way that instructions and invitations are formed that can allow for those things to come through. We did in the end, coincidentally, run into an anti-war protest during the performance in Exeter and they may have mistaken us for a counter-protest, but I liked this enigmatic moment.

TW: I was on that walk with you and although it did look quite bewildering – the anti-war protesters suddenly confronted with cowboys and cowgirls – it couldn't be easily reduced to a pro-war or pro-American image because of this rather frivolous yodelling and line-dancing that was going on, so it remained in an inexplicable zone.

MM: Yes. I'm interested in challenging categories, generalizations, fixed identities and throwing them up in the air to play with them.

TW: In that piece, because you were working with the line-dancers moving through in the city, and yourself in costume and you had quite a large group of walkers with you, it took a conspicuous form in the city. In other works, with a few walkers, it's not so conspicuous.

MM: Yes, but sometimes that conspicuousness would appear in these more seemingly discrete performances. For instance, as part of a development of *way* *from home*, I set up walking dialogues between public officials and refugees in Plymouth. I facilitated a walk with a police officer and a young refugee, who was 18 or 20 at the time and teaching break-dancing as part of an initiative to promote racial equality. The young man felt that walking with a police officer in this convivial way was not something he did in his daily life.

TW: The police officer was in uniform?

MM: Yes. In our discussion about his experience after the walk, the young man described how he noticed people's expressions of surprise seeing them smiling and talking to each other, instead of him being handcuffed. He commented how common it was for him to confront this assumption in the street that he is a criminal because he is black and of the way he dresses. So it set up a conversation that may not otherwise happen.

TW: The representation of a fictional American identity in *Yodel Rodeo* and addressing assumptions about the identity of refugees in *Take me to a place* and *way from home* are all concerned with mediated versions of identity, aren't they? There's the Hollywood films or the news about Iraq versions of being American and images of refugees in the media. Your work brings out individual identities as opposed to reductive collective identities and stereotypes. It brings out lived experiences.

MM: Yes, and the particularity of an individual experience. The refugee support organizations recognized this as the potential of what we could do with the walks. The walks became a radio broadcast and this online digital work. They were interested in using these modes to disseminate an alternative representation to the media stereotypes of refugees. At that time there was a lot of negative press for refugees and asylum seekers in the UK. The work was able to offer these narratives that don't focus on the trauma of that experience in a voyeuristic way, all focused around the journey: how did you get here? It allowed the people to tell what they wanted to tell about their experience and to focus more about living here now and trying to make a life and new home here. I am interested in creating what I think of as mesh-works of narratives where individual paths and stories can be exchanged and juxtaposed and shared within this meshwork so that a collective experience made up of particularities is communicated, not a generalization.

TW: A series of *way from home* walking conversations were broadcast on the Today radio programme. Have you used the media in other works?

MM: In the past in my early work, yes. In my very early career as a performer I worked with a group of artists in San Francisco [SF] called Random Acts Theater creating enigmatic actions that would catch the media's attention in response to political issues or moments of political tension, such as when the SF police started arresting Food Not Bombs for feeding homeless people on the streets. I'm interested in employing different media as sites or modes of presenting the work. The locus of expression in the work for me is in the conversation. The media or mode of presentation sometimes depends on collaborators and the skills and desires of the people involved. For example, involving the BBC in *way from home* was the idea of the refugee support organizations and it was driven by their interest in finding outcomes that were significant for them. The digital artwork came about through an AOL Innovation in the Community Award. I worked with Refugees First and limbomedia to propose the online project as an idea that successfully won the award for the refugee organization. This award included capital that could be used for computers and Internet access, something they desperately needed in order to better serve their clients. I wasn't working with a specific outcome in mind at the beginning, but was opportunistic. Arts funding wouldn't have been able to provide them with the direct economic outcome they received indirectly through the artwork. I wanted to create an outcome that would respond to the needs expressed by the organization and would be developed with them.

TW: Your work has these many different forms and phases: instructions, drawings, sketch maps, conversations, wanderings and then allowing a re-presenting and re-experiencing by another layer of audience through audio recordings combined with maps, a CD that people could walk around with, a digital interactive artwork online. Talks and publications are also further forms of disseminating.

MM: And workshops.

TW: The secondary audience can look at the experience of the first participants but you also create egress for them to have their own primary experience as well.

MM: I'm interested in the primary, the ephemeral, engagement and trying to recreate that in the documentation or the secondary experience, and keeping it a live experience requires a negotiation between different forms of media. I've just recently consulted on the participatory research project Transnational Communities: Towards a Sense of Belonging led by Maggie O'Neill (Department of Sociology, University of Loughborough) and Phil Hubbard (Department of Geography, University of Loughborough), and the methods developed through *way from home* were adapted and explored in an event aimed at initiating the process of research through creative practice involving four arts and refugee and asylum seeker organizations in four cities and towns in the Midlands. I facilitated a day of walks and a workshop based to act as a catalyst for participants to create their own artworks that will be exhibited at the Bonnington Gallery in Nottingham at end of the project.

TW: So the work stays open in the beginning, middle and end.

MM: A photographer and a refugee inhabitant of Loughborough made a website using Flickr out of the Transnational Communities project. That is an example of how the work becomes open-ended, self-organizational, and continues to multiply outside of my own control.

TW: Does that present you with a problem about authoring and intellectual property?

MM: In some way it's challenging when you are trying to operate within academic research environments or the art world where authorship matters. I'm interested in contesting that, but I also have to operate within it. I'm interested in the collective act of conversation, mutuality, collaborative authorship, and too much emphasis of the artist's signature can undermine that intention or upset the gravitational centre of the work. So sometimes it is difficult to locate or articulate what my role is in this transient way of working. But this is a model that is becoming more familiar in our communication-driven society, and the institutions will inevitably have to catch up.

TW: You are usually working with the social experience of the environment of the city – Exeter, Plymouth, Penzance – rather than the intimate refuge space of the house in that sense of home. You're not concerned with what Gaston Bachelard called the nest-house or the garment-house.[11] Is that because you see that individual home space as a Western space, or you are more interested in that interaction between private and public in the environmental sense of space?

MM: Yes, I'm definitely interested in the public space as the context for the work. It's not the place that has historically been constructed as the domain of women in Western society, so perhaps the work presents a challenge to that perception. But the work also involves an aspect of home-making that confounds the usual expectations of that activity; this home-making that interests me is one that occurs in the social sphere. It is concerned with a sense of survival that depends upon the neighbour, the community, the external relationships. An interest in cultural exchange is always driving my work. I'm interested in my own culture and where I've come from and that exchange with another. What happens in those moments of exchange: how we understand one another. And that is an exchange that happens outside of the home or outside of the familiar comfort zone. However, I'm also interested at the moment in how we communicate transnationally through that home-nest. How families, like mine, for instance, who are spread out across the world, talk to each other through Skype. I'm interested in where that interstitial space opens out and cultural exchange happens then within the home, the family, the intercultural marriage, like my own.

TW: Web cam turns the home back into a performative stage.

MM: Yes. I'm interested in how we stage those conversations.

TW: Have specific issues come up around women in the projects?

MM: Yes, in *way from home* and *Take me to a place* my movement and interaction with men in public space was not an experience that could be shared by some women refugees and asylum seekers given their concerns about being persecuted for their different appearance in the streets of Plymouth, such as for wearing a head scarf, or their cultural rules of behaviour, which prohibited them from socially interacting with men other than family. In some instances these prohibited, limited or excluded their participation in the artworks. I developed connections with women through going to community events and would invite them to participate, but they didn't turn up for the walks. In the recent work as a consultant with the Transnational Communities project in the Midlands I did walk with a group of women from the Nottingham African Women's Empowerment Group. They decided to walk together in pairs following one woman's favourite route along the River Trent. This reinterpretation of my original instructions transformed it into a social event and suggested a form for that work that might make it more accessible for some women in the future.

TW: How much is the work about the city? I'm originally a Londoner and now in London I'm often struck by how inhospitable the city is unless you have money. The whole city is colonized by commercialization. You have to spend money to sit down or be warm. How much is urban theory something you are interested in? Perhaps this is just a hobby horse of mine because I'm now a rustic! A lot of people you are working with are coming from rural situations to the city. In a village you do know your neighbours and they help you out and that is often not the case in the city.

MM: My work is not exclusively about the urban, but my recent work has been made in urban contexts, and therefore urban experience is part of its concerns. The designated 'dispersal areas' for asylum seekers and refugees in the UK are urban centres, so this aspect of the context of my work is significant. And what you've said about the city being inhospitable if you don't have money is definitely an issue this population is confronted with. When I consulted on the Plymouth welcome booklet, I saw my walking instructions as something that could be potentially useful as a set of strategies for getting out of the house and interacting with the city without money, without engaging with the market.

TW: That's all you're presented with in Western cities.

MM: Yes, and I'm interested in creating alternative spaces and situations for people.

TW: The homeless participant you mentioned earlier, with the question mark, eventually found the public library as the place he could think of as home. Those places in the city are becoming rarer and rarer, and closing down. You have talked about how bodies build places, about embodied encounters in the city. That's a kind of Michel de Certeau idea?[12]

MM: Yes and Edward Casey.[13]

TW: Are you exploring the mutual impact between the moving experiencing body and the environment it is immersed in? How use impacts on the shape of the city?

MM: Yes, and in particular I'm interested in the migrant's impact on the shape of the urban environment. I have co-opted Tim Ingold's notion of 'inhabitant knowledge' to think differently about what or who constitutes 'local knowledge'.[14] I'm interested in the knowledges and experiences of place that the migrant inhabitant brings to a place as they make a home there. In *way from home* I became interested in how places were perceived differently, how they were transformed, what kinds of places were important, like the library and how those became subverted to people's own purposes. A grocery store might become a kind of community centre. What happens in the back rooms of those spaces? The welcome booklet started to document that. A student of mine took over that project and invited people to take photos of those kinds of places. It revealed the unofficial community spaces that exist and the social capital that circulated amongst those communities.

TW: What are your motivations for doing this work? How did you come to it?

MM: I've always been interested in cultural exchange and social engagement in my work, the exchange and understanding of different, sometimes conflicting, cultural and political perspectives. Growing up in the southern US I lived in a culture of conflict, where racial violence and hatred were a part of the everyday fabric of life. At university in the late 1980s in Alabama and later in Washington, DC, I began working as an anti-white-supremacy activist and studying politics. But I became more interested in understanding different cultural world views and went on to study anthropology, while beginning to make work as a dancer and performance artist. I always wanted to get as far away from the South as I could at that time in my life. But then I found that I kept trying to get back to it, because that culture and the process of conflict and change that it was going through was what made me and what I cared about most passionately. So my work kept taking me back in a way. I became interested in how my art could be a mode of cross-cultural exchange of knowledge and actively engage in effecting political or social change. That is something that I have continued to investigate and develop throughout my career as an artist and have now formalized as a methodology in my recently completed doctoral research. All this has led me to create work that acts as a context for dialogue or as an agent of exchange and/or change.

Presently, it's part of my everyday life in a different way. I've lived in a foreign country for over a decade and in a culturally diverse family, where different world views are constantly negotiated. I've lived away from my country and culture for so long now that, when I do go back there, I sometimes feel like a foreigner and it feels foreign to me. There is no going back the way I came, but I have to find a different way home that is a kind of advancing forward all the time, a homing. That's also my favourite kind of walk – more a circle than retracing steps.

Notes

1 Some of Misha Myers' works and publications are not specifically noted in this interview, but are relevant to the themes discussed: Misha Myers, 'Homing Devices', *Leonardo Electronic Almanac* 14/3 (2006), Locative Media Special Issue, unpaginated (online), http://leoalmanac.org/journal/vol_14/lea_v14_n03-04/mmyers.asp; *Homing Place*, 2006, website, www.homingplace.org; 'Along the Way: Situation-responsive Approach to Education and Participation', *International Journal of the Arts in Society* 1/2 (2006), 1–6; 'Situations for Living: Performing Emplacement', *Research in Drama Education* 13/2 (2008), 171–80.

2 See Misha Myers, 'Journeys to, from and around: Founding Home in Transition' in Graham Coulter-Smith and Maurice Owen (eds), *Art in the Age of Terrorism* (London: Paul Holberton Press, 2006), pp. 213–27. For further information about this project, see: Misha Myers, *way from home*, digital artwork, 2004, www.wayfromhome.org; Misha Myers and Dan Harris, 'way from home', *Performance Research* 9/2 (2004), 90–1 and DVD supplement.

3 Misha Myers, *Take me to a place*, performance, Barbican Theatre, Plymouth, UK, 4 June, audio CD, recorded Music Zone, Plymouth, UK, 11 June 2004.

4 Misha Myers, *Yodel Rodeo*, place-specific performance and installation, *Homeland*, Spacex Gallery and Relational, Exeter, UK, 17 April–16 May 2004.

5 Misha Myers, 'Walk with Me, Talk with Me: The Art of Conversive Wayfinding', *Visual Studies* 25/1 (April 2010), 59–68.

6 For a discussion of the range of uses to which 'participation' has been put in contemporary art practice, see Claire Bishop (ed.), *Participation* (London and Cambridge, MA: Whitechapel and The MIT Press, 2006).

7 Umberto Eco, 'The Poetics of the Open Work' in ibid., pp. 20–40.

8 See Claire Bishop, 'The Social Turn: Collaboration and its Discontents', *Artforum* (February 2006), www.artforum.com/inprint/id=10274, accessed 1 August 2009.

9 Nicolas Bourriaud, *Relational Aesthetics*, trans. Simon Pleasance and Fronza Woods (Dijon: les presses du reel, 2002).

10 Françoise Collin cited in Rosi Braidotti, *Nomadic Subjects: Embodiment and Sexual Difference in Contemporary Feminist Theory* (New York: Columbia University Press, 1994), p. 15.

11 Gaston Bachelard, *Poetics of Space* (Sussex: Beacon Press, 1992).

12 Michel de Certeau, *The Practice of Everyday Life*, trans. Steven Rendell (Berkeley: University of California Press, 1984).

13 Edward Casey, *Getting Back into Place: Toward a Renewed Understanding of the Place-World* (Bloomington and Indianapolis: Indiana University Press, 1993).

14 Tim Ingold, *The Perception of the Environment: Essays in Livelihood, Dwelling and Skill* (London: Routledge, 2000).

On foreign discomfort: *Magdalena Makeup* Live Art Event 4

Lena Simic

'*Magdalena Makeup* Name Post Card Encounters Journey Home' was the name of a performance paper delivered at 'Diasporic Futures: Women, the Arts and Globalization', a one-day conference at the Victoria and Albert Museum (V&A) in London, July 2006. The performance paper was inspired by my own work *Magdalena Makeup* Live Art Event (2004), which took place at Art Workshop Lazareti, Dubrovnik, Croatia and Lark Lane Community Centre, Liverpool, UK. Drawing from that, this chapter addresses my own position as a foreign artist in the UK within a live art / performance art context. It briefly outlines the Arts Council England (ACE) policies on cultural diversity and criticizes a certain kind of 'box-ticking' that goes on with 'culturally diverse artists' like myself. Written from an artist's position the chapter proceeds to disclose my own tactical take on my Foreigner subject position as a certain arts-making methodology. Finally, this chapter discusses *Magdalena Makeup* Live Art Event as an example of a self-reflexive, feminist, transnational arts practice which aims to connect with its audience members differently than prescribed by dominant globalization processes.

The British live art scene thrives on the presence of the category of 'Otherness'. 'Otherness' in arts has been tackled on many levels: through institutional policies on cultural diversity namely prioritising funding for 'culturally diverse' artists (for example the ACE initiative 'decibel', which first started in 2003 and still runs as an ongoing biennial showcase of performing arts), curatorial projects that address issues of cultural difference (for example, *You Are Here* [2002], a specially commissioned programme of Live Art for the Liverpool Biennial, as developed by the Bluecoat Arts Centre in collaboration with the Live Art Development Agency; Artsadmin calendar *Performing Difference* [2005]; and *Necessary Journeys* [2005] project, developed out of the 'decibel legacy') and finally, thematically, by artists themselves (for example, Kazuko Hohki, Stacy Makishi, Silke Mansholt and Oreet Ashery).

During the years 2003–06, the time when I developed and performed *Magdalena Makeup* Live Art Event, ACE placed 'cultural diversity' as one of its top priorities. In its manifesto document entitled 'Ambitions for the Arts' that was released in February 2003 after 'a period of radical reform' in the summer of 2002, with the appointment of a new Council, 'culturally diverse arts' are 'at the very least promised to make more funding available to them'.[1] In 2003 ACE defined 'cultural diversity':

> The term 'cultural diversity' can be interpreted in many different ways. We will take a broad and inclusive interpretation, as meaning the full range and diversity of the culture of this country. In some cases our focus will be on race and ethnic background and in others on disability, for example.[2]

Cultural diversity (with the focus on race and ethnic background) has been on the Arts Council's agenda for three decades: from the 1976 seminal report *The Arts Britain Ignores* by Naseem Khan and the term 'ethnic minorities' arts' through conferences between ACE and the British Council 'Re-inventing Britain' (1997) and 'Connecting Flights: New Cultures of the Diaspora' (2002), which introduced 'cultural studies' discussions to art administrators, policy makers and artists, to the more recent ACE publication *Navigating Difference*.[3] This publication gathered articles from forty arts managers, policy makers, practising artists, academics, audience members and commentators, all of whom dwell on cultural diversity and cultural identity in the arts.

With the production of 'Great Art for Everyone', a ten-year-long vision starting in 2008, ACE replaced the term 'cultural diversity' with 'diversity'. In the epilogue of *Navigating Difference*, Tony Panayiotou, Director of Diversity, ACE, writes:

> Arts Council England is working on a paradigm shift to allow it to explore, discuss and respond to diversity in its broadest sense – and it will no longer use the term 'cultural diversity' … This strategic and philosophical re-alignment would see Arts Council England doing more arts-related work on issues such as age, class, faith, gender and sexuality; working with refugees and asylum seekers; and responding to issues around community development such as urban regeneration, anti-poverty initiatives and the whole rural agenda.[4]

Current ACE ambitions are outlined in the booklet *Achieving Great Art for Everyone*,[5] with 'diversity' being listed as one of the five desired outcomes of ACE work alongside 'excellence', 'reach', engagement' and 'innovation'. In collaboration with the journal *Third Text* a new publication *Beyond Cultural Diversity*, compiled and edited by Richard Appignanesi, critiques the state funding of 'cultural diversity'.[6] I see the dropping of 'cultural diversity' as a term from the ACE vocabulary as an affirmative step. Initiatives like 'decibel' help profile 'culturally diverse arts and artists' and introduce them to the mainstream,[7] but by being grouped together the artists are constrained to deal mostly with identity politics. In 2003 Samenua Sesher, director of 'decibel', argued against the view of 'cultural diversity' as box-ticking:

> The Arts Council's done a lot to prioritise cultural diversity – it's an ongoing priority for us, not a box to be ticked. With decibel we have a budget and a moment in time, to not only get people talking about the issues, but to identify gaps and address some key needs of the sector.[8]

However, while ACE policies on the inclusion of 'culturally diverse artists' look appealing on paper, 'real artists' with 'real culturally diverse' backgrounds might be sensitive about being bracketed within it. Additionally, the term 'culturally diverse artists' has often become interchangeable with Black and Asian British artists, partly due to the ACE initiatives like 'decibel' (2003–04) that concentrated specifically on the promotion of African, Caribbean and Asian artists in England and thus lumped them all together. A 'culturally diverse' artist would thus need to develop a sense of irony about her own position within the system or tactically ignore that positionality and thus avoid working with the themes of identity politics.

As long as there have been strategies in place for cultural diversity there has been cultural commodification of difference. Cultural and feminist theorists have addressed this issue while artists themselves have looked to ways of subverting this commodification through employment of their very own cultural tactics (see the work of Kazuko Hohki, Stacy Makishi, Silke Mansholt and Oreet Ashery among others). Feminist theorist Sara Ahmed has argued against provisional acceptance of difference into the standard by its requirement to be different and thus 'allow the nation to imagine *itself* as heterogeneous (to claim their difference as "our difference")'.[9] The ACE publication *Navigating Difference*, which addresses cultural diversity, includes articles (Ghiraldi, Williams) that promote a shifting of the agendas of top-down models of policy making by taking into consideration examples of cultural diversities as found in local communities. However, like any institution, ACE, on the whole, just by being what it is, the organization responsible for the implementation of cultural strategies at a national level, is very unlikely to hand over its executive powers to the artists and arts organizations themselves, ACE's subjects. On the other hand, artists and arts organizations themselves need to understand that ACE, or any other institution, is not the 'be all and end all' of their arts practices. Cultural diversity is consequently not given top-down as a strategy, but rather emerges through 'us', and 'we' emerge through it. Ahmed suggests that '[t]hinking about multiculturalism must begin, therefore, with an undertaking that the coherence of the "we" of the nation is always imaginary and that, given this, such a "we" does not abolish cultural difference, but emerges through it'.[10] The 'we' of the nation need not be defined by the Arts Council strategies on cultural diversity but cut across the binaries of citizenship and non-citizenship, immigrants and locals, strangers and friends, black and white, gay and straight, disabled and abled, and as Trinh Minh-ha suggests include the inappropriate Other within every I.[11] The production of my 'I' contains the Other. I am produced by the Other. In this sense a nation emerges through Others and artists can help refigure that always imaginary, possibly even violent 'we' of the nation.[12] *Magdalena Makeup* Live Art Event is an attempt at a refiguration of the nation, within the local community, and a call to think through art transnationally rather than solely in terms of the nation.

In devising my own terminology for myself and my artwork in response to current arts trends and conditions in the UK, I have used the label of 'Foreigner'. I have chosen Foreigner as a subject position: my 'privileged' social identification, as an anomaly, something most limiting in the eyes of society and most tactically useful for my artistic interventions. The Foreigner is my chosen specific, tactical 'difference', a 'difference that matters'.[13] The term Foreigner distinguishes me from the group whilst informing my social and artistic identity.

Having crossed international borders many times, lived in different countries, been exposed to different interpretations of histories and cultures, I have decided to carve out a space for political comment through my arts practice. My particular positioning, a certain self-identification as a Foreigner is tactical and always operates within a given socio-political context, in this case, in the north west of England (Liverpool, where I live) and in Dubrovnik, Croatia (my hometown, which I often visit). As a Foreigner, I like to think of myself as peeking out from the ticked box of the 'Other White European', educated, privileged position. As I assess my right to claim the Foreigner difference, I am aware that my arts and academic context has produced this position as much as the lived experience of my locale. Within the 'arts and academic world' I accept the Foreigner label as a convenient position from which I embark upon my practice-based research. The Arts Council (north west England branch) and academia (the Arts and Humanities Research Council funds my research) embrace me as a Foreigner. They might be ticking their boxes or responding to the multicultural criteria prescribed 'from above', but monies have been committed to the Foreigner to embark on her arts projects and research. I am using the funding systems instrumentally whilst at the same time reflecting critically on my Foreigner label and position.

What I start working from is my 'critical difference' and multilayered understanding of culture and identity. Trinh Minh-ha writes: 'Otherness becomes empowering critical difference when it is not given, but re-created'.[14] While 'otherness' is inevitably given to me as a 'label' and commodified not only by contemporary society, which serves multiculturalism as a product, but also by different curatorial projects and art strategies, I work my often superficially exoticized 'Otherness' into 'critical difference'. Creative 'critical difference' allows the possibility of a reflexive space for and with others; it moves us to think beyond the spatial limits of the nation-state and to think through issues differently, through an arts practice.

My 'Foreigner' figuration and the artwork produced through it enable me to act within the local community. Even though at first as a Foreigner I might be considered an excluded element in my community, through my arts practice I am bringing my action into it. By involving the community in my artwork I am acting upon it and opening it up beyond its locale. The interactions between the Foreigner and her locale inform and transform one another. The boundaries of the Foreigner are open. The Foreigner is not an entity, and will inevitably enter into the process of her own re-figuration during the period of creating, delivering and reflecting on her arts practice. The social and the Foreigner will change through their encounters with each other. They modify and mediate each other. *Magdalena Makeup* Live Art Event is an example of that interaction.

In the tradition of feminist interventions into the canon, *Magdalena Makeup* intervenes into the figure of Mary Magdalene (the penitent whore archetype) while at the same time destabilizing the fixed notion of home. *Magdalena Makeup* Live Art Event was originally devised as a series of one-to-one sessions between individual members of the audience and myself as the performer in my Mary Magdalene figure: an exotic Other in a red silk dress and makeup. During each fifteen-minute session the audience member enters a small enclosed space with the performer, watches a ten-minute autobiographical film about my connection to Mary Magdalene figure through my given name Magdalena and gets to have their feet anointed, a ritual reminiscent of the biblical act that Mary Magdalene supposedly performed for Jesus. Through the figure of the exotic Other, *Magdalena Makeup* explores the notion of 'home' as an attempt to connect/juxtapose two cities: Liverpool (artist's resident home) and Dubrovnik (artist's place of birth). These two cities become connected through the act of sending postcards, initiated by the members of the audience. Each member of the audience is handed a stamped and addressed postcard with my face on it and asked by the performer to post the postcard 'back home where I belong'.

Magdalena Makeup Live Art Event first took place on 28 August 2004 from nine in the evening till three in the morning in Art Workshop Lazareti, as part of 'Karantena – Multimedia Arts Festival' in Dubrovnik, Croatia and on 6 November 2004 from eleven in the morning till five-thirty in the afternoon in the Old Police Station, Lark Lane Community Centre, in Liverpool. During these two events, a series of one-to-one sessions between individual members of the audience and myself, in my Mary Magdalene figure, I anointed forty-four pairs of feet. In addition, *Magdalena Makeup* was re-produced as a performative paper at 'The Articulate Practitioner – Articulating Practice' forum in Aberystwyth in July 2005 and at 'Diasporic Futures: Women, the

Arts and Globalization', a one-day conference at the V&A in London in July 2006.

In the following paragraphs I will describe my encounter with the audiences at the V&A in London in July 2006 and my subsequent gathering of the postcards sent by the audience members. I entered the stage as the Mary Magdalene figure, in a silk red dress, purchased in Super Savers Liverpool Oxfam for five pounds, a blond wig given to me by my uncle in Dubrovnik and ruby lipstick. I carried with me an alabaster jar purchased for 350 kunas in a Dubrovnik antique shop. I spoke into the microphone. I told the audience about the costume I was wearing and props I was carrying.

I said to my V&A audience that through my performative act I prostituted myself as Magdalena, as an eroticized and exoticized female, as an artist, as a performer, as a Foreigner, as an alien, as Other, as the named one. I told them that in her introduction to *Performativity and Belonging* Vikki Bell pointed out that 'taking the temporal performative nature of identities as a theoretical premise means that more than ever, one needs to question how identities continue to be produced, embodied and performed, effectively, passionately and with social and political consequence'.[15] I said that I pushed my temporal performative identity of the Magdalena name (dis)identification into theatrical practice and invited questions around this newly constructed 'prostitute' identity. I said that the process of the transformation of Lena, the 'everyday improper' me, into Mary Magdalene became transparent both through the video footage on film as well as during the encounter. My audience got to watch the short homemade film about the whole process of my transformation into the figure of Mary Magdalene (the images of Dubrovnik, my collecting of the costume and props in these two cities, my conversation with my mother and grandmother), as well as witness my actual dressing and makeup application in order to become the Mary Magdalene figure for their 'intimate pleasure'.

I read the text from my flyer/postcard:

> I am from Dubrovnik.
>
> My name is Magdalena, after my grandmother, and inspired by my name, I assume Mary Magdalene's Biblical status as a penitent whore and stage encounters between you and me.
>
> Witness the process of my transformation into Mary Magdalene in Dubrovnik, always my other home. I am offering you an audio-visual individual encounter with my 'Other' culture. I bring you a bit of 'Other'.
>
> I possess perfumed ointment contained in an alabaster jar. I smell divine. I have marked my space with cloth and odour. I anoint your feet. Experience the contemplative and tangible space of a Biblical ritual. Beware, this is a contemporary experiential enactment.

> I have constructed myself as an object of desire. I invite your gaze upon me. I touch …
>
> I am foreign and sensual. I am making myself up for you. Pay me a visit …
>
> Call 07963769108 to book your private session. Limited availability.

I said that in *Magdalena Makeup* I juxtapose my two homes and transverse their geography. I told them about having created an imaginary postcard of 'Liverpool and Dubrovnik combined'. I claimed that the live art event itself allowed me to be in two places at once. Magdalena physically brought a bit of Liverpool into Dubrovnik and vice versa (the costume, the props, the video images). Magdalena, the performer, invited Lena, resident of Liverpool / born in Dubrovnik, to be in two places at once. It was the constructed Magdalena who held the tickets for the journey in between two homes. I said that Ahmed offered a definition of the alien as 'only a category within a given community of citizens or subjects: as the outsider inside, the alien takes on a spatial function, establishing relations of proximity and distance within the home(land)'.[16] Through me, a self-proclaimed alien, I charged the audience with the task of re-establishing 'relations of proximity and distance within the home(land)' as well as invited them into an act of movement *between* my home(land)s. The journey between the V&A in London and Dubrovnik is

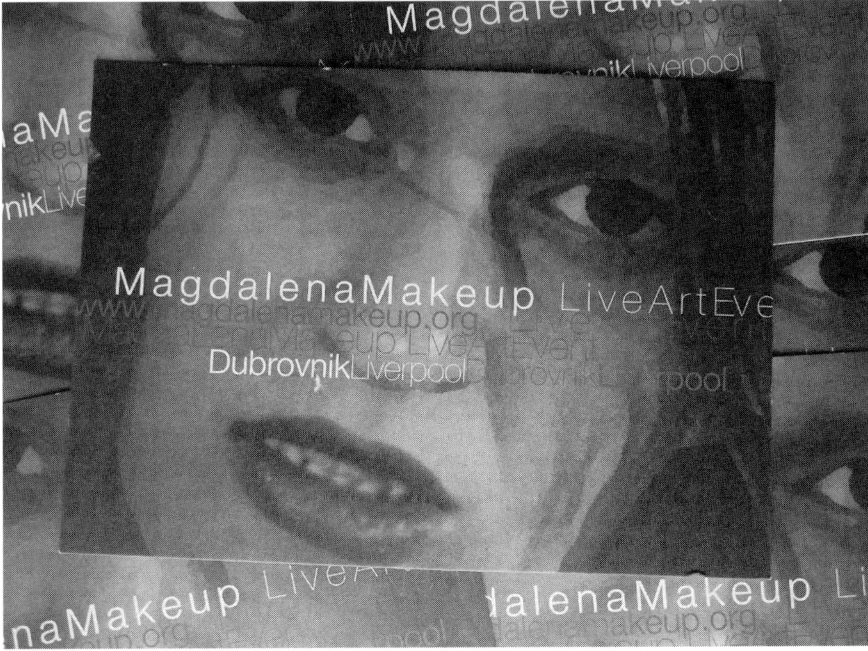

Lena Simic, *Magdalena Makeup Postcard.* 4.1

taken in the form of a postcard whose movement is initiated by the members of the audience. Magdalena postcards create a space between two cultures.

At that point I handed out my sixty-seven postcards, some of which have already been used. I explained that I wasn't being paid for the participation at the conference and therefore could not afford to print a new set of flyer/postcards. They were all stamped and addressed to my Dubrovnik home. I asked them to be so kind as to send me back home. I showed them my video film about previous postcards travelling from Dubrovnik to Liverpool and back again. Seventeen audience members will send my postcards. I will collect them all in Dubrovnik.

The flyer/postcard for *Magdalena Makeup* is my photographic portrait filtered by paintbrush with additional lipstick and makeup on it (Figure 4.1). I, the photographed Lena, became a further representation, *Magdalena Makeup.* I, Magdalena, am read as a place of address and as a future possibility. I offer my postcard (stamped and addressed) for posting. I, Magdalena, invite a member of the audience to send me back home where I belong. As my Other address / my Other home (Od greba zudioskih 4 in Dubrovnik) is inscribed on the postcard I offer my contact details aware that I present myself as a Foreigner, someone whose address is elsewhere across international borders. I remind a member of the audience that I do not belong *here*, but *there.* I invite him or her to reconsider the space I occupy. I provoke him or her to reassess my position: I am a Foreigner, with a Foreign address, a prostitute artist, a female, Magdalena/Lena, an immigrant, possibly an infiltrator, a terrorist, an anomaly. I enter the current political debate on immigration; I call on my audience members to reconsider a Foreigner's position within local time and space, in one's own neighbourhood. However, I also offer the postal idea of travel, of the in-between zone between two homes, an abstract idea of free movement:

> To post is to send by 'counting' with a halt, a relay, or a suspensive delay, the place of a mailman, the possibility of going astray and of forgetting (not of repression, which is a moment of keeping, but of forgetting).[17]

The act of sending embraces both *here* and *there*, *now* and *then.* Postcards transgress boundaries of time and space. The act of sending is a generous act; it entails forgetting about itself; it erases evidence. The 'responsibility' lies with the act of sending, with each member of an audience and the postal system. Trust is placed not only with each individual member of the audience but also upon a stamp that will be marked by the date and place of departure and delivered by the recipient's Other postal system. The tax duty has been paid to both legal states that named Magdalena in the first place and continue to name her. Two postal systems are in agreement. The Other home is expecting the 'sent'. My Other address is correct: the Other time/space is assured. I, Lena, will travel through space and time to intercept the 'sent'.

The danger of the act lies with the possibility of going astray, of getting lost in the process of travel between Liverpool and Dubrovnik, in never reaching one's destination. Not all the postcards are expected to arrive at their destination. I am happy to play with the possibility of *losing* most of them; I am happy to forget. My postcards reach my Other address altered, modified (dis)figured. They have slipped through time and space and my face on them, in makeup, is also (dis)figured. In this context my face connotes my 'name dis-identification'.

When I, in my corporeal body, travel from Dubrovnik to Liverpool or vice versa I always *reach* my destination. Travelling in between these two particular places is my familiar state of being. By looking at post, travel and myself in between I created a space that is in between Liverpool and Dubrovnik. Ahmed states that 'the journey between homes provides the subject with the contours of a space of belonging, but a space that expresses the very logic of an interval, the passing through of the subject between apparently fixed moments of departure and arrival'.[18] I aimed to involve such space through the idea of a postcard with my face on it, through its imaginary travel, through its possibility of never having a fixed moment of departure (I never knew when or if each postcard was sent nor could ever be entirely sure of its destination). My space of belonging in between homes is an interval, as unstable as the destiny of those postcards:

> What does a post card want to say to you? On what conditions is it possible? Its destination traverses you, you no longer know who you are. At the very instant when from its address it interpellates, you, uniquely you, instead of reaching you it divides you or sets you aside, occasionally overlooks you. And you love and you do not love, it makes of you what you wish, it takes you, it leaves you, it gives you.[19]

There exists a possibility of communication, of further relationship between me and you. This postcard is also a 'feedback space' as I ask the audiences for palimpsestic writing[20] over my flyer. This betokens an important change: pre-encounter, the flyer worked as an advertising call card; post-encounter, the same piece of paper, transformed into a postcard, has become a means of further communication. The act of sending calls for a message. I was pleased to offer my flyer words as a background for further intervention around the conceptual ideas of Mary Magdalene, arts, home, travel and encounter.

I said to my V&A audience that by having previously set this live art event 'inside' both of my homes, Dubrovnik and Liverpool, I alluded to my 'alien' position of a dislocated 'outsider' within these two places. I told them I leave 'Od greba zudioskih 4', my Dubrovnik address, and arrive at '19 Livingston Court' in Liverpool every year at least twice, more likely three times. I said I always return to both places. I have lived away from my original home of Dubrovnik since the age of sixteen, but I have always been obliged to return *home*. I have always travelled back *home* from my different residential homes. Discussing journeys between homes, Lynne Pearce notices that 'the repeated travel *between* these homes, old and new, affords those of us granted this privilege the opportunity of "measuring" the differences and similarities between location and communities'.[21] Journeys between homes allowed me to unfix the notion of home as stable. They shifted my perspective. While in the past Dubrovnik has always been there for me to stay the same by offering me stability through its supposed fixity, 'other places' of my accidental residences kept changing (Bastrop, Long Beach, Zagreb, Bratislava, London, Bratislava again, Tomintoul, Liverpool, Bangkok, Liverpool again). Over time, Dubrovnik itself has changed because of being compared to these 'other places', and finally, took on the role of the Other place. Being exposed to life in new places and always aware of their supposed non-existence before my arrival, I started to question Dubrovnik's own authenticity in my prolonged absence. Through annual visits to Dubrovnik, I became aware of my physical and mental changes: while Dubrovnik people remarked upon my changes, I remarked upon 'the changed Dubrovnik'. Dubrovnik became Foreign ground for me. We alienated one another.

I told the V&A audience that when I did *Magdalena Makeup* in Lark Lane Community Centre in Liverpool I thought of the individual encounters between me and the members of audience as a gift to my L17 community. I 'Othered' the community using my local and personal connection to the area. I performatively 'prostituted' my Foreign position, aware that it carries certain preconceptions, in order to have a change of mind, to transgress the preconceived 'authenticity' of an Other. I made the issue of my Foreign descent into a spectacle; I 'prostituted' it through my live art event, and finally raised money because of it for a worthy local charity. That morning I occupied Lark Lane Pre-School staff room. I placed my props, smells and live embodiment over the pre-existent functional community room. The occupation was agreed upon and I offered to collect some donations for the Pre-School, which had recently lost its Liverpool City Council grant, in exchange for the room. However, I would argue that my artistic occupation stimulated more change in the community than fifteen pounds in change gathered during that Saturday. *Magdalena Makeup* Liverpool existed solely within its context of L17. It was a parallel event to a birthday party taking place in the hall next door. Many members of the audience were 'snatched' from the party. My staff room became a place of rest, contemplation, difference. It was an excuse to leave the kids behind for fifteen minutes and indulge in something unusual: the epic archetypal figure of Mary Magdalene waited around the corner, and presented herself as being written over by myself and the L17 community.

Each neighbourhood – in this case, Liverpool 17 – is trying to create its own sense of identity (through specific local shops, restaurants and pubs, community centres and their programme of events). However, the achieved identity of L17, as a bohemian, student-centred, quirky part of Liverpool, puts it in direct opposition to its neighbouring postcode of L8, which gets to be bad, dangerous and rough, and L15, the more 'real' residential area with a multicultural twist on Smithdown Road. I concluded there were invisible borders everywhere. I am taking driving lessons and the instructor is talking about getting familiar with the driving centre's catchment area. The schools need to be situated within the catchment area. Even though these invisible borders that exist between postcodes or even within them could be celebrated as 'difference' with local autonomy from larger governmental structures, they are always forced to define each other. Moreover, they provide a shield against any kind of accountability towards larger city structures unless those are beneficial for that particular neighbourhood.[22]

I said that as I started to live in the community of L17 and L17 'accepted' me locally – with warm feelings and obligatory name-tags such as a foreigner, a mother, an artist, an Other – I consequently, yet unwillingly, joined in the playing of the borders game. My escape route became my performance work. I recognised my ability to *act* in the community and thus give 'my acceptance' back. I made myself visible. I staged (as an act of reciprocating the acceptance I had received) the *Magdalena Makeup* encounters in the toddlers' group and Pre-School staff room at the Old Police Station, Lark Lane Community Centre. I made a 'local public place' into my intimate and politicized space. I occupied the local public space intimately but with political agency as an artist. I felt I had the right to do it because I was acting as one of the locals belonging there. I even collected some donations for the Pre-School. However, there is a danger that my arts event might be read as only reinforcing the borders of this particular space and providing the selected group of local people with 'something special'.

I thought that the reality of organizing 'arts in the community' is in understanding 'local intrigues and politics'. My aim was to get a locally owned space at the Old Police Station, Lark Lane Community Centre, and transform it into an artistic one. However, I was denied access to a 'healing room', the most suitable place for my event. I was advised to meet Jacki, the events manager of the 'healing room', during the Healing Day, an event run by a group of local hippies. I had to drop my cultural Saturday afternoon life and act as one of the locals at the 'Healing Day do' with aromatherapy, organic goods and numerous massages. I still did not get their 'healing room'. I guess it had to do with my 'inappropriate' appearance, makeup and red laptop bag – I was silly enough to come to the Old Police Station straight from a Tate Liverpool event where I was attending a book launch. Can one do both in a single afternoon and get away with it? This string of events, and the danger that *Magdalena Makeup* in L17 might have seemed to reinforce the invisible borders, made me think twice about the implications of doing arts in the community.

Doreen Massey's article 'The Strangers Beyond the Gates' is a provocation to understanding our own implications within the processes of globalization.[23] Massey takes on Alan Read's quote from the material he circulated before the Civic Centre Symposium (April 2003) where she delivered the paper. The quote reads: 'Theatre, after all, has always been an act of proximity and presence seeking the global and international within its own neighbourhood.' Massey follows by arguing for the inseparability of local place and global space. She warns us against the privileging of the local and reminds us that the 'global space is equally real, grounded, meaningful, as is place'.[24] She writes:

> The lived reality of our daily lives actually is incredibly dispersed and widespread in its sources, in its resources, in its contacts and most certainly in its repercussions. I don't think we can seriously posit space as the outside of place as lived. … If we really think space relationally, then it is no more than the sum of all those relations, engagements, interactions that encircle the globe. It is utterly everyday and grounded and it may go round the world. It is everywhere local but altogether it is global.[25]

In connection to that intersection between the local and the global, Massey urges us to consider distant strangers, beyond our cities and our immediate surroundings. Raising 'the potential wider geographies of our social and political responsibilities',[26] she reminds us that cultural diversity is not only here and now, but somewhere else as well:

> But cultural diversity, cultural difference, alterity, *is* implacably *also* far away and in different and distant lands. In our current concern for hybridity at home we must not forget that wider geography. It used to be called internationalism, and there are now different ways in which we can frame it and think it. But it seems to me that we have to put it much more firmly back on the agenda in the disciplines in which we work: the cultural, the performative, the social. I want to pick up Alan's argument, in the quote that I gave you before. He talks about theatre and its integral relation to proximity and presence, but he then goes on to raise the possibility of linking foreground and distance, and of thinking internationally.[27]

My position as Foreigner compels me to think in broader terms than the local community. Thus, I refrain from calling L17 my home. I fear the locality of my performance work might do more to reinforce those invisible borders. The movement in between postcodes is possible and, therefore, I am eager to understand home as my position in the system rather than the experienced locality. Home becomes about having a mission, in my case an artistic one. My journeys in between homes have taught me to put things in perspective and, therefore, even though I might experience locality as my temporary home, I must learn to consider it in larger socio-political relations. Furthermore I must learn to consider my arts practice 'beyond home'.

In *Magdalena Makeup* I *indulged* the local community. In the face of being unable to challenge any larger power structures my aim with *Magdalena Makeup* was to act intimately and change things locally. I attended too many community-based events and ate too many sweet homemade cakes sold for local charity initiatives, but I still believe that artwork, aware of its own positionality and the social structures that underpin them, might be capable of refiguring the local and the lived in the service of incremental social transformation.

Notes

1 Arts Council England, *Ambitions for the Arts 2003–2006* (London: ACE, 2003), www.artscouncil.org.uk/downloads/ambitionsfull.pdf, p. 4.
2 Ibid.
3 H. Maitland (ed.), *Navigating Difference: Cultural Diversity and Audience Development* (London: ACE, 2006).
4 Ibid., pp. 208–9.
5 Arts Council England, *Achieving Great Art for Everyone: A Strategic Framework for the Arts* (London: ACE, 2010).
6 R. Appignanesi (ed.), *Beyond Cultural Diversity: The Case for Creativity: A Third Text Report* (London: Third Text Publications, 2010).
7 For more information about decibel past and current showcases, see www.decibel-pas.com/press-room/what-is-decibel.
8 N. Khan (ed.), 'Reinventing Britain' in *ACE decibel and The Guardian*, special edition (London: ACE, 2003), p. 15.
9 S. Ahmed, *Strange Encounters: Embodied Others in Post-Coloniality* (London and New York: Routledge, 2000), p. 96.
10 Ibid., p. 101.
11 T. M-H. Trinh, 'Not You/Like You: Post-Colonial Women and the Interlocking Questions of Identity and Difference', *Inscriptions* 3–4 (1988), http://culturalstudies.ucsc.edu/PUBS/Inscriptions/vol_3-4/minh-ha.html; and 'Outside in, Inside Out', in T. M-H. Trinh, *When The Moon Waxes Red: Representation, Gender and Cultural Politics* (New York and London: Routledge, 1991), pp. 65–78.
12 For further discussion about the problems of using 'we' in feminist contexts see E. Aston and G. Harris, 'Feminist Futures and the Possibilities of "We"?', in Aston and Harris, *Feminist Futures? Theatre, Performance, Theory* (Basingstoke and New York: Palgrave Macmillan, 2006), pp. 1–16.
13 S. Ahmed, *Differences that Matter: Feminist Theory and Postmodernism* (Cambridge: Cambridge University Press, 1998), p. 192.
14 Trinh, 'Outside in, Inside Out', p. 71.
15 V. Bell (ed.), *Performativity and Belonging* (London: Sage Publications, 1999), p. 2.
16 Ahmed, *Strange Encounters*, p. 3.
17 J. Derrida, *The Post Card: From Socrates to Freud and Beyond*, trans. A. Bass (Chicago: University of Chicago Press, 1987), p. 65.
18 Ahmed, *Strange Encounters*, p. 77.

19 Derrida, *The Post Card*, back cover.
20 Palimpsest – n. a manuscript written over a partly erased older manuscript in such a way that the old words can be read beneath the new.
21 L. Pearce (ed.), *Devolving Identities: Feminist Readings in Home and Belonging* (Aldershot: Ashgate, 2000), p. 177.
22 In *The Fall of Public Man*, Richard Sennett claims that 'community has become both emotional withdrawal from society and a territorial barricade within the city', which consequently means that 'this new geography is communal versus urban; the territory of warm feeling versus the territory of impersonal blankness'. He continues by stating that 'the community must turn toward the larger structures of city and state which have actual power, the community is so absorbed in itself that it is deaf to the outside, or exhausted, or fragmented' and proceeds to warn that 'localism and local autonomy are becoming widespread political creeds, as though the experience of power relations will have more human meaning the more intimate the scale – even though the actual structures of power grow ever more into an international system.' In R. Sennett, *The Fall of Public Man* (London: Faber and Faber, 1993, originally published in 1977), pp. 301, 310, 339.
23 D. Massey, 'The Strangers Beyond the Gates', *Performance Research: On Civility* 9/4 (2004).
24 Ibid., p. 119.
25 Ibid.
26 Ibid., p. 118.
27 Ibid., p. 121.

5 'How we live today …'

Florence Ayisi in dialogue[1] *with Mo White*

Introduction

Florence Ayisi is a documentary filmmaker with a growing international reputation for representing Africa in a different light. Her films provide insights that challenge stereotypical notions of both Africa and African women, showing diverse communities and experiences whose dynamism differs from those portrayed in the Western news media.

Ayisi comes from Cameroon, Central Africa, and studied English at the University of Yaoundé, before moving to England to study at a private television studio in London, the University of Hull and University of Leicester. Further studies followed at the Northern School of Film and Television before she took up teaching positions at University of Sunderland, Coventry University, University of Glamorgan and the University of Wales, Newport in 2000, where she has remained and is currently a Reader in Film Practice.

Her first feature-length documentary film *Sisters in Law: Stories from a Cameroon Court* (2005) was co-directed with Kim Longinotto and won over twenty-six international film awards. These included the prestigious Prix Art et Essai at Cannes Film Festival in 2005 and others at Santa Barbara Film Festival and Bologna Human Rights Film Festival, to name but a few. Ayisi followed that success with the setting-up of her own company, Iris Films (UK), and she has directed and produced a further three films to date: *My Mother: ISANGE* (2005), *Our World in Zanzibar* (2007) and *Zanzibar Soccer Queens* (2007). The last of these has toured to a number of major film festivals since its release and continues to gather plaudits as it goes.

Storytelling is at the heart of Ayisi's filmic practice and it is from contemporary African literature that her initial inspiration comes. Given the different perspectives that Ayisi's films have produced it can be seen that along with other African filmmakers, as well as contemporary African writers, she is imagining a new version of Africa.

Mo White: Let's start by talking about your background a little and what brought you to England, and latterly to Wales. I see that at degree level you studied English. Were film and television studies, and perhaps African film studies, part of that course, and is that what inspired you to become a filmmaker?

Florence Ayisi: My first degree was in English – major subjects were English literature and linguistics, with options like drama and theatre arts, American literature and African literature, but we never looked at film as part of the course. Although, when I was younger, I used to spend my summers in the cinema with my school friends, watching Kung-fu films and Indian melodramas! The cinema was just shouting – that's how people watch films in a lot of African countries. Along with my friends we took part in the narrative. The way that we watched films was more of a collective process in which our reactions were often explicit, either through verbal responses or emotional displays. We were in a sense 'participating' in telling the story. We would go along with the actors and wait for the moment when the main actor appeared on the screen and then we would all scream 'that is the actor!' You were proud to recognize the actor on the screen and we would say to one another 'how did you know this actor?' and the answer would be 'I know this actor because I saw them in the last film!' That is how cinema was for me then. At the time there was very little African film for us to see. When I first went to university, if we saw posters at the cinemas in Yaoundé with any black faces on, the cinema would be packed. The queues would be so long that the film would be finished and people would still be queuing.

There's a history of oral storytelling in our tradition – stories that are handed down by parents and retold around the fireplace. I experienced that myself as my grandmother and grandaunts would tell us fables, and then tell us about things that were happening in the village using the same style, using dramatic tension and irony to tell contemporary stories about what is happening in the village. I grew up feeling I wanted to tell stories. I loved telling the stories of the films I had seen to my school friends who were from more remote areas and did not have the luxury of going to the cinema. I kept telling my big brother I wanted to do 'mass communication'! That, to us, was radio – as television only came to Cameroon in 1985. That's where my yearning to tell stories came from and I can see now that this desire has followed me all the way along.

In the mid-1980s the Ministry of Higher Education was sending a lot of young people abroad, especially to France and the UK. When television started in Cameroon in 1985 some scholarships were given to young people to go and study film and television. So when I was offered the scholarship to study in UK, I took it and shifted to study film and television.

MW: So the idea was that you were being funded by the government to go to the UK to study film and television, with the intention that you would go back to Cameroon and work in the developing television industry?

FA: Exactly, that was a good intention! However, sometimes good intentions don't get fulfilled. I studied at the Television Training Centre in London, and then I went to do a masters in theatre and media production at the University of Hull.

Early films and influences

MW: You've won many awards for your films and this started quite early in your career. An early film of yours, *Where the Cows Go* (1991), won an award – can you talk about that?

FA: Yes, it was a film I made at the university; it won an award at the Chicago Film Festival in 1992. I studied for another Masters in film production at the Northern School of Film and Television in Sheffield, which was run by Leeds Metropolitan University and supported by Channel 4 Television. We were the first batch of students and you went in as a writer, sound-recorder, editor, director or producer. I went in as a producer and produced two films; one was *Where the Cows Go* and the other, *A Red Hat* (1991).

Where the Cows Go is about this woman being in prison in the 1930s because she kissed another woman and her being ostracized because she was different. We shot some scenes of the film on location around the Yorkshire Dales, so I started following this tradition of shooting outside. I like the realist tradition of African cinema where most of the filming is done on location. Even though I make documentary films, I watch a lot of fiction films and they inspire me. For example, the Italian neo-realist films, the French New Wave, the British kitchen sink dramas. So the two films that I made at Northern School of Film and Television gave me the scope to film on location.

MW: This is very different from my own background as an artist working with film and the moving image where, as an artist, you do everything. Of course your perspective is one that follows an industry-led model …

FA: Yes, on some of my courses, I had studied camera, sound, editing and so on, but now when I make films I would prefer to leave the actual craft skills to a cinematographer, sound person and editor. Of course, I have and I do use the camera when I go to do my research work, and I shot some of the scenes in the film about my mother, and *Our World in Zanzibar*, but I am not a cinematographer. I would not risk it, particularly when I'm working with a big budget. I just want to think about the content of the film, listen to what the people we are shooting are saying, how they are relating to us, because it's a two-way process. I prefer not to worry too much about how to shoot it, because we discuss how I want it to look and sound before we start the filming.

MW: We might talk now, generally, about what informs your film practice and what you were looking at or interested in when you were making those early films at university. You have mentioned the French New Wave and African cinema and I am wondering what specifically …

FA: Yes, but I think that coming from a background in literature – Nigerian writers like Chinua Achebe, Wole Soyinka, Francis Bebey – the Cameroonian artist, writer and musician – and Ngugi wa Thiong'o, the Kenyan writer, were my early influences. In some of Wole Soyinka's work, especially *The Interpreters* (1965), the concept of individual responsibility is highlighted; that for change to happen you must cleanse yourself first and then you can go with a group of other people who have also cleansed themselves and together you can bring about change. So change starts with an individual. On the other hand, Ngugi wa Thiong'o talks about the struggle of the masses or mass action, and that change comes when people mobilize. In one of his plays, *The Trial of Dedan Kimathi* (1976), he makes that community feel that for change to happen they need the masses to mobilize and become one. These two writers are saying truthful things but I feel as an individual that first of all I have to understand what the problem is and then we can come together as a community and be stronger. Generally speaking, most of the African literature I read involved very realistic stories and settings that reflect how we live; you imagined yourself relating to the ordinary characters, you share their fears, their dreams and so on. I saw these thematic elements in the short film scripts that I produced on my film course; that's why I chose the scripts.

In terms of African film the work that has influenced me is Safi Faye, the first woman in sub-Saharan Africa to make a long film. Sita Bella from Cameroon made a very short film in the 1960s called *Tam-Tam à Paris*. In *Kaddu Beykat* (1975), which means *Letter from My Village*, Safi Faye used both drama and documentary to tell the story of her village. She is concerned about her community, and how they should speak for themselves, rather than just showing us stereotypes. This is a really important film, but of course it's very rare that you can get to see it.

Then you have Ousmane Sembène's first film *Borom Sarret* (1963). This is a strong critique of life in a recently independently African country. The poor state of affairs that he presents in this fantastic twenty-minute film is still here today, as it was soon after independence. He wrote literature before becoming a filmmaker. He stopped writing because he felt that the people he wanted to communicate with cannot read or write and so he turned to cinema. Cinema, for him, was like having a conversation with his people; the ordinary people who need to understand why things are the way they are. Ousmane Sembène is important to me, and so is Souleymane Cissé, who in the book *African Cinemas: Decolonizing the Gaze*[2] laments the fact that the white camera doesn't represent Africans like humans. I agree with him when he suggests that we have to take responsibility to speak about ourselves in ways that we want to be seen. In a sense, we need to 'humanize' African people, both for ourselves and for 'others', particularly in this postcolonial and post-independence era. When you see anthropological films that speak about Africa and any kind of people who have been colonized or dominated they are always spoken *for*. I feel strongly that people in my films should speak for themselves. They should tell you how they feel, what it means to get up in the morning and go to the farm. During one of my film research trips a woman tells me 'Two years ago I didn't have a gas cooker – the smoke from the firewood spoils the lungs, that's what my educated sons have told me. Now I have a gas cooker – my life will never be the same again.' I want to hear her say that for herself. I don't want to narrate it: 'you see this woman in this farm, today she is using a gas cooker because of the successful agribusiness she started with microcredit finance.' No! I want to hear it from her, in the tone of her own voice because you can hear how proud and determined she is. When it comes from her it's something completely different – let her use her own voice, which adds another dimension in the different ways we dream and aspire wherever we are in the world today, especially in this globalized context.

MW: Would you describe the way in which you construct the narratives in your films as being auto-ethnographic? That is perhaps one of the terms you could use, where people speak for themselves, where there is no narrator, either disembodied or one that is behind the camera encouraging them …

FA: I spend time with the people who appear as subjects in my films – that is why I value the research period – and it's important for me that they understand the process, and they can trust me. This is a crucial part of the way I work so that the people I film see that they have choices – and can see that they can affect the work. Most mainstream documentary and ethnographic films tend to objectify African people. It's important for me that the people are central to the *mise en scène*; they shape the story; they reflect and think. They are visible, not as objects, but subjects who 'speak' and are active participants of what is going on, and they present challenging viewpoints in what they say.

Sisters in Law

MW: Let's talk about what is, in some ways, your best-known film, *Sisters in Law: Stories from A Cameroon Court*. I'm interested in the collaboration with Kim Longinotto, the well-known documentary filmmaker. I'm interested in what your role in the film was.

FA: Let me speak briefly about how the collaboration worked and my role. I came with the idea and access to people and the courts in Cameroon; Kim came with her access to Channel 4 Television funding, and her extensive filmmaking experience. I don't think I went in naïvely thinking we were going to be on the same footing with regards to our individual roles and contributions. However, in the process of developing ideas and making a film there is a context and a system of understanding – where did the idea come from? How was it set up and developed in terms of the choice of people, and locations? How do you gain the trust of the people to the point where they allow you to film them during vulnerable and challenging times in their lives? What choices are made and how do these affect and shape the content?

In brief, my role was crucial despite the disparity in our filmmaking experience. I had established a relationship with the women before we started shooting; before Kim arrived with Mary Milton[3] these women had felt comfortable with me. They saw me as one of 'them', which I am, even though I live in the UK. I also understood the sensitive nature of some of the cases that I decided would be good to film – through speaking with the Women's Legal Aid Clinic who, though not featured in the film, were instrumental in supporting the women to take their cases to court. Throughout the filming itself, my relationship with the women enabled us to gain their trust and confidence.

Actually, the life of *Sisters in Law* started at Sheffield documentary festival in October 2001 where I was watching a Kate Davis film, *Southern Comfort* (2001), about transgender. Amazing film! We were expecting a 'Q & A' with her after the film. Then, Alan Fountain (former Commissioning Editor for Channel 4 TV) announced that Davis wasn't there because many Americans weren't flying so soon after 9/11. They brought Kim Longinotto to talk about her work – I was excited. I had seen a couple of her documentaries, *Divorce Iranian Style* (1998) and *The Day I Will Never Forget* (2002). I liked *Divorce Iranian Style*, particularly the way that some of the film's subjects will occasionally talk directly to the camera/director.

I met Kim after the 'Q & A' and shortly after this meeting we started communicating about some of my ideas that she was interested in. The idea of women judges in Cameroon stood out. I went to Cameroon for research, and also to obtain an authorization from the Minister of Justice (Ahmadou Ali). When the Minister gave me the permission letter – this was the defining moment for me in the process of making *Sisters in Law*. Channel 4 TV (Peter Dale) had informed Kim that they were keen on the idea of women judges in Cameroon, but they needed to see evidence of 'access' to the country and also to film in the courts. The Minister of Justice told me he was extremely proud of women's work in the judicial system. There is no perfect legal system in the world, but women are particularly strong in Cameroon, and their presence ensures that women 'victims' get a chance to have someone to look at their problem in a more sympathetic manner. So the women in that film (the State Prosecutor, Ngassa Vera, and the Magistrate Court Judge, Ntuba Beatrice) are just the tip of the iceberg – they are not the only women in the judiciary [Figure 5.1]. I believe that the Minister also realized that making the film would be a way to honour and acknowledge women's role in the judicial system.

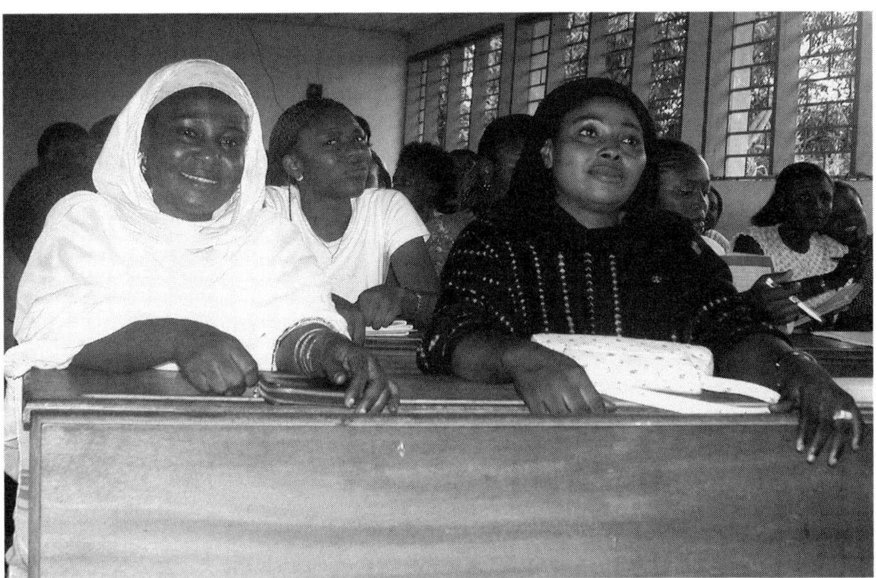

Florence Ayisi, *Sisters in Law: Stories from a Cameroon Court* (2005). Production still. 5.1

MW: That is one of the ways in which the film could be seen as problematic. There is no narration or scene setting. As a viewer, you are delivered straight into the film and because no context is provided I use my own knowledge of the judicial system – one that is based on a Western European system and that is largely male dominated. My impression then was that these are really unusual women, and as a member of the audience I am offered no other information.

FA: I believe that the women are not unusual only in the sense that there are many other women like them, administering justice strictly and fairly. Even for many Cameroonians who may understand this context, it is unusual to actually see the women in action; doing what they do. Going to the courts to listen to proceedings is not part of people's day-to-day experience. On another level, they are unusual because of the exceptional and intelligent manner in which they solved the cases – swiftly applying the law, as it should be. This is far removed from how many people imagine women's roles, positions and status in Africa. Also, getting a conviction for domestic violence cases involving resilient Muslim women is extraordinary, especially so because for them as it was the first time the two women judges had succeeded in doing so in their own careers. Moreover, how often are we presented with African women like this on television? Even the women (Amina and Ladi) and children (Sonita and Manka) who are the victims of violence show strength and courage to face their aggressors in court. I believe that it's also because Western audiences had not been privileged to see such strong African women on the screen that makes them so unusual to the point where viewers at Cannes were asking for their autographs. These new images of strong African women have contributed to the huge success of the film – the two women judges in the film have had, and continue to have celebrity status wherever the film is screened, especially when they are present during the screening.

MW: Looking at *Sisters in Law* in comparison with your solo work – it is striking how those films are handled in a different way. The camera in *Sisters in Law* is very close, very intimate. It does take a 'slice of life' without any context. A context does exist in your own work where you provide the viewer with a way in. In *Sisters in Law*, the people are subject to the camera in quite a revelatory way. It seems to be a very intrusive approach to filmmaking, and when it's a white European director doing the filming it is surely problematic.

FA: The most important thing is that within that 'space' we get to see 'new' and different images of brave African women and children – which is my clear agenda and vision for making films. As an emerging filmmaker, you sometimes have to negotiate and compromise because you want to get past some of the hurdles that film school cannot teach you. However, in my process of finding new ways in which Africans can be imagined differently, I have also shared the concerns that underpin the politics of representation in terms of not just what is represented – but also how that content is meditated. This lies at the heart of what Souleymane Cissé says in *African Cinemas*. He has a concern for how Africans have been portrayed, and a call for the need to redress the way to 'look' and construct the African subject when he says 'Those who came to film us never showed the people here as human beings. They came to show us to their audiences as though we were animals. They saw us with their eyes. They filmed us any old how. We know the camera can give a positive image of human beings. This White camera shows Africans as not belonging to the human community. They film wild animals with more respect'![4] He goes on to suggest that 'the first task of African filmmakers is to affirm that people here are human beings and to make known those of our values which could be of use to others'.[5] I fully agree with Souleymane Cissé here because it brings a very different kind of dialogue to the screen. For example, coming back to my film practice, this is one of the reasons why I was attracted to some of Kim Longinotto's work when I saw a particular scene in *Divorce Iranian Style* where a woman turned to the person behind the camera and talked to her.

MW: ... and the woman's gaze was returned – but this is something that doesn't happen in *Sisters in Law*.

I think it's important to talk here about what happens when you do that kind of collaboration with an established filmmaker who has such a track record of working in a particular way. A recent article by Paul Basu, in *Rethinking Documentary: New Perspectives, New Practices*,[6] is not totally critical but it does hint at an important problematic here. Basu compares the BBC programme *Tribe* with Bruce Parry to Kim Longinotto's documentary film practice and their differing approaches to ethnographic film. Even though the comparison obviously works quite well in Kim Longinotto's favour, the point is still raised – and her track record seems to bear this out – that the subjects she investigates are made possible only through her links with people who are closer to or from that particular culture.

FA: Kim is an accomplished filmmaker, and accessing production funding is guaranteed with her track record. Funding is crucial in realizing any film project, so too is access and knowledge of subjects, people, locations, the cultural context. As is having a vision that provides a new perspective on how we live today in this process of making films. *Sisters in Law* is a combination of all these factors.

Our World in Zanzibar

FA: In 2005, soon after *Sisters in Law* was screened at Cannes and won a prestigious award, I was inspired to carry on finding stories that presented a different picture of life in Africa, especially the lives and experiences of women. I had an idea that I wanted to do something about women's autobiographies. I was invited to the Zanzibar International Film Festival to work with the Women's Panorama section on a project about Western women who have migrated to Zanzibar. The theme for that year's festival was 'Histories and Migrations'. My biggest question was what is Africa offering a woman from America, the richest country in the world? I thought that if these Western women have chosen to live in Zanzibar, then Africa must have something to offer them – then Africa is beautiful. This fed my clear agenda of showing that there is another side to Africa that is not negative – so I jumped on the bandwagon!

I made *Our World in Zanzibar* (2007) there. This was based on workshops organized by Alice Aida Ayers, an African-American artist, now living in Zanzibar. The women – from Britain, The Netherlands, USA and Spain/Peru – told their very personal and sometimes painful stories of what led them to move away from their supposed 'comfort zones' in the West. One of the ideas was to find connections between women's lives; between African women and their sisters from the West. The migrated women wrote stories in the form of written journals and African women performed these through the spoken word, mime and movement. The documentary, *Our World in Zanzibar*, combines the women's migration stories and staged performances.

Zanzibar Soccer Queens

MW: Was it when you were in Zanzibar that you found out about The Women Fighters Football Club that became the subject of your next film, *Zanzibar Soccer Queens* (2007)? I really enjoyed watching that film and it made me laugh a lot. I thought those women are brilliant and I'm jealous of them too because I would have liked to be playing with them – but I belong to the wrong generation and I'm in the wrong country!

FA: Yes, I was there for five weeks and I watched the Zanzibari women from a distance, going about elegantly to the market in nice bright colours of the Khanga. I see the women in the shop and in the street but I don't know what their voices sound like. The day before I left Zanzibar I met this guy and I lamented that I knew nothing about the local women – he was quick to say that they may cover their head, neck and face, but Zanzibari women are dynamic. They play soccer and netball, and they are in business. That underneath that veil or hijab, there is a fiery woman. So I said tell me about the soccer bit! So this guy took me to meet Nassra J. Mohammed at ten in the morning and my flight was at two o'clock in the afternoon! I met this very quiet, calm and unassuming woman who wore a black hijab. She was sitting at her desk in the immigration office – and we talked. I am very curious because

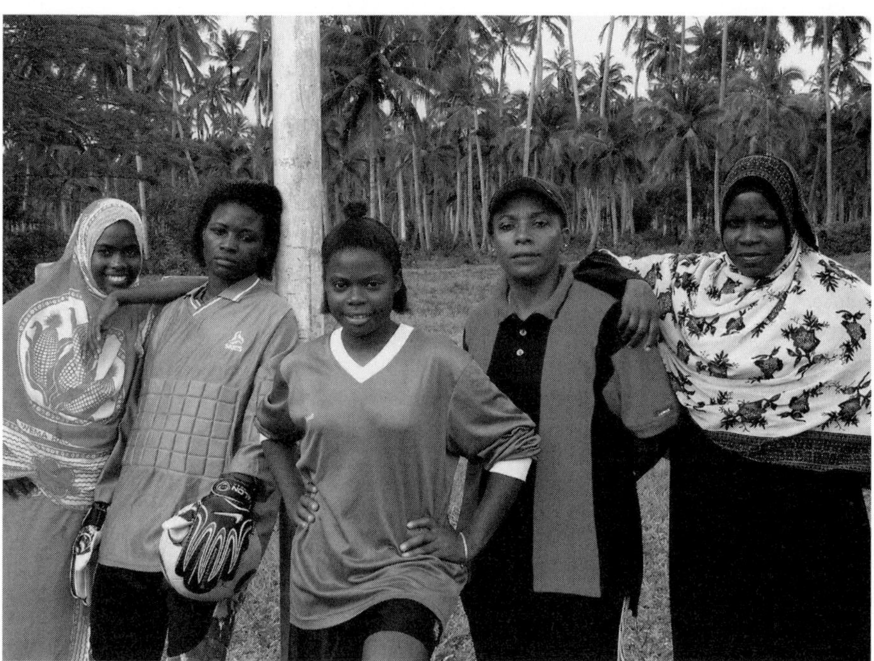

5.2 Florence Ayisi, *Zanzibar Soccer Queens* (2007). Production still.

I love football. She spoke to me for forty-five minutes non-stop. I came away and thought she has never spoken before. You know, from the age of seventeen Nassra had won so many trophies as Badminton Champion and she had represented her country numerous times. I had never heard of her before or about what she had done for her country and I asked her – why haven't I heard about you? She said it is because I am a woman. So I decided to go back and make a film about Nassra and the team of women she coaches, Women Fighters. What I saw in this woman, Nassra, was what I can only refer to as a determined individual taking the responsibility and having the courage to pursue what she believes in – in that process, the young women see her as a leader, and because they too have a passion for football they are encouraged. They have someone, a 'big sister', who has shown them the light, and together they can achieve something special – the freedom to be themselves and have dreams. Nassra in her position knows that a lot of the women cannot afford to buy the basic sports gear they need for training and so on. But they want to play! So she takes the responsibility to enable them to do this. As a team of women, they are strong and determined to experience something special, something outside of their everyday existence [Figure 5.2].

I have a specific agenda for cinema as an African woman. I want to explore, investigate and show things that have been absent in the mainstream media in today's globalized context – the diversity and complex socio-cultural experiences of modern Africa. I want to show how people struggle and succeed. Shortly after I arrived in Britain from Cameroon in the mid-1980s, I quickly became aware of the conspicuous absence of images and ideas that I was familiar with. What I was confronted with were media representations of Africa that were simplistic and limited to the negative stereotypical images of disease, poverty, debt and corruption; a place where there are famines and wars that could only be helped by Bob Geldof and Live Aid. It was a terrible affront to my dignity as an African person. Such representations undoubtedly reinforce a particular kind of reality and perception of the continent and its people. What I saw was an inability of the media to see beyond news headlines, or to accept that another reality existed in Africa. I kept wondering why such representations were devoid of the complex political and economic relationships that still exist between most Western countries and their former colonies – the neo-colonial relations that are the stranglehold or barriers to some aspects of socio-economic development in Africa. I became aware of the various media theories and concepts in analysing the mass media. It was clear to me at that time, as it is now, that one such theory – the classical view of the media theory of Karl Marx and Frederick Engels – is still relevant today in relation to the power of the media setting the agenda and disseminating ideas and world views of the few who own and control the means of material production.

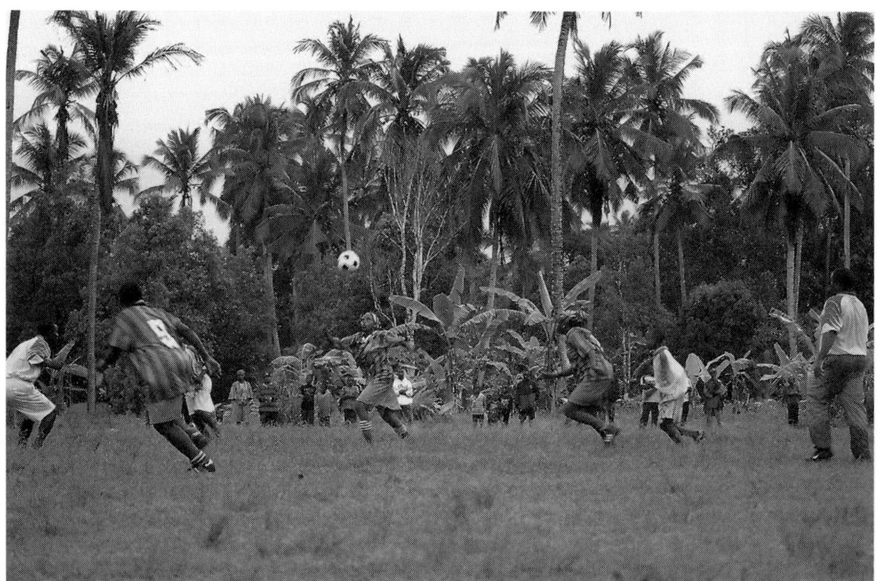

5.3 Florence Ayisi, *Zanzibar Soccer Queens* (2007). Production still.

While I do not deny the sad state of socio-economic problems experienced by people in many African societies I am interested in unravelling the myriad of untold stories of struggle, hope and success. There are stories that celebrate the lives and experiences of the people that you will never otherwise hear about. In a sense, these challenge the status quo. So if you see a community that is suffering I am interested in showing a little bit of sunshine, although I am not refuting that these people are suffering at the same time. I am interested in showing that this is not a big deal for them.

When I saw the Zanzibari women playing soccer with very limited gear, I was not concerned about asking, you're playing soccer barefoot – how do you feel? Why should I ask them about playing soccer barefoot? I wanted to know why they play soccer; what it means to them. You can see she is playing soccer barefoot so why should I ask her about it? Why should I ask her about the obvious? She is training five days a week, in spite of the fact she doesn't have boots – she plays [Figure 5.3].

I came back to the UK and decided to raise the money from my own funds to make the film. I decided that even if I made a short film just about Nassra that will be worth it. She had spoken with such passion. I thought that her story – what she's done for her country, as a woman, and how she inspires and supports the younger women – would be forgotten in twenty years' time. I thought that she deserves to be remembered. So, I took a bank loan and my partner and I re-mortgaged our house. I worked with an ex-student who had just finished his post-graduate course in Royal Holloway, University of London. He was keen to work with me on the project and set about advertising for a crew by posting on independent film network websites. We shot for four weeks over the Easter holidays in 2006. During this time, the sound recordist became ill and we didn't have enough material. Luckily, we had production insurance; we were covered for the days we lost. So we went back again and shot for three weeks in the summer.

By early October we had a 110-minute rough cut, which I decided to send to the Gothenburg International Film Festival. I knew by the time the festival started in February 2007 the film would be finished. Four days later, an email came. They loved the film and they'd like to show it – and they invited me to attend too! So we finished editing the film and we took it to Sweden. The film was shown three times at the festival and the cinemas were packed!

It has since been to other film festivals. It was shown at the Institute of Contemporary Arts, London as part of the Black Film Festival. Then I started looking for distributors and that was hard. The film was too long for television. It was 87 minutes by that time and they wanted 52 minutes. I had no more money to edit. At that point some friends in London put up some funding to get the film re-edited. Now it has a distributor in London, and I am delighted that the Filmmakers' Library in America has acquired the film – that's the latest acquisition from the distributors and it's great news for the film and the efforts of our independent production.

MW: What have audience reactions to the film been like?

FA: It has been amazing. People cheer – like football audiences! In Gothenburg, New York, Taiwan, Oslo, Toronto … everywhere, people respond really well to seeing beautiful, strong women playing soccer, expressing their passion for the game, their dreams and frustrations, and how important it is in their lives.

It has been shown in Zanzibar. That was so amazing. I was very scared because these women are marginal in their society. The country is over 90 per cent Muslim. I was nervous for two reasons – the fact that a Koran teacher said that men are weak when they see a woman's legs and body exposed when they wear football shorts. The second thing was that nobody had seen these women on the beach in swimming costumes. Nassra has parties for the team from time to time – either in her house or on the beach party. They have music with a small band, they eat, and they swim. This is important to them and it's how they live, so I included a sequence of the women enjoying themselves at the beach party. In the longer version of the film there is more swimming and dancing – and quite sexy dancing! I wondered what the audience in Zanzibar would say when they see the women in their swimming costumes. So I was scared about this. The screening at the Zanzibar Film Festival took place at the open-air cinema in Old Fort, Stone Town, under the stars with an audience of over 1,000 people. When the Koran teacher came on the screen and talked about men being tempted when women wear shorts, the audience booed. I started feeling comfortable! Then a player's mother says in the film 'we are currently going by science and … and the whole crowd said "technology!"' I have never seen anything like it. The audience were shouting, cheering and I wondered what I had been worried about.

MW: Were The Women Fighters FC there?

FA: Yes, they hadn't seen the film before. The Festival Director did invite the women onto the stage and some of them wore their shorts and sports attire. It was an amazing atmosphere as the audience cheered and shouted the names of the players – they looked so proud!

Another important thing about the film was the soundtrack. When I was doing the research in December 2005 I said to them that I would like to use the popular Zanzibar Taarab music in the film so I asked them to select some songs. So they chose songs that meant something to them. Taarab music is predominantly about love songs and what the women are doing is shifting this to their love of football – subverting the meaning of the songs. During the screening, the audience reaction was particularly noisy when the Taarab songs came on. Sometimes it felt like one big party.

When the film was shown in New York, this guy from Zanzibar came up to me when the film had finished and he said, when you show this film in Zanzibar the men will feel very kicked in the balls with that last song. So they are very clever women. Overall, the film has been very well received. I'm glad you like it too!

MW: I do! It is seeing what I can only describe as the unbridled joy of the women in the team when they are playing. You get a real sense of the liberation that they are experiencing in playing the game and that is very moving.

FA: The process of filming was also a very moving experience for us; we saw pain, joy and strength. In this process, we felt it was important that the women also had their input into how and where their interview was shot. It was up to them how they could be interviewed – in their house, on the pitch, on the beach. The goalkeeper said 'I want the sea behind me'. One of the ex-players insisted that her kitchen is her new reality and it was important for her that we filmed her in that space.

I did warn the women to be certain that what they say on film is okay for them, because it will be seen in Zanzibar. One woman, she said on film 'Men and women are equal – it is only religion that separates them'. It is such a pleasure when you produce a documentary film that you were not expecting. That's the beauty about making documentaries – not knowing what you will get when you put a camera in front of people, especially people who have never been filmed before. When such people get a chance to speak, you get another dimension of their reality, directly from them. What these brave women dream of is justice and equality – a just society where they can be free to express themselves and achieve their personal ambitions beyond their prescribed roles. Underneath their calm and determined desire to play football is the call for improved socio-economic conditions that will allow them to progress – you get this message in a subtle manner through their own voices in the interviews. But what I was particularly enchanted about was the fact that they just got on with finding ways to play despite the odds. Their simple portraits and challenging personal views present a slice of the complex and diverse experiences of how women live today in Africa – it's not just food they need. They too worry about keeping their bodies physically fit, and some dream to travel the world and maybe meet Ronaldo. It was a privilege for us to be allowed into the lives of the players – to interview them and to have them tell me what they think and feel, their pain, fears and hope. Maybe Paula Rabinowitz captures this better when she says that 'by bringing the images of daily life and ordinary people into public view, photography remakes vision and in so doing produces (or reproduces) new forms of (class) consciousness'.[7]

My Mother: ISANGE

MW: So lets move on to talk about *My Mother: ISANGE* (2005), which you made at about the same time as *Sisters in Law*. It is a very different film from *Sisters in Law*. It is a much more personal film where you have used your family album, archival material and you have made use of a rostrum camera. It is obviously made with a much smaller budget than *Sisters in Law*. For all that it is a very direct film and quite raw, in the best sense, and very effective. I certainly was very moved when I watched it.

I have a particular interest in this area of filmmaking and this is something that I've touched upon in my doctoral thesis when I was looking at a few feminist filmmakers making work in the 1970s and 1980s. I looked at the work of Michelle Citron and Su Friedrich, for example. This is a 'theme' taken up again more recently by Chantal Akerman in her work that was shown at Camden Arts Centre earlier this summer (2008). It is also a 'theme' I have made moving image work about – a triptych titled *On Stones I Draw* (2002–05) that, as a whole, reflects upon the experience of Irish migration. In one part of this triptych my mother appears – or rather the back of her head does, much to her amusement! However, generally the mother–daughter relationship as a theme is not celebrated and is largely ignored in the mainstream film industry, at least for serious treatment. I wonder is this something that you have also found? Your film is dedicated to your – now deceased – mother and has been shown at the Black Film Festival in Cardiff in 2007, the Real Life documentary festival, Ghana in 2007, and the Afrika Eye film festival, Bristol in 2008. So how did the project come about?

FA: Valley and Vale Community Arts (Celfyddydau Cymuned Cwm a Bro), an access project based in Bridgend invited me – and other women – to make a film about my relationship to my mother and how my life was similar or different to my mother's life. This film was first shown as part of International Women's Day 2005 at the National Museum Wales.

My mother died in 1984 and I wasn't at her funeral. I was at the university in the capital city, Yaoundé, far away from where my family lived. I was in the middle of writing exams. So when she died my family felt that if they told me then I would fail my exams, so they told me ten days after she was buried. That was devastating. And today, twenty-four years later, she is not dead to me. I am still looking for her so that I can say goodbye. My uncles used to call my mother 'Mister Catherine'. My mother was a strong woman who spoke her mind and made sure that her brothers or other male relatives did not trample on her. She did not go to college because her father thought that a women's education would only end in the kitchen. When I was growing up, the word feminism was not familiar to me, but this woman fought hard to make sure all her children were educated. There were times when she had no shoes – when she walked barefoot but she didn't care. She would say 'I want pencils and if it means I don't get sandals – that's what you get'. So, the result was that all of us, her children – there are ten of us, could read and write. This was an opportunity that she had been denied. She used to say 'I didn't do it, but you people will do it'.

I had photographs of my mother that I brought with me to the UK. Then I discovered a lot more photographs of her that were in colour taken before I was born by Rev. Werner Keller, a Basel Mission Pastor from Switzerland, in the 1950s. When Valley and Vale asked me to do this I jumped at the opportunity to use these photos. It was a chance to think about my mother, to lament her and to remember her. The photographs of her are a big part of the memory I have of her and a significant footprint of my past and heritage. There is a recent book by Malin Wahlberg called 'Documentary Time: Film and Phenomenology', where she talks about how you can arrest time that is passed by using recovered film footage.[8] You can bring back the past in this way, and this is what I tried to do with this film. Recently I saw a film called *Boogie Woogie Papa* (2002) by Eric Bafving, a Swedish filmmaker. Through a series photographs, the filmmaker narrates a father–son relationship and the tragic end to his father's life – he commits suicide. It's amazing how this story is told and what a powerful film this is. Whoever said that there is no narrative in documentary filmmaking has completely misunderstood the medium. Using the still photographs in *My Mother: ISANGE* gave me a chance to think and to reflect on our relationship – framing a particular time and memories [Figure 5.4]. I was also exploring ideas about autobiography, about storytelling and self-representation, and what we can say in public about our private selves that may mean something to the experiences of others.

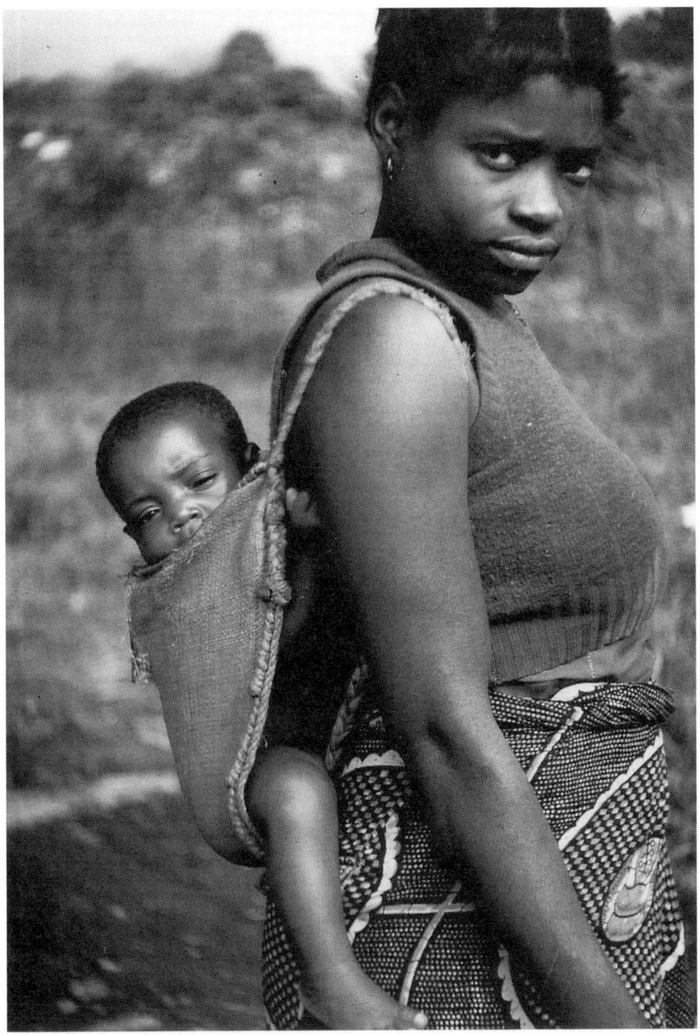

Florence Ayisi, *My Mother: ISANGE* (2005). Production still. 5.4

MW: The work by Chantal Akerman that I mentioned before, *Marcher à côté de ses lacets dans un frigidaire vide* (2004),[9] works with the same subject matter. It was shot in a very lo-fi way on something like a Mini DV camera, in black and white. It was shot in Akerman's mother's home, so it was a very intimate domestic setting – with just Akerman and her mother there. This was completely appropriate as they were discussing traumatic events about Akerman's grandmother, who had died in Auschwitz. The camera was on auto-focus and, as a result, constantly going in and out of focus as Akerman and her mother moved. This didn't detract from the work, in fact it added to it – and it was very moving. Perhaps not unlike your own experience with this subject matter, work that addresses the mother–daughter relationship does not have a significant profile even – or especially – in contemporary art practices. On the whole, male critics don't value work that speaks to this theme.

Filmic practice

MW: Let's talk about your cinematic style; the codes and conventions you use. In your own films your camera is not that close to the subject – there is always a context around the subject. Can you tell me more about your approach to this?

FA: In my film practice, I am constantly thinking of different ways to speak about and construct the subjects in my films; finding a position from which to speak differently. When I was planning and developing *Zanzibar Soccer Queens* I decided that we would use wide-angle lens so that the landscape and the characters are in close harmony. I also decided against using soft focus. The context of a film in terms of where you see the subject plays an important role in providing an unspoken narrative. In *Zanzibar Soccer Queens*, and in another film I am currently editing (*Women Artists in Cameroon*), we film in such a way that the 'place' is where the context of the stories and experiences of the women are grounded in the landscape and space that is part of their identity. How can I separate them from the background, no matter how simple? We are also defined by the textures of the landscape, the vegetation, the sea and the modern architecture and so on. Having soft focus is like denying the context of their existence. In *Zanzibar Soccer Queens*, the women's bodies are permanent fixtures to the textures and echoes of the spaces in which they play. These aspects of *mise en scène* provide another layer of their stories.

Even when doing interviews with film subjects I relate quickly to what a film critic like Roy Armes[10] has said about African filmmaking. The voice becomes really important because African people have not been allowed to speak for themselves. They have always been spoken for so, in terms of the postcolonial context, hearing people speak about themselves is crucial.

Through the use of interviews, I emphasize the 'Voice' in a specific context where the subject is directly communicating something. African people have barely spoken about their experiences. It is through the women's individual interviews in *Zanzibar Soccer Queens*, for example, that the women narrate themselves; this is one of the ways in which subjectivity is constructed and reproduced. The structure of each story comes from the woman's desire to express and speak about her life, which is rooted within her socio-cultural context. In *Women Artists in Cameroon* I go one step further to experiment with looking into the camera. So apart from the interviews which function as a narrative thread they also 'look' at camera/audience. Through their look and voice, I feel that the women have a strong presence that makes them subjects rather than 'silent' and passive objects.

MW: Something that you have mentioned before is how you can change discourses about how Africa can be imagined and how these concerns are brought into your work.

FA: My filmmaking practice is part of my research and through this I hope my work will give the audience new ways to perceive Africa. I decided that rather than write about some of the issues I am interested in, showing these other images of Africa is more effective. The challenge is how these ideas become manifest in visual representations – so this brings me to the point of how I construct my documentary films. The general perception of women's experiences in African societies is that they are oppressed, but there are pockets of resistance, as in Cameroon, where the women judges sit and apply the law. In Zanzibar, too, where a woman can play soccer and despite the fact that there may be opposition to it, she has made that space. In Africa, the only needs are not just food, shelter and medicines. So my question is – can we shift the dominant discourse? Can we look at other things apart from poverty, war, famine and misery? Through my practice-based research I am looking at the other side, at other stories from an African perspective showing the other complexities and rich cultural heritage that are hidden. My approach is that we can think about this differently and produce a counter-discourse that opens up new subjects and provides new knowledge.

MW: On this question of how you conceptualize or think about your film practice – generally how do you regard yourself as a diaspora filmmaker? Do you feel in any way aligned to black filmmakers working in this country – for example, Isaac Julien and Sankofa, Black Audio Film Collective and John Akomfrah, whose work has been touring recently from FACT, Liverpool.[11] Do you feel you are located in the same way in that Black British film context as you obviously do in an African film context?

FA: In many ways, yes, we do have a commonality but theirs is a different context. Maybe it would be best to first of all speak about the framework and context of my practice-based research work that engages with and explores creative practices in documentary and ethnographic filmmaking. The general agenda and questions of my film practice focus on exploring and constructing 'new' perspectives and knowledge as well as new frames of referencing the complex realities of modern Africa – an entirely new reality that is different from some of the prejudices borne out of the histories of colonialism and slavery.

I have been living away from my home country since 1986. As an African my work is a reaction to the myriad of negative stereotypes and simplistic representations of African people. In this sense, I believe that I can situate myself within the context of African cinema where the experience of film production –

emerging from anti-colonial struggles and thriving within the postcolonial era, its political impulse and cultural location – places it within the broad framework of Third Cinema. My work can also be seen within the broader context of the 'social realist' movement of African cinema according to Manthia Diawara's classification – films that deal with themes relating to current socio-cultural issues. So, I feel that my work belongs to that broad agenda and process of 'decolonization' of culture – challenging and interrogating the status quo.[12]

At the same time, I can say that I am equally located in the diaspora here in Britain because I did discover with great disappointment that the representation of ethnic minorities, especially African Caribbean, was also of great concern to that community. Soon after I arrived in the mid-1980s I discovered the work of filmmakers like Horace Ove (*Pressure*, 1975 and *Playing Away*, 1987), Menelik Shabazz (*Burning an Illusion*, 1981), Isaac Julien (*Territories*, 1984; *Looking for Langston*, 1989) and John Akomfrah (*Handsworth Songs*, 1986). Their films offered a variety of perspectives and a wider context on the contemporary Black experience. Looking at their films I could not help but see that our positions and concerns were connected in many ways. Our work predominantly engages with the politics and questions of representation – redefining and constructing aspects of our different cultures, identities, sexualities and ethnicities that have heretofore been misrepresented, under-represented or absent in the popular and dominant media of Europe and the USA in particular. We share common historical experiences located in slavery, colonization and racism. We are 'Others' in the West, and the contemporary cinematic and visual representations of people in the diaspora embody some manifestations typifying postcolonial and anti-racist struggles around identity and difference. We are reshaping, questioning and redefining through our films and other forms of art practice. We are resisting the possibility that we could be forgotten through misrepresentation or absence. Generally, filmmaking by filmmakers in the diaspora – or who are in countries that have experienced any form of domination – is an act of resistance, resisting the different forms of our cultural denigration. We are constructing new forms that speak differently about our histories, memory and identities 'today' as well as 'yesterday'. But what is important for me as an emerging filmmaker in the diaspora – in this process of shifting the cinematic lens in order to produce alternative cultural forms – is to feel that my work is part of the bigger project of decolonizing how we have been portrayed.

Future projects

MW: You obviously have a very busy schedule, juggling a career as a filmmaker and being a full-time academic, but what new projects are you involved in at the moment?

FA: The two roles are not in opposition! My research feeds my teaching and my teaching feeds my research. The energy the students put into their work and the topics they come up with really does feed my own ideas and work. Then I use my own concerns to draw their attention to the politics of representation with specific reference to issues around 'absence' and different forms of 'misrepresentation'. I am also able to do a lot of my own work because I am here at the university and I wouldn't be able do this – at least, in this way – without their support. It's a place to think and rethink!

I have a film, *Art of this Place: Women Artists in Cameroon* (*Art de ce lieu: Femmes artistes au Cameroon*) that is in post-production.[13] It will be finished in a couple of months. The film presents a rare insight into the rich variety of women's creative expressions in the visual arts in contemporary Cameroon. From wood sculptures to different forms of paintings and ceramics, the women's work reflects their visions and passion for the arts. The Minister of Culture in Cameroon has commissioned it. She said to me, you must make this film so that women's creative talent can be known, and people can acknowledge their work, which was part of an exhibition in the National Museum. It is the first time that a group of women have had such an exhibition. It will be shown on Cameroon television but I have made it so that people beyond Cameroon will also find it interesting. In the film one of the artists says that her work is a testimony of our time and I relate to that strongly. My work is also a testimony, so that we may know how we live today because tomorrow we will be forgotten, but if a film is there we are saying this is how we are now.

Notes

1 The start of this process was an interview that took place in Newport at the University of Wales, where Florence Ayisi teaches. It continued in an impromptu meeting on a train following the Cine 25: Women in Film and Media Showcase (Women's Studies at University of York) weekend at City Screen, York in February 2009. This was followed by mail exchanges – hence a more accurate description is, as titled, a dialogue.

2 Oliver Bartlet quotes Souleymane Cissé in *African Cinemas: Decolonizing the Gaze* (London: Zed Books, 2000), p. 5.

3 The sound recordist on the production of *Sisters in Law* (2007).

4 Quoted in Bartlet, *African Cinemas*, p. 5.

5 Ibid, p. 13.

6 P. Basu, 'Reframing Ethnographic Film', in T. Austin and W. De Jong, *Rethinking Documentary: New Perspectives, New Practices* (Maidenhead: Open University Press, 2008), p. 95–107.

7 P. Rabinowitz, *They Must Be Represented: The Politics of Documentary* (London and New York: Verso, 1994), p. 35.

8 M. Wahlberg, *Documentary Time: Film and Phenomenology (Visible Evidence)* (Minneapolis: University of Minnesota Press, 2008).

9 Translated into English as *To Walk Next to One's Shoelaces in an Empty Fridge.*
10 Roy Armes is author of *African Filmmaking: North and South of the Sahara* (Edinburgh: Edinburgh University Press, 2006) – the most recent book amongst many others.
11 K. Eshun and A. Sagar, *The Ghosts of Songs: The Film Art of the Black Audio Film Collective* (Liverpool: Liverpool University Press and Foundation for Art and Creative Technology, 2007).
12 Examples of Third Cinema can be seen at Kim Dodge, *What is Third Cinema?* (2007), http://thirdcinema.blueskylimit.com/thirdcinema.html, accessed on 19 September 2011.
13 This film was completed in 2011.

6 Here, there and in-between: South African women and the diasporic condition

Marion Arnold

They hang suspended in space – two small dolls – clipped and threaded to a rope. They hang between large plants, a black *Aeonium* 'Zwartkop' from Africa and a white iris from Europe. The black woman doll, wearing a red dress and green head scarf, holds a blue bag. She bears a grey bundle on her head and a baby is strapped to her back. The white girl doll is devoid of clothes but wears a bonnet, delicately modelled. She is damaged: her head is perfect but her legs are broken and she has no arms. Below these female figures two black and white guinea fowl confront one another, their distinctive red heads engaged in dialogue above a small, crocheted white mat. Two other *hanga*[1] turn their backs on the argument. The bottom of this painting (Figure 6.1) – for I am describing painted realities – is filled with an embroidered cloth patterned with brightly coloured, stylized pigs, crocodiles and words.

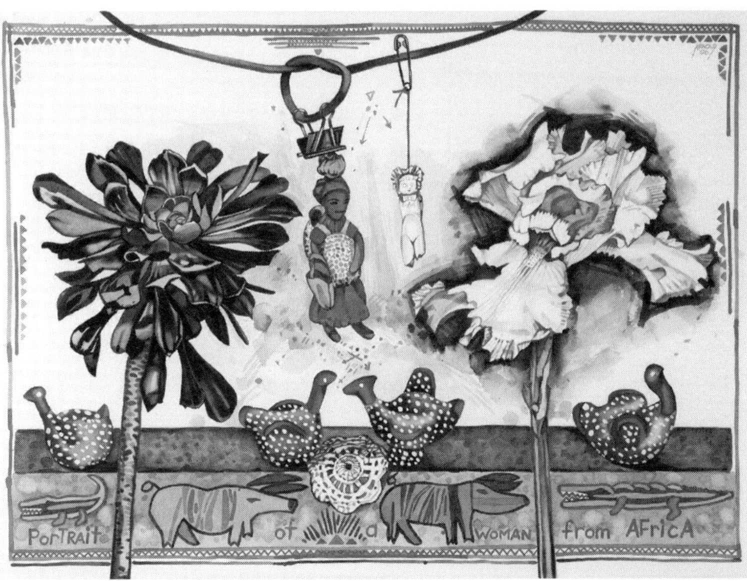

Marion Arnold, *Portrait of a Woman from Africa* (2006), watercolour. **6.1**

The words spell out 'Portrait of a Woman from Africa'. But there are two female forms – a girl-child and an adult woman – so which is the woman *from* Africa? Does 'portrait' refer to the painted likeness of the white girl, who will become a woman, or to the black mother, or is the painting a 'portrait' of a woman artist 'from Africa'? The title suggests that verbal language complicates visual meaning. We cannot presume that all Africans are black, especially in the south of this immense continent. African history is characterized by myriad peoples and virtually unceasing, seemingly endless migrations; people are always from somewhere and are going to somewhere else, through choice or compulsion. They are here, then there, or are in-between.

In the West the term the 'African diaspora' has become synonymous with the trans-Atlantic slave trade and its consequences within the Americas and Caribbean. This is only one African diaspora but it is the one that is best known, due largely to African-American scholars. Living in a country richly endowed with universities, departments of African Studies and academic publishers, they have the resources to research, write and circulate their history. To a lesser extent black Britons also explore an African diaspora characterized firstly by the westward passage of people to the Caribbean, and then by the twentieth-century entry of West Indian Commonwealth citizens into Britain, commencing with the arrival of the *Empire Windrush* in June 1948.

Africa is a huge continent.[2] In addition to experiencing significant diaporas out of its land mass, it has known innumerable internal migrations, which are not linked by common heritage, racial descent or shared meanings of terminology such as nation, migration, immigrant, emigrant and diaspora. The historical settlement of peoples in west and central Africa was very different to the migrations within the eastern and southern regions, which continued well into the nineteenth century and the age of colonialism, serving to complicate ideas about race, tribe, ethnicity and, ultimately, nation.[3]

Since the diasporas of southern Africa, and their manifestations within visual culture, have received relatively little critical academic attention outside of the region,[4] this study focuses on diaspora within historical and contemporary South African society, and specifically on the ways in which the diasporic condition has affected South African women. While the original meaning of diaspora defines the process as one of *enforced* dispersal, I will consider the intersection of individual and social circumstances which suggest that choice (personal agency) and compulsion (imposed action) cannot be neatly separated when investigating the reasons generating dispersal or relocation.[5] Although diaspora is a historically verifiable movement of people, I suggest that the *diasporic condition* is the experience and subsequent narration of processes of disruption, dispersal, relocation and adaptation to new experiences of place and domicile. It is, therefore, shaped by individual and collective memory (consciousness of past places, behaviours and cultures) and current lived experience (actual interaction with physical space and place). Being within the diasporic condition, aware of both 'here' and 'there', compels acknowledgement of both past and present in order to predicate a future based on the potential to reconcile identities determined by ethnicity, gender, religion, language and generation.

Modern South Africa, originating as a British dominion created by the Act of Union in 1910, is uniquely positioned to demonstrate that diasporas are not homogenized packages of causes and predictable effects but are historically, geographically and culturally specific. South Africa's population comprises white settlers (predominantly of Dutch, British and French Huguenot ancestry), nine major black groups,[6] a mixed-race 'coloured' group, and Asian people, mainly of Indian ancestry. There is a plethora of origin and dispersal narratives, inflected by geography, power struggles and ideology, and these are articulated in eleven official South African languages. Multiple versions of the contested past are ever present in many guises.

The borders of many modern African nation states are not defined by the natural boundaries of physical geography or by settlements of different ethnic/linguistic groups, but were the results of nineteenth-century imperialism and political mapping. At the 1884–85 Berlin Conference the great European powers divided the African continent into spheres of influence established by arbitrarily drawn borders. Ethnic groups were artificially divided, and political and cultural realities were positioned in opposition to one another. South Africa was not part of this dispensation; the concept of 'nation', equally fraught, was different and had a long, complex origin. Indeed, the modern Republic of South Africa generates all the difficulties of identifying the constituents of a 'nation'.[7]

Settlement histories

The original inhabitants of southern Africa were nomadic hunter-gatherers, the San (still commonly called the Bushmen), who were partially displaced by the pastoralist Khoekhoen (popularly called 'Hottentots' by European colonists). While negroid, Bantu-speaking peoples moved southwards down Africa's east coast, the southern tip of the continent, sparsely populated only by the Khoesan (a term encompassing both San and Koekhoen), was settled by Europeans – the Dutch, who established a garden at the Cape of Good Hope in 1652. Their eyes on the lucrative spice trade in the Far East, the Dutch wanted access to fresh fruit and vegetables for their sailors, and Jan van Riebeeck was charged by the VOC (Vereenigde Oostindische Compagnie) with establishing a base at the Cape. The settlement became a Dutch colony in 1679 and, during the Napoleonic wars, from 1795 to 1802 the Cape Colony was occupied by the British.

The second British occupation of the Cape in 1806 was permanent and it created lasting friction between Dutch and English settlers. Ultimately this contributed to the epic white diaspora, the Great Trek, which began in the 1830s. Disgruntled with British rule at least 12,000 Voortrekker Boers and their servants moved out of the Cape Colony to the African hinterland, encountering the Xhosa on the eastern frontier and the militant Zulu further north, and fighting battles which were subsequently mythologized in Afrikaner history. They also fought the peoples whom the strong Zulu kingdom had dispersed in the *Mfecane* (the crushing or scattering).[8] This nineteenth-century southern African diasporic displacement of black groups, fomented by the powerful Zulu king Shaka, made land claims difficult to substantiate; no single ethnic group could demonstrate permanent, stable settlement of particular regions north of the Cape Colony.

One of the results of the *Mfecane* was to increase the supply of slaves to traders operating from Indian Ocean ports. This diasporic slave trade out of eastern Africa, especially from the ports in modern Tanzania, fed the South American and Indian Ocean slave markets and brought African slaves to Cape Town during the Dutch administration to join other slaves who had originated in Angola.[9] The Cape slave community was constituted of Black Africans and Malays from Indonesia and thus the colony was the final place of domicile of different diasporas whose people contributed to the mixed-race Afrikaans-speakers, the 'Coloureds' (originally the Cape Coloureds) of modern South Africa.[10]

Under British administration the Cape Colony was populated mainly by British and Dutch settlers, mixed-race and freed slaves, and a small population of indigenous Khoesan. Bantu-speaking Xhosa, moving through and settling in the Eastern Cape, were fighting frontier wars with the British. The balance between the different racial groups altered in the 1820s and 1830s. The British government actively promoted emigration to the Cape and a scheme to populate the newly proclaimed Albany district in the Eastern Cape saw the arrival of over 4,000 Britons in the first half of 1820. In the mid-1830s the Dutch *boers* (farmers) began the Great Trek and moved north to found independent Boer republics. The earliest was the short-lived Republic of Natalia; the two that endured were the South African Republic (or Transvaal, recognized by Britain in 1852) and Orange Free State (recognized in 1854).

In 1842 Britain gained additional territory – Natal. A few traders and hunters had settled at Port Natal in 1824, maintaining a working relationship with the Zulu under Shaka. The Voortrekkers established the Republic of Natalia in 1839, it submitted to the British three years later and the formal annexation of Natal to the Cape was proclaimed in 1845. The regional population – British, Voortrekker, Zulu, and people displaced by the *Mfecane* – was in flux and the issue of settlement and land ownership under British administration was contentious and complex. The racial mix of Natal was enriched by the arrival of another immigrant group – Hindu Indians who began arriving as indentured labour in 1860. Contracted as agricultural workers, they could get free passage back to India after ten years, but those who completed their contracts could choose to remain and provision was made to allocate land to them. Indian immigration increased; by the end of the nineteenth century about 100,000 Indians were settled in Natal including Muslim traders, as well as the young lawyer Mahatma Gandhi.

The Second South African (Anglo-Boer) War (1899–1902) resulted in the defeat of the Boers and surrender of their independence. In 1910 the four British colonies south of the Limpopo river were subsumed into the Union of South Africa, an expedient move to create a 'nation' constituted of provinces subject to both provincial and centralized government and forged from fractious and diverse regional identities with separate histories of migration and settlement, contradictory political agendas, a wide range of cultures and different ethnic populations. The new Union of South Africa was a British dominion until 1961 when it severed ties with the United Kingdom and declared itself a republic. It withdrew from the Commonwealth of Nations, to which it was readmitted only after the 1994 democratic elections.

The final chapter of twentieth-century South African history in which diaspora plays a significant role occurs under the Afrikaner Nationalist government, which ruled the country as a white minority regime from 1948 until 1994. A key component of Nationalist ideology was apartheid – racial separation[11] – and its implementation led to the forced removal of peoples deemed to have a 'homeland' other than the place where they currently resided. Re-zoning legislation also resulted in the forced removals of established urban black and coloured communities, notably those of Sophiatown in Johannesburg and District Six in Cape Town, to areas on city peripheries. In effect this social engineering attempted to consolidate white economic power, ensure that the white population farmed the most productive land, and disempower urban black people. Hendrik Verwoerd's 'separate development' policies caused wholesale disruption of cohesive communities, and urban–rural resettlement compelled black people to re-establish their lives in remote *Bantustans* (homelands) that were literally foreign but were conceived by white legislators to have been places of historic origin. Eventually the Nationalists conferred 'self-government' and subsequently 'independence' on their patchwork of homelands.[12]

An adjunct of apartheid legislation and illiberal Nationalist government was a diaspora out of Africa in the late twentieth century as people – black, white and coloured – who opposed apartheid left South Africa by choice or to avoid arrest for their political activities.[13] This dispersal saw South Africans seeking refuge in the United States, the United Kingdom, Europe and African countries. For some this was exile during which they pursued the liberation struggle until they returned in 1994; for others it was permanent relocation. For all who left South Africa, the diasporic condition was a reality.

This brief outline of settlement patterns within South Africa indicates that migration and movement are characteristic of the region. The concept of diaspora has been and still is a reality for much of the population, being part of collective memory, apartheid history and contemporary experience. Within South Africa all ethnic groups can claim ancestral diasporic identity (coming from somewhere) and many have personal experiences of dispersal (being forced to go somewhere else).

Diaspora, apartheid and visual culture

Diaspora entails movement. Bodies move from familiar spaces to new, unfamiliar realities; a sense of belonging is replaced by an awareness of being foreign or different. But the spirit and imagination have the capacity to construct and occupy a mental space between past and present for far longer than the body which must adapt and locate shelter, food, water, the bus route and so on in the here-and-now. While external, strategic processes of adjustment and survival occur, and feelings of loss and alienation are processed, individuals may also exist in the space in-between where they are cognizant of an immediate reality and, simultaneously, are suffused by memories. Thus observed images of the here-and-now (the look of the street where one lives or the appearance of the corner-shop owner) jostle with visual memory flashes of 'home'. 'There' and 'here' intermingle as a stream of consciousness in the inner eye.

Homi Bhabha's useful theory of social hybridization as a negotiation of cultural identity in the face of encounters with difference emphasizes not what can be determined – two cultures, two places – but what is amorphous, which he identifies as 'the in-between' or 'the third space'.[14] The use of space as a trope, helpful when discussing cultural acclimatization, is almost self-evident with reference to visual art, which is characterized by and situated in space. Moreover, to be a visual artist is to know that meaningful art is invariably produced by hybridization – fusions of influences, recontextualized appropriations, combinations of old and new – these things make art. The challenges for the diasporian artist become: how do I use my personal circumstances positively to facilitate the development of a hybrid artistic identity which reconciles past and present, heals divided consciousness and fuses memory with new experiences? How do I *represent* my relationship with places of domicile and different cultures, and express my ideas and perceptions visually and spatially? These issues can be discussed with reference to representations of South African women and work by South African women within art and visual culture.

After the Nationalist government assumed power in South Africa in 1948, racial classification resulted in duplicated facilities, unequal in quality ('white' beaches were sandy; 'non-white' beaches were rocky and sometimes polluted), or denial of resources for black and coloured people if the white government considered them to be inappropriate. Coloured and black children received inferior educations to those provided for whites, and 'art' (as opposed to 'craft') tuition was available only to white children at government schools. separate tertiary education denied black students opportunities to study art until a Department of Fine Art was established at Fort Hare University in 1971. For much of the twentieth century South African art was defined as painting, sculpture and printmaking produced by white artists and the small minority of black artists who had been educated at mission schools and through non-governmental initiatives.[15]

During the late 1970s, when legitimate channels of political action were banned, art imagery became increasingly politicized; cultural work by artists and writers, often using strategies of encoded or metaphorical expression, commented on the racist ideology underpinning apartheid. Since the phenomenon and practice of racism were intimately related to historical settlement patterns and forced removals it is possible to discern a critique on diaspora within South African visual culture.

Women and the diasporic condition under apartheid

When the Nationalist party came to power in 1948, part of apartheid ideology was the 'different but equal' mantra, but the absurdity of this utterance is nowhere better demonstrated than when considering the socio-cultural position of women. Whatever their racial classification, women were subject to patriarchal discrimination by men. So dominant was the issue of race within South African politics that gender issues were marginalized in public debates and feminism was, to its detriment, invariably positioned in opposition to nationalism. This was accepted by many women including conservative Afrikaners who supported apartheid, and black women working within struggle politics.[16]

Opportunities to unite women through interracial contact became increasingly difficult once apartheid legislation took effect. Interaction functioned most effectively within the trade union movement and ineffectually in the cultural arena. Here, white women, belonging to the privileged ruling minority, had access to art tuition while coloured and black women had almost no opportunities to engage with the western-oriented South African art world. Moreover, their production of traditional artefacts, such as ceramics, basketry and beadwork, was not considered to be 'art'. Within this framework of inequality it is possible to locate evidence in visual art of the power of collective memory originating in historic migrations, and politically engaged visual statements about identity under apartheid. Such art speaks of the condition of being 'here, there and in-between'.

In the history of White South Africa, the Great Trek (1835–54) assumed mythic status within Afrikaner memory. This movement of thousands of Voortrekkers was a classic diaspora because the trekkers claimed that British rule and conflict with the Xhosa had made their lives in the Cape Colony intolerable, compelling them to leave their homes to seek new territory in the hinterland where they could establish self-government. The Great Trek narrative, which shaped Afrikaner identity, emphasized courage and resilience; it told tales of wagons and oxen moving over difficult terrain, of heroic male leadership and battles won by god-fearing people who triumphed over fierce, heathen warriors.[17] The stories were laced with the conviction that the British were perfidious, the blacks were uncivilized, and the trekkers were righteous people who had a god-given right to land and nationhood in Africa.

The centenary of the Great Trek was celebrated in 1938 with a re-enactment of the historic migration. Wagons, with men, women and children in nineteenth-century dress, criss-crossed South Africa, and were accorded a tumultuous and emotional reception by Afrikaners countrywide. The final celebrations were held at Monument Hill on the outskirts of Pretoria on 16 December, the Day of the Vow, and the cornerstone for the Voortrekker Monument was laid. Inaugurated in 1949, the authoritarian Monument was designed to symbolize Afrikaner nationhood and memorialize Great Trek history. Sixty-four synthetic-granite ox wagons, circling the cubic Monument, form a symbolic *laager* acknowledging the battle of Blood River and the covenant with God, which was believed to have granted victory over the Zulu. Marble reliefs in the Hall of Heroes tell the story of the Great Trek, foregrounding the male protagonists. At the Monument entrance, a large stature of a Voortrekker mother and children by Anton van Wouw (1862–1945) depicts the *volksmoeder* (mother of the nation). With one exception, Laurika Postma (1903–87), the architect and sculptors associated with the Monument artworks were men. After considerable debate, women were permitted to execute a narrative frieze of tapestries designed by artist W.H. Coetzer.[18] Installed in the Monument basement in 1961, the tapestries were removed from this unsuitable space in 1966 and sent to the Voortrekker Museum and, in 2000, they were reinstalled inside the Monument in the room containing Piet Retief's cenotaph.

So successful was the 1938 re-enactment of the Great Trek that it generated a replica to celebrate the 150th anniversary of the Trek in 1988. Fifty years had made a huge difference to the politics of remembrance. The centenary celebrations were held before the Nationalists came to power; in 1988 they had governed for forty years, implemented apartheid and ensured that their job reservation policy provided Afrikaners with employment. However, South Africa was a pariah in the world: cultural, sporting and economic sanctions had been imposed; the Black Nationalist and Communist parties were banned and their leaders were imprisoned or in exile; the army was fighting a guerrilla war and emergency regulations were in place to contend with internal unrest. The country was also experiencing economic stagnation, high unemployment and record inflation. Pressure to initiate reforms was increasing but the government also faced the problem of Afrikaner extremism. Schisms within the ranks of the *volk* emerged openly in the early 1980s when right-wing Nationalists, distrustful of what they considered to be the reformist inclinations of P.W. Botha, broke away from the Nationalist Party.[19] By 1988, as Grundlingh and Sapire observe, the government knew a reform programme 'required the support of English speakers and "moderate" black groups, precisely those historically portrayed as "enemies" in traditional "Great Trek" representations. Because of the need to reach new audiences, it was no longer possible to beat the ethnic drum.'[20]

Eric Hobsbawn notes that 'invented tradition' is invoked more frequently when a society feels threatened by change,[21] and in 1988 Afrikaners had either to adapt to changed circumstances and acknowledge the need for socio-political reform, or re-commit themselves to values inherited from the past, which were believed to offer a moral compass and definition of white nationhood. The nature and objectives of the historic diaspora were contested and the Trek re-enactment was used selectively by different Afrikaner factions to support different versions of trekker identity, namely forward-looking adaptability or backward-looking reassurance. Divisions within Afrikanerdom were not overcome and there were two rival versions of the Trek, each with their own memorabilia, rhetoric and interpretations of the past but using the same symbolism – wagons and 'traditional' dress. Documentary photographs of the 1988 Great Trek[22] re-enactment render a complex political commentary on the ways in which the historic white diaspora was used as the origin of political myth and 'invented tradition', and simultaneously reveal the politics of 1988.

Photojournalist Louise Gubb's[23] colour photograph of the Great Trek re-enactment (Figure 6.2) has the caption 'December 1988. Traditionally attired Afrikaner women have their hair done at a portable salon while celebrating the 150th anniversary of the Great Trek.' The exclusive focus on women is unusual in the Trek imagery of art and popular culture. Even when idealized as *volksmoeders*, women are invariably portrayed supporting male enterprise, but here we have an all-female situation juxtaposing past and present. Women, participating in the staged Trek in period costumes, utilize the services of a modern hairdresser equipped with a hand-held electric hairdryer (left foreground) and surrounded by innumerable commercial hair products in plastic containers.

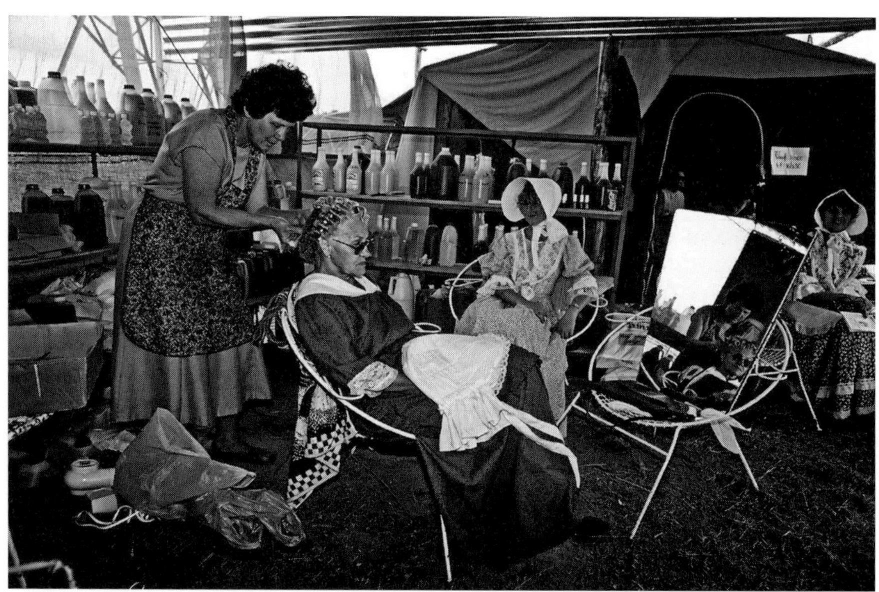

6.2 Louise Gubb, *Great Trek Re-enactment* (1988), photograph.

The attention devoted to hair is significant on several levels. Dominating the centre space, the older woman is having her hair set on rollers, a procedure which will create disciplined waves appropriate for middle-aged femininity but this luxury, unknown to her pioneer forebears, will be hidden under the object that dominates the photograph literally and symbolically – the traditional white *kappie* (bonnet). The central focus of the image, it is reiterated on the heads of the younger seated women, already fully costumed for their performances on the Trek wagons. The *kappie* was practical. Made of white fabric it reflected heat and protected the face but it also enforced tunnel vision and this, metaphorically, gave Afrikaner women a narrow perspective on life.

The photo's spatial structure sustains the dialogue between 'here' (the modern world, and 'there' (the evidence of the past and its enduring hold on collective identity). Mediating between past and present, the mirror offers the space for reflection: the hairdresser and her client confront themselves – the hairdresser works with modern professionalism but her client has committed herself to affirming historical values that must be given physical presence. A tent, functioning as a temporary dressing room for the forthcoming performance, is where the women contrive their appearances as trekkers, relinquishing personal identity to assume the *volksmoeder* stereotype. Although the collision between modern and 'authentic' historical femininity is acted out in the hair salon, this setting renders a deeply ironic comment on Afrikaner identity and their commitment to racial classification.

The Population Registration Act of 1950 required South Africans to be registered as white, black or coloured. When there was doubt – an abandoned baby for instance, or an application for reclassification – the pencil test decided the issue. Negroid peoples have tightly curled hair; Caucasians tend to have straight or loosely waved hair. If a pencil was stuck into hair and it fell out, it 'proved' that the person was white; if it was retained in *kroes hare* (frizzy hair) the person was 'non-white'. Many white Afrikaners held family secrets of ancestors who had children with slaves and some families were constituted of both white and coloured members. Both whites and coloureds spoke Afrikaans but whites *were* white – according to official evidence – and had to preserve their appearances. The 1950 legislation (amended) stated that a white person was 'a person who in appearance obviously is a White person ….'[24] So, here in the hair salon in 1988 bigger issues than vanity are at stake: appearance matters; hair signifies.[25]

Louise Gubb's photograph – through its formal orchestration of colour, the stark, symbolic white *kappies*, the mirror and the chair frames containing the white women – was for a series produced for an illustrated feature article in the *Telegraph*, but this particular document can be read as a nuanced, layered critique on the conflicted nature of Afrikaner female identity. Three women have elected to commemorate their diasporic heritage which, in 1988, could not be divorced from the political present of a society under stress. They exist in a provisional space, erected for temporary activity, and in a space in-between the romance of the past and the reality of the present. This is the moment in-between, a time to reflect. The future was to reformulate South African politics: two years later Nelson Mandela walked to freedom. Six years later democratic elections ended long years of apartheid oppression and made an iconic black man the President of the 'new' South Africa.

While white Afrikaners looked to their nineteenth-century migrations to offer the bedrock of their collective identity, the Nationalist government used this same migratory history to control the movements and opportunities of black and coloured South Africans in the mid-twentieth century. The declaration of 'historic' homelands in rural South Africa and the proclamation of separate residential areas for different races in urban centres subjected many South Africans to the trauma of forced removals. As artists began to realize that the visual arts offered opportunities for political activism, forced removals, dislocation and nostalgia for the past occasioned by experiences of loss emerged as expressive subjects and realist commentary. As previously indicated, black and coloured people had limited opportunities to study art, and amongst those who completed a formal training course there were very few women. Bongiwe (Bongi) Dhlomo (b. 1956) is one such artist.[26]

She studied at Rorke's Drift, the common usage name of the Evangelical Lutheran Church of Southern Africa's Art and Craft Centre. Started in 1961 by

Swedish printmaker Peder Gowenius, and based at Rorke's Drift in KwaZulu-Natal from 1963, the Centre was the only residential art and craft school for blacks in South Africa. The art school itself was established in 1968 (weaving and ceramics were taught as 'crafts'), and about fifty students graduated before the 'fine art' school closed in 1982.

Dhlomo, from a rural, Christian, Zulu background, applied to Rorke's Drift because her job as a typist/clerk lacked challenges and promotion prospects and she had become aware of the emotional power of visual imagery. In conversation with Michael Godby, she recalled,

> On Sunday, June 20, 1976, I bought the *Sunday Times* newspaper .... On this day I bought the newspaper specifically to catch up on the news of the unfolding students' upheavals in Soweto, Johannesburg. As I opened the newspaper I remember very vividly the shock I experienced from the images spread over more than four pages – all the images were black and white and very graphic in their depiction of what had happened on the 16th of June and the three days thereafter.[27]

Dhlomo was clear on why she wanted to be an artist, telling Brenda Atkinson, 'The photographs of the Soweto uprisings had influenced my thinking about images: I wanted to be part of that community that captured history. I believed capturing the same history in images to be as important as writing books, to make sure these events are never forgotten.'[28]

Studying at Rorke's Drift from 1978 to 1979, Dhlomo was exposed to images by the first generation of printmakers (all men) such as John Muafangejo (1943–87), Azaria Mbatha (b. 1941), Dan Rakgoathe (1907–2004) and Vuminkosi Zulu (1943–96), who had helped to establish the national and international reputation of the Centre. Although the 1960s printmakers had favoured religious imagery (which sometimes referred obliquely to the present), the politicized artists of the late 1970s – such as Dhlomo, Kay Hassan, Pat Mautloa and Sam Nhlengethwa – located their narratives within the arena of daily events. Recalling her student days in a 2002 interview with Hobbs and Rankin, Dhlomo testified to the increasing politicization of the student body, and commented on enthusiasm for the Black Consciousness Movement and its charismatic leader, Steve Biko (killed in detention in 1977).[29] By the time she graduated from Rorke's Drift, Bongi Dhlomo saw herself as a representational artist whose objective was to document history, and in the early 1980s she produced a body of linocut prints on the theme of forced removals.

These images, a raw and explicit comment on diasporic upheaval, deal directly with a situation which was common throughout South Africa during apartheid. Trained as a printmaker, concerned with telling the stories of her time, committed to the liberation struggle, and attracted by the stark clarity of black and white images (in documentary photographs as well as prints),

Dhlomo used a simplified realism with symbolic overtones to structure her message – intense pictorial space. This space probes the experience in-between the familiar and the new, the space of the diasporic condition. Dhlomo does not represent a direct autobiographical experience of diaspora but, working as a politicized black artist, she was painfully aware of the situations inflicted on her community. The descriptive titles of *Removals I–VII* sustain her visual reportage: *The Past ... The Future; Bulldoze the Blackspot; Resettlement; Against our Will; From here ... where to?; Aftermath; People Are Living here.*

In *Aftermath* (1983) (Figure 6.3) Dhlomo portrays the havoc wrought by bulldozers that demolished an informal settlement and wrecked communal living. In the aftermath people will be relocated. A man, two women and a child dominate the foreground, pushing into a dark space between what was, and what will be. This black region divides the presence of home (a few belongings) from the absence of home (demolished shacks). As they are depicted from the rear, we do not engage directly with the figures' anguish. We see what they see, sharing their roles as witnesses of a broken cultural landscape. 'Things' become eloquent: pieces of corrugated metal sheeting that formed shelters; the aggressive bulldozer on the left; remnants of domestic life in the foreground. A pot, kettle, small cupboard, boxes and a black bundle

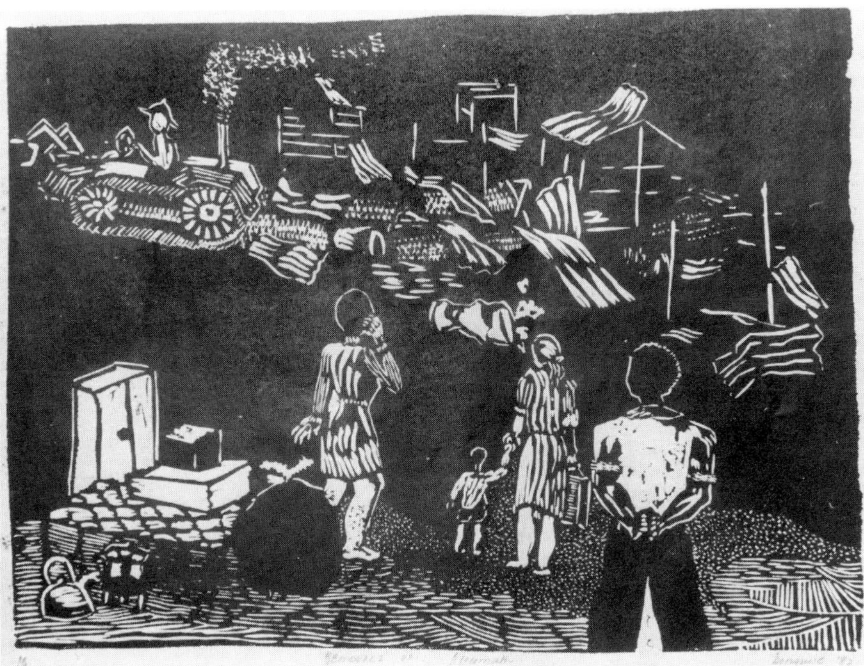

Bongi Dhlomo, *Aftermath* (1983), linocut print from *Forced Removals* series. **6.3**

salvaged from the demolitions constitute the only neatly organized element in the picture. Broadly delineated, with an economic use of detail, this image does not portray sensationalized drama but offers testimony of destruction. The physicality of relief printmaking and surface violation by tools that cut and gouge allow Dhlomo's energized lines to transmit emotion and interpret pain and loss in a starkly tonal manner. The work and the series embody the ways in which black and white dominated all South African lives.

Although the *Removals* series was not directly autobiographical, another print draws on an incident that touched Dhlomo's life: *Cemetery Unrest – Premature Resurrection* (1983). When exhibited at The Art Centre, Durban, in 1983 the print bore the caption: 'dedicated to the artist's late father, who up to his death in 1979 was against people being uprooted in the Bergville area. The cemetery that was uprooted in 1981 is in an area where he was Minister – most of the people were buried by him.'[30]

Dhlomo, grieving for her father, pays tribute to him and the people he served; her print makes a poignant comment on the unfeeling state. Executed on an irregularly shaped format symbolizing the damage inherent in the depicted incident, the pictorial structure is filled with flat silhouettes and busy, patterned shapes. Resurrection, imagined so often within Western religious imagery, becomes a bizarre South African reality peopled by white soldiers in camouflage holding weapons, black people as witnesses, bones, skeletons, and open and closed coffins. The 'unrest' of the title refers to the dead whose eternal peace has been disturbed, not the living, immobile under a watchful military gaze.

The significance of Dhlomo's *Removals* series lies in her subject matter, the time of production – the early 1980s – and the reception accorded to her political images. Her work was shown in 1982 at the Botswana National Museum and Art Gallery during the Gaborone conference, 'Art Towards Social Development and Change in South Africa', and it generated a passionately argued paper by Thami Mnyele, who was to be killed in 1985 during a cross-border raid by the South African Defence Force into Botswana.[31] Mnyele appealed for collective, community-based cultural activism to create art which would empower and inform communities.

The rupture of lives caused by the forced removals of the apartheid era made 'home' a provisional place. Art helped to define the presence of absence and offered a space for remembrance and contemplation. Amongst women artists who interpreted forced removals are Peggy Delport, a University of Cape Town lecturer, who executed a large mural in District Six in 1984–85, and a collective of former District Six residents, who made an appliqué commemorating their former home in 1992.[32]

Post-apartheid South Africa and diaspora

South Africa's coloured people, whose very existence was born of diaspora, understand the oppressions and challenges of hybridization. Their ancestors, from here, there and everywhere, moved south across Africa or arrived at the Cape after long ocean voyages, bringing their languages, cultural memories, oral histories and artefacts. As racial classification was made mandatory under apartheid, some coloureds accessed family genealogies to determine if they might claim white identity. Others referred to themselves as black and made commitments to resistance politics.

In 1994 South Africa elected a black government after universal suffrage elections. While the post-apartheid era brought political freedom to all South African citizens it conferred a particularly precious freedom on artists – the liberation of imagination. Throughout the 1980s, artists endured pressure to make didactic or propagandistic 'struggle art'. In the post-apartheid era they could choose their subjects and materials, escape the confines of didacticism and engage with the aesthetic concerns and strategies of art practice. Not all artists made the transition to creative freedom with ease or had the confidence to loosen the shackles of South African politics or political correctness. One woman artist who did so with assurance and now has an international profile is Cape-based artist Berni Searle (b. 1964).[33]

Searle's heritage is 'coloured'. she has used this to play with and play on the connotations of being coloured, and to examine her own diasporic extended family as well as the coloured community and its relationship to South African history. In so doing she transforms heritage into art images inflected by postcolonial theory but resolutely visual and transformative in their concerns.

Having trained as a sculptor Searle learnt how to use space and materials to articulate both form and content, but she made her reputation working with installation and lens-based media. Her photographic projects, digital prints and videos require collaboration with photographers (notably Jean Brundrit) and film-maker Alberto Iannuzzi. Conceptually, Searle's work benefitted from postgraduate studies of contemporary art theory, particularly the writings of British cultural theorist Stuart Hall, and his articulation of black Britons' responses to Caribbean diasporic experience. Searle, coming to maturity as an artist in the post-apartheid era, was well positioned to put the past in perspective and to engage with global as well as local concerns. Her work deals eloquently with issues pertinent to global diaspora – loss, concepts of home, being here and there – and, significantly, it uses art as a space for creative action and meditation, and for investigating what we see as well as what we know.

One of Searle's important early photographic series originates in local politics, being based on the artist's identity as coloured. According to the

Population Registration Act 1950 (amended), the coloured category has seven sub-categories: Cape Coloured, Malay, Griqua, Chinese, Indian, Other Asiatic and Other Coloured.[34] *Red, Yellow, Brown* (1998) from the *Colour Me* series (1998–2000) features Searle's motionless, recumbent, naked body covered on three different occasions with coloured, fragrant spices: red paprika, yellow turmeric, and dark brown cloves (on a visual level there is little to differentiate Searle's use of spice from the powdered pigments used by British artist Anish Kapoor). Searle comments,

> I presented myself for observation. I include the number of the exposure along the edges of the prints, drawing attention to the ethnographic role of photography in justifying perceived differences between people, particularly in relation to the racialised and gendered body. The idea of a specimen for inspection is reinforced by the enclosed box of spices below the image of the body, the colours of which don't entirely correspond with the colours of the spice sprinkled over the body (even though its the same substance). I have also incorporated colour test charts at the bottom of each image that are slightly out of focus and as such are not to be relied on.[35]

Searle's 'coloured' body, transformed by coloured spices, turns stigma into a celebration of one of the diasporic strands of coloured community identity – the Malays from the Far East, renowned for their spicy cooking, now considered thoroughly South African. In its use of spices the work also evokes fragrance and flavour: food as nourishment and as a component of social ritual.[36]

This is emphasized in *Traces* (1999), another configuration of the *Colour Me* series, which alludes to acts of tracing/defining and residues. Three large digital prints of the artist's spice-covered body, photographed from above, confront three images with only the traced imprint of the body discernible in the coloured spice powders.[37] Below the latter are three scales filled with spices, but the dials on the scales are fixed and fail to register the spices' weights. The *Colour Me* spice images relate to personal and community identity: one of Searle's maternal great-grandfathers was a cook from Mauritius and another came from Saudi Arabia (the history of East Africa acknowledges the role of Saudi Arabian traders from medieval times).[38] Searle's representations of presence and absence refer to historical knowledge and gaps in memory, to three-dimensional volumes signifying the realities of people and flat shapes that suggest the two-dimensionality of stereotypes.

The communicative power of Searle's works originates in the primacy she accords to the senses. Sight and touch dominate. When she is the subject her eyes are open – she looks, and looks back at the viewer as in *Untitled* (1998) (Figure 6.4 and colour reproduction on the book cover) from the *Colour Me* series; when she is the object her body feels the powder that masks its

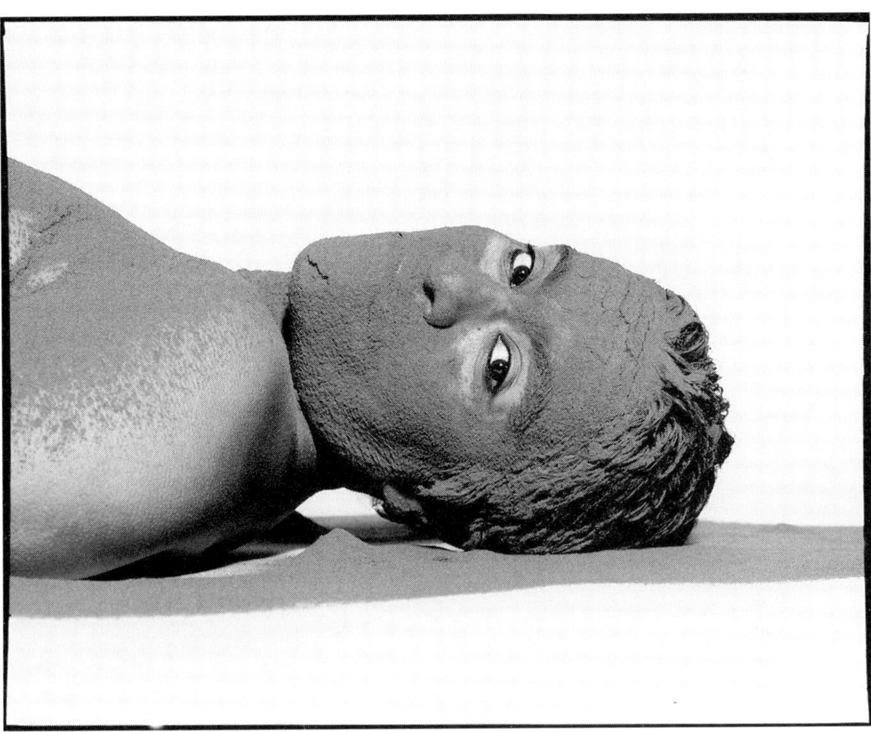

Berni Searle, *Untitled* (1998), handpainted colour photograph from *Colour Me* series. 6.4

sexuality, concealing eroticism. Although she can smell the spices, her mouth is closed and she neither tastes the spices nor indicates that she is a speaking subject controlling the act of interpretation. That is for the viewer.

The *Colour Me* series does more than refer to South Africa's obsession with race and skin colour. It manifests the liberating power of colour within life and art. The rock artists of Europe and Africa used earth pigments not unlike Searle's spice palette to create their images. Their configurations and Searle's representations of the body are not executed tonally in black and white but in colour. *Colour* me, says Searle in her title, using a verb. Her use of the personal pronoun is also important. She places herself in all her works, functioning as 'still life' or object in *Colour Me* and the *Discoloured* series (1999–2000),[39] and as participant in her video projections, although she is no more a performance artist than was Ana Mendieta or is Cindy Sherman. Searle's female body is at the service of Searle the creative artist.

This body was used poetically in a significant double projection video installation dealing directly with journeying in ways that speak of African diasporas and the twenty-first-century diasporic condition. *Home and Away* (2003),[40] framed in elegantly orchestrated sequences of rhythmic colour and form, was produced during a residency in 2002 at the Montenmedio Arte Contemporaneo Foundation, situated in Vejer, at the southern tip of Spain. The film was shot in the Strait of Gibraltar, which has seen innumerable arrivals and departures of people moving east and west, and between Europe and Africa. Today that ocean witnesses journeys by desperate economic migrants, fleeing Africa for Europe.

Searle located ways of affirming her regional identity on the toe of Africa where the sea is a constant presence because, at the northern tip of the vast African continent, she encountered the same relational histories of land, water and people. What she knew as a South African resident of Cape Town could be translated into a meditation on the human condition of journeying from choice or compulsion. The Mediterranean, an area of multicultural contact and trade, was used to conceptualize a filmic narrative: Searle, dressed in a red skirt with white overlay, piped with polystyrene to make it float, drifts in blue water. One projection features the body moving in and out of the frame, the fabric creating abstract, rhythmic, coloured patterns, while the other projection presents the wide sky, distant coast, and ocean. Visually the imagery is seductively beautiful.

The lyrical quality is enhanced by words whispered in English. The verbs, 'to love, to fear, to leave' are conjugated: 'I love, you love …' but when 'I fear' is voiced, black dye is released, darkening the water and signifying the dangers of its depths and the risks of sea passages. The ocean becomes the space of displacement, between here and there, and the video ends as the boat on which the camera has been mounted speeds off, replacing intimacy with panoramic emptiness.[41]

Diaspora touched and still touches South African lives in different ways. Historical migrations and conflicts were co-opted by twentieth-century geopolitics to keep enmity and uncertainty alive and well. Louise Gubb's Great Trek re-enactment photographs recorded the way memories of a historical white diaspora were manipulated for political display, while Bongiwe Dhlomo's interpretations of contemporary, diasporic forced removals refer directly to the racial power struggles between a black majority and white minority in apartheid South Africa. In the post-apartheid era Searle chooses to work with ideas that transcend the regional and national issues characterizing South African life. Her concepts originate in her own experiences as a South African woman but she is primarily an artist who, knowing the pain and loss generated by diaspora, dispersal and resettlement, examines not the particularity of specific events but the passage of time and the evocation of places in the spaces of art. Redolent with suggestion, her still and moving images put history in a space where it can be accessed but has lost the ferocious power with which it once controlled South African life and influenced art.

There is a future after diaspora; every journey has an end. The new political dispensation in South Africa required artists to place art and politics in a new relationship in order to give a future to South African art. Bongiwe Dhlomo, discussing these issues, observed that her politicized images of the 1980s might assume a different imperative after ten years of democracy – 'if the same work is seen by people during the ten years of democracy celebrations [in 2004], it should be able to communicate something else to them, like, "Never, never, never again …"'. She then added, 'I know that we fought and won the war but as an artist I am now faced with the many battles that confront me in South Africa. The role of the artist has not changed: The circumstances have altered. The tools are still the same but the call is to utilize our art as a building block for reconstruction.'[42]

And what about the two dolls suspended in space in *Portrait of a Woman from Africa*? Now in England, they are both from Africa, although in the nineteenth or early twentieth century the broken white-paste doll journeyed from Britain to the Cape, and was excavated from a mole hill on Rondebosch Common, Cape Town, by an energetic Jack Russell terrier. Both dolls subsequently went to England with the artist. The painting is a representation of plants and objects, including small black and white dolls, and portrays the artist who was – I was – reluctant to abandon everything which had been collected after decades in Africa.

Born in England, I lived my childhood and young adulthood in a place that no longer exists, Salisbury in Rhodesia (now Harare in Zimbabwe). I migrated. A university post took me to Pretoria in South Africa. Then I relocated to the mother city – Cape Town. From there the ocean drew me over water, back to the northern climes of my ancestors, where the culture and heritage was familiar but the landscape was new and strange. My migrations, undertaken by choice, weighed against circumstance, produced experiences of the diasporic condition.

If you are from 'there' and live 'here' then the space in-between is filled with memories colliding with new realities. For artists this can be productive territory. As an outsider or onlooker you notice things, see sharply, observe what others take for granted. And, looking back through the lens of memory, you negotiate with the past so that it becomes a resonant presence not a belligerent bully. Then past and present, here and there, can meet the imagination in the space in-between.

Acknowledgements

I wish to thank Jenny Stretton, of the Durban Art Gallery for providing information and images, and Louise Gubb, Berni Searle and Bongi Dhlomo for their communications with me and for allowing me to reproduce their work.

Notes

1 *Hanga* is Shona for the helmeted guinea fowl found throughout Zimbabwe. In the 1970s rural Zimbabwean women started to model and paint guinea fowl for sale at the roadside.

2 Africa occupies about 20 per cent of the earth's total land area. In 2006 the population was estimated to be about 885 million, roughly 20 per cent of the world's population. About a thousand languages are spoken in Africa.

3 Just as West and Central African peoples constitute the focus of slave trade studies so West and Central African art features prominently in American-dominated research, leading to the erroneous assumption that the peoples of Eastern and Southern Africa produced little 'art' and had impoverished material cultures. See the discussion in my Introduction in M. Arnold (ed.), *Art in Eastern Africa* (Dar es Salaam: Mkuki na Nyota Publishers, 2008).

4 I attribute this to two reasons. American scholars are, understandably, interested in their own origins rather than African political and cultural history *per se*. But there is another reason for the neglect of South African diasporas – politics. During the apartheid era, the cultural boycott of South Africa inhibited the free circulation of knowledge. Whilst Western academics considered that they were making an effective moral protest against the apartheid regime by severing contact with South African academics and denying them access to conferences and publication opportunities, they also limited their own knowledge of what was happening within South African cultural politics. As a result they had scant understanding of the role that cultural activism played within South Africa, where it became an effective component of resistance politics. When South Africa was readmitted to the global community in 1994 the West evinced interest in post-apartheid art and culture rather than in the complex multifaceted stories of earlier South African cultural activities.

5 I deviate from Gilroy who, in advancing a definition of diaspora, proposes that 'the word connotes *flight following the threat of violence* [Gilroy's emphasis] rather than freely chosen experiences of displacement': P. Gilroy, 'Diaspora and the Detours of Identity', in K. Woodward (ed.), *Identity and Difference* (London: Sage Publications, 1997), p. 318.

6 The nine major black groups are Zulu, Xhosa, Tswana, Venda, Sotho, Ndebele, Tsonga, Swazi and Pedi.

7 South Africa admirably demonstrates the characteristics of a nation as the 'imagined community' articulated by Benedict Anderson, *Imagined Communities: Reflections of the Origin and Spread of Nationalism*, revised edition (London and New York: Verso, 1991). Under apartheid, only imagination could have yielded the bizarre patchwork of so-called independent states located within the boundaries

of the South African state which supposedly demonstrated the 'separate but equal' concept within apartheid ideology.

8 The Zulu term is interesting since it is virtually the same as the original Greek meaning of diaspora – a scattering. Davenport and Saunders note that 'The Sotho equivalent, [of *Mfecane*] *Lifaqane* (pronounced *Difaqane*) conveys the notion of forced removal': R. Davenport and C. Saunders, *South Africa: A Modern History*, fifth edition (London: Macmillan, 2000), p. 13. The origins of the *Mfecane* are complex but it was essentially a power struggle between various African kingdoms from which the Zulu king, Shaka, emerged as the dominant protagonist.

9 The British banned the slave trade in 1807 and emancipated slaves in 1834. Only in 1873 did the British force the Sultan of Zanzibar to close the slave markets on the island and mainland although slavery remained legal within his empire.

10 The slave population rose from 14,641 in 1783 to 36,278 in 1834, the year when emancipation was enacted (Davenport and Saunders, *South Africa*, p. 25). Afrikaans is not a language derived exclusively from Dutch. Having many origins, slaves communicated in a shared tongue; fusions of their Dutch masters' language and their own native languages resulted in Afrikaans, officially recognized as 'Afrikaans' in 1925 and spoken by white and coloured South Africans, but resisted under apartheid by black South Africans who considered it 'the language of oppression'.

11 Apartheid was constructed of legislation that determined territorial segregation, political representation and urban living. It built on earlier 'native policy', including the 1913 Land Act, which deprived Africans of the right to own land outside of designated reserves that constituted only about 13 per cent of the land. The blatantly racist legislation of apartheid includes The Prohibition of Mixed Marriages Act (1949), the Population Registration Act (1950) and the Group Areas Act (1950). The population was registered as African, white and coloured.

12 By 1984 Gazankulu, Kangwane, Kwa Ndebele, KwaZulu, Lebowa, Qwaqwa, Ciskei, Bophuthatswana, Transkei and Venda were 'self-governing'.

13 After the Sharpeville shootings of 1960 and the Soweto uprising in 1976 emigration from South Africa increased notably.

14 See Homi K. Bhabha, *The Location of Culture* (London: Routledge, 1994), especially pp. 1–9 for the theory of hybridization and 'the in-between', and J. Rutherford, 'The Third Space: Interview with Homi Bhabha', in J. Rutherford (ed.), *Identity, Community, Culture, Difference* (London: Lawrence and Wishart, 1990).

15 Rorke's Drift (KwaZulu-Natal) and Polly Street (Johannesburg, Guateng) were established to teach art to Africans and became well known for the students and work produced. See, Rorke's Drift, E. Rankin and P. Hobbs, *Rorke's Drift: Empowering Prints. Twenty Years of Printmaking in South Africa* (Cape Town: Double Storey Books, 2003), and, on Polly Street, E. Rankin, 'Teaching and Learning: Skotnes at Polly Street', in F. Harmsen (ed.), *Cecil Skotnes*. Published privately in conjunction with the 1996 *Cecil Skotnes Retrospective* exhibition at the South African National Gallery.

16 For an exposition of the relationship between nationalism and feminism see S. Hassim), *Women's Organisations and Democracy in South Africa: Contesting Authority* (Madison: The University of Wisconsin Press, 2006). Hassim (p. 32) notes, 'The dominant position within the ANC until the late 1980s was that the

emancipation of women was secondary to and contingent upon national liberation'. For the historical engagement of women with resistance to apartheid see M. Arnold, *Women and Art in South Africa* (Cape Town and Johannesburg: David Philip, 1996), especially pp. 100–3, 113–20; 131–47; and M. Arnold and B. Schmahmann (eds), *Between Union and Liberation: Women Artists in South Africa 1910–1994* (Aldershot: Ashgate, 2005), pp. 4–9.

17 On 16 December 1838, 470 Voortrekkers confronted 10,000 Zulus at Blood River; 3,000 Zulus were killed and only three trekkers were injured. The victory was attributed to the power of God, and the Day of the Covenant was celebrated as a public holiday in South Africa under Nationalist rule.

18 For the debate around the tapestries and a comprehensive analysis of the visual articulation of the *volksmoeder* see L. Van der Watt, 'Art, Gender Ideology and Afrikaner Nationalism: A Case Study', in M. Arnold and B. Schmahmann (eds), *Between Union and Liberation: Women Artists in South Africa 1910–1994* (Aldershot: Ashgate Publishing, 2005), pp. 94–110.

19 See R. Davenport and C. Saunders, *South Africa: A Modern History*, fifth edition (London: Macmillan, 2000) for the formation of breakaway Afrikaner parties such as the Conservative Party, the Afrikaner Weerstandsbeweging (AWB), Aksie Eie Toekoms and Blanke Bevrydigings Beweging (White Liberation Movement).

20 A. Grundlingh and H. Sapire), 'From Feverish Festival to Repetitive Ritual? The Changing Fortunes of Great Trek Mythology in an Industrialising South Africa, 1938–1988', in R. Hill, M. Muller and M. Trump (eds), *African Studies Forum*, vol. 1 (Pretoria: Human Sciences Research Council, 1991), p. 293. In my discussion of the 1988 Trek I am indebted to these authors for their insightful analysis of the re-enactments and the politics of the day.

21 See particularly E. Hobsbawn and T. Ranger (eds), *The Invention of Tradition* (Cambridge: Cambridge University Press, 1983), pp. 4–5.

22 The *Vrye Weekblad* newspaper sponsored an exhibition of Trek photographs by Gideon Mendel entitled *Beloofde Land* at the Market Galleries, Johannesburg.

23 Louise Gubb has worked as a photojournalist for three decades, covering South Africa's turbulent struggle for democracy and the Mandela presidency while working for prominent international news magazines including *Time*, *Newsweek*, *Stern Paris* and *Match*. Her photographs have been featured in several books and exhibited internationally. In 2002 she was Assignment Editor and one of a hundred photographers for *Day in the Life of Africa* photobook produced to benefit HIV/Aids consciousness-raising activities in Africa.

24 Cited in E. Boonzaier and J. Sharp, *South African Keywords: The Uses and Abuses of Political Concepts* (Cape Town and Johannesburg: David Philip, 1988), p. 101.

25 The significance of hair in the Coloured community became the subject of performance works by Tracey Rose. In *Span II* (1997) she sat naked in a glass case, shorn of all body hair, preoccupied with knotting a mass of dark hair. For discussion on *Span I and Span II* see A.E. Coombes, *History After Apartheid: Visual Culture and Public Memory in a Democratic South Africa* (Johannesburg: Wits University Press, 2004), pp. 254–9.

26 Dhlomo completed a one-year National Secretarial course in 1975, worked as a typist/clerk in 1976, and studied at Rorke's Drift in 1978–79, graduating with a Fine Art

Diploma. She has held many administrative and curatorial positions (including at the Federated Union of Black Artists gallery FUBA, the African Institute for Contemporary Art, the Alexandra Multi-Arts Factory and the Thupelo project), and was the administrator of the 1st and 2nd Johannesburg Biennales. She is married to artist Pat Mautloa. She is also known as Bongiwe Dhlomo-Mautloa; I have chosen to use the shorter version of her name under which she made the prints I discuss.

27 M. Godby, 'Art and Politics in a Changing South Africa: Bongi Dhlomo in Conversation with Michael Godby', *African Arts* (Winter 2004), p. 62. Available online at http://findarticles.com/p/articles/mi_m0438/is_4_37/ai_n13775097.

28 B. Atkinson, 'Bongi Dhlomo-Mautloa interviewed by Brenda Atkinson', in B. Atkinson and C. Breitz (eds), *Grey Areas: Representation, Identity and Politics in Contemporary South African Art* (Johannesburg: Chalkham Hill Press, 1999), p. 118.

29 Cited in P. Hobbs and E. Rankin, 'Rorke's Drift: Imprints of Resistance', paper delivered at *Impact 2003, 3rd International Printmaking Conference*, Michaelis School of Fine Art, University of Cape Town, August, 2003).

30 *Cemetery Unrest: Premature Resurrection* is reproduced in Ann Oosthuizen (ed.), *Sometimes When it Rains: Writings by South African Women* (London and New York: Pandora, 1987), p. 146. It was one of ten linocut prints which Dhlomo supplied for the text.

31 Mynele's paper was published posthumously in 1988: T. Mnyele, 'Thoughts on Bongiwe and the Role of Revolutionary Art', in A. Olifant and I. Vladislavic (eds), *The Years of Staffrider* (Johannesburg: Ravan Press, 1988). Essay first published in 1986.

32 Peggy Delmont, *The District Six Mural*, Holy Cross Centre, Cape Town, 1984–85. Acrylic and PVA on plastered masonry walls, 850 x 785 cm, illustrated in Alexander and Cohen (1990: 137, plate 113). F. February, Y. February and F. Mathews, *District Six, Where We Lived* (Fabric, Collection: South African National Gallery, 1992), illustrated in Arnold and Schmahmann (eds), *Between Union and Liberation*, Colour plate 26.

33 Bernadette (Berni) Searle studied at the Michaelis School of Fine Art, University of Cape Town, completing a Masters degree in 1995. She received the Standard Bank Young Artist Award for Visual Art in 2003, and has won a number of international prizes and awards. She has exhibited on many group shows within South Africa and internationally. For a full listing of exhibitions see E. Baderoon, L.A. Farrell and C. Kellner), *Berni Searle Approach* (Cape Town: Michael Stevenson Gallery; Tampa: Contemporary Art Museum/Institute for Research in Art; Johannesburg: Johannesburg Art Gallery, 2006), www.stevenson.info and www.bernisearle.com/Berni_Searle/Current.html.

34 See Martin West, 'Confusing Categories: Population Groups, National States and Citizenship', in E. Boonzaier and J. Sharp (eds), *South African Keywords: The Uses and Abuses of Political Concepts* (Cape Town and Johannesburg: David Philip, 1988), pp. 100–10, for the extraordinary convolutions of the legislation. West includes a table of reclassifications for 1986. Some members of Berni Searle's extended family were classified as whites.

35 In Rory Bester, 'Floating Free', in *Berni Searle*, Standard Bank Young Artist Award catalogue (Cape Town: Bell Roberts Publishing, 2003).

36 Searle's references to food inform her video *Snow White* (2001), where she is covered with off-white pea flour that falls from above and is then used to make dough, and *A Matter of Time* (2003), where she attempts to walk on glass covered with olive oil.
37 Searle observes (in Bester, 'Floating Free'), 'I think it's important to note that most of my works are not exhibited as photographs, but as digital prints of the photographic images which have been scanned and printed on different media such as backlit paper, vellum or transparencies. So while the work draws on the photographic image, it also moves away from the medium at some point. But when I have the photographs taken, the photographer is capturing a subject who has had some say in how she wants to be portrayed and what she is doing while the photograph is being taken. I'm also in a position to determine the way in which the work is presented. Once it is in the public arena though, I have to relinquish control!'
38 Searle also has British and German European ancestry.
39 In the *Discoloured* series Searle used Egyptian black henna to stain parts of her body, such as her hand in *Lifeline* (1999). The henna resembles bruising and indicates the body's vulnerability. See Coombes, *History After Apartheid*, for discussion on these works. For examples of Searle's works see www.bernisearle.com/Berni_Searle/Current.html, www.michaelstevenson.com, and Baderoon, Farrell and Kellner, *Berni Seale Approach*, plate 32.
40 *Home and Away* was first shown in 2003 when Searle was the Standard Bank Young Artist Award Winner for Visual Art and her exhibition travelled throughout South Africa. It is available on YouTube. Related to the video are two series of prints, *Waiting* and *By Night*.
41 Water continues to feature prominently in Searle's works. *Alibama* (2007) is a two-screen video projection that explores the landscape of Cape Town as a vantage point for viewing the Atlantic Ocean which brought the Confederate raiding ship, the *Alabama*, to Cape Town in the early 1860s. The well-known Afrikaans folk song *Daar Kom die* Alibama (Here Comes the *Alibama*) provides the sound track for a wistful conflation of American and Cape histories, connected by slave ownership. See Garb 2008 for an account of this work.
42 In M. Godby, 'Art and Politics in a Changing South Africa: Bongi Dhlomo in Conversation with Michael Godby', *African Arts* (Winter 2004), p. 65. Available online at http://findarticles.com/p/articles/mi_m0438/is_4_37/ai_n13775097.

Image-making with Jeanne Duval in mind: photoworks by Maud Sulter, 1989–2002

7

Deborah Cherry

In 2003, Maud Sulter curated a major exhibition at the National Galleries of Scotland in Edinburgh, entitled *Jeanne Duval: A Melodrama*.[1] In the accompanying catalogue, she wrote:

> My ongoing visual fascination with Jeanne Duval began in 1988 with a visceral response to a Nadar photograph captioned *Unknown Woman*. There she stared at me willing me to give her a name, an identity, a voice. So for over a decade I have been image making with her in mind, from *Calliope* in *Zabat*, 1989 to *Les Bijoux*, 2002.[2]

The photograph in question portrays a young woman. Unlike many of Nadar's sitters she is not attired in formal or bohemian dress. She is swathed in deep folds of velvet. She wears no jewellery. Her hands are not visible. Her hair is untied and undressed, falling soft and full from a centre parting. One side of her face is artistically cast in shadow, and she looks out directly, regarding those who look at her.[3] Out of Sulter's encounter with this photograph came writings, large-format self-portrait photographs including *Calliope* from her *Zabat* series (1989), *Les Bijoux* and *La Chevalure* (both 2002), and photomontages, notably *Syrcas* (1994) and *Jeanne: A Melodrama* (1994–2002).

Maud Sulter (1960–2008) was an artist, an exhibition curator, an award-winning poet, a writer and a publisher, the founder of Urban Fox Press and the gallery Rich Women of Zurich in London's Clerkenwell district.[4] She exhibited widely and internationally in solo shows or exhibitions such as *The Thin Black Line* (Institute for Contemporary Arts, London, 1985), the European Photography Awards (Berlin, 1991), *Pictura Britannica* (Sydney, 1997), *Transforming the Crown: African, Asian and Caribbean Artists in Britain, 1966–1996* (New York, 1996–97) and *Black Womanhood: Images, Icons and Ideologies of the African Body* (Hood Museum of Art, Dartmouth College Hanover, USA, 2008). She won the British Telecom New Contemporaries Award in 1990 as well as the MoMart Fellowship at Tate. With *Syrcas* she represented Britain at *Africus*, the Johannesburg Biennale of 1995. Her work is to be found in numerous private and public collections, including the Scottish Parliament, the Arts Council Collection, the Victoria and Albert Museum and the UK's National Portrait Gallery, by whom she was commissioned in 2001 to photograph children's writers. Maud Sulter's art engages a rich range of references to Scotland and Ghana, the two locations of her heritage, and more widely to the interconnections between Europe and Africa. Distinctive to her work is her preoccupation with movements between Africa and Europe over the past six centuries and more, and the longevity of African diasporas in Europe, their multiplicities and specifities – in 1999 she emphasized the significance to her of 'the west African diaspora'.[5]

Diaspora and disappearance are recurring themes in her work:

> This whole notion of the disappeared, I think, is something that runs through my work. I'm very interested in absence and presence in the way that particularly black women's experience and black women's contribution to culture is so often erased and marginalised. So that it's important for me as an individual, and obviously as a black woman artist, to put black women back in the centre of the frame – both literally within the photographic image, but also within the cultural institutions where our work operates.[6]

Hysteria (1991) explores the life, art, and histories of the nineteenth-century African-American sculptor Edmonia Lewis, offering clues, hints and traces of her creative practice, her social circles, and her last sighting.[7] Sulter has often spoken of the vital importance of recognizing 'the fact that Black people have been in Europe for over four hundred years'.[8] *Alba*, a complex installation of 1995, was inspired in part by William Dunbar's poetic references to a resplendently attired black woman who participated in a tournament at the court of James IV of Scotland (1488–1513) then suddenly vanished.[9] In tracking the traces of the missing, she 'often approaches her work with the tools of a detective', scrutinizing archives and materials, investigating the formations of knowledge, and questioning evidence and identifications.[10] As Alice Walker famously stated: 'As a black person and a woman I don't read history for facts, I read it for clues.'[11]

Through a focus on her image-making with Jeanne Duval in mind, this chapter looks at Sulter's examination of the central significance of African diaspora women and African art to the formations of European modernity. I set out here an experimental exploration of her diaspora aesthetics, drawing on Lubaina Himid's proposal of 'gathering and re-using' as a strategic creative practice that enables resistance and change.[12] Sulter investigated the artistic possibilities for the visual representation of women like Jeanne Duval whose creativity, experience and histories have all too often been missing or marginalized. And this in turn prompted her preoccupation with disappearances and returns, explored here in relation to Jacques Derrida's contemporaneous interests in spectres and revenants.

Who was the woman in the photograph; the woman in the studio of the nineteenth-century photographer Gaspard Félix Tournachon, invariably known by his adopted name of 'Nadar'; this 'unknown woman', who is after all only unknown to us? Sulter considered that the sitter whom Nadar had photographed may have been Jeanne Duval, though she was cautious, wary of definitive conclusions. In *Zabat Narratives*, prose poems published alongside the display of *Zabat*, the photographic series which, in *Calliope*, includes her first address to the imagery of Jeanne Duval, she wrote:

> Well anonymous was to be a blackwoman in this blackwoman's case cause sure enough doesn't history forget to record which of Félix's photos document the beauteous Black muse. Now we know that she is Black, we know she is alluded to as Venus, but what we decide that we don't remember is that she is not the coal Black wench of Victorian fantasy but a straightforward coloured girl like many another. This is not to say that I am not happy that my daddy's skin is as dark as you can get but it galled me to think that that fucking stupid little glass plate that (i) Félix managed to keep without breaking and (ii) has survived all this time, is attributed to Unknown Woman when any idiot would know how to put two and two together to make five.[13]

In an interview ten years later she stated: 'Well, I don't agree that it is *the* photograph of Jeanne Duval. The problem of identifying a photograph of Jeanne Duval … Well, how is it the Unknown Woman? Have you checked the archives? It is recorded as the Unknown Woman in one particular book, and then being recorded as the Unknown Woman repeatedly, it has become history itself. It is like Edmonia Lewis disappearing. The texts repeat themselves that Edmonia Lewis has disappeared.'[14]

Nadar certainly knew Jeanne Duval, one of several diaspora women who circulated in Parisian literary and artistic circles in the mid-nineteenth century.[15] If Nadar is best known today for his portrait photography, Duval's fame usually rests on her role as the model, muse and long-standing companion of the poet Charles Baudelaire. Although she appears frequently in Baudelaire's letters, and is often discussed in nineteenth- and twentieth-century accounts, biographies and reminiscences of Baudelaire and Nadar, there is relatively little documentation on which to reconstruct her biography, and none of her letters survive. Discovering that there is no consensus on her birth place, her appearance, her names, her character or her death, Maud Sulter asked:

> Who is this Jeanne Duval? A beautiful black woman who inspired Baudelaire to write some of the finest poetry and prose poems ever written; miracles of language which explore her sensuality, sexuality and ethnicity observed by the poet as the Western world stood on the cusp of modernity itself. And therein lies the crisis point for the vast contradictions in how she is perceived and portrayed.[16]

Undertaking extensive independent research in Europe, North America and the Caribbean, Sulter began to map a life story for this 'inspiring woman of African descent with a recorded if partially erased existence',[17] negotiating the wide disparities in her numerous appearances in the existing literature to discern 'a loving daughter, an actress on the French stage, an inspired editor – to quote Baudelaire himself – a trusty archivist, devoted friend, and Baudelaire's one true love'.[18]

By 1988 Duval was already a highly contested figure in accounts of French literature, studies of Baudelaire's life and analyses of his poetry, especially the 'Black Venus' cycle in *Les Fleurs du mal.* Art historical studies have had something to say about her, asking if it is she who is depicted in Eduoard Manet's painting of a woman reclining in a voluminous crinoline, which is said by some – but not all Manet scholars – to portray Jeanne Duval,[19] and considering the several sketches and drawings of her that survive. The literature on, about and around her is now substantial, with lengthy biographies, more focused studies, and seemingly inexhaustible argument over her representation in and influence upon Baudelaire's poetry. Across the period of Sulter's 'image making with her in mind', Duval became increasingly discussed and desired in feminist and post-colonial theory as scholars cited and took issue with each other in staging their debates. Christopher Miller cautioned against an elision of the person with the poems, emphasizing that the representation of an exoticized, eroticized black femininity in Baudelaire's modernist poems recycles and renews a longstanding trope of western racism.[20] Mieke Bal warned of the propensity of literary critics to 'fall from Baudelaire's phonetic and metaphoric charms straight into the arms of his Afro-European mistress Jeanne Duval, whose attraction for critics needs some explaining'.[21] Griselda Pollock combined careful attention to the texts on Duval that might constitute a biography for her with analysis of representations generated by 'unquestioned racism' and 'a virulent misogyny': Western high culture has, she asserted, 'coloured, bestialised, stupefied and hated Jeanne Duval, aligning her with the key images of night and death, hence of imaginary blackness: the prostitute and the vampire'.[22] In Spivak's elegant dissection she is, like Sulter, reading for clues. Spivak takes Baudelaire's poem 'Le Cygne' as one of three texts that, along with responses to it, will offer 'a mirror of our performance of certain imperialist ideological structures even as we deconstruct the tropological error of masculism celebrating the female'.23 As she explains however, the 'price of learning such a tropological deconstruction of masculism, however, was the performance of a blindness to the *other woman* in the text' (pp. 151–2). Baudelaire's line 'Je pense à la négresse' (I am thinking about the negress, line 42 for Spivak) sets up a problem in interpretation: 'we might look at the naming of the negress … She might of course "be" Jeanne Duval' (p. 153). Spivak resists this line of enquiry, and follows a 'textual clue', noting that the poet borrows two lines from another of his poems, 'À une malabaraise', ostensibly about 'one of two women Baudelaire encountered in Mauritius and the island of Reunion respectively' whom the poet 'misplaces' to the generalized domain that he ascribes to 'la négresse': 'la superbe Afrique' (superb Africa, p. 154). Recognizing that '[u]nder the principles of New Criticism it is not permitted to introduce such extraneous considerations into a reading of the poem', Spivak argues for their necessity if she is to 'develop a strategy (rather than a theory) of reading matching the situation of reading that might lead to a literary critique of imperialism' (p. 153). The dangers otherwise are of 'ignoring the inscription of the "negress"', and neglecting to develop 'the native informant perspective', by summoning Baudelaire as sympathetic observer of exile, by bringing in 'precisely the details about Jeanne Duval or the elusive *malabaraise*, without attending to the way the negress is displayed in the poem', or by suggesting that this figure is Baudelaire's dark double.[24] Introducing Jeanne Duval is thus both a necessity and a distraction to an analysis the poem's exoticism of *la négresse*; seeking an explanation through Baudelaire is only a diversion.

Writers and artists have also re-imagined Jeanne Duval. Angela Carter's *Black Venus* (1985) portrays Jeanne Duval in an intertextual reworking of Baudelaire's poems.[25] Carter's text has garnered debate: is *Black Venus* citation, appropriation, subversive critique or complicit with what Rebecca Munford identifies as Duval's 'historical displacement'?[26] For Lorna Sage, Carter is 'mischievously engaged in supplementing the canon – writing round the edges of the known, resurrecting (by means of invention, naturally), materials that didn't quite make it into the record, and voices that we didn't get to hear'.[27] Carter's revisions and rewritings may also be identified with a feminist trajectory that reads against the grain to give voice to figures otherwise silenced and re-animates characters in canonical works of art or literature. Eunice Lipton's searches for Victorine Louise Meurent, the woman painter who modelled for *Olympia*,[28] or the painstaking documentation of Laure, an African diaspora woman who also modelled for this painting, undertaken by Nancy Proctor and Griselda Pollock, come to mind.[29] Given the extensive attention to Jeanne Duval, it might be said that, far from disappearing, she, or more precisely the sign 'Jeanne Duval', has been excessively invoked, so much so that 'Jeanne Duval' becomes the sign of difference, comes to represent difference. Jacques Derrida's concept of *différance* as both distinction and delay helps to explain the doubled meanings that are at work in the sign 'Jeanne Duval': 'On the one hand [*différer*] indicates difference as distinction, inequality, or discernibility; on the other, the interposition of delay, the interval of *spacing*, and *temporalizing* that puts off until "later" what is presently denied'.[30] *Différance* thus speaks precisely, as Derrida indicates, of 'difference as distinction, inequality, or discernibility' and it also captures the restless and disruptive proliferations of meanings that are always delayed, deferred, unfixed, open to (re)interpretation. Derrida's suggestion of delay, as I argue later, is also at work in his reflections on ghosts who belatedly return from the past to haunt the present. 'Jeanne Duval' thus became a highly contested sign. For the artist, she was not only an 'inspiring woman of African descent with a recorded if partially erased existence',[31] but a powerful sign of the longevity of the African diasporas in Europe: 'Jeanne Duval signifies the continuing African presence at Europe's cultural heart and the simultaneous denial and erasure of that presence.'[32] Investigating her history, her appearance and disappearances has, she believed, a critical relevance for the present.

> Signifying as her life does the continuing Black presence in Europe over centuries, in her we see illuminated the politics of gender, racism and class endemic in the world in which she inhabited and also all too present in the repercussions of cultural imperialism, which echo to us in our present lives and times.[33]

Jeanne: A Melodrama is composed of four scenes, rearranged by the artist in a varying sequence on different occasions.[34] As a whole they encompass the period of Duval's life in Paris, from the later 1830s to the mid-/later 1850s. Two focus on her early career on the Parisian stage, while two others mark the years in which she moved in artistic and literary circles in the French capital.

Nadar's photograph appears in each of the four images. Throughout, viewers are aware that fragments of this image are taken from somewhere else, that they travel with the traces of their past. The image is snipped unevenly, even erratically, with awkward cuts and angles that deliberately draw attention to their excision. Segments of a woman's face, of her face with her hair, of her head with part of her upper body encased in velvet drapery, register a diasporic trace, the cultural migration of the image. The fragments of Nadar's

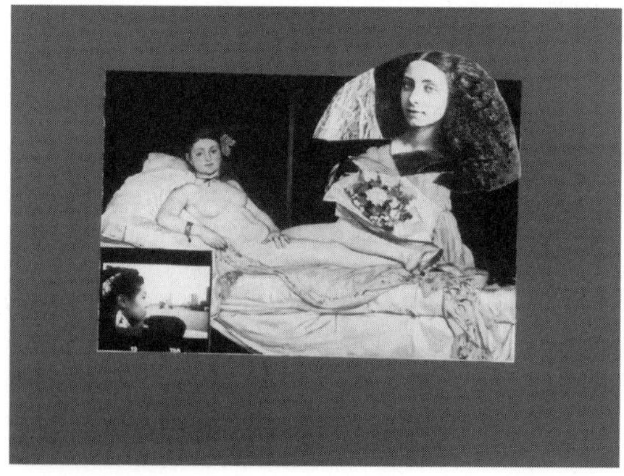

7.1 Maud Sulter, *Jeanne: A Melodrama, I* (1994–2002), photographic print.

photograph double as Jeanne Duval and as the uncertainty of identification – that is, as her presence and her lost history. The image is at once a visual record, a document, and an unsettled, proliferating sign: in what follows *Jeanne Duval* refers to this multiple potential.

Jeanne: A Melodrama undertakes a radical deconstruction of European modernism. Two scenes focus on urban spectacle, the theatre and popular entertainment, another on the commoditization of women, in an address to art historical scholarship that has defined modernity through the rise of new forms of city pleasure and leisure.[35] All four are concerned with the presence of African diaspora women in the creative heartlands of modern Paris.

In *I* the head of *Jeanne Duval* is introduced into a reproduction of Manet's *Olympia* (painted 1863, exhibited 1865, Paris, Musée d'Orsay) in the place of Laure, the black attendant (Figure 7.1). This insertion immediately disorients the scale of the painting, since Jeanne's head is at least twice the size of Olympia's. Breaking through the border of the print, it is at once inside and outside the reproduction of Manet's painting. Its insertion dislodges what has conventionally been viewed as the painting's primary regard – from the white model to the spectator – aptly characterized by Jennifer deVere Brody in an inspiring and thought-provoking article as Olympia's 'confrontational, even glaring gaze'.[36] Rebecca Schneider compellingly suggests that Olympia's gaze marks not her active seeing, but her focus for the gaze of others: 'there is not reciprocity – the seen does not see back', she writes, continuing, 'what is acknowledged by the direction of her gaze (whether defiant or compliant) is the viewer's sight marking her as seen. She can only acknowledge that she is seen, but she cannot author vision, cannot see back'.[37] In Manet's painting Laure appears to be watching the supine woman, whereas in scene *I* of *Jeanne: A Melodrama* the spectator is now equally regarded by Jeanne Duval. Her insertion destabilizes polarized oppositions in the painting between two women differentiated by skin colour as well as (un)dress, along with readings that stage Olympia in difference to Laure. One of several black scholars to bring radically new perspectives to the analysis of the performance of race in *Olympia*, Jennifer deVere Brody's incisive study concludes: 'The black female body is the vehicle needed for the (re)productive performance of "white" sexuality, … to make the white figure whiter via her constructed, contrasting difference'.[38]

Jeanne: A Melodrama is not the artist's first address to Manet's *Olympia*. In an outstanding essay on Maud Sulter's art of 'political collage' Angela Rosenthal considers that *Thalia*, one of the *Zabat* series which shows Alice Walker as the muse of comedy holding a profusion of flowers, reconfigures the bearer of Olympia's floral tribute.[39] Sulter is one of several black feminists to defamiliarize this celebrated painting and its figural dispositions. Highlighting writings by Harryette Mullen and Lorraine O'Grady, Jennifer deVere Brody draws attention to the ways in which 'Black feminist readings revive the black figure, erased in the title of the painting, and reveal her presence … to show how she grounds the figure of whiteness.'[40] Harryette Mullen's poetic re-reading of *Olympia* beautifully exposes the interplay worked on chromatics:

> A light white disgraceful sugar looks pink, wears an air, pale compared to shadow standing by. To plump recliner, naked truth lies. Behind her shadow wears her color, arms full of flowers. A rosy charm is pink. And she is ink. The mistress wears no petticoat or leaves. The other in shadow, a large pink dress.[41]

Mullen plays on / preys on slippages between pink, the spectrum of tones, vacillations between dark and light, valencies of shadow and illumination.

Sulter's photo-montage plots a counter-move. Her conjunctions tend to dissolve the oppositions on which the painting and subsequent analyses have depended. Writing in 1989, in the passage quoted earlier, Maud Sulter remarked that for her Duval was 'not the coal black wench of Victorian fantasy, but a straightforward coloured girl like many another.'[42] Why does she say this? One reason might be the continual preoccupation with Duval's skin colour.[43] In 'Blood Money', the prose poem published in the catalogue to *Syrcas*, Sulter wrote passionately about the dangers and futility of racial categorization, confounded by the long intimacies between Africans and Europeans.[44] Duval was African and European, a woman born from long histories of interracial contact between colonizers and colonized, travellers, settlers and migrants moving between the global north and south. In *Jeanne: A Melodrama* the interplay of colour is worked out not through the dramatic staging of skin colour, but rather through the play of monochromes against the rich crimson of the mounts. Scene *I* deploys a colour reproduction in a brilliant deconstruction of colour and its uses. The reproduction of the painting has faded; the once dazzling pink of Laure's dress is here almost indiscernible in hue

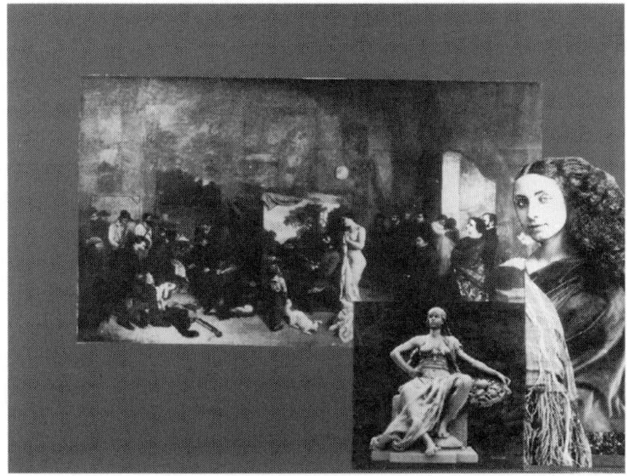

7.2 Maud Sulter, *Jeanne: A Melodrama, IV* (1994–2002), photographic print.

from the leached-out body tones of the reclining body, designated 'white', or the crumpled scarf beneath her. In *I*, colour is re-coded, displaced to a dynamic interplay across an unlike 'colour' reproduction unevenly placed on its crimson mount, across the sepia tints added to a historic photograph and a monochrome contact print.

Low down on the left, and counterpointing the introduction of the snippet of Nadar's photograph, is a black and white contact print depicting the artist, her face turned away, almost in profile. Sulter wears a striped head-scarf, reprising that worn by the missing Laure, returning her to the present in a new guise. She is looking out over the Seine with the Eiffel Tower in the distance, underlining the location of Paris, centre of Western modernity, and now of its museums, archives and collections, the destination for anyone in search of Jeanne Duval. These additions interrupt the staging of the painting, undo its logic, unravel its field of vision. Here, as in all four, *Jeanne Duval*'s face looks out; slight variations of cut and tilt shift the angle of her quizzical regard.

The partner of *I* is *IV*, which features another key image of European modernity, Gustave Courbet's *The Painter's Studio: A Real Allegory Determining Seven Years of My Life as an Artist* (1855, Paris, Musée du Louvre; Figure 7.2).This is a significant association – between *Olympia*, one of the most famous images of a female nude and a renowned portrayal of artistic practice depicting a workroom peopled with friends, colleagues, allies, models with, centre stage, the artist at his easel; standing behind him is that key sign of artistic endeavour as masculine, the unclothed, female model, whose drapery only emphasizes her nudity. A grainy, low-resolution monochrome print of Courbet's painting provides the semiotic ground for the insertion of *Jeanne Duval* to the right, cutting up against the diminutive figure of Charles Baudelaire, seated to the edge of the group, reading. According to some accounts, a figure representing Jeanne Duval was once included in Courbet's *Atelier* adjacent to Baudelaire, only to be painted out/over at the poet's request.[45] All that remains at the site of her disappearance are, as Jill Matus so nicely puts it, 'the ghostly traces of her effacement'.[46] In Sulter's reduced replica, it is deliberately hard to discern the principal characters in the painter's studio, let alone a set of indistinct marks on a side wall. Sulter's placing of *Jeanne Duval* echoes that of the European model standing behind Courbet, emphasizing once again the central place of African women in Western modernity. As in *I*, her presence is magnified, at odds with the scale of the reproduced painting, and again breaking the border between print and mount. But here *Jeanne Duval* moves beyond and outside the frame, simultaneously in front of the painting and beside it. This figure becomes a supplement, working within 'logic of the supplement' proposed by Derrida. Alluding to the double meaning in French of *supplément* as addition and replacement, Derrida indicates that the supplement is disruptive and even dangerous: 'Its sliding [or slipperiness, slithering] slips it out of the simple alternative of presence and absence. That is the danger.'[47] This dangerous supplement, he contends, 'breaks into the very thing that would have liked to do without it, and which allows itself to be simultaneously cut into, violated, filled and replaced, completed by the very trace through which the present augments itself in the act of disappearing into it.'[48] Derrida's concept of the supplement allows an understanding of the force of this belated re-insertion of the photographic fragment: *Jeanne Duval* intervenes, pushes in/between and against this representation of modern European artistic practice and its networks of sociability, breaking into its frameworks, disruptive and destabilizing.

IV is a composite assemblage that includes two other significant elements, both inter-textual references to *Syrcas*, a series to which I return later. One is an image, a grainy reproduction taken from the *Syrcas* catalogue, of a *fin-du-siècle* sculpture of *Europa* in which the European continent is represented by an African/diaspora woman, rather than the more familiar European figure in, nevertheless, the usual sexualized and exoticized manner.[49] This image is juxtaposed to the figure of the white woman standing at the centre of Courbet's studio. The second element is a slice of an image of an acrobatic dancer of *Ikhien-ani-mhim* in Ishan, Benin.[50] This figure is an insistent presence in *Jeanne: A Melodrama*, segments appearing in colour in *III* as well as in *IV*, bidding viewers to complete the image, to recognize the reference, to see the grounding presence of African art, culture and peoples in Western modernity, to acknowledge the close and recurrent proximities of contact and exchange.

I and *IV* are counterpointed by *II* and *III* (Figures 7.3 and 7.4), both of which allude to Duval's early career on the Parisian stage; this is after all *A Melodrama*, and Jeanne Duval was one of many women who worked as theatrical artistes. In *II* and *III* she is the protagonist of the performance staged

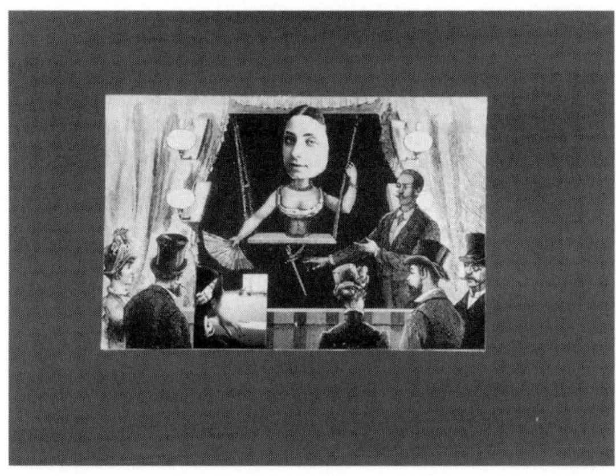

7.3 Maud Sulter, *Jeanne: A Melodrama, II* (1994–2002), photographic print.

before us. Popular in the early nineteenth century, melodrama takes its name in part from melody, musical accompaniment to spoken drama. The scene once again is modern Paris, with its growing entertainment industries, theatres, cafes and bars. In *III* Jeanne Duval appears as a performer, attired in the costume of Pierrot, the tragic clown in Europe's *commedia dell'arte*. She is followed by a mysterious figure in black whose face is concealed by the upper part of the Benin mask, a conjunction that acts as a reminder, once again, of the contacts between Africa and Europe while marking culturally distinct forms of dance. And this time it is the snippet of the mask that breaks into the crimson mount, stretching beyond the frame of the appropriated nineteenth-century image. In *II* Jeanne Duval's face is sutured into a print of a theatrical entertainment that seems to portray a popular magic trick in which the lady vanishes. Slipped in between the figures of the audience is another of the contact prints of the artist gazing out across Paris, this time turned away from us, her hand resting on a balustrade before her, a visual gesture which once again problematizes the relay of glances between viewers and viewed. It is as if her audience then and now both witness and are complicit in the disappearance of Jeanne Duval. Hands are prominent in *II* and *III*, their gestures reanimating the hands hidden in Nadar's photograph: Pierrot's right hand; the artiste holding the fan and the swing support; the impresario's signal – 'now you see her, now you don't'. The prominence of Sulter's left hand reminds the viewer of the hand of the artist holding the scissors. In the sequence published in 1994 this was the last image, a position in the series that underlines the precariousness of Jeanne Duval's historical existence. Just as she becomes visible, she is at risk of disappearing.

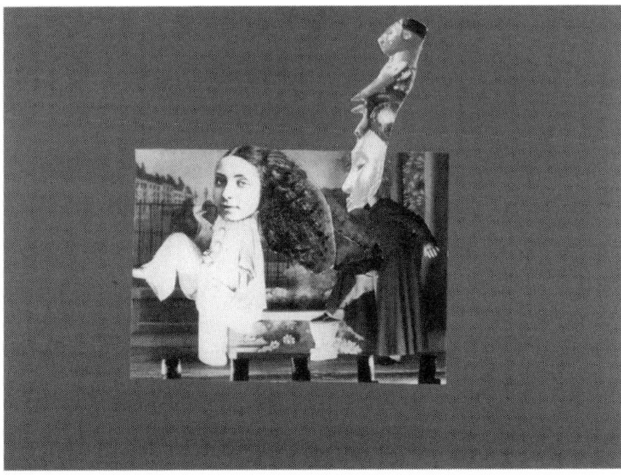

Maud Sulter, *Jeanne: A Melodrama, III* (1994–2002), photographic print. 7.4

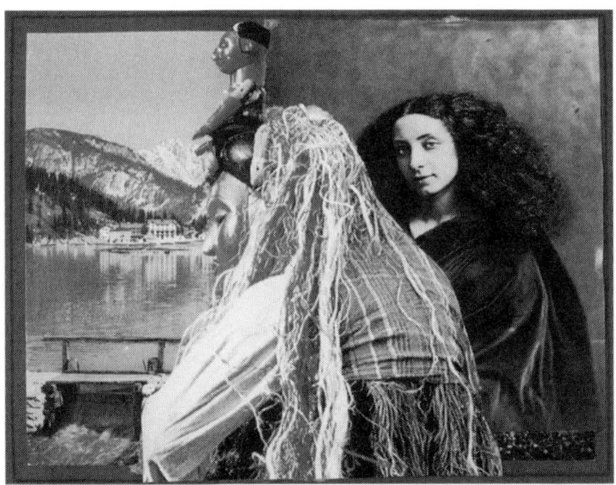

7.5 Maud Sulter, *Duval, from Dumas et Duval, Syrcas* (1994), photographic print.

Syrcas (1994) and *Jeanne: A Melodrama* are both made using photo-montage, a visual form with avant-garde and modernist precedents, acknowledged political purpose and a distinguished history. Sulter had certainly read and consulted Maud Lavin's absorbing study of Hannah Höch's work in the interwar years.[51] Sulter emphasized her deliberate choice of this medium in the winter of 1993: 'it was that time of contemplation, rest, being in one place that made the "working around the kitchen table" an interesting thing to do'.[52] She continued, 'the actual practices of cutting and pasting pieces together, it has west African roots to it. ... Montaging and collaging is a very intense process'.[53] For *Syrcas* she made small-scale paper collages that were photographically reprinted on a larger scale for exhibition. Photo-montage provides the visual form for Sulter's incisive dismantling of modernist perspectives on African art: its aestheticizing and othering as 'primitive'; its inclusion in modernist displays; artistic borrowings and appropriations by artists such as Pablo Picasso or Man Ray (in *Syrcas* Sulter often selects the precise examples); and modernist juxtapositions of white bodies and African masks, as in Höch's *From an Ethnographic Museum* (1924–34). *Syrcas* and *Jeanne: A Melodrama* are closely related, elements of the first series reprised and reworked in the second. In both the artist draws powerfully on photo-montage's propensities for temporal disjunction and spatial disturbance as she counterpoints diverse printed materials, some from popular culture, the staple of the medium, some from high art.

In the 'haunting poetic images of SYRCAS with their subtle allusions and startling juxtapositions'[54] West African masks and art objects excerpted from books on African art, illustrated largely with examples in Western collections, are laid onto European images – well-known paintings, nineteenth- and twentieth-century photographs, picture postcards, scraps of travel imagery. *Syrcas* is a complex work that reflects on violence and genocide, on the disappeared and the unseen, on perceptions of minorities, on the longevity of the West African diaspora in northern Europe, and the intensity and complexity of cross-cultural contact between the peoples of the world. Its protagonist is Monique, 'a woman of African and European descent' who was born in Cameroon and becomes a performer in a French circus in the 1920s to the 1940s.[55] Her life and family are jeopardized by racism, the rise of fascism, the ethnic cleansings of modern Europe. As Sulter reminds us, this past has particular relevance for our present: 'Monique may be near you right now.'[56] With its first display in Wrexham in Wales, she selected a Welsh word, *Syrcas* meaning circus, for the title. According to the artist: 'The work uses a series of landscape postcards from sort of unspecified European Alpine-type scenes, montaged onto which are African masks, African objects. … In a way it's a testimony to the black experience within the Holocaust and it's also hopefully functioning in the present as a reminder of individual responsibility.'[57] In one section, the diptych entitled *Duval* and *Dumas, Duval* is fashioned in five layers which are evened out in the exhibition print: a purple card with deep red border as a ground to the whole, a sepia-toned print of Nadar's photograph occupying most of the right half, beneath a small strip of patterned paper, to the left a sparkling tourist view of a lake bordered by chalet-style houses and mountains (Figure 7.5). At the centre is a segment of the image of the acrobatic dancer of *Ikhien-ani-mhim* that also appears in *Jeanne: A Melodrama*. In *II* and *III* of *Jeanne: A Melodrama* Sulter appropriates prints of popular theatre whereas in *I* and *IV* she works with reproductions of two paintings. Their vintage quality and the scrappy edges suggest removal from books, emphasizing not the singular work of art but its dissemination, circulation, access and availability for audiences outside the museum, the profound divergence between original and copy. Throughout the series, a central image is laid on a crimson mount as if prepared for framing, again highlighting the social lives and manifold uses of images. While well within the visual syntax of photo-montage, there is in *Jeanne Duval: A Melodrama* an uncanny echo of Aby Warburg's *Mnemosyne Atlas* (1925–29) and its reflections on the afterlives of images.[58]

The mid-1990s were a highly productive period for the artist. In photo-montages, film and installation, Sulter elaborated a diaspora artistic practice of gathering and re-using. *Plantation* is a forty-minute video work with poetry, music, and appropriated clips from the 1944 film of Charlotte Brontë's novel *Jane Eyre* (USA, director Robert Stevenson), a Gothic romance starring Orson Welles and Joan Fontaine. These are laid onto / cut into a documentary film of the artist's abdominal surgery in November 1993: four gloved hands work together to cut, pare away, reveal and remove a tumour and finally suture and stitch.[59] The title unmistakably summons the territories of slavery, geographically distant yet intimately connected to Britain as Edward Said magisterially analysed in his discussions of 'overlapping territories, intertwined histories' in *Culture and Imperialism*, first published in 1993.[60] *Plantation* ends with the artist's voice asking over and over again, 'Can women have wishes?', until finally: 'Cleopatra was found dead lying on a bed of gold.' *Alba* conjures time and space, assembling images of fourth-century Egyptian porphyry (The Tetrarchs from San Marco in Venice), five colour portrait photographs, twelve black-and-white photographs of plates from a seventeenth-century alchemical treatise, massively enlarged in scale and floating on the walls, and African art exquisitely arranged on plinths. A soundtrack played contemporary, traditional and ceremonial African music, and the artist reading 'The Alba Sonnets', which she had written.

Writings on diaspora cultural production have emphasized two key characteristics: multilocational, intercultural appropriation and adaptation, defined by Paul Gilroy as a dynamic cultural syncretism,[61] alongside 'an urgent and acute link to politics'.[62] In an essay on 'everyday Black creativity and its relation to political change', Lubaina Himid emphasized the importance of 'the artistic practice of gathering and re-using'. Citing as one example the quilting of the Zamani Soweto Sisters Council she wrote of 'the power to create anew from what was discarded or what exists as something else, [that] equips the maker with the power to make political change'. She summarized: 'Gathering and re-using is an essential part of Black creativity ... Each piece within the piece has its own history, its own past and its own contribution to the whole, the new function.'[63] As she indicates, this double movement creates an art of resistance.

Sulter's installations and photo-montages are heterochronic and heterotopic arts of assemblage that participated in a contemporaneous alertness to, in Jane Beckett's analysis, the 'precariousness of historical survival, as well as the pluralities and insecurities entailed in the processes of historical interpretation'.[64] In the mid-1990s, Sulter gathered and reused objects, images, fragments and c(l)ues which diasporically migrated; there was no fusion, hybridization or creolization, rather awkward tensions, unpredictable collisions, and incommensurate confrontations that are deliberately puzzling, enigmatic even incomprehensible.

The recurring image in *Jeanne: A Melodrama* is an archival photograph, and the series can be situated within the well-established impulses of archival art. According to Hal Foster, archival art employs found materials: 'These sources are familiar, drawn from the archives of mass culture, to ensure a legibility that can then be disturbed or *detourné*; but they can also be obscure, retrieved in a gesture of alternative knowledge or counter-memory.'[65] Archival art, he contends, works to 'probe a misplaced past, to collage its different signs, ... to ascertain what might remain for the present' (p. 21), and, in the case of Thomas Hirschhorn, to recover 'radical figures' (p. 11). Much of this analysis, especially the retrieval of counter-knowledges and an emphasis on the constructed nature of the archive, accords with Sulter's artistic practices, although she does not arrange her materials according to a 'quasi-archival logic' or within 'quasi-archival architecture' (p. 5). And *Jeanne: A Melodrama* essays much more than the recovery of a radical figure. Like *Syrcas*, this series has the moral urgency ascribed to archival art by Okwui Enwezor and Ernst van Alphen. Moreover, as Sulter remarked on several occasions, Duval is not confirmed as the sitter for *Unknown Woman*. The desire for identification (the photograph is Jeanne Duval) sits uneasily beside the recognition of the difficulties of establishing her identity for certain. Hovering in this uncertainty, the photographic trace signifies Duval not only as a knowable individual, but as a ghost, a revenant who is conjured by the artist to haunt the places and times from which she disappeared. The effect is electrifying, disturbing, as Sulter stages the spectre of Jeanne Duval, the woman of the African diaspora who is haunting European visual modernity and its belated histories.

Maud Sulter was not the only one thinking about ghosts in the early 1990s. Ghosts haunt Derrida's *Spectres of Marx*, published in 1994. Derrida begins with his reflections on 'the historic violence of Apartheid'.[66] He dedicates the book to Chris Hani, leader of the South African Communist Party and key figure in the African National Congress, who was assassinated in 1993. The threshold to *Spectres* is thus violent racial conflict. For Derrida, the ghost is predicated on return and repetition, on coming again to haunt places once frequented. It is, he explains: 'A question of repetition: a specter is always a *revenant*. One cannot control its comings and goings because it *begins by coming back*' (p. 11). Yet this is no simple repeat appearance, he contends, no revisitation of the same. The spectre is not resurrection of what once was, but a conjuration, summoned to the present on behalf of the present and the future 'in the name of *justice*' (p. xix). There can be no possibility of a future without disjointing time, 'without this *non-contemporaneity with itself of the living present*, without that which secretly unhinges it, without this responsibility and this respect for justice concerning those *who are not there*, of those who are no longer or who are not yet *present and living*' (p. xix). At the outset Derrida calls on his readers 'to learn to live *with* ghosts. … To live otherwise, and better. No, not better, but more justly. But *with them*. … And this being-with specters would also be, not only but also, a *politics* of memory, of inheritance, and of generations' (pp. xviii-xix). Although an extended translational encounter between *Spectres of Marx* and *Jeanne: A Melodrama* (emergent in the same year) is beyond the scope of this chapter, a provisional beginning suggests that this encounter disjoints the histories of western modernity, its legacies and genealogies. Sulter's citational collage, as much as Derrida's, construes this '*non-contemporaneity with itself of the living present*'. Both the philosopher and the artist are concerned with conjuring ghosts in the name of justice, with revenants who disturb and disrupt the trajectories of time, from past to present to future. Jeanne reappears where once she was, but not in the same guise. She returns in the form of a fragment of an image that perhaps represents her, with all the difficulties that representation entails. Her belated re-appearance is summoned in the 'name of justice'. If there is, as Derrida suggests, a 'politics of memory' in summoning ghosts, there is just as importantly, for the artist and the philosopher, a politics of the future that calls for European societies to co-exist hospitably, to 'live with' difference.

Self-portraiture has been a consistent theme in Sulter's art.[67] *Zabat* is a series of nine dye destruction [Cibachrome] prints, each depicting one of the muses. For the centrepiece the artist (who is also a published poet) both becomes and is possessed by the muse of epic poetry. *Calliope* is staged as if in an early nineteenth-century portrait photographer's studio. On a small round table, akin to the photographer's studio property, are a pair of framed daguerreotypes, diminutive by comparison to the majestic figure wrapped in velvet and rapt in thought, whose visual form echoes Nadar's portraits of Jeanne Duval and of Sarah Bernhardt. The parallel prose poem 'Calliope' (included in *Zabat: Narratives* is in the first person, as if spoken by Jeanne Duval. In an interview in 1992, Sulter outlined her approach to this image of herself:

> I chose to cast myself as 'Calliope, the Muse of Heroic Poetry.' I suppose that's rather flattering to my poet side – but there was a sort of representation, a recreation of a photograph by the French photographer Nadar which is entitled 'Unknown Woman', and I played about with the idea that this portrayal of the unknown woman was actually a photograph of Jeanne Duval. Now Jeanne Duval has been historicized as the exotic muse of Baudelaire's poetry, the Black Venus, and I wanted to play around, especially in the text [of *Zabat: Narratives*], with the idea of how black women's creativity is present then disappears, the notion of the disappeared creative person. Jeanne Duval disappears – we know not where she is buried, so on and so forth. … So that invisibility, even where there is a presence, was something that I wanted to express through that portrayal of the artist recreating herself in the role of Calliope.[68]

Conventionally presented in the history of Western art as white women, in *Zabat* the muses are portrayed by black women writers, artists, musicians and strategists. Reflecting on this move, Sulter stated:

> I would contest that classical history has a European root. … the root of classical history lies in Egypt … when the Alexandrian shrine of the Muses, the great Alexandrian Library was destroyed during the Crusades, so much of that bridge between Africa and Europe was destroyed.[69]

These are sumptuous, densely layered and strikingly beautiful images, portraying, for example, Alice Walker as Thalia, the muse of comedy, Lubaina Himid as

Urania, the muse of astrology, and singer Ysaye Maria Barnwell as Polyhymnia, the muse of sacred song. Far exceeding the personage who haunts the frame, sitter and figure supplement one another as model and muse. Here the artist explores a diaspora aesthetics of 'gathering and re-using' that adopts, adapts and re-signifies images, objects and visual forms in an allegorical mode of representation that both invokes historical precedent (Maud Sulter *as* the muse of epic poetry) and re-imagines an 'allegorical impulse' which Craig Owens associated with appropriation, with the 'fragmentary, the imperfect, the incomplete', and which he characterized by 'its capacity to rescue from historical oblivion that which threatens to disappear'.[70] *Calliope*'s complex levels of representation – of the artist, of a historical individual, of a constituency – participated in the debates on one of the key issues for feminist thinkers in the later 1980s. Differentiating between *Vertretung* ('stepping in someone's place', the political representation of a community) and *Darstellung* ('proxy and portrait'), Gayatri Chakravorty Spivak concluded the two are so closely enmeshed that 'in the act of representing, you actually represent yourself and your constituency in the portrait sense, as well'.[71] *Calliope* initiated a representational strategy in which the artist 'recreat[ed] herself in the role' of the muse of epic poetry, in which she both took up the place of Jeanne Duval and imaged herself as Jeanne Duval. And, depending on a strategic essentialism articulated by Spivak as necessary to feminist representation, in which Duval came to represent a community, signifying 'the continuing black presence in Europe over centuries'.

In two series of 2002, *La Chevelure* and *Les Bijoux*, Sulter returned to image-making with Jeanne Duval in mind and to the theme of the muse. This time she faced the camera to 're-figure myself as Jeanne Duval not as previously in *Zabat* as an active muse and artist, but in a funk of postmusedom'.[72] In the diptych of *La Chevelure* and the suite of nine that make up *Les Bijoux* the titles point to poems by Baudelaire included in *Les Fleurs du mal*, but there are few direct parallels. In *La Chevelure* there is none of the cascading mane saluted by the poet, one of several signs of exoticism, excess, of a heightened, sexualized Orientalism, as the poet dreams of a vast global space: 'All languid Asia, blazing Africa/ a whole faraway world that is absent, almost dead survives in the depths of this forest of aromas.'[73] Sulter resists this fascination with abundant hair. One photograph portrays a woman whose hair is tightly drawn back from her face. The other depicts a woman who holds a skein of hair in one hand, and in her left the bag in which it will be sold and kept by its new owner. In mid-nineteenth-century France, inspired by Empress Eugénie, the styling of fashionable women demanded lustrous, gleaming dark hair, with elaborate twists, braids, and plaits; then as now extensions and additions were much in demand, supporting a brisk trade. Whereas, for some historians, Baudelaire 'more than once … sold her jewels and her furniture', in her narratives about Duval, Sulter considered that in her continual support for her lover 'Duval sold her jewels, and possibly her hair, to keep herself and Baudelaire … . I admire Jeanne Duval for that.'[74] Despite its title, in *La Chevelure* hair is not on display, but severed; it is packaged, ready for sale. Equally, in *Les Bijoux*, the model's hair is pulled back close to her head, almost disappearing into the shadows of the b(l)ackground (Figure 7.6).

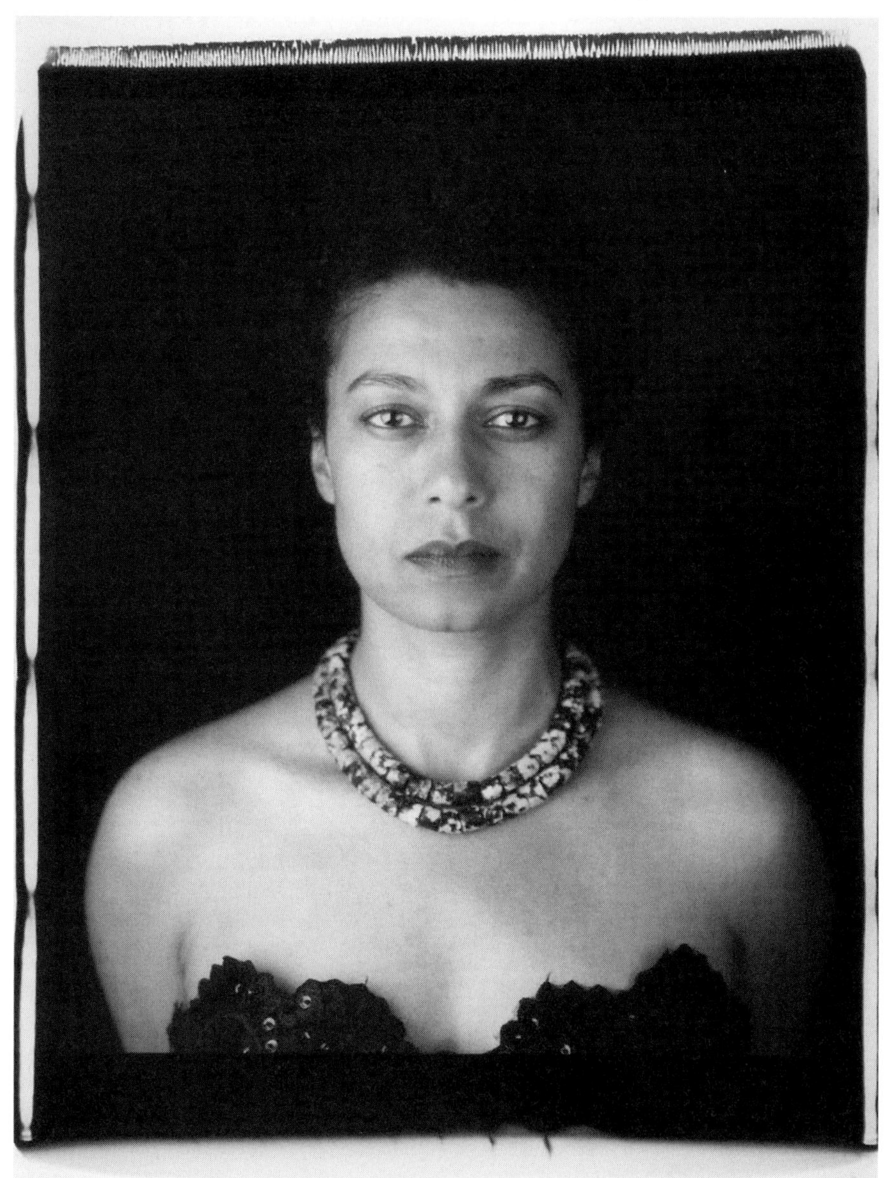

7.6 Maud Sulter, *Les Bijoux* (2002), photographic print.

In Baudelaire's poem *Les Bijoux*: 'My beloved was naked, and knowing my heart's desire, had kept only her sonorous jewels on.'[75] By contrast Sulter's photographs portray a woman attired in magnificent dresses and gorgeous adornment; if her shoulders are bare she is never nude. The figure wears three elaborate evening gowns, each with its own distinctive jewellery. Across the series, the jewels are as much constraint as they are decoration, as she tugs at the gorgeous gleaming skeins. There are, perhaps, references to neck restraints once used on slaves, a clue embedded in Baudelaire's comparison of his beloved to 'les esclaves des Mores' or Moorish slave women, although the references are by no means so straightforward. At times the figure faces outwards, at others she is in profile, or looking at an angle. A range of powerful emotions plays across her face: desire, grief, anguish, pain and loss.

For Mark Sealy these 'confrontational and sensuous self-portraits' have a 'strong undercurrent of sexual power … intensified by the possibility of both violence and rejection', as the figure turns away, or tugs at her necklaces 'threatening to break with the conventions of desire'. Sealy also highlights the now familiar theme of the African diaspora, arguing that for *Les Bijoux* the 'key function is to remind the viewer of how critically close African and European cultures have historically been and that the complexities of these encounters cannot be simply reduced to simplistic understandings of white encounters with the other'.[76] Sulter explores here the predicament of the model whose presence is inspirational to creative practice. Much has been written about the modernity of Baudelaire's poetry inspired by an erotic fascination with an African diaspora woman. In these performative self-portraits Sulter investigates the possibilities for understanding Jeanne Duval's relationship with the poet, the wide spectrum of emotions engaged in a tumultuous long-term relationship that moved from a passionate intensity when Duval was a muse and inspiration, to distance and parting. The figure in the frame is Maud Sulter and Jeanne Duval. Sulter appears *as* Duval. Performance runs through her image-making with Jeanne Duval in mind as she summons Duval – on stage, into the frame. *La Chevelure* and *Les Bijoux* are spectral performances in which the ghost of Duval, embodied by Sulter, haunts the frame.

In *La Chevelure* and *Les Bijoux* Sulter has created images that address the nature of beauty, an abiding concern in aesthetics and one that has been too often implicated racializing difference. In her analysis of African and diaspora aesthetics, Sarah Nuttall has traced 'the inscription of Africa in dominant western aesthetic discourses as the figure of the ugly' alongside characterizations of African women as exotic and the savage in anthropology, art history and ethnography.[77] Sulter confounds such visual inscriptions by transforming a specific photographic format preferred by the institutions of the state, the 'mug-shot' in which the head and upper torso appear frontally and directly. The beauty of the model is combined with a simplicity of means, intricated through variation and repetition, in which the photographer skilfully modulates the fall of light and shadow to articulate a counter-vision of beauty to that proposed by *Olympia*. Beauty and explicitly African beauty is the theme of *African Beauty*, also known as *Akwambo: A Good Spirit Always Looks after Her Young* (2001, Edinburgh, Scottish Parliament), a triptych that uses the same portrait format. Three large-format Polaroid photographs show an *akua'ba* figure between two portraits, one of the artist, the other of the musician Miles Ofuso Danso. For Sulter this conjunction of a Scots-Ghanaian and a French-Ghanaian with an image of Akan and Asante ideals of female beauty, fertility and health, is a 'playful portrait, a trope of the continuing 500-year exchange between Africa and Europe'.[78]

Maud Sulter was an artist well versed in photography's histories and critical theories. Running through her art and her writings is an address to photography, its past and its future. The clues in *Calliope* and *Hysteria* point to encounters in the nineteenth-century photographer's studio, whereas in her art of the mid-1990s she took up photo-montage, reviving a twentieth-century visual form renowned for its relation to politics, making an artistic move at odds with mainstream pictorial photography or the return to documentary. Sulter was well aware of Roland Barthes' dictum: 'the same century invented History and Photography'. There is too I suggest another link to Barthes. In the pages in *La Chambre claire*, in which he explores the connections between history and photography, Barthes discovers 'another *punctum* (another *stigmatum*) [other] than the "detail"'. He explains that 'This new *punctum* is no longer of form but of intensity'. This new punctum, he confirms, 'is Time, the lacerating emphasis of the *noeme* ("that-has-been"), its pure representation'.[79] This punctum – of intensity, of Time, of 'the lacerating emphasis of the *noeme* ("that-has-been")' – is undoubtedly at work in Sulter's recounting of her 'visceral response' to a photograph of an 'unknown woman', as much as in her sustained and evocative image making with Jeanne Duval in mind.

Acknowledgements

Warmest thanks to Lubaina Himid for generously discussing this essay with me, to Stephen Bann and Sophie Berrebi for their thought-provoking discussions of Nadar; to Farida Guseynova and Zippora Elders for their research assistance; and to the editors for their helpful feedback on an earlier version.

Notes

1 M. Sulter, *Jeanne Duval: A Melodrama* (Edinburgh: National Galleries of Scotland, 2003). She originally proposed an extensive display, setting her own work alongside major works of European modern art.

2 Sulter, *Jeanne Duval*, p. 11.
3 The photograph is in the Départment des Estampes et la Photographie, Bibliothèque nationale de France, Paris and is often reproduced.
4 On her curating see D. Cherry, 'With Her Fingers on the Political Pulse: The Transnational Curating of Maud Sulter', in A. Dimitrakaki and L. Perry, *Feminism and Curating: Politics in a Glass Case* (Liverpool: Liverpool University Press, 2013).
5 Interview with S. Choi-Park, in *Maud Sulter's* Syrcas*: The Space of Archives*, unpublished MA dissertation, University of Sussex, 1999, pp. 47–58, (p. 52).
6 www.vam.ac.uk/vastatic/microsites/photography, accessed 27 July 2009.
7 On *Hysteria* see S. Malvern, 'The Muses and the Museum: Maud Sulter's Retelling of the Canon', in M. Biddiss and M. Wyke (eds), *The Uses and Abuses of Antiquity* (Bern: Peter Lang, 1999), pp. 227–41.
8 Sulter quoted in R.E. Wilson and G. Somerville-Arjat (eds), *Sleeping with Monsters* (Edinburgh, Polygon, 1990), p. 29, quoted in J. Mabon, 'Europe's African Heritage in the Creative Work of Maud Sulter', *Research in African Literatures: The African Diaspora and Its Origins*, 29/4 (Winter 1998), 148–55.
9 On *Alba* see D. Cherry, 'Troubling Presence: Body, Sound and Space in Installation Art of the Mid 1990s', *Revue d'Art Canadienne / Canadian Art Journal*, 25/1–2 (1998), 12–30.
10 L. Himid, 'A Brief Introduction of the Magical World of Maud Sulter's Photoworks', in *Maud Sulter: Syrcas* (Wrexham: Wrexham Library and Arts Centre, 1994), p. 34.
11 Quoted in Sulter, 'Clio' *Zabat: Narratives*, 1989, privately printed limited edition, unpaginated.
12 L. Himid, 'Fragments', *Feminist Arts News*, 2/8 (1988), 8.
13 Sulter, *Jeanne Duval*, p. 60, first published in 'Calliope', *Zabat: Narratives*, unpaginated.
14 Interview with S. Choi-Park, p. 53.
15 Nadar, *Charles Baudelaire intime* (Paris: Blaziot, 1911). Denise Murrell's PhD, 'Seeing Laure: The Iconographic Legacy of Race as Modernity in Manet's *Olympia*', Columbia University, New York, is investigating these women's histories as part of her research on Manet's *Olympia* and its inspiration for modernist and postwar black artists. My thanks to Denise for a stimulating conversation.
16 Sulter, *Jeanne Duval*, p. 21.
17 Ibid., p. 24.
18 Ibid., p. 22.
19 *Baudelaire's Mistress Reclining* (1862, Budapest, Szépmüveszeti Museum). J. Adhémar dissents, in 'À propos de *La Maîtresse de Baudelaire* par Manet (1862), un problème', *Gazette des Beaux Arts*, 102 (November 1983), p. 178. T. Dolan, 'Skirting the Issue: Manet's Portrait of Baudelaire's Mistress, Reclining', *Art Bulletin* 79/4 (December 1997), 611–29, gives a careful study of various interpretations of the painting and its sitter. She claims that 'Doubts about the identity of the subject may be justified' though she bases this on her view of 'the complex and strained relationship between the poet and his mistress in the early 1860s' (p. 611). She notes a distance between Duval and Baudelaire after 1861, and that there is no mention of her in his letters after 1864 (p. 613).
20 C. Miller, *Blank Darkness: Africanist Discourse in French* (Chicago: Chicago University Press, 1986), p. 69.

21 M. Bal, 'Three Way Misreading: Review of Gayatri Chakravorty Spivak, *A Critique of Post-Colonial Reason: Toward a History of the Vanishing Present*', *Diacritics*, 30/1 (2000), 2–24; p. 21.
22 G. Pollock, *Differencing the Canon: Feminism and the Writing of Arts Histories* (London: Routledge, 1999), pp. 247–315; (p. 269).
23 G.C. Spivak, *A Critique of Post-Colonial Reason: Toward a History of the Vanishing Present* (Cambridge, MA: Harvard University Press, 1999), pp. 148–56; (p. 148). Further references to this work will be given as page numbers in the text.
24 Ibid.
25 A. Carter, *Black Venus* (London: Vintage, 1985), pp. 1–14. Sulter notes both *Black Venus* and *Alias Olympia* in *Jeanne Duval* (p. 14).
26 R. Munford, 'Representing Charles Baudelaire/Re-presencing Jeanne Duval: Transformations of the Muse', *Forum for Modern Language Studies*, 40/1 (2004), 1–13; p. 6.
27 L. Sage, *Angela Carter* (Plymouth: Northcote House Publishers, 1994), p. 44.
28 E. Lipton, *Alias Olympia: A Woman's Search for Manet's Notorious Model and her Own Desire* (New York: Cornell University Press, 1999). See also M.M. Siebert, *A Biography of Victorine-Louise Meurent and her role in the art of Eduoard Manet* (Ohio State University, PhD Dissertation, 1986). http://etd.ohiolink.edu/view.cgi?acc_num=osu1217266489.
29 Pollock, *Differencing the Canon*, pp. 247–315.
30 J. Derrida, *Speech and Phenomena and Other Essays on Husserl's Theory of Sign*, trans D.B. Allison (Evanston, IL: Northwestern University Press, 1973), p. 129. Derrida's emphases.
31 Sulter, *Jeanne Duval*, p. 24.
32 Ibid., back cover.
33 Ibid., p. 24.
34 I take here the order in ibid. A different sequence is given in *Art History*, 17/4 (December 1994), 513–16, where each is accompanied by a short text: *III* [Pierrot] is first, with the text 'noir noir noir/ Na pas plus noir/ comman ou gate dehor'; followed by *I* [*Olympia*] with the text 'Ti mi mi/ vin condur moi/ a cause dehor y fair noir'; then *IV* [*Atelier*] with the text, 'Tanto, tanto mon mair/ Tanto'; and finally *II*. Accompanied by the words 'Tanto dans soro zanana/ Tano mon mari tanto/ Tanto dans soro jaunana'. These short texts are quotations from Sulter's poem 'East', which opens with the lines 'You sing to me a song/ from East African/ islands' and continues to tell of rape, colonial brutality, and the reparation of love. M. Sulter, *Zabat: Poetics of a Family Tree, Poems, 1986–89* (Hebden Bridge: Urban Fox Press, 1990), p. 47.
35 T.J. Clark, *The Painting of Modern Life: Paris in the Art of Manet and his Followers* (London: Thames & Hudson, 1984).
36 Jennifer deVere Brody, 'Black Cat Fever: Manifestations of Manet's *Olympia*', *Theatre Journal*, 53/1 (March 2001) 95–118; p. 99.
37 R. Schneider, *The Explicit Body in Performance* (London and New York: Routledge, 1997), p. 67.
38 deVere Brody, 'Black Cat Fever', p. 105.
39 Angela Rosenthal, 'Calliopes Reisen: Maud Sulters politishe Collagen', in Annegret

Friedrich et al.,(eds), *Projektionen: Rassismus und Sexismus in der Visuellen Kultur* (Marburg: Jonas Verlag, 1997), pp. 243–61; p. 253. She traces Calliope's journeys from *Zabat* through *Hysteria*, *Jeanne: A Melodrama* and *Plantation*.

40 deVere Brody, 'Black Cat Fever', p. 103. The artist Lorraine O'Grady produced studies for a 16-diptych photo installation 'Flowers of Evil and Good'. She is, she states, 'not so much interested in the literal Jeanne as the figurative one – the hybrid woman caught up in the dilemmas of diaspora'. Her essay, 'Olympia's Maid: Reclaiming Black Female Subjectivity', appears in J. Fruch et al. (eds), *New Feminist Criticism* (New York: Collins, 1994), pp. 152–70. See: www.lorraineogrady.com. H. Mullen, *Trimmings* (New York: Tender Buttons Press, 1991).

41 Mullen, *Trimmings*, p. 15, quoted in de Vere Brody, p. 103.

42 'Calliope', in *Zabat: Narratives*, unpaginated.

43 See Pollock, *Differencing the Canon*, pp. 261–77.

44 Sulter, *Syrcas*, p. 35.

45 Dolan, 'Skirting the Issue', p. 163 credits A. Bowness, 'Courbet and Baudelaire', *Gazette des Beaux Arts*, 90 (1977), 198.

46 Jill Matus, 'Black, Blonde and Hottentot Venus: Context and Critique in Angela Carter's *Black Venus*', in A.M.J. Easton (ed.), *Angela Carter* (Basingstoke: Palgrave Macmillan, 2000), pp. 161–72; p. 167.

47 J. Derrida, *La Dissémination* (Paris: Seuil, 1972), p. 124, translated by B. Johnson in *Dissemination* (Chicago: University of Chicago Press, 1981), p. 193.

48 Derrida, *La dissémination*, p. 126, my translation.

49 Sulter, *Syrcas*, p. 8.

50 This is identified as an acrobatic dancer of *Ikhien-ani-mhim* in Ishan, Benin in Frank Willett, *African Art: An Introduction* (London: Thames & Hudson, 1971), p. 203.

51 M. Lavin, *Cut with the Kitchen Knife: The Weimar Photomontages of Hannah Höch* (London and New Haven, CT: Yale University Press, 1993), listed in the bibliography of Sulter, *Syrcas*, p. 37. For longer considerations of Syrcas, see Rosenthal, 'Calliopes Reizen'; Maria Lind, 'In the Margin of the Margins', *Portfolio* 19 (1994), 42–3; and on Sulter's 'scrap-book style', Jane Richards, 'A Cut Above the Rest', *Independent*, 23 August 1994.

52 Interview with S. Choi-Park, pp. 54–5.

53 Ibid., pp. 57–8.

54 M. Barlow, 'Foreword', *Syrcas*, p. 7.

55 www.vam.ac.uk/vastatic/microsites/photography/story.php?storyid=ph052&row=3. Accessed 9 August 2009. Sulter, 'Blood Money', *Syrcas*.

56 Sulter, 'Blood Money', *Syrcas*.

57 www.vam.ac.uk/vastatic/microsites/photography, accessed 9 August 2009.

58 Georges Didi-Huberman, *Atlas ¿Cómo llevar el mundo a cuestas?* / Atlas: How to Carry the World on One's Back? (Madrid: Museo Nacional Centro de Arte Reina Sofia, 2011). With thanks to Alison Green for this reference.

59 A lengthy description by Wayne Baerwaldt is provided at www.locusplus.org.uk/suteress.html. The artist also titled her operation video *UK Plantation 1* (private collection).

60 E. Said, *Culture and Imperialism* (London: Vintage, 1994), p. 112.
61 P. Gilroy, *There Ain't No Black in the Union Jack: The Cultural Politics of Race and Nation* (London and New York: Routledge, 1987, 2002), and *The Black Atlantic: Modernity and Double Consciousness* (London: Verso, 1993).
62 V.S Kalra et al., *Diaspora and Hybridity* (London: Sage, 2005) p. 40.
63 Himid, 'Fragments', p. 8.
64 J. Beckett, 'History (Maybe)', in *History: The MAG Collection: Image-Based Art in Britain in the Late Twentieth Century* (Hull: Ferens Art Gallery, 1997), pp. 139–41.
65 H. Foster, 'An Archival Impulse', *October*, 110 (Fall 2004), 3–22; p. 4. Further references to this title will take the form of page numbers within the text.
66 J. Derrida, *Spectres of Marx: The State of The Debt, The Work of Mourning, and The New International*, trans. P. Kamuf (London and New York: Routledge, 1994), p. xv. Further references to this title will take the form of page numbers within the text; emphases in original.
67 Although for Stuart Hall ('Black Diaspora Artists in Britain: Three "Moments" in Post-war History', *History Workshop Journal*, 61 (2006), pp. 1–24) self-portraiture is a consistent theme, Sulter's art bears comparison to self-imaging by her contemporaries, including Cindy Sherman.
68 M. Haworth-Booth, 'Maud Sulter: An Interview', *History of Photography*, 16/3 (autumn 1992), 263–6; (pp. 264–5).
69 Ibid., p. 264.
70 C. Owens, 'The Allegorical Impulse: Toward a Theory of Postmodernism', *October* 12 (Spring 1980), 67–86; (pp. 68, 70).
71 G.C. Spivak, *The Post-colonial Critic: Interviews, Strategies, Dialogues* (London and New York: Routledge, 1990), interview 1988, p. 108.
72 Sulter, *Jeanne Duval*, p. 15. *Les Bijoux* were exhibited in *Reading the Image: Poetics of the Black Diaspora* (Halifax, NS: Mount St Vincent Art Gallery, 2007).
73 C. Baudelaire, 'La Chevelure', transcribed and translated in Sulter, *Jeanne Duval*, p. 17.
74 Dolan, 'Skirting the Issue', p. 613. Sulter, *Jeanne Duval*, p. 15.
75 Baudelaire, 'Les Bijoux', transcribed and translated in Sulter, *Jeanne Duval*, pp. 32–3.
76 *Next Level*, no. 12 (November 2007), www.marksealy.com, accessed 6 June 2008.
77 S. Nuttall, 'Introduction: Rethinking Beauty', in *Ugly/Beautiful: Africa and Diaspora Aesthetics* (Durham, NC: Duke University Press, 2006), pp. 8–27.
78 www.scottish.parliament.uk/visitandlearn/24481.aspx.
79 R. Barthes, *La Chambre claire* (Paris: Seuil, 1980), trans., R. Howard as *Camera Lucida* (London: Vintage, 1993), pp. 93, 96.

Alison Lapper Pregnant: embodied geographies, post-imperial identities and public sculpture in London's Trafalgar Square

8

Rosemary Betterton

> Visual space is, *in the first instance*, a set of social relations; it is never innocent, nor does it merely reflect, either directly or through contrived mediations, 'real' social relations located elsewhere.[1]

It seems that most mornings now I wake up to a cacophony of politicians and policemen, commentators and academics, who articulate increasing anxiety about the nature of contemporary 'Britishness'. Migration, citizenship and multiculturalism, crime and security, white working-class youth and 'home-grown' terrorism, the vulnerable environment and the unstable economy, erosion of local place and community, all make up elements of an increasingly confusing and conflicted discourse about what binds the nation together, contributing to a feeling that 'being British' is somehow in crisis.[2] Common British values have become the site for the government's rhetorical attempt to define a shared national belonging in relation to a citizenship policy that increasingly defines 'difference' as a threat.[3] Beneath this surface noise lies the sound of the unequal 'geographies of power' shifting,[4] as old certainties dissolve and feared new consequences emerge in an era of an uncontrolled global capitalism. Unsure about the past and uncertain of the future, a troubled relation to different cultural histories and global identities appear to make the present place and time seem almost untenable. Doreen Massey argues that these experiences of disorientation and uncertainty are linked to the vast reorganizations of capital, the formation of new global space and new technologies of communication that occurred at the end of the twentieth century, which have produced a 'new disturbing placelessness',[5] felt by those for whom identity is no longer confirmed by place.[6] Within this unstable global geography, I ask just whose identities are secured by a sense of 'place' and, in turn, which places help to secure a sense of (national) identity? By examining one contemporary sculpture, *Alison Lapper Pregnant* by Marc Quinn, 2005 (Figure 8.1) in the iconic British location of London's Trafalgar Square, I want to explore whether a specific embodied geography can illuminate questions of national place and identity in contemporary Britain.

I shall argue that Quinn's statue of Alison Lapper marked the entry of an embodied maternal and dis/abled subject into a highly charged domain of military heroism and cultural nationalism, in a way that disturbed its spatial politics.[7] The significance of this sculpture lies both in its symbolic location at the heart of nation, and in its provocation of debates about visibility and public forms of embodiment. Through a close reading of the sculpture I open up questions about the representation of an embodied other – female, pregnant and dis/abled – within a national heritage site previously inhabited in sculptural terms by the bodies of male heroes. What does it mean for a historically excluded body to enter into public space, and what somatic norms can define citizenship in our post-imperial times? I borrow from the work of feminist geographers to argue that a sense of place is always contingent, dynamic and open to contestation by different social groups.[8] Being 'in place' and feeling 'at home' in the world are never unmediated experiences and are differently affected by class, ethnicity, age, sexuality and gender.[9] My interest emerges in relation to the interdisciplinary field that Rosalyn Deutsche calls 'the field of spatial politics',[10] a visual space that she argues is characterized by social conflict and structural exclusions that condition urban existence.[11] Deutsche suggests that we need to reconfigure the field of spatial politics to account for different sets of relations between situated subjects and objects in space within a 'psychic economy' of vision.[12] The commissioning of *Alison Lapper Pregnant* marked a deliberate intervention into a site of spatial politics, Trafalgar Square, with, I suggest, some unintended effects in its psychic economy. Deutsche's formulation is particularly helpful in thinking through the embodied geographies of public sculpture in ways that can account for both an imaginary social cohesion *and* the exclusion of particular bodies from national space. How does resistance to new forms of embodiment reveal the desire to fix the meanings of place within familiar aesthetic and cultural certainties? And, what can such 'out of place' bodies tell us about national cultural identity?

Trafalgar Square: 'An iconic site of immense symbolic significance'

> All attempts to institute horizons, to establish boundaries and, to secure the identity of places, can in this sense therefore be seen to be *attempts to stabilize the meaning of particular envelopes of space-time.*[13]

Doreen Massey argues that attempts to fix the identity of a particular place are always challenged by changes in social power. She identifies this as 'the site of social contest, battles over the power to label space-time, to impose the meaning to be attributed to a space, for however long or short a space of time'.[14] She continues that claims to the particular heritage of a site 'seek the identity of a place by laying claim to some particular moment in time-space when the definition of the area and the social relations dominant within it were to the advantage of that particular claimant group'.[15] As Massey suggests, readings of space and place are always constructed in relation to an elsewhere, which she calls 'the presence of the "outside within"'.[16] In the case of Trafalgar Square this was the former empire and its colonies, which shaped its monuments and architecture. As Deborah Cherry has shown, both its physical boundaries and symbolic identity were 'unsettled and contingent',[17] the products of discontinuous histories of planning and rebuilding until the mid-nineteenth century when it was stabilized as the national site of Nelson's memorial at the height of British imperial power.[18] The dispute over the form and location of *Alison Lapper Pregnant* thus hinged in different ways on its performance as a public sculpture in 'an iconic site of immense symbolic significance'.[19]

Indeed, 2005 was the bicentennial year of Nelson's death at the Battle of Trafalgar in 1805, which was marked by naval celebrations and renewed attention to questions of how Britishness might be defined. As Cherry explains, there had been a series of debates in the nineteenth century over the design and remodelling of Trafalgar Square, beginning with John Nash's grand plan in 1814 to transform the whole area from Regent Street to Pall Mall. The Square was rebuilt between 1830 and 1845 and the National Gallery was completed in 1838 in order to house the national collection of art; at this time the Square was being imagined as a forum dedicated to the arts and the sciences. St Martin in the Fields marked yet another aspect of the square's role as a haven for the homeless from the nineteenth century onwards.[20] It only became the focus for naval commemoration and military display with the erection of Nelson's Column, which was completed in 1868. From that date until 1939, the Square was a monument to British colonial ambition with the erection of memorial statues on two other plinths to 'soldier heroes' of the British Empire,[21] and the building of Canada House (1925–31) and South Africa House (1931–33).[22] Trafalgar Square is therefore richly invested with symbolic meaning as the centre of national memorial and colonial display: 'a site that spatializes imperial history and the global theatres of its activity', but also 'of contested histories and memories'.[23] The installation of *Alison Lapper Pregnant* under the aegis of a socialist mayor and a liberal arts establishment contributed to the process of contesting Trafalgar Square's imperial identity, part of Ken Livingstone's explicit intention of re-mobilizing the political and democratic spaces of London.[24]

However, Trafalgar Square was already the site of continuous tensions between imperial narratives and the politics of dissent to which the Fourth Plinth debate adds a further cultural dimension. The Square became the focal space for free speech and national protest in the nineteenth and early twentieth centuries, including the mass demonstrations by trades union, socialist and suffrage movements. In more recent times, this history has included marches against unemployment and the banning of Irish Republican demonstrations

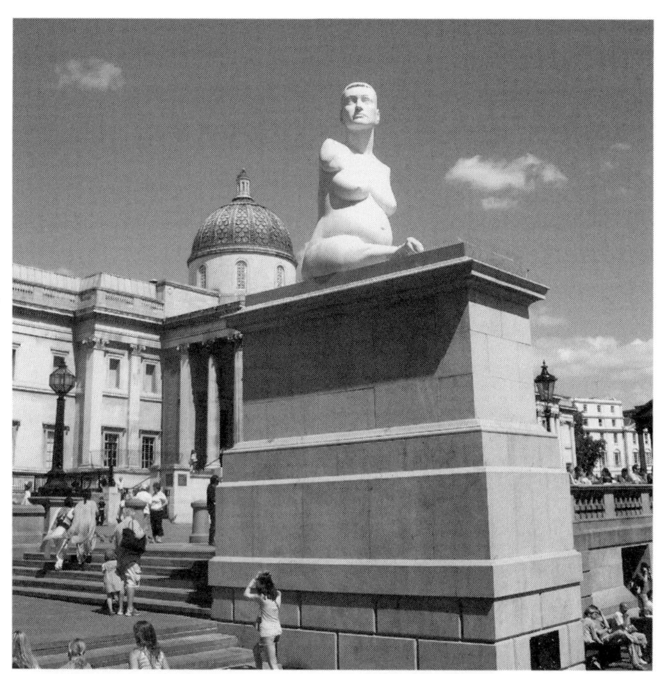

8.1 Marc Quinn, *Alison Lapper Pregnant* (2005), marble, Trafalgar Square, London.

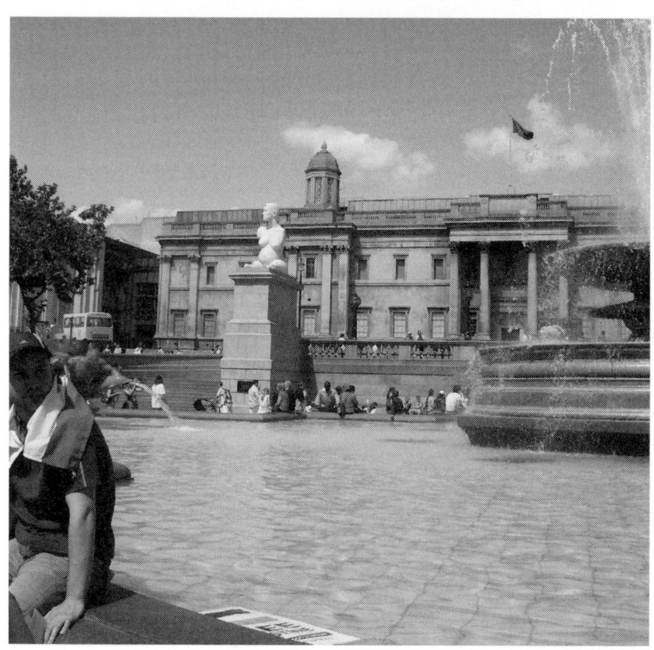

8.2 *View of Trafalgar Square with Alison Lapper Pregnant* (2006).

in the 1980s, the Poll Tax 'riots', and anti-apartheid and pro-Nelson Mandela demonstrations in the 1990s, and protests against the war in Iraq in 2003. On the hot July day in 2006 when I went to photograph the Lapper statue, I found myself part of a demonstration against the Israeli invasion of Lebanon. The Square was politically charged with the presence of Lebanese and English, Palestinians and Orthodox Jews (amongst others) as the multi-inhabitants of a shared space. In my photograph, a man sits on the edge of a fountain wearing a Lebanese flag draped around his neck while a placard floats in the water and, behind the statue of Alison Lapper, the Union Jack floats over the National Gallery to produce a contradictory space of signification (Figure 8.2). In addition to being the focus for political dissent, the Square's other role as London's landmark tourist location and the scene of national celebrations also identifies it with multifarious experiences of leisure, pleasure and enjoyment. Within this complicated context, the reception of the Lapper sculpture was never going to be simple. It stands in relation to what Cherry identifies as a tripartite relationship between 'monuments, urban space and the subject … Memorials are thus not only about the subject of their representation, the figure depicted, but also about the subjects who encounter them in the everyday life of the city.'[25] If Alison Lapper is the subject of the representation, what is the nature of the encounter with various other 'subjects' in the Square?

Alison Lapper Pregnant: 'Sculpture's unveiling is pregnant with meaning', *The Guardian*, 16 June 2005[26]

On 15 September 2005, Marc Quinn's marble sculpture *Alison Lapper Pregnant* was unveiled on the Fourth Plinth to the left of the National Gallery façade in Trafalgar Square to mixed acclaim and opposition. On his unveiling of the sculpture, Mayor of London, Ken Livingstone, commented that 'Alison's life is a struggle over much greater difficulties than the men who are celebrated here.'[27] It was acclaimed by its supporters, but the response from the tabloid press was more ambivalent: the headline in the influential *London Evening Standard* on the announcement of the commission read, 'So, Is This Really What We Want on Trafalgar Square's Empty Plinth?'[28]

The unveiling of the statue had generated much interest and was trailed in national news media, and in television documentaries about the making of the sculpture and about Lapper herself. Alison Lapper has a medical condition called phocomelia, which means that she was born without arms and with shortened legs. Her exceptional life story had already attracted a great deal of media attention since 2000 and she appeared with her infant son in the prestigious BBC documentary series *A Child of Our Time* and in Channel 5's *Extraordinary People* series, as well as in lifestyle features in the press. Her autobiography *Alison Lapper: My Life in My Hands* was launched in 2005 to coincide with the installation of Quinn's sculpture. Lapper's media presence therefore derived primarily from her profile as a highly articulate working-class mother with severe limb impairments, rather than from her own professional practice as an artist.[29] But, by asserting her presence as a maternal body within the media *and* as an artist working in photography and digital imaging, Lapper challenges the boundaries that confine physically impaired maternal bodies to invisibility. She insists on her physical presence in order to question aesthetic perceptions of what constitutes beauty in the human body, as well as

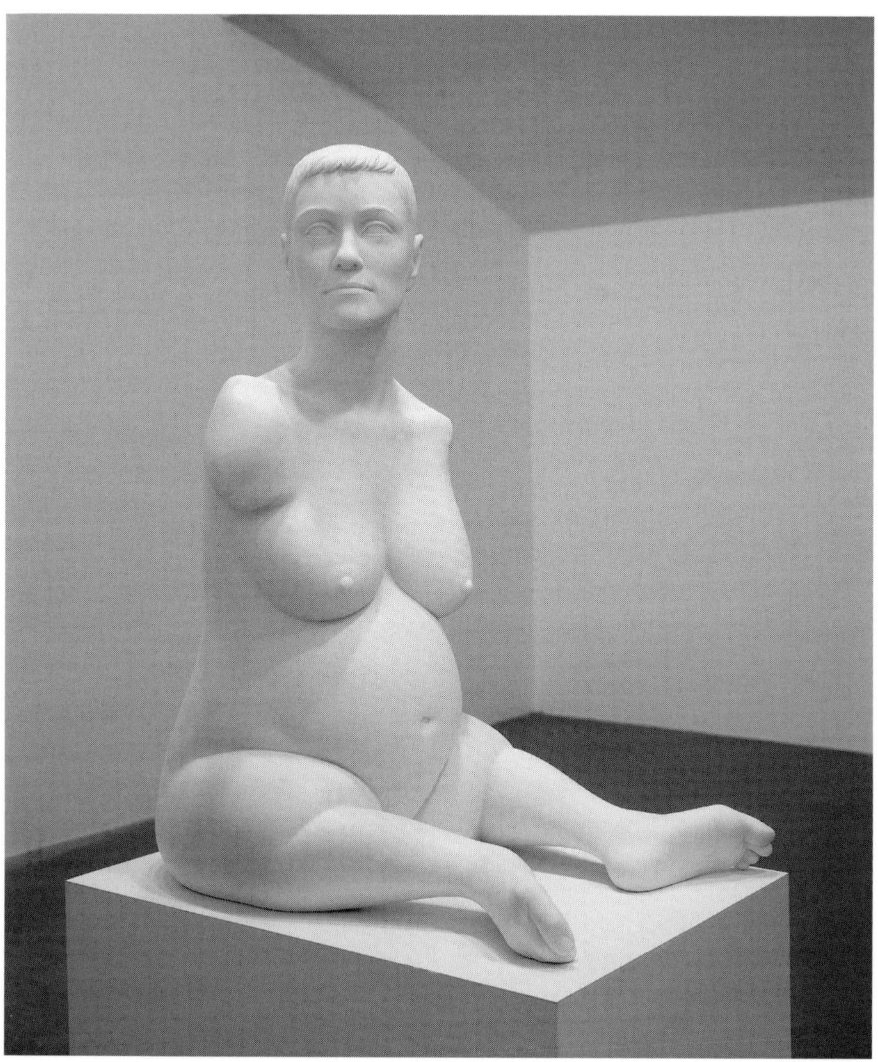

8.3 Marc Quinn, *Alison Lapper (8 Months)* (2000), marble and plinth.

those who would deny her role as a mother, thus raising the issue of the rights of women with disabilities to bear children.[30]

Lapper's portrait by Marc Quinn began as a smaller marble sculpture entitled *Alison Lapper (8 Months)*, made in 2000 as one of a series of sculptural portraits of people with limb impairments, mainly artists, writers and musicians (Figure 8.3).[31] As the original title suggests, it represents Lapper not only as pregnant, but visibly in the last stage of pregnancy. The female body frequently appears in public sculpture in the guise of nymph or muse, but an individual portrait of a naked woman, emphatically pregnant and dis/abled, is literally without precedent. Quinn drew on a model of beauty defined in Greek classical sculpture and, by choosing to portray Alison Lapper he challenged aesthetic preconceptions that connect notions of the ideal with a certain bodily norm. He invites us to consider whether a physically fragmented body that is readily accepted in the Venus de Milo can be recognized in a portrait of a living woman with no arms, thus 'using the weight of tradition to undermine itself'.[32] His stated intention in choosing white marble as the medium for the work was to find a means of representation that would confound the viewers' expectations. Quinn's original sculpture was thus intended to question the nature of public responses to the sight of disability and pregnancy through reference to academic sculptural traditions. Lapper collaborated with Quinn as his model and saw the sculpture as a significant statement on her own behalf. Indeed, she used her visibility in Quinn's portrait to establish her own career as a professional artist: 'The sculpture provided a platform for my work. But hopefully it is being exhibited on its own merits because it has taken a long time to achieve some acceptance that images of a naked disabled woman can be considered as art.'[33]

The Fourth Plinth debate: 'A new model of female heroism'

The new version of Quinn's portrait, re-titled *Alison Lapper Pregnant* and enlarged to 3.55 metres high, was installed in 2005 as part of a continuing debate about what befits a monument for London's most famous public square. The question of how to fill the empty Fourth Plinth in Trafalgar Square was the subject of ongoing dispute about the appropriateness of contemporary art as a form of national monument.[34] In 1998 the Royal Society of Arts had commissioned three contemporary artists to produce temporary sculptures for the empty plinth which had occupied it in successive years: Marc Wallinger's naked male statue *Ecce Homo* was installed in 1999; Bill Woodrow's figurative *Regardless of History* in 2000, and Rachel Whiteread's abstract monument, *Plinth*, in 2001. In 1999 the Greater London Authority took over responsibility for the commission and it was under the influence of the newly created office of Mayor of London that Quinn's statue was commissioned. The Fourth

Plinth Commissioning Group was led by Sandy Nairne, Director of the nearby National Portrait Gallery, who recommended the installation of Quinn's sculpture to the Greater London Authority in 2004:

> The debate about public art is one of the most valuable aspects of this project. While no single commission – and no single use for the plinth – will please everyone, contemporary work that gets people engaged with this vital public space is extremely valuable.[35]

Initial reactions to the statue focused on the legitimacy of Lapper's figure as a representative of nationhood in relation to the existing sculptural monuments in Trafalgar Square. How could a sculpted portrait of a pregnant woman with limb impairments occupy a public site encoded as heroic and masculine, and signified as such by Nelson's Column? One trope that recurred throughout the controversy was the gender reversal enacted by Quinn's statue and Lapper's status as a 'female hero'. This emphasis was made by Charles Saumarez Smith, Director of the National Gallery, in his suggestion that 'Alison Lapper is much more beautiful than Nelson. The colour of the stone is wonderful and the proportions are perfect.'[36] This view was summed up by Greg Hilty, Director of Visual Arts and Literature at Arts Council England, who claimed that the 'work considers questions of idealism, heroism, femininity, prejudice and identity'.[37] Lapper's own comment on the statue reflected on these themes: 'I regard it as a modern tribute to femininity, disability and motherhood. It is so rare to see disability in everyday life – let alone naked, pregnant and proud.'[38] All of these comments echoed those of the sculptor himself, who made the following statement when the sculpture was unveiled:

> At first sight it would seem that there are few if any public sculptures of people with disabilities. However, a closer look reveals that Trafalgar Square is one of the few public spaces where one exists: Nelson on top of his column has lost an arm. I think that Alison's portrait reactivates this dormant aspect of Trafalgar Square. Most public sculpture, especially in the Trafalgar Square and Whitehall areas is triumphant male statuary. Nelson's Column is the epitome of a phallic male monument, and I felt that the square needed some femininity, linking with Boudicca near the Houses of Parliament. Alison's statue could represent a new model of female heroism.[39]

Quinn draws attention to Nelson's own disability as a 'dormant aspect' of the Square – indeed, it is well nigh invisible at the top of the 'phallic male monument' – and he connects Lapper to the 'feminine' presence of Boudicca nearby in Parliament Square. This comparison is highly charged, since Boudicca was the first national heroine and legendary Queen of the Iceni who led a rebellion against the Roman occupation of Britain. Quinn thus presented the statues of Lapper and Boudicca as similarly gendered, albeit differently embodied, ideals of an imaginary feminine national identity. His comment taps into the controversy over the notable absence of any monuments to recent historical women in Trafalgar Square, for example, wartime heroines or suffragettes, but Quinn elides this debate in a reference to a semi-mythical gendered national past.[40]

To sum up this debate, *Alison Lapper Pregnant* had the endorsement of the political authority for London and of the English arts establishment as a celebration of female heroism and disability and as a valuable public sculpture. At the same time, the public visibility of a sculpture of a woman's heavily pregnant and dis/abled body became an issue for the press and wider public.[41] Quinn's statement reveals what was at stake: whose bodies are deemed appropriate to represent the nation and what forms should these bodies take? I want to examine the terms of this debate more closely for what it reveals about the encoding of white imperial masculinity and the counter representation of pregnancy and disability in a national site.

'Ghosts of modernity': white space and somatic norms[42]

In *Space Invaders: Race, Gender and Bodies Out of Place*, Nirmal Puwar discusses the idea of subjects 'out of place' in relation to what she terms an 'invisible, unmarked and undeclared somatic norm'.[43] Citing an earlier debate over the positioning of a statue of Nelson Mandela in Trafalgar Square, she argues that '[t]he moment when the historically excluded is included is incredibly revealing … this is a presence that prods us to look again at … the production of national space'.[44] Inviting us to consider somatic norms in racialized as well as in gendered contexts, Puwar suggests that 'the coupling of particular bodies with specific spaces is at the heart of this conflict, even though the issues are declared to be of a purely aesthetic nature'.[45] The Mandela statue, also championed by Ken Livingstone, was intended to be situated on the north side of Trafalgar Square.[46] And, like the debate over Quinn's sculpture, disputes about the positioning and scale of the Mandela statue were primarily articulated in aesthetic terms: the Public Arts Committee of Westminster City Council rejected the sculpture on the grounds that it found 'the size and shape of the hands disagreeable'.[47] After its rejection from Trafalgar Square, Ian Walters' statue was finally unveiled by Nelson Mandela himself in October 2007 in a different site in Parliament Square, thus situated symbolically in the context of the democratic, rather than the imperial state.

Puwar suggests that there is 'a notable metonymic shift in the increased presence of women and racialised minorities into spaces in the public realm which have been predominantly occupied by white men'.[48] In this process, she argues, 'women and non-whites are instead highly visible as deviations from the norm and invisible as the norm'.[49] Just as the black figure of Mandela challenged the white space and body of the nation, *Alison Lapper Pregnant* makes visible the unmarked somatic norm that maintains English national identity as already classed and gendered.[50] In the case of Trafalgar Square, the deviation is from the previously unmarked norm of white masculinity of the imperial figures that populate it. The statues erected on two other plinths commemorate military figures: General Charles Napier (1856), who had commanded the British army in India, and Major General Sir Henry Havelock (1861), who was responsible for savage reprisals after the Indian Mutiny in 1857. Both men thus played a key role in establishing British imperial power at a crucial historical moment in the mid-nineteenth century. The visible presence of Lapper's maternal-feminine body throws these bronze sculptures of masculine military 'heroes' into relief, causing us to reflect again on their presence.[51] They become visible anew as representatives of a colonial past unified through visual, cultural and political references to the virtues of empire. As Cherry notes, the visual language of Neo-Classicism and the Roman Empire is not only articulated in the pose and drapery of the statues, it is embedded within the sculptural and architectural decoration of the Square as a whole. I shall suggest that these symbolic and aesthetic references are extended, as well as contested, in Quinn's depiction of Lapper.

The cult of the soldier hero focuses on the exceptional individual whose actions exceed the norm and who thus becomes the agent of history. As we have seen, Quinn's description of Alison Lapper as 'a new model of female heroism' echoes this familiar trope of exception and destiny. Likewise, his use of white marble in the style of classical sculpture takes on new meaning when transferred to the highly charged context of Trafalgar Square. The plinths on which all three statues stand are simple monoliths in plain granite and Quinn reconfigures the relation between the plinth and his sculpture by massively enlarging the latter's scale, although the figure conforms to academic sculptural convention in pose and style.[52] Sculptural practices have frequently offered means of thinking through relations and modes of embodiment and, indeed, offer a material site for reformulation and resistance to traditional values. The classical tradition of sculpture offered powerful models for the public, heroic and ideal masculine body, and in the modern period a fascination with the private, erotic and fragmented female body emerged. Quinn's work stands in dialogue with these two traditions: the modelling of Lapper's head and torso including the treatment of her eyes and hair follow a classical type, while the morphology of her body is distinctly individual. Traditionally only certain types of body were accorded the privilege of representation in public sculpture and the form of the monumental nude was not open to all: it is the white and able-bodied subject which constitutes the sculptural ideal. In *Vital Signs: Feminist Reconfigurations of the Bio/logical Body*, Margrit Shildrick and Janet Price argue that: 'Insofar as it is taken as the grounding of the autonomous subject in modernity, the body must appear invulnerable, predictable and consistent in form and function, above all free from the possibility of disruption.'[53] The particularity of the Lapper's dis/abled body and its 'morphological irregularity' challenges this conception of a unitary body and self. If the male statues that populate Trafalgar Square represent the emergent nineteenth-century subject of the British Empire with their emphasis on contours, limits and a manly confinement of interiority, then the visible contrast of *Alison Lapper Pregnant* simultaneously makes reference to and disrupts that unmarked ideal.[54] As a visibly dis/abled body given monumental form, *Alison Lapper Pregnant* disrupts the metaphorical relationship that connects the rational, coherent self to a unified body shape and, furthermore, does so as a visibly pregnant female subject.

If disability is rarely represented in monumental sculpture, then it is also unusual for pregnant bodies, unless they are young, white, able-bodied and heterosexual, to achieve public visibility. The display of pregnancy in celebrity culture has now become an eroticized norm following the notorious photograph of Demi Moore by Annie Leibovitz on the cover of *Vanity Fair*, but the appearance of a naked, dis/abled woman who is heavily pregnant is clearly very different. While it is easy to forget just how transgressive Moore's image was and the hostility that it met in 1991, it is still the case that only limited types of maternal body are accorded the privilege of representation in public space and, in general, pregnant bodies that do not conform to the normative ideal are rendered invisible.[55] The spatial taxonomy of the pregnant body is one of concealment and revelation; it is private and yet subject to constant public scrutiny. The pregnant woman occupies a space of multiple attachments and investments both in relation to her unborn child and to a wider community of partner, family, friends and other citizens. Pregnancy seems to belong naturally to the 'intimate relations of private personhood',[56] and yet it is always publicly mediated and subject to intense regulation. This scrutiny defines a pregnant woman either as normative, heterosexual, able-bodied and in a stable relationship or, as in the case of Alison Lapper – a single working-class mother with disabilities – as deviating from the norm.[57] The entry of Lapper's unique pregnant body into a privileged public site in 2005 therefore invites the question: why now and why here? What does this body 'out of place' tell us about 'the constellation of agency, identity and embodiment'[58] in relation to national citizenship?

Affective icons: Britishness and 'the intimate public sphere'

In her analysis of citizenship at the end of the twentieth century, Lauren Berlant develops the concept of 'the intimate public sphere'[59] to describe how privatized and familial concerns have come to dominate public political life in the

United States. I shall suggest that the concept of public intimacy can be also traced within debates about national identity in Britain, and see whether this provides a way of further thinking through the complex discursive location of *Alison Lapper Pregnant*. The term 'intimate public' neatly captures the shift in Lapper's own status from a private subject to a public citizen between 2000 and 2005 in the interval between the two versions of her sculpted portrait. It also serves as a metaphor to map the sculpture's physical relocation from the relative intimacy of a gallery space to its new visibility as a public monument in Trafalgar Square. This is not an intimate or local space, nor is it a space of the everyday that Massey suggests has been coded as feminine and maternal.[60] Public civic space has historically been the domain of male achievement and agency, and the transposition of the statue on an enlarged scale to a public site seems to expose the figure's vulnerability to the gaze. My contention is that the contingency of its new emplacement simultaneously renders the statue as potentially disruptive of gendered spatial politics *and* vulnerable to a hostile gaze. As I have already suggested, not all responses to the sculpture were positive, and this is exemplified in the comments on Quinn's statue by the art critic Robert Simon, editor of the *British Art Journal*:

> I think it is horrible. Not because of the subject matter I hasten to add … I think she is very brave, very wonderful, but it is just a rather repellent artefact – very shiny, slimy surface, machine-made, much too big.[61]

Simon's embarrassment is palpable, caught between the desire not to be seen to attack Lapper herself – the patronizing, 'she is very brave, very wonderful' – and his evident horror at the 'very shiny, slimy surface'. Simon's critical confusion seems to stem from a displacement of the political, 'the subject matter', onto the aesthetic, 'a rather repellent artefact', thereby thinly masking his antipathy to the sight of the visibly pregnant body of a dis/abled woman. He articulates the disturbance that Deutsche suggests is characteristic of 'a masculine being … who actually occupies a position of threatened wholeness in a relation of difference'.[62] Deutsche defines the position of the voyeur in relation to urban visual space as: 'Distancing, mastering, objectifying – the voyeuristic look exercises control through a visualization that merges with a victimization of the object.'[63] Without ascribing Simon's comments too much critical weight, they can be seen as indicative precisely of a failure to maintain sufficient distance between himself and his object of vision – as well as of Alison Lapper's refusal to become a victim. *Alison Lapper Pregnant* comes too close; it is 'much too big' and ceases to be mastered by his voyeuristic gaze.

My own initial impression on seeing *Alison Lapper Pregnant* a few weeks after its unveiling was indeed that the huge scale and whiteness of the statue was shocking. This context is very different from that in which I first saw Quinn's *Alison Lapper (8 Months)* in the Tate Gallery Liverpool in 2002.[64] In contrast to that solitary, silent and relatively private viewing, in the setting of the Square I viewed the statue against passing crowds, London buses and the National Gallery: a hybrid site of the mixing of English and foreign bodies, of people and pigeons. *Too* big and *too* white, it seemed to be incongruous within the visual space of the Square. While traditionally public sculpture mediates between the scale of surrounding buildings and that of the human body, this statue stands out; it is literally larger than life. So, what do I make of my response to its size and excessive whiteness? I can rationalize my response in aesthetic terms: the over-lifesize figure is out of scale with the other statues and humans in the Square; the gleaming white of the marble stands out against the dull grey of weathered stone and the London sky. But I also recognize that my discomfort, like Robert Simon's, stems from an affective response rather than an aesthetic judgement. My reaction feels more akin to embarrassment, a sense of (something) being exposed, or put in Lauren Berlant's terms, of the intimate being made public. Within this psychic economy, the sudden intimacy with the representation of a larger than life white, naked, pregnant and physically impaired body produces a discomfort in my encounter that I find hard to explain. On the one hand, its spectacular performance of whiteness in the spatial politics of the Square means that the sculpture does not merge decorously with the existing statuary and thus helps to contest the latter's claim to authority. On the other, the statue reminds me of Angela Rosenthal's account of white female skin as a sign of feminine purity within a racial visual discourse in neoclassical art:

> [A]nxieties about embodiment … led to particular attention being paid to the white female body as a marker of ideal selfhood and nationhood. The body in representation was seen less as a safe harbour for identity than as a cultural battleground of diverse competing claims to gendered, nationalized and racialized selfhood.[65]

Quinn's choice of opaque Macedonian marble, usually associated with memorial art, has an opposite visual effect from the translucent blushed skin of the paint surfaces that Rosenthal brilliantly describes in late eighteenth-century British portraiture. Does *Alison Lapper Pregnant* bear a similarly explicit value in the context of current anxieties about a gendered and racialized British identity? Against a backdrop of Trafalgar Square, does this image of an emphatically white, albeit physically different, female body denote any equal shift in public feeling?

In her mapping of public intimacy in the USA, Berlant claims that, 'the political public sphere has become the intimate public sphere' in a way that redefines citizenship and 'locates the nation's virtue and value in its intimate zones'.[66] She argues that, in reaction to the citizenship claims of different racial, sexual and economic minorities, a new 'public rhetoric of citizen trauma' has emerged, through which the image of the nation has been re-shaped.[67]

According to Berlant, the fetus has become the exemplary citizen of the United States: 'a national stereotype and … a vehicle for the production of national culture'.[68] In the discourse of fetal rights, it both exemplifies 'the subject position of the national victim' and, at the same time, 'produces the anti-madonna, the mother who poisons or aborts her child, as newly traumatized national icon'. Berlant suggests that in order to understand this fracturing of the pregnant woman and fetus, we need to think further about 'how the national norms of corporeality work, and about the nation-making function of the minority stereotype'.[69] While I argue that Alison Lapper's active agency does not conform to an icon of the 'anti-madonna', the issue of severe disability and abortion has similarly produced a conflicted discourse around the rights of the fetus and child versus those of the mother, and which has complicated responses to *Alison Lapper Pregnant*.[70] However, Berlant's words suggest to me a link with another 'traumatized national icon' who, as a mother, figured significantly in the emergence of a renewed sentimental public culture in Britain, Diana Princess of Wales.

Media and political discourses in Britain became similarly saturated with public feeling in a shift that has been identified with the 1997 election of a New Labour government under Prime Minister Tony Blair, followed swiftly by the mass-mediated narrative of the death of Diana Princess of Wales, which demonstrated 'a very un-British affectivity'.[71] The political commentator Andrew Marr suggested that the 'Diana moment' provoked 'an emotional revolution',[72] which brought about a revived culture of public sentiment.[73] This popular emotionalism became the hallmark of New Labour under Tony Blair and was exploited in his famous speech at Diana's funeral in which he suggested 'She *was* the people's Princess', and 'Diana taught us a new way to be British'.[74] In 'Princess Diana: A Sign of the Times', Rosalind Brunt argues that the death of Diana 'marked the entry of icon into the vernacular',[75] suggesting that through this process her image became an 'indexical-democratic' sign that also paradoxically incorporated postmodern spirituality. The subsequent outbreak of public mourning in the form of massed flower tributes and personal memorials focused on national sites, particularly Parliament Square and Kensington Gardens in London, demonstrating a performative grief that spatialized emotion within a different affective geography from that usually associated with public political culture. Linda Grant further suggests that the 'illusion of Diana as a transracial, transcultural icon', fostered by her embrace of Dodi Fayed, was 'a symptom of anxieties produced at the interstices of nation, race and culture in the global economy'.[76] British identity thus simultaneously embraced public trauma and mapped the politics of intimacy within its 'intimate core of national culture'.[77] I suggest that the monument to Lapper as a heroic, dis/abled mother, may be read, like the image of Diana, as an 'indexical-democratic' sign, but in a form that Berlant argues now permeates public life in the USA. She suggests that marginality has become the basis for new national stereotypes that function by virtue of their exception from the hegemonic public culture:

> [T]hese 'positive' icons of national minority represent both the minimum and the maximum of what the dominating cultures will sanction for circulation, exchange and consumption ... As iconic minority subjects ... they represent heroic autonomy from their very identity.[78]

Berlant's model of the permitted tolerance of minorities within national life resonates with contemporary debates in Britain about the place of minority ethnic, sexual and disability cultures.[79] If we are looking for a public image of the national body in relation to new affectivities of Britishness, the statue of *Alison Lapper Pregnant* is not so much 'a new model of female heroism', as Marc Quinn suggested, but a 'minority exception' that represents 'heroic autonomy'. In this narrative, a doomed princess and a dis/abled mother could both become affirming icons within a national sentimental culture.

Re-imagining embodied geographies

I have argued that Lapper's limbs and pregnancy threaten the masculine and imperial domain of the nation and, simultaneously, reveal its continuing symbolic norms. The entry of a dis/abled and pregnant female body into the privileged space of Trafalgar Square raises aesthetic and political questions about which bodies are deemed appropriate to be represented in national sites and what forms these should take. I have explored how certain somatic figures come to embody the nation in our post-imperial times, both in contemporary cultural discourses and in material sites of visual and political significance. And, if 'visual space is, *in the first instance*, a set of social relations', Trafalgar Square is a representation of space that is a palimpsest of gendered and racial politics. The entry of *Alison Lapper Pregnant* reveals how this embodied geography can be symbolically and materially inhabited by different gendered and raced bodies in ways that reconfigure its spatial politics. As Irit Rogoff puts it, certain works of public art 'agitate public space and undo its certainties'.[80] Quinn's sculpture intervenes within the social and psychic relations through which embodied subjects are situated and situate themselves in visual space. It provokes anxieties about a woman's pregnant and dis/abled embodiment in public and the disavowed difference that her visible agency provokes. In contrast to the 'liberal' arts establishment, and in opposition to the rhetoric of 'common British values', I suggest that *Alison Lapper Pregnant* acts as a lightning rod for competing claims by different national citizens to gendered, racialized and dis/abled selfhood.

Acknowledgements

My thanks to Gail Lewis, whose comments on an early version of this chapter made me think much more carefully about 'whiteness', to Imogen Tyler, Josie Dolan, Dot Rowe and Gill Perry, who invited me to give papers on it, and to all those who gave me feedback.

Notes

1 Rosalyn Deutsche, *Evictions: Art and Spatial Politics* (Cambridge, MA: The MIT Press, 1998), p. 197.

2 The phrase 'broken Britain' was coined by Conservative Prime Minister David Cameron, and has been echoed in the writing of a number of formerly radical commentators who now attack the liberal left and multiculturalism, for example, Melanie Phillips *Londonistan* (New York: Encounter Books, 2006) and Nick Cohen, *What's Left?: How Liberals Lost Their Way* (London: Fourth Estate, 2007). As David Edgar noted, critics used an attack on multiculturalism to mask a reassertion of hierarchic and traditionalist values ('With Friends Like These…', *The Guardian*, 19 April 2008).

3 Anne-Marie Fortier (*Multicultural Horizons: Diversity and the Limits of the Civil Nation* [London and New York: Routledge, 2008[) argues that a new imaginary landscape of multiculturalism has emerged that is increasingly defined by promoting community cohesion rather than increasing diversity. She cites the government document *Building on Progress, Volume 4: Security, Crime and Justice* (2007), which states that 'British common values must be promoted to those who wish to live in Britain permanently', with the implicit threat of expulsion if they do not conform. A debate about contemporary Britishness was also provoked by the fortieth anniversary of Enoch Powell's infamous 'rivers of blood' speech in 2008. Recent artworks that question assumptions about a coherent British identity include Christine Borland, *English Family China* (1998), Lubaina Himid, *Swallow Hard: The Lancaster Dinner Service* (2007), and Faisal Abdu'Alla, *The Browning of Britannia* (2007).

4 Doreen Massey, *Space, Place and Gender* (Minneapolis, MN: University of Minnesota Press, 1994), p. 160.

5 Ibid. p. 164.

6 Massey cites David Harvey, Fredric Jameson, Anthony Giddens and Jean Baudrillard as critical theorists who cite 'the condition of postmodernity' as a source of cultural and political pessimism, which she suggests reflects the experience of a cultural elite that feels itself to be displaced: she asks 'is this a predominantly white/First World take on things?' (ibid. p. 165).

7 I follow Janet Price and Margrit Shildrick (eds), *Vital Signs: Feminist Reconfigurations of the Bio/logical Body* (Edinburgh: Edinburgh University Press, 1998) in their use of 'dis/abled' to signal the false binary that demarcates physical and mental abilities. I use the term 'post-imperial' rather than 'postcolonial' both to signify the specificity of the sculpture's location in bringing the empire 'home' and to distinguish my approach from postcolonial writing that highlights borders, hybridity and migration (Homi K. Bhabha, *The Location of Culture* [London and New York:

Routledge, 1994]; Gayatri Chakravorty Spivak, *In Other Worlds: Essays in Cultural Politics* [London and New York: Routledge, 1988]).

8 From the extensive body of work by feminist geographers on the gendering of space and place, I have consulted Gillian Rose, *Feminism and Geography: The Limits of Geographical Knowledge* (Oxford: Polity Press, 1993); Massey, *Space, Place and Gender*; Nina Laurie, *Geographies of New Femininities* (New York: Longman, 1999); and Lorraine Dowler et al. (eds), *Gender and Landscape: Renegotiating Morality and Space* (London and New York: Routledge, 2005). As Laurie put it: '"Place" not only shapes "gender", femininities in turn are part of what shapes those places' (p. 12).

9 Massey notes that for many peoples colonization over centuries has been accompanied by the loss of place and identity and the sense of 'home' being under threat of invasion (Massey, *Space, Place and Gender*, p. 165). She cites bell hooks' critique of 'home' (*Ain't I a Woman: Black Women and Feminism* [Cambridge, MA: South End Press, 1992]) and Toni Morrison's *Beloved* (New York: Alfred Knopf, 1987), both of which call into question the correlation between place, home and identity.

10 Deutsche, *Evictions*, p. 207.

11 In her essays 'Men in Space' and 'Boys Town', Deutsche makes an extended critique of Harvey's *The Condition of Postmodernity* (1989) on epistemological and political grounds. She argues that, by excluding feminist theories of representation and sexual difference, Marxist critics of postmodernism can only offer 'totalising visions of society' (Deutsche, *Evictions*, p. 205) based on a historical materialism that relegates 'other subjectivities to positions of subordination or invisibility' (p. 198).

12 Ibid., p. 212.

13 Doreen Massey, *For Space* (London: Sage, 2004), p. 5.

14 Massey, *Space, Place and Gender*, p. 5.

15 Ibid. p. 169.

16 Ibid.

17 Deborah Cherry, 'Statues in the Square: Haunting at the Heart of Empire', *Art History* 29/4 (September 2006), pp. 660–97; p. 665.

18 See ibid. for a detailed account of the re-shaping of Trafalgar Square and its changing symbolism. The National Gallery was sited on the north side with the Royal College of Physicians (1823–25) on the west side of the Square. Doreen Massey quotes Edward Said on national identity as 'an invented object, with a history of struggle and conquest behind it that it is sometimes important to represent' (Massey, *Space, Place and Gender*, p. 6).

19 Cherry, 'Statues in the Square', p. 662.

20 Street people were shown in the context of Trafalgar Square in *The Illustrated London News* and in paintings in the nineteenth century. I am grateful to Anna Greutzner-Robins for pointing this out to me.

21 Dawson, 1994

22 Cherry notes that in addition to these 'white settler territories', other developments in nearby Whitehall including George Gilbert Scott's Foreign, Colonial, India and Home Offices (1868–73), contributed to the 'spatialization of empire' in the environs of the Square (Cherry, 'Statues in the Square', p. 67). Another addition since its independence is the Ugandan Embassy.

23 Ibid. p. 664.

24 Ken Livingstone's project as Mayor of London was to transform the symbolic space of Trafalgar Square through public events, animation and sculpture just as he had earlier done in the 1980s on London's South Bank as Leader of the Greater London Council.

25 Cherry, 'Statues in the Square', p. 684.

26 www.guardian.co.uk/uk_news/story/0,,1571296,00.html.

27 Ibid.

28 As quoted in *The Independent*, 17 March 2004.

29 For example, in Lapper's *Angel* 2000, her naked and winged torso projects into a dark void in which floats an ultrasound image, the whole being a digital self-portrait made when she was pregnant in 1999. See my discussion of Lapper's artwork in R. Betterton, 'Promising Monsters: Pregnant Bodies, Artistic Subjectivity and Maternal Imagination', *Hypatia: A Journal of Feminist Philosophy*, special issue, *Maternal Bodies* 21/1 (winter, 2006), 80–100.

30 In the documentary film 'The Woman with the Remarkable Body' on Channel 5 (2005) Lapper recounted the constant scrutiny of herself and her son to see if she was a 'fit' mother. The problems for disabled women in pregnancy have been addressed in feminist disability studies: see Nasa Begum, 'Disabled Women and the Feminist Agenda', *Feminist Review* 40 (Spring 1992), 71–84; and Jenny Morris, 'Personal and Political: A Feminist Perspective on Researching Disability', *Disability, Handicap and Society* 7/2 (1992), 157–66.

31 A companion portrait *Alison and Parys* in 2001 showed Lapper with her infant son, Parys, was also sculpted life-size in crystalline marble. Quinn's *Kiss* (2001), in Sheffield City Art Galleries, represents portraits of the dis/abled artists Catherine Long and Mat Fraser and is based on Rodin's *The Kiss* (1901–04).

32 Quinn quoted in Tate Gallery 2002, un-paginated. Lapper also used the Venus de Milo as a model for her self-portrait photographic series, *Untitled* (1999). Mary Duffy had previously used the statue as a prototype in her self-portrait photographic installation, *Cutting the Ties that Bind* (1987), to critique media images of disabled women and to represent: 'My identity as a woman with a disability … that is strong, sensual, sexual, fluid, flexible and political' (quoted in Lynda Nead, *The Female Nude* [London and New York: Routledge, 1992], p. 77). Claudine Mitchell discusses the way in which the Anti-Corset League in France before the First World War also appropriated the statue to represent the 'natural' body 'against the mutilation of the body by the corset': C. Mitchell, 'Style/*Ecriture*: On the Classical Ethos, Women's Sculptural Practice and Pre First World War Feminism', *Art History* 25/1 (2002), 1–22; p. 8.

33 Quoted in *The Independent*, 14 May 2004. Lapper's new visibility included an invitation onto BBC2's *Newsnight Review* to give her views on the unveiling of the statue. She said: 'I am very hopeful this sculpture will make a difference. If you look at it, it is very beautiful as a piece of art. Disabled people are not vulgar or ugly or grotesque, and hopefully people will recognise that.' www.guardian.co.uk/uk_news/story/0,,1571296,00.html.

34 The Fourth Plinth was designed by Sir Charles Barry in 1841 and was left unfilled due to lack of funds.

35 www.london.gov.uk/view_press_release.jsp?releaseid=2782 (last accessed 12 May 2008). For details of past Fourth Plinth commissions, see www.london.gov.uk/fourthplinth/about.
36 www.guardian.co.uk/uk_news/story/0,,1571296,00.html.
37 www.fourthplinth.co.uk/unveiling.htm (last accessed 12 May 2008).
38 Ibid.
39 www.fourthplinth.co.uk/marcquinn.htm
40 The representation of women in the form of public statues in Trafalgar Square had already been debated, following an unsuccessful proposal by women Members of Parliament to commemorate the women of the First and Second World Wars on the Fourth Plinth. See Nirmal Puwar, *Space Invaders: Race, Gender and Bodies Out of Place* (Oxford: Berg, 2004), p. 6.
41 Quinn noted the hostile response to the sculpture's embodiment of difference, which he claims was the conceptual genesis of his subsequent work *Evolution*, a series of nine pink marble sculptures representing the growth of the human embryo and foetus during its gestation. See M. Quinn, *Evolution* (London: Mason's Yard, 2008).
42 '[T]he ghosts of modernity, whites could assume power as the norm of humanity, as the naturally given. Unseen racially, that is seen as racially marked – or seen precisely as racially unmarked – whites could be everywhere' (D. Goldberg quoted in Puwar, *Space Invaders*, p. 55).
43 Ibid., p. 8.
44 Ibid., p. 5.
45 Ibid., p. 4.
46 Puwar and Cherry give slightly differing accounts of the dispute over Mandela's statue. Westminster Council's rejection of the attempt backed by Ken Livingstone to erect it in Trafalgar Square led to a public enquiry in 2005 (obituary of Ian Walters, 'Sculptor and Socialist', *The Guardian*, 18 August 2006, p. 38).
47 Puwar, *Space Invaders*, p. 5.
48 Ibid., p. 7.
49 Ibid., p. 59.
50 Vron Ware suggests that the critical project of making whiteness visible 'requires an acknowledgement of the way that other complex factors – notably gender, sexuality, class, and geography – compound social identity and hence produce a complex configuration of whiteness.' Vron Ware and Les Back, *Out of Whiteness: Color, Politics and Culture* (Chicago: University of Chicago Press, 2002), p. 284.
51 Ken Livingstone called for the removal of these two Victorian generals to a different location on the basis that they no longer hold any symbolic value for contemporary Londoners. Citing Livingstone's call in 2002 for recognition of the Square as a continuing forum for free speech, Cherry suggests that it has been 're-fashioned as the people's square' (Cherry, 'Statues in the Square', p. 690).
52 Angela Rosenthal notes the symbolic value of white marble in her discussion of the Pygmalion myth in 'Visceral Culture: Blushing and the Legibility of Whiteness in Eighteenth Century British Portraiture', *Art History* 27/4 (September 2004), 563–92.
53 Writing about the female nude in art, Lynda Nead has also argued that 'the

notion of unified form is integrally bound up with the perception of self, and the construction of individual identity' (Nead, *The Female Nude*, p. 7). In her dialogue with Margrit Shildrick on the dis/abled body in *Vital Signs*, Janet Price says, 'I felt, effectively, invisible and/or "Othered", fixed by a single/unitary identity that labelled me as "disabled", as "wheelchairbound"' (Price and Shildrick, *Vital Signs*, p. 232).

54 Henri Lefebvre links the spaces of modernity to 'phallic solitude and the self-destruction of desire' (Lefebvre, *Critique of Everyday Life: Foundations for a Sociology of the Everyday*, trans. John Moore (London: Verso, 2002), p. 223.

55 This point is explored in detail in Imogen Tyler's essay on the Demi Moore photograph: I. Tyler, 'Skin Tight: Celebrity, Pregnancy and Subjectivity', in S. Ahmed and J. Stacey (eds), *Thinking Through the* Skin (London and New York: Routledge, 2001). For a discussion of pregnant pornography, see A. Schriefer, 'Conceptualization of the Pregnant Body and Pregnant Women's Subjectivity in On-Line Pregnant Pornography', www.gwu.edu/-medusa/pregnant.html (accessed 14 November 2007).

56 L. Berlant and M. Warner, 'Sex in Public', in L. Berlant (ed.), *Intimacy* (Chicago: Chicago University Press, 2000), pp. 311–30; p. 319.

57 See I. Tyler, '"Chav Mum Scum Mum" Class Disgust in Contemporary Britain', *Feminist Media Studies* 8/1 (2007), 17–34.

58 Lauren Berlant, *The Queen of America Goes to Washington City* (Durham, NC: Duke University Press, 1997), p. 101.

59 Ibid. p. 4.

60 Massey, *Space, Place and Gender*; see also Jane Beckett and Deborah Cherry, 'Modern Women, Modern Spaces: Women, Metropolitan Culture and Vorticism', in Katy Deepwell (ed.), *Women Artists and Modernism* (Manchester: Manchester University Press, 1998), pp. 36–54; Rosemary Betterton, 'Women Artists, Modernity and Suffrage Cultures in Britain and Germany, 1890–1920', in Deepwell (ed.), *Women Artists and Modernism*, pp. 18–35; Janet Wolff, *Feminine Sentences: Essays on Women and Culture* (Berkeley and Los Angeles: University of California Press, 1990), on the gendering of modernity, urban space and cultural practices.

61 http://news.bbc.co.uk/1/hi/england/london/4247000.stm

62 This comment is in the context of Deutsche's critique of Harvey's totalizing vision of urban space in *The Condition of Postmodernity*, which she identifies as voyeuristic: 'urban discourse continues to construct space as a feminised object surveyed by mastering subjects' (Deutsche, *Evictions*, pp. 201, 215).

63 Ibid., pp. 212–13.

64 As a work of art it suffers from the translation of scale into a large monument, which renders some of the modelling crude and exposes a certain weakness in sculptural form.

65 Rosenthal, 'Visceral Culture', p. 579.

66 Berlant, *The Queen of America*, pp. 4, 261.

67 Berlant cites the role of the Reaganite right followed by the Clinton era in reinstating 'family values' and the 'citizen child' at the heart of American politics (ibid., pp. 261, 2).

68 Ibid., p. 148.

69 Ibid., p. 154.
70 Very different responses to the statue were evident from the reactions of audiences to my paper. These ranged from pleasure and celebration of the visibility given to Lapper's body to a questioning of her figure as positive for women. One friend recounted how, having photographed the sculpture in Trafalgar Square, she showed it to her mother who reacted with a silence she took to be disgust.
71 J. Richards, S. Wilson and L. Woodhead (eds), *Diana: The Making of a Media Saint* (London: I.B. Tauris, 1999), p. 9.
72 Andrew Marr, *A History of Modern Britain* (London: Macmillan, 2007), p. 47.
73 Marr is unsympathetic to this sentimentalization of Diana: 'she had all the modern disorders – bulimia, self-hatred, celebrity' (ibid.). The continuing obsession with Diana's death is evident from the reopening of the inquest in London in October 2007 on its tenth anniversary and the success of Stephen Frears' film *The Queen* (2006), which focused on Elizabeth II's reaction. The tenth anniversary was also marked by a public memorial service and a Wembley rock concert organized by Princes William and Harry.
74 Quoted in Rosalind Brunt, 'Princess Diana: A Sign of the Times', in Richards, Wilson and Woodhead (eds), *Diana*, p. 29.
75 Ibid., p. 22.
76 Linda Grant, quoted in S. Wilson, 'The Misfortunes of Virtue : Diana, the Press and the Politics of Emotion', in Richards, Wilson and Woodhead (eds), *Diana*, p. 51.
77 Berlant, *The Queen of America*, p. 5.
78 Ibid., p. 156.
79 Specific examples include ongoing debates about British Muslim identity within the context of global terrorist activities, the status of homosexuals within the Church of England, and the question of rights of physical access for wheelchair users to the English countryside (BBC Radio Four, *Today*, 1 December 2007).
80 Irit Rogoff, *Terra Infirma: Geography's Visual Culture* (London and New York: Routledge, 2000), p. 27.

9 Diasporic unwrappings

Lubaina Himid in conversation with Jane Beckett

Lubaina Himid (Figure 9.1) was born in Zanzibar, an island off the coast of East Africa, part of Tanzania, moving as a child first to Blackpool, then London where she grew up. She studied at Wimbledon College of Art (BA Theatre Design 1972–76) and the Royal College of Art (MA 1982–84). Lubaina Himid works in painting, drawing, installation and printmaking. She first came to prominence with *Freedom and Change* in *State of the Art* at the ICA in 1986 and with a series of important exhibitions she curated in the 1980s, including *The Thin Black Line* (ICA, 1985–86). Since the late 1980s her signature works have been large-scale cut-out figures in intricate sardonic installations, including A *Fashionable Marriage* (Pentonville Gallery, London, 1986); *Naming the Money* (Hatton Gallery, Newcastle upon Tyne, 2004); and *Uncomfortable Truths* (Victoria and Albert Museum, London, 2008), although she also works on canvas (e.g. *Revenge*, Rochdale Art Gallery 1992). Her exhibition *Plan B* followed a residency at Tate St Ives. She has exhibited widely in the UK and internationally, in Europe and in the USA, representing Britain at the 5th Havana Bienalle in Cuba. She has paintings, cut-outs and drawings in numerous private collections and is represented in several public collections.[1] Lubaina Himid lives and works in Preston in the north west of the UK and is Professor of Contemporary Art at the University of Central Lancashire.

Jane Beckett: Lubaina, we have talked often about contemporary art practice and curating; initially about your signature cut-out pieces, and about your work in many contexts. The interpretative and critical readings of your work have located it as history painting, or in feminism, or memorialization. Are these your aims as an artist?

Lubaina Himid: Yes, the aim has always been to engage in dialogue with an audience, to exchange and build on ideas about ways we could collaborate in a life-long project to make the invisible threads of certain historical narratives part of an everyday conversation. The history painting label helped me to define my practice at the time. It was Mike Tooby who first asked me whether I was a history painter and when I said yes he asked me to be in his *Depicting*

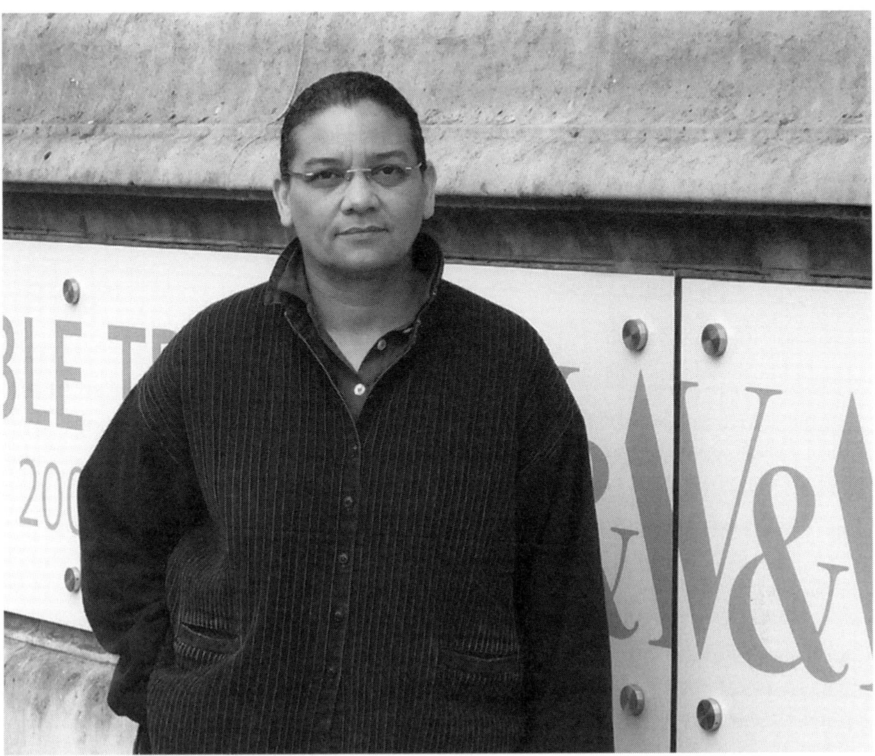

Photograph of the artist Lubaina Himid (2007). 9.1

History for Today show at the Mappin in Sheffield.[2] I made the fifteen-piece watercolour series *Toussaint L'Ouverture* (1988)[3] – I was making work a great deal about Toussaint, Yaa Asantewa, Harriet Tubman, Bessie Smith: heroic figures, special iconic people, leaders. The thought was that by making paintings or cut-outs the way was open for discussion, argument at a number of levels.[4] No one but black artists and black political writers/leaders talked about these figures then. These figures needed to be a central subject for debates around racism in education, the media or the police; this was my way of trying to make history or at least change how the history of now would be told in future.

Narrative is a driving force, yes: I am interested in the minute details of people's lives and use their stories in my work much like a novelist does, imagining, mixing and matching, but not at all like a historian. I am not interested in the facts as recalled by distant witnesses from the outside; this seems too unreliable somehow – the emphasis is more on the feelings and memories, learned behaviours, and tiny habits as experienced from the inside which then go on to inform future small personal actions.

The later work – *Cotton.Com* (2002), *Naming the Money* and *The Lancaster Dinner Service* (2007)[5] – centres much more on the insignificant narratives of insignificant people engaged in the struggle to manage their everyday lives, lived as part of monumental and global strategies for power and wealth. How do the small, vulnerable and ordinary still make a difference to the whole picture? How do we ensure that our contribution is at least acknowledged if not rewarded?

JB: By seeking new solutions for visualizing 'history'?

LH: The old solutions did not seem to allow for creative imaginings nor did they enable the black woman's story to take its place amongst the other voices. Her story is complex and constantly interwoven through the whole, yet is often told simply and by others as that of a silent victim. The device of placing two black women in a painting together was an early method I used to counteract this assumption that there was only one story *and* that the black woman never spoke. The use of pattern and dress to tell the story has always been important too; I am constantly exploring the notion that textile design could be a secret and yet visible language between women. The making of the life-sized cut-out who stands in a room rather like a piece of furniture, taking space like a sculpture but occupying the role of a painting, has also engaged me for many years. I have probably made about two hundred of these by now. How do you create a conversation piece but not in the polite sense? Perhaps rather as a visual gate crasher who has the sense to bring a gift to the party.

JB: In two recent – related – shows, *Swallow Hard: The Lancaster Dinner Service* (2007)[6] and *Kanga and Other Stories* (Peg Alston, New York 2008) you re-explore issues of greed, memorialization and history.

LH: And in the project which I am working on at the moment and which will launch in April 2010 in Liverpool, the *Sweet Jelly Mould Monument* project.

JB: *Swallow Hard* was a double installation: dinner service settings on a table, sideboard, mantelpiece and window sills, so there is an unstable horizon line and the viewer is constantly repositioned and cannot see the work as a whole.

LH: In fact it's in two parts. You are describing the display in the kitchen of the Judges Lodgings, which was indeed on several surfaces as you describe. However, the main dining room display covered every inch of an eighteen-foot Caribbean mahogany table made by Gillow, the famous Lancaster furniture maker/slave-ship owner. You never see the work as a whole and are never sure which pieces are real and which are fake. You have to stretch and lean, peer and squint to take it all in [Figure 9.2]. In fact there are even hidden texts inside the tureens and jugs giving the names of the slave servants painted on the outside. No one ever sees these at all. Many of the pieces, especially the jugs, are quite fine late nineteenth-century ceramics that I found in junk shops and antique markets across the region (north west England). Some pieces, mostly the small plates, are simply twentieth-century rubbish over painted to look old and expensive. A number of visitors were not aware at all that the pieces were contemporary art and engaged with them as satirical narratives painted on English tableware circa 1807.

JB: So the spectator is conscious of being spatially contained in a domestic setting and re-positioned in terms of race, gender and class?

LH: The spectator in the small regional museum is often visiting for a pleasant hour of nostalgic engagement with the past glories of English heritage. The work is part of a strategy to inject a shot of unease into the complacent visitor, a sort of tickly cough that suddenly needs to be dealt with, that shakes you out of your dreamy wandering.

JB: Is there a doubling of lives in *Swallow Hard* – a doubling of places at the table – of black and white lives?

LH: White sits at the table. Black serves/waits at the table. White is there to be covered in food and eaten off; is painted on plates. Black is there to contain; is painted on jugs and tureens. The English in the city are merchants, lawyers, clergy, ship builders, politicians, in favour of or appalled by abolition. The Africans are the observers speaking through signs to each other about life as servants in the city, unacknowledged participants in the struggle for abolition.

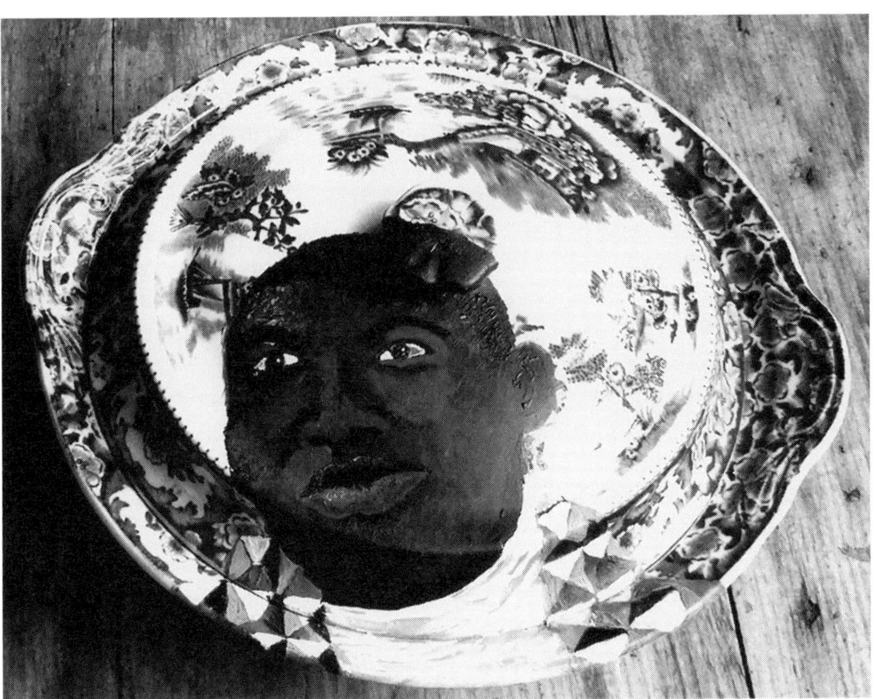

Lubaina Himid, *Swallow Hard: Lancaster Dinner Service* (2007). Tureen. 9.2

The black slave servants painted on the jugs and tureens are all either invented people, remembered people and people I saw in the streets of Lancaster and the north west of England, or people who have appeared in paintings which now hang in the museums of Europe, Britain and North America. Inside each jug or tureen I painted the name of the person depicted on the outside. You could not eat off the ceramics with black people's faces; they are 'contained' rather than displayed. The point I am often exploring vis-à-vis the black experience is that of being so very visible and different in the white Western everyday yet so very invisible and disregarded in the cultural, historical, political or economic record or history.

I hope this the last piece I will ever make which has the overt stain of slavery all over it. The black person as 'slave who must be freed' is too cosy a concept and is not as powerful or useful as the thread which has driven me forward in most of the work I have made during the past twenty-five years or so and that is that people of the African diaspora have made significant contributions to the cultural landscape of Britain, continue to do so and must be acknowledged and rewarded.

JB: What were the processes in making this work – selecting objects and overpainting?

LH: The process of buying, choosing and painting took around twelve months. The histories of Lancaster are hidden, covered, disguised and remade in a quaint and elegant, very English way and this directly informed the decision to make *The Lancaster Dinner Service* for the Judges Lodgings Museum in Lancaster, a project in which over-painting is a serious and consistent working method. Over-painting in my work is a recent development and stems from a realization that much of my life has been spent trying to correct past mistakes. Making the dinner service using layers of Liquitex acrylic paint and dozens of small brushes I would work on several objects at the same time while waiting for layers to dry or the light to improve the better to develop details. The work was done at any and every opportunity at the studio in my house. When making large-scale projects I work early in the morning from 5 until 8, all day at the weekends and most evenings for a couple of hours during the lighter evenings. As each plate was complete I hung it on the wall; as the tureens or jugs were finished they were placed on available surfaces all around the house. The patterns were often invented but also copied from numerous cloths, books, postcards and photographs in my studio. The maps were copied from engravings housed in the Lancaster archives; the buildings were painted from photographs taken during the previous year on my information-gathering walks around every inch of the city.

JB: The range of references in the over-painted images sets up a dialogue between your work and eighteenth-century paintings and cartoons – was this a conscious dialogue?

LH: I could indulge in all of my preferred ways of making; the buying of a hundred plates, tureens and jugs from markets, junk shops, car boot sales and antique shops across the region allowed me to spend money on painting surfaces; copying, re-using and altering the work of James Gillray, George Cruikshank, John Newton, William Hogarth, D.C. Thompson comics and cartoonist Steve Bell to depict the merchants, ship owners, lawyers and political figures of the city in compromised positions allowed me to explore ideas about satire, comedy and laughter in drawing, giving me the perfect excuse to mock and tease the contemporary hypocrisy of twenty-first-century liberalism while at the same time making truly humiliating images of people who showed little regard for those whom they bought and sold.

JB: Your pursuit of jokes and satire may surprise some people and maybe is an uneasy fit with the docketing of your work as 'history' painting.

LH: The work has always had satire at its heart, from the naked cut-out men with enormous penises made in the early 1980s, through the Hogarth cut-out installation *A Fashionable Marriage* made later in the decade. Even the paper works depicting the life of Toussaint L'Ouverture were not entirely serious and were designed to be enjoyed by very young people keen to see how, for instance, a hero did his washing.

JB: What job does laughter do in the works and their display?

LH: Its place in the work is to mock those who take themselves especially seriously but also to make a space for an exchange of views without coming to blows. Having witnessed and documented, for two decades, the constant mocking and ridicule aimed at black men in the music industry, for instance, I feel justified in returning some of the fire and ire. Everywhere across advertising and the broadcast and printed media there are references to black men and 'bling', black women and 'warbling' or black sportsmen and their 'animal magnitude', 'womanizing' or 'laziness', black women in sport and their 'venom' or 'ugliness' or 'maleness'. As an artist I can protest earnestly and be ignored, or turn the tables, laugh and reclaim the images.

JB: So are the white figures on the plates of Swallow Hard who are shown as excessive – in aggressive stances, overfed and on horseback, tittering, vomiting – suggesting through exaggerated, grotesque portrayals the social and moral decay of the eighteenth century or are they part of a strategy, like Steve Bell, to mock and tease the contemporary hypocrisy of twenty-first-century liberalism?

LH: If we don't point out the hypocrisy of twenty-first-century liberalism and its 'say a lot but do nothing' policies we will find ourselves supporting ill-thought-through strategies that allow whole sections of the poor and badly educated population into a state of imagined neglect and real marginalization.

It is not in the interest of the twenty-first-century liberal to understand and act upon the wrongs they know to be wrong. But they would have to be idiots if they have not realized that we know their game. In case they are idiots, my mockery, satire and subsequent laughter is designed to be a little wake-up call.

JB: Are these an echo of your earlier work on William Hogarth, such as the contemporary politics you explored in the *Fashionable Marriage* installation cut-outs and the exhibition at the Victoria and Albert Museum (1998)?

LH: I am still very involved in an examination of the work of Hogarth and spend time studying both the paintings and the engravings, playing with ideas about another re-working to match my *Fashionable Marriage* installation. An invitation has come for me to re-make *Fashionable Marriage* for an exhibition in the USA in the near future and because several major pieces from the original installation have been lost there is an opportunity to develop some of these ideas in the re-make. They were pretty tame when compared to the eighteenth-century images, and very tame indeed when compared to the images of black people in the eighteenth-century cartoons held by the National Maritime Museum at Greenwich. But I am very interested in discussing possible ways of showing these images.

At one point I discussed and even had an exhibition date for showing the whole of *Naming the Money* at the National Maritime Museum alongside a collection of James Gillray cartoons and a collection of slave accoutrements such as chains, shackles, branding irons and other items donated to the museum by a collector of material connected to British shipping. It came to nothing in the end. I never found out why; curators move, priorities change.

JB: So there is a complex process of representation at play here – a constant making and remaking of black identities – the eighteenth century morphing into a twenty-first-century presence in the display, while at the same time rendering this unstable and flickering across historical moments – images on plates, over-painting on paper.

LH: Perhaps what I am trying to do is make images that are clearly twenty-first-century fabrications but that carry visual clues culled from the past few hundred years to imply that had I been working as an artist across this time span these are the images I would have made. There is a seductively cruel quality to the English eighteenth-century cartoon, an outrageous disregard for the balanced view, that is still very present today, which hovers beneath the surface in public art gallery or museum dialogue, but that is full frontal in the world of stand-up comedy and YouTube. A black identity in a European setting is obviously an extremely complex and richly layered skin to be in but the bottom line is that we inhabit this continent because there is a long history of Europeans rampaging through ours. It's astonishing that where you come from and how long you have been here still matter so deeply both inside and outside your head. Questions around why African people still come to Europe are interwoven into the fabric of the flags, and flash across the everyday conversation, the newspaper page, the music lesson and the sports event all the time. Teachers and lawyers, architects and engineers, doctors, dancers, whatever, all of us have to engage with our 'Africanness' somewhere beneath the surface of our professions, each day that we develop our careers here. It's a double life lived in two halves, two languages, two states: the separate and the merged. Interesting but hard work.

JB: A recent issue of *The Voice* posed the question: 'Black and British: Are we suffering from a crisis of identity?' Do you agree?[7]

LH: I don't think we as African diasporas are suffering a crisis of identity at all: we know who we are, we know why we are here. The crisis surely is located in the very real often internalized feeling that many people in Britain would be much happier if we were not here at all, even now after all this time. How like *The Voice* to posit the question in terms of self-blame.

It's clear to me that the so-called indigenous British people cannot decide who we are or admit the facts of why we are here. This is the crisis of identity. I have made project after project in an attempt to interrogate issues and narratives about the desire to belong. All the pieces I have written and made about monuments and commemoration are centred around achieving recognition for the cultural contribution we have made to this nation during the past several hundred years.

JB: Would you, then, locate your work in Franz Fanon's concept of 'passionate research' in making visible colonial experiences and at the same time making visible/producing black identity within an overall unificatory project?[8]

LH: Yes, if making visible colonial experiences is making visible everyday life in the twenty-first century for those of us drifting about the globe with a colonial rucksack on our backs. I do not usually try to create an imagined life in the past with the work but rather attempt to make a space for a conversation. The colonial experience haunts and holds back the numerous strategies for creative involvement that intelligent and energetic black diasporas are making the effort to develop.

JB: Is this a black diasporic unwrapping and/or a migratory aesthetics?

LH: My work engages with how we are pictured, how we picture ourselves, how we are very visible, but our cultural contribution is not seen. I want to talk about what it feels like to conform and rebel, to see and yet be invisible, to contribute and not be recognized, to give and not be rewarded. I don't wish to nurture the notion of unbelonging, of transience and longing for/reference to 'home' but it hovers around the work I made in the 1990s; it ended with *Naming the Money*. If I had to choose between the two it would be to say that the project is concerned with how we are now, how we are seen now, and has at its heart how we deal with this in visual conversations with each other. Black diasporic unwrapping feels more like cultural exploration from the inside than migratory aesthetics, which sounds more like social anthropology, the 'other' viewed from the outside.

JB: Black diaspora or Black Atlantic?

LH: Black diaspora whenever possible.[9] The Black Atlantic project is not in opposition to my project but I would rather try to deal with how we survive the aftermath. After the mourning comes revenge, being here. We do carry the weight of the drowning, the killings, the rapes and the centuries of injustice that have been executed in the name of European church and state, but the fact is people from all of the fifty-two African countries across the continent do survive and attempt to flourish all across the world, whether as the sons and daughters of slaves, or the descendants of those who allowed them to be taken, or even the descendants of those few who have never been affected by the European project. We survive, we contribute, we enrich the human experience.

JB: Has your work changed again in the past decade? Modified between *Revenge* (1992) and *Uncomfortable Truths* (2007)?[10]

LH: It's interesting that you see this as a modified stance; I think it's more a strategic move away from the art gallery and into the museum. It's a move from a site of extreme and overt racism in which the black is exotic and sexualized or plays the part of the dandy and the fool, or is dead and therefore absent from the room, to a site of covert racism that wishes to be seen to be inclusive and to engage in acts of teaching and learning. The over-painting of the multi-layered narratives simply reflects the mysterious and neglected collections, the controlled displays and the obsessive worship of the antique artefact. I play with the fixed idea of history and make fakes or paint over valuable ceramics as in *Swallow Hard: The Lancaster Dinner Service* or ask to place my history work next to another rather more revered strand of history, in the way that I did with *Naming the Money* in *Uncomfortable Truths* at the Victoria and Albert Museum. It's possible to love the museum with a passion and to be dismayed by its inability to flow with the changes as fast as the world of the street. I see it as my job to help to introduce a much more diverse set of people to this incredible world of beautifully made pieces of furniture, ceramic, tapestry or metal work and jewellery but to place a different and more politically critical narrative alongside the voice of the museum.

JB: In a recent discussion of cultural identity and politics, Stuart Hall explored the complexity of a play of 'difference' within identity, suggesting that its possible to rethink the positioning and repositioning of Caribbean cultural identities.[11] While his analysis necessarily turns on Caribbean identities, it could be explored in relation to the fact that you are both English/European and Zanzibari/African.

LH: I have always thought of myself as an East African brought up by English women. My mother and aunt are women who spent their time as students at the Royal College of Art and Trinity College of Music making friends with a whole range of other London students from all over the world. Those friends included journalists, lawyers, artists, musicians and writers, and many of them were from East Africa. I am both Zanzibari in that I was born there (though my father was from the Comorian Islands) and English/European. There are great advantages to this heritage – a richness of experience, an absolute necessity to be creative and the ability to develop a balanced overview – but it's a real struggle if you have any issues with 'belonging'. I don't think the parents of dual heritage children have any idea how much terrible pain this journey to an understanding of self can be.

JB: Should *Double Life* (Bolton Museum and Art Gallery, 2001) and *New Robes for MaShulan* (Rochdale Art Gallery, 1987) be positioned in this context?[12] *Double Life* uses texts that form a fragmentary tale of personal histories and the installation included photographs of looms, bars and gents in 1930s clothing, glass cabinets of dusty beer bottles and twelve delicate, gridded double paintings of everyday objects – forks, flowers, door keys, etc.

LH: *New Robes for MaShulan* was an exhibition title invented by Maud Sulter. I would have entitled the exhibition *No Maps*: it had very little to do with my grandmother and was much more a show about the terror of being in transition; me cut adrift from friends and family and about to live in Yorkshire at the end of the 1980s.

Double Life, on the other hand, was designed by me to be a celebration of the childhood of two annoying but determined old ladies, my mother and my aunt, both of whom in their time had the nerve to take what was given to them and run with it. They are the daughters of a family of Lancashire publicans and lived a privileged life in the midst of between-the-wars poverty. Shirley Temple meets *Angela's Ashes*. The museum in which *Double Life* was first shown is only a few miles away from where they lived. The paintings are all re-enactments, re-imaginings of tiny moments and snippets of conversations they had related to me all my life. Differently because essentially they see and hear the same incidents slightly differently. It gave me an excuse to spend hours with them pretending to check details and verify facts. We just laughed a lot actually.

JB: *Kangas and Other Stories* [Peg Alston, New York; Figure 9.3] consisted of paper works and seems to relate to the double-life concept and to your mother's work as a textile designer; you also maintain a strong interest in African cloth and textiles, don't you?

LH: *Swallow Hard* (2006) was a series of painted paperwork exhibited one year before the *Lancaster Dinner Service* in the same location, The Judges Lodgings, Lancaster, but on the walls of the coffee shop and along the corridor. I love the language of pattern, its immense potential for movement, illusion, colour experiments and subliminal political messaging. This exhibition is just a part of the exploration of how to imply invisible influences without explanation but without slipping into the abstract. The patterns are narratives as I have said many times before. My mother's influence is there quite strongly

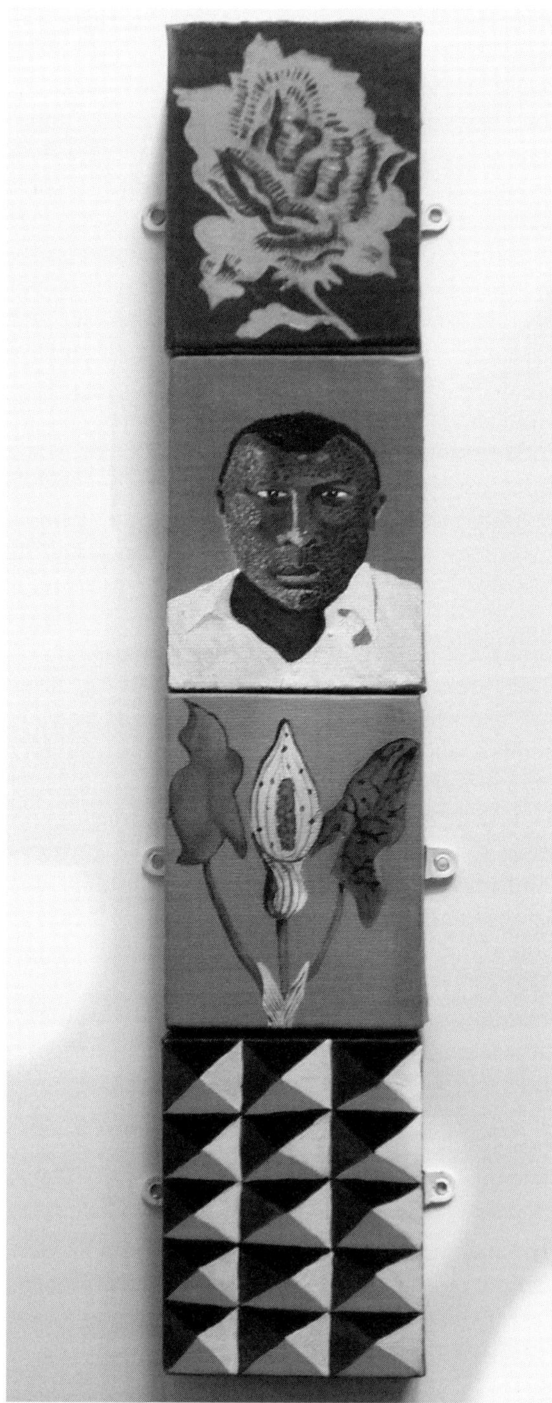

9.3 Lubaina Himid, *The Architect* (2005–07), from *Kangas, Common Wild Flowers and Other Stories.*

but I am not a textile designer; it's such a precise skill, so mathematical. At its most thrilling textile design is perfection, I love to play with this perfection. The influences are many; from Persian miniatures to Austrian soft furnishings through West African weaving to the inevitable East African printed Kanga.

The *Kanga* project really started with the series *Zanzibar* (1998/99) painted at the same time as *Plan B*. However, in its present form it started in about 2005 when I decided to paint patterns over dozens of my old paintings. Not obliterating them entirely but changing them to suit the thoughts I was having at the time about the futility of storing hundreds of good paintings which would never be shown again. I painted over the bad ones, the painful ones and the ones that had failed outings. It is an ongoing project and eventually I hope to get through the whole lot.

JB: Is the exploration of identity one narrative of the work?

LH: I have explored the identity of the coloured girl for fifty years and how subtly she/we differently deal with this 'in-between' and 'double' life. It's not a particularly clear or consistent story but the relationships that develop in a woman's life as a consequence of trying to belong somewhere 'racially' in addition to the usual decisions and journeys we make are still interesting to me yet somehow exhaustingly and strangely predictable. She looks around a room in a public setting to find herself but is not always reassured when she does. However, she is often very likely to seek out other coloured girls for private and strategic conversations, which then take place over many years.

The black male identity is something so important to unpack creatively, left to the scrutiny and care of others during the past thirty years the results have been very disappointing to me. I am only now really closely engaging with what it means to represent a black man visually. I cannot know from the inside so the investigation is severely limited and reduced to an outsider's study of how it has been done and by whom and where and why.[13] My work on this so far is then a kind of crude correction of what has gone before. I am working on it.

Negative/Positives: Guardian Paper Works is a series of pages from *The Guardian* newspaper taken from almost every issue published since January 2007. It examines the visual representation of black people in this newspaper and includes photographs and accompanying texts relating to sports people, politicians, soldiers, the dead, criminals, heroes and fashion models, ordinary people and royalty.

I have collected hundreds of pages and so far have completed around fifty over-paintings. The patterns I have imposed attempt to 'reclaim' the image of the black person and highlight the strange and inappropriate use of image and language juxtaposition in which they find themselves [Figure 9.4].

JB: In what ways has black male identity been explored creatively and disappointingly by others in the last thirty years; surely Donald Rodney's work was very perceptive and subtle in this respect?

LH: Of course there is some marvellous even breathtaking work around this subject but it's impossible for me to attempt to describe an overview of thirty years work as part of this interview. We would have to discuss the work of not only Donald Rodney but also Eddie Chambers, Glenn Ligon, Kerry James Marshall, Keith Piper, Chris Ofili, Steve McQueen, Yinka Shonibare, Hew Locke, Eugene Palmer, Denzil Forrester, Stan Douglas, El Anatsu, Cherry Samba, Isaac Julien, John Akomfrah, Trevor Matheson, Raimi Gbadamosi, David A. Bailey, Fred Wilson and David Hammons, just for starters!

I am tired of seeing black men depicted as dead or wounded victims, angry idiots or vacant jesters or drugged-out killers and often with identities determined by their imagined sexual prowess. It is the everyday visual offer from broadcast and printed media that is full of this stuff; as soon as black men became visible in these worlds they were forced to assume this, and only this, narrow range of possible identities. The visual artwork produced during the past thirty years always had a struggle to redress this imbalance.

JB: Black men were a key part of the *Uncomfortable Truths* installation in the Victoria and Albert Museum, weren't they? Your cut-out black servant figures were located throughout the British galleries in conversation, in dialogue with a range of historical works and attitudes.

LH: The experience of working with the Victoria and Albert Museum was interesting in that the original invitation was to show all one hundred cut-outs in *Naming the Money* in the temporary exhibitions galleries. This idea shifted and changed over several years and sixteen figures became a central element of the exhibition *Uncomfortable Truths*. The figures were eventually shown at various points chosen by the curators throughout the British galleries. The process was lengthy and painful but because I was able to choose which cut-outs were shown and many of the locations were spectacular the resulting irony of my black slave servants, nameless and silent, being placed in subservient positions to great and expensive 'stolen' objects owned by the British aristocracy in the V&A was just about bearable (Figure 9.5).

There are sixty men painted as part of *Naming the Money* and forty women; when we displayed sixteen of the cut-outs as part of *Uncomfortable Truths* there were ten men and six women, so they were in the majority but the emphasis was not gender biased. The men are dancers, viola da gamba players, mapmakers, shoemakers, dog trainers and drummers. The women are ceramicists, herbalists, toy makers and painters. Looking back through the videos we made of these installations I have studied the formations and the placing: the men do not hold key positions but they do make more noise; twenty of them are musicians.

I spent a decade painting women almost to the exclusion of men (though in the 1980s I painted Toussaint L'Ouverture several times) and eventually felt that I had drifted away from my father's influence and creativity. This could be an attempt to reconnect.

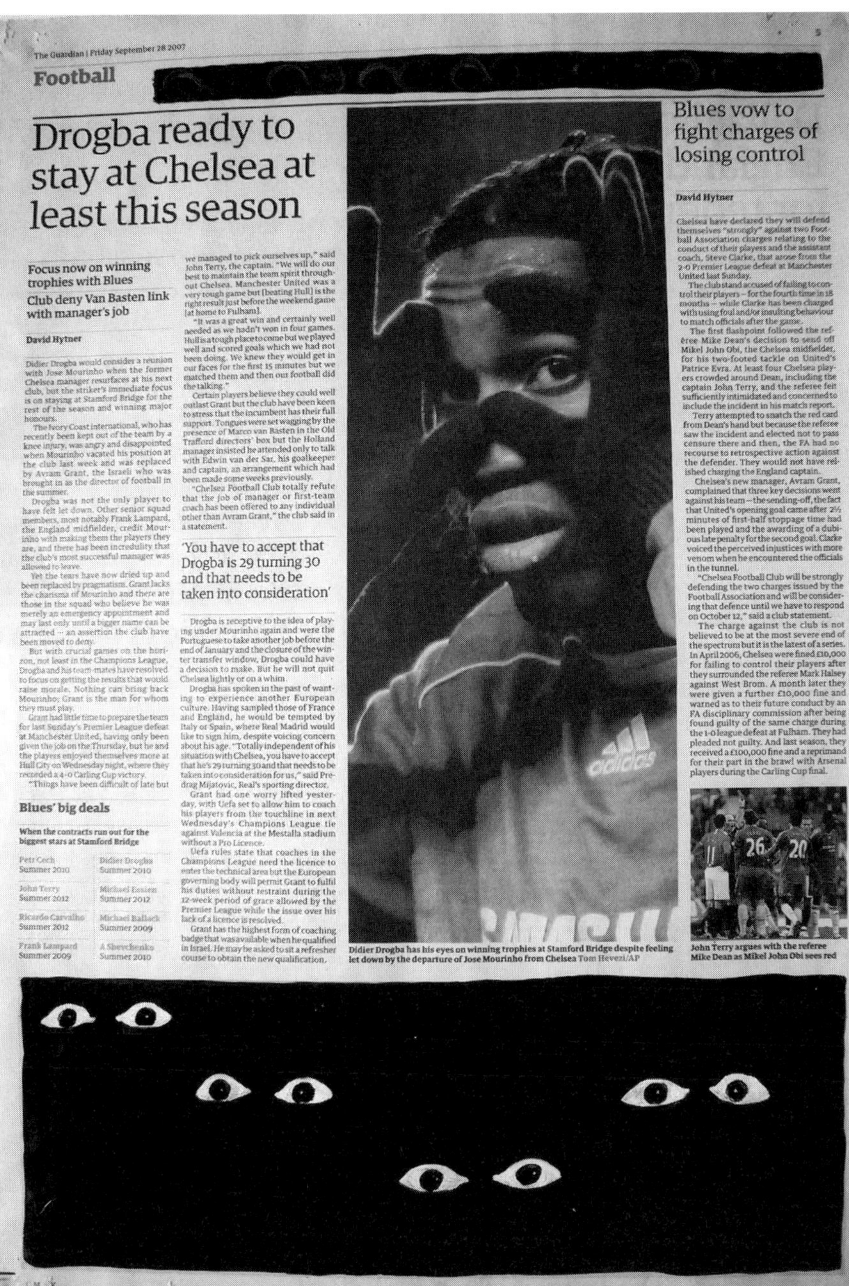

The Guardian | Friday September 28 2007

Football

Drogba ready to stay at Chelsea at least this season

Focus now on winning trophies with Blues

Club deny Van Basten link with manager's job

David Hytner

Didier Drogba would consider a reunion with Jose Mourinho when the former Chelsea manager resurfaces at his next club, but the striker's immediate focus is on staying at Stamford Bridge for the rest of the season and winning major honours.

The Ivory Coast international, who has recently been kept out of the team by a knee injury, was angry and disappointed when Mourinho vacated his position at the club last week and was replaced by Avram Grant, the Israeli who was brought in as the director of football in the summer.

Drogba was not the only player to have felt let down. Other senior squad members, most notably Frank Lampard, the England midfielder, credit Mourinho with making them the players they are, and there has been incredulity that the club's most successful manager was allowed to leave.

Yet the tears have now dried up and been replaced by pragmatism. Grant lacks the charisma of Mourinho and there are those in the squad who believe he was merely an emergency appointment and may last only until a bigger name can be attracted – an assertion the club have been moved to deny.

But with crucial games on the horizon, not least in the Champions League, Drogba and his team-mates have resolved to focus on getting the results that would raise morale. Nothing can bring back Mourinho; Grant is the man for whom they must play.

Grant had little time to prepare the team for last Sunday's Premier League defeat at Manchester United, having only been given the job on the Thursday, but he and the players enjoyed themselves more at Hull City on Wednesday night, where they recorded a 4-0 Carling Cup victory.

"Things have been difficult of late but we managed to pick ourselves up," said John Terry, the captain. "We will do our best to maintain the team spirit throughout Chelsea. Manchester United was a very tough game but [beating Hull] is the right result just before the weekend game [at home to Fulham].

"It was a great win and certainly well needed as we hadn't won in four games. Hull is a tough place to come but we played well and scored goals which we had not been doing. We knew they would get in our faces for the first 15 minutes but we matched them and then our football did the talking."

Certain players believe they could well outlast Grant but the club have been keen to stress that the incumbent has their full support. Tongues were set wagging by the presence of Marco van Basten in the Old Trafford directors' box but the Holland manager insisted he attended only to talk with Edwin van der Sar, his goalkeeper and captain, an arrangement which had been made some weeks previously.

"Chelsea Football Club totally refute that the job of manager or first-team coach has been offered to any individual other than Avram Grant," the club said in a statement.

'You have to accept that Drogba is 29 turning 30 and that needs to be taken into consideration'

Drogba is receptive to the idea of playing under Mourinho again and were the Portuguese to take another job before the end of January and the closure of the winter transfer window, Drogba could have a decision to make. But he will not quit Chelsea lightly or on a whim.

Drogba has spoken in the past of wanting to experience another European culture. Having sampled those of France and England, he would be tempted by Italy or Spain, where Real Madrid would like to sign him, despite voicing concern about his age. "Totally independent of his situation with Chelsea, you have to accept that he's 29 turning 30 and that needs to be taken into consideration for us," said Predrag Mijatovic, Real's sporting director.

Grant had one worry lifted yesterday, with Uefa set to allow him to coach his players from the touchline in next Wednesday's Champions League tie against Valencia at the Mestalla stadium without a Pro Licence.

Uefa rules state that coaches in the Champions League need the licence to enter the technical area but the European governing body will permit Grant to fulfil his duties without restraint during the 12-week period of grace allowed by the Premier League while the issue over his lack of a licence is resolved.

Grant has the highest form of coaching badge that was available when he qualified in Israel. He may be asked to sit a refresher course to obtain the new qualification.

Blues' big deals

When the contracts run out for the biggest stars at Stamford Bridge

Petr Cech Summer 2010	Didier Drogba Summer 2010
John Terry Summer 2012	Michael Essien Summer 2012
Ricardo Carvalho Summer 2012	Michael Ballack Summer 2009
Frank Lampard Summer 2009	A Shevchenko Summer 2010

Didier Drogba has his eyes on winning trophies at Stamford Bridge despite feeling let down by the departure of Jose Mourinho from Chelsea Tom Hevezi/AP

Blues vow to fight charges of losing control

David Hytner

Chelsea have declared they will defend themselves "strongly" against two Football Association charges relating to the conduct of their players and the assistant coach, Steve Clarke, that arose from the 2-0 Premier League defeat at Manchester United last Sunday.

The club stand accused of failing to control their players – for the fourth time in 18 months – while Clarke has been charged with using foul and/or insulting behaviour to match officials after the game.

The first flashpoint followed the referee Mike Dean's decision to send off Mikel John Obi, the Chelsea midfielder, for his two-footed tackle on United's Patrice Evra. At least four Chelsea players crowded around Dean, including the captain John Terry, and the referee felt sufficiently intimidated and concerned to include the incident in his match report.

Terry attempted to snatch the red card from Dean's hand but because the referee saw the incident and elected not to pass censure there and then, the FA had no recourse to retrospective action against the defender. They would not have relished charging the England captain.

Chelsea's new manager, Avram Grant, complained that three key decisions went against his team – the sending-off, the fact that United's opening goal came after 2½ minutes of first-half stoppage time had been played and the awarding of a dubious late penalty for the second goal. Clarke voiced the perceived injustices with more venom when he encountered the officials in the tunnel.

"Chelsea Football Club will be strongly defending the two charges issued by the Football Association and will be considering that defence until we have to respond on October 12," said a club statement.

The charge against the club is not believed to be at the most severe end of the spectrum but it is the latest of a series. In April 2006, Chelsea were fined £10,000 for failing to control their players after they surrounded the referee Mark Halsey against West Brom. A month later they were given a further £10,000 fine and warned as to their future conduct by an FA disciplinary commission after being found guilty of the same charge during the 1-0 league defeat at Fulham. They had pleaded not guilty. And last season, they received a £100,000 fine and a reprimand for their part in the brawl with Arsenal players during the Carling Cup final.

John Terry argues with the referee Mike Dean as Mikel John Obi sees red

Lubaina Himid, *Didier Drogba* (2008), from *Positive Negatives*. **9.4**

JB: And is there also a gender issue in the work?

LH: The work I make is black art and it is feminist art. I am not just an artist. I am a black artist and a feminist. If I wasn't there would be no need for me to make things. It's still very important to me that the things I see I see because of who I am and how I am seen. Being visible and invisible at the same time is an everyday state of being for women. How we deal with this and whether it matters seems now to be an individual issue.

JB: On the Tate website your *Between the Two My Heart Is Balanced* (1991) appears under the banner 'Feminist art', juxtaposed with Cindy Sherman, *Untitled No.97* (1982) and Helen Chadwick, *Eroticism* (1990) – are you comfortable with this bracketing?

LH: Being juxtaposed with Cindy Sherman and Helen Chadwick is amusing and if you think it means anything you are right, but it means that they needed to put a black artist there as a signifier. They have not yet managed to collect the work of Maud Sulter, whose work speaks directly to these two artists; when and if they do I will be usurped from this position of sandwich filling, and she will replace me. I would rather be in a sandwich between Stan Douglas and James Tissot or Bridget Riley and Yinka Shonibare but this is a bit sophisticated for Tate.

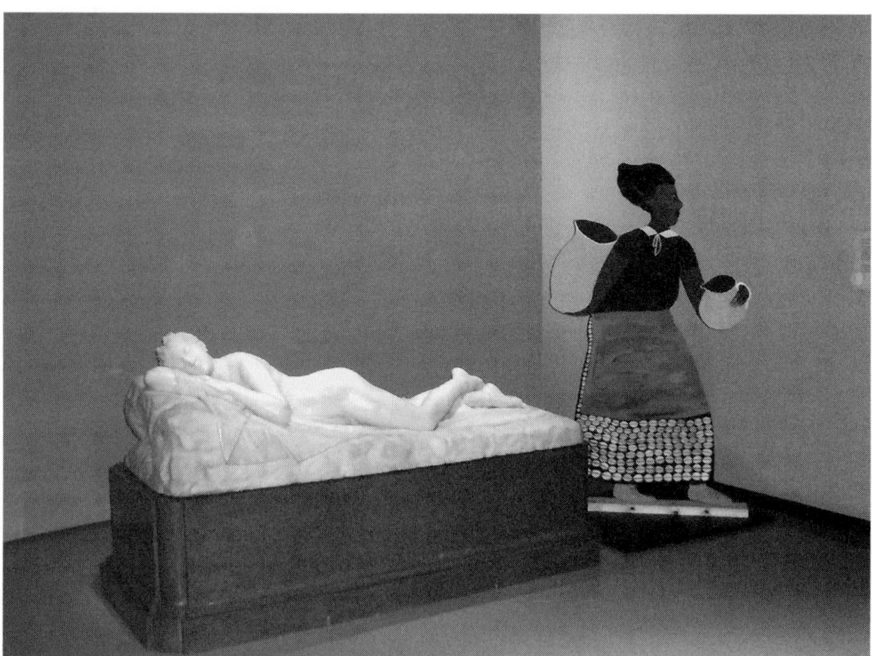

9.5 Lubaina Himid, *Asiza the Ceramicist* from *Naming the Money* (2004) (exhibited at *Uncomfortable Truths*, V&A Museum, 2007).

JB: You have done an immense amount of work in writing, organizing exhibitions and speaking in support of black woman artists – is this still part of your projects?

LH: I have been very hurt both mentally and physically by working in support of black women artists but it remains something I do; it is part of who I am. Now I work with a group of artists in Preston on small-scale exhibition projects, funding applications, educational projects and publications both DVD and text based.

JB: Display, accessibility to collections and collection per se has been a recurrent part of your work, from *Mrs Salt's Collection* (1990) to *The Point of Collection* and *Open Sesame- Making Histories Visible* (Tate/Uclan, 2005).

LH: Collection and display have always been very important to the work I make. Museums have been central to my life since childhood and it has always been an everyday experience for me to visit them. I would rather be in a museum than a department store but the two types of location merge for me into one looking, walking, talking, comparing, dreaming, peopled experience. I have probably in early work made rather simplistic comparisons to the way that people are collected and displayed, used as signifiers of wealth, liberal thinking, intellect, and the way that tapestries, paintings, ceramics and jewels are collected. Much of my work has been an attempt to examine what belonging is, why it matters, who decides, how you decide when it does and doesn't matter to you. I want to belong.

JB: What about *The Point of Collection* and *Open Sesame* projects?

LH: The two DVDs, the first *Open Sesame* and the second *The Point of Collection*, made with Susan Walsh in collaboration with the Tate Liverpool education team, are known as the *Making Histories Visible* project. The whole project is part of the work I do at the University of Central Lancashire with black artists and students to try to push my whole idea of recognition for contribution forward. The first DVD *Open Sesame* records every occasion on which Tate has shown the work of African/Asian/Caribbean artists in its four galleries. The text publication that accompanies this gives the contact details of galleries who represent the exhibited artists and gives web addresses at which you can find out more about more artists.

JB: Some of the filmic structure (water, rivers, narrative voice-over) and the structure of the narrative in *The Point of Collection*, and even the mellifluous narrative voice seem to be aware of Patrick Keiller's film *London*,[14] and the project is also, like Keiller's film, 'essay, document, critique, poem'.[15]

LH: It does have glimpses of Patrick Keiller and I am a great fan of the still camera filming the moving scene. I want the work to be very calm and very unlike television, much more like a painting. The mellifluous voice cannot be helped but I'd forgotten how alike he and I sound.

They are essays; they are also information packs and instruction manuals, and were made to help diverse audiences open up dialogues with the national collections at Tate. They were made to be used. It is true that only just below the surface is a critical element. Tate does not do enough to reflect the substantial and significant work being made by artists from the black diaspora. The references to water are all through both works; one reason is because all four Tates are next to water – the Thames, the Mersey and the Atlantic – but also tides and trade, floods and drowning, shipwrecks and drains and stolen loot seem to flow and swirl about the buildings themselves and the politics of collecting in the British context. I miss London, long for London life, but otherwise the city isn't really the central player in these works.

The second DVD *The Point of Collection* is a much more satirical affair. It has taken many years to understand that Tate is focused on the object and not the artist, that collecting for them is only interesting when they can make connections between the objects. It is an essay, a document but much more of a poem of smiling despair. I was trying to be funny too and annoying. It is still a useful document and tells you what the Tate have in their collection – how many works by each African/Caribbean/Asian artist. The numbers are very sobering: so small and so many artists not represented. It is certainly meant to be a strong critique but this always has to be seen in the context of other major European collections. The Tate scores rather well when held up against collections in Europe.

JB: You have also worked as a curator – *The Thin Black Line* (1985–86),[16] your own independent venue, The Elbow Room, and at Rochdale Art Gallery – and so are aware of display tactics and the politics of collection and display. Could this be rooted in your training in theatre design – in the setting and staging of arguments and ideas? And there is a theatricality in curatorial work – the setting of scene, the initiation of a narrative – setting the scene for a performance perhaps?

LH: The concern with collection and display is more related to the curating experience. It has been easy for me to show and promote other people's work and ideas, and I've even been successful at getting other people's work shown at quite prestigious and beautiful venues, but I have always been hopeless at getting anyone to buy it. My training in theatre design affects almost everything I do, so there are possibilities in your suggestion. The setting for *Swallow Hard: The Lancaster Dinner Service* was like a stage set in which the artworks were the players. *Naming the Money* was absolutely a theatrical piece in which the artworks spoke, sang, danced and interacted through colour and pattern. The audience walked amongst the 'players' in the same way that I imagined the role of audience for the street/outdoor theatre pieces I designed in the 1970s.[17]

JB: A setting of space and place, of possibilities, was present in your installations *Naming the Money, Ballad of the Wing* at the Chisenhale Gallery, London and also Stoke Museum (1990), and *Vernet's Studio* at the Transmission Gallery in Glasgow and at the 5th Havana Biennale in 2004.[18]

LH: *Ballad of the Wing* was a series of paintings surrounded by objects on plinths with labels plus a wall painting and the best invite ever (a credit card). In retrospect it should have been a series of paintings with a small book of photos/texts of the exhibits on plinths as a catalogue.[19]

Vernet's Studio was definitely an installation: you walked amongst it; forgot bits of it as you went through; shouted the answers; showed off to your friends if you knew more answers than your friends. You needed patience to be able to engage with looking and trying to piece the thing together, then some desire to seriously think about what it means/meant to be an artist; you needed a sense of humour and a map.

Naming the Money was/is an installation; the figures have to be shown as a group, though the group size can vary.[20] The people represented speak to each other, relate and engage with each other, which they would do whether you entered the room or not, and then you walk amongst them looking at them, reading their stories and listening to the sound track. Then they bring you into the conversation. It's the strongest and best and last installation.[21]

Naming the Money tries to bring all the old dialogues I have had in my work about the injustice of slavery and the neglect of black histories and interweave them with the new conversations about belonging, integration, belonging and migration and the struggle to make visible and real a recognition of the rich and complicated contribution to the culture and the economy made by those who have come from somewhere else.

JB: If museums and galleries have co-opted installation art back into the institution, it seems to me that *Naming the Money* has resisted this, particularly in its form at the Victoria and Albert Museum – maybe even exposed the workings of capitalism in the art world.

LH: The workings of capitalism in the art world are exposed by the galleries and museums themselves. They are in love with the price of art, are under the spell of the dealers and the auction rooms. They want to show the work which has been bought by celebrities so that stars may attend their opening launch parties. Artists themselves are the workings of capitalism. The people depicted in the installation *Naming the Money* simply acted as signifiers for the wealth of the nation as they have always done. It's not the way the work was designed; it was never meant to be a work which repeated the scenario of the slave/servant trapped in the houses of rich, highlighting European wealth and African servitude. In its original setting it took up an enormous amount of space across three gallery spaces, through which the audience had to negotiate a path in order to experience a world in which those who had contributed their everything were given a voice to say what it felt like to have come from somewhere else and then be destined to spend their lives negotiating the dangerous political terrain working for nothing disguised as pieces of furniture and ornaments.

JB: The title, particularly the reverberations of the word 'money', has a lot of resonance to popular culture.

LH: Yes, a better title would have been *Show Me the Money*.

JB: Actually I understood 'the money', in *Naming the Money*, to refer to a professional painter's/artist's possibilities – to work, to sell and to show work.

LH: Yes that was a very real issue for me at the time and I did talk about that in the catalogue, but it's obvious really that my project was always about showing and telling and never about buying and selling. I do sell paperwork to private buyers and large works to museums but not often. I was in the process of moving twenty-five years' worth of artworks from a horrible dirty storage unit to a beautiful but very expensive, beautifully lit, heated studio/store 8 metres square with huge doors just round the corner from my house. It was the sixth or seventh time I'd moved the work during the past twenty-five years. It's a wonderful space but I am not clear why I am keeping the five hundred or so pieces of creativity stored there, hence the over-painting project.

JB: Are you making any more installation pieces?

LH: I am working now on *The Jelly Moulds Pavilion* in collaboration with Liverpool Museums Service, an installation in the form of an architectural competition display.[22] Thirty or so nineteenth-century ceramic sweet jelly moulds painted on the outside, with African patterns and portraits of African men and women, sit on a long table as maquettes for a potential public monument. Each is surrounded by tiny figures to help a sense of scale [Figure 9.6]. Around the walls of the room, which looks out over the Mersey, are photographs, drawings and prints depicting the city of Liverpool with a range of these jelly mould pavilions, dotted about in their potential locations. Several more jelly moulds located in other sites across the museums service and across the city are the outriders, each on a simple plinth presented as a part of the competition to decide on a temporary decorative space to commemorate the contribution of several generations of Africans to the health, wealth and architectural splendour of the city.

JB: Why did you want to become an artist?

LH: I wanted to become a journalist really and believed that newspapers could change the world. Then I wanted to be a stage manager and organize the schedules, costumes, props back stage. In the end because I could make art, had O level and A level art and had made drawings, paintings, sculptures and photos every day of my life thus far, plus my mother was an artist, I applied to go to art school to do a foundation with the idea of going on to do theatre design. It was a plan B really and a struggle from the beginning, not an enjoyable period of my life – too competitive.

I didn't plan to become an artist, I was one already and was encouraged by some good teachers and my mother to train to be a professional. I was a useless theatre designer because I found it very difficult to work with other people in a team and was much too political at the end of the 1970s when I left art school to fit comfortably into the world of ballet and opera, which is where most of my fellow graduates found most of their early work. I was rather humourless and serious and driven towards Brechtian theatre and European film but had not been strategic enough to make contacts in these fields.

All through the late 1970s in London I made some attempts at designing for fringe productions for a very political and serious Greek Cypriot theatre company, then moved onto working a little with Yvonne Brewster on some black theatre productions with the Talawa Theatre Company.

At the same time I designed the interiors (furniture and décor and menus, etc.) for innovative and almost revolutionary (at the time) eating places in Waterloo and Covent Garden. This then turned into a very serious campaign to make my own exhibitions of paintings and drawings and cut-outs and to facilitate exhibitions of other people's work. I learned most of what I know about this from Vera Russell at the Artists Market in Covent Garden. Ultimately I applied to the RCA to write a thesis *Young Black Artists in Britain Today* (1984)

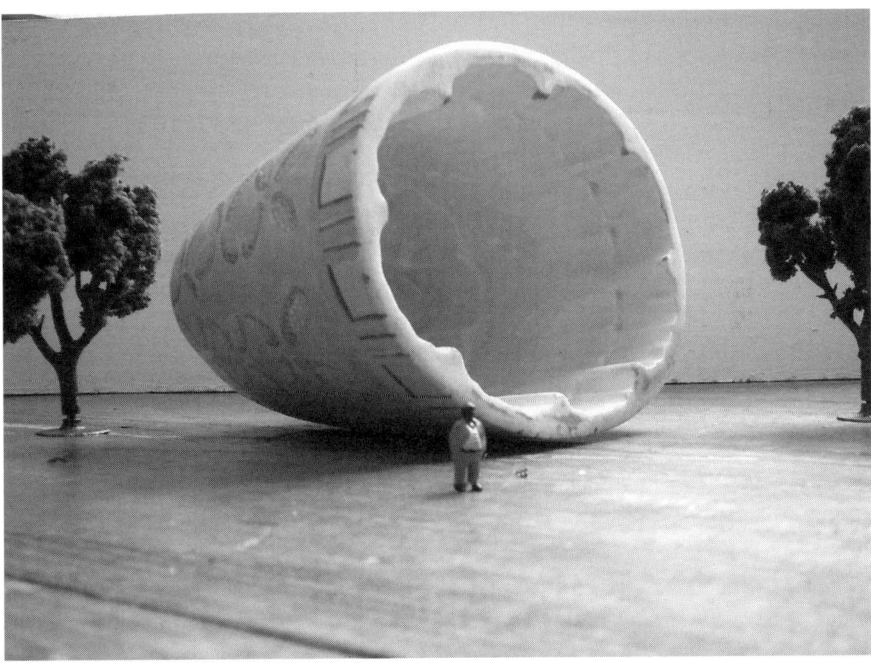

Lubaina Himid, *Liverpool Sweet Jelly Mould Monument Project* (2010). Maquette for Falkner Square. 9.6

to combine my passion for this and my absolute conviction that black people could be important artists. At the time everyone thought this was the maddest and most impossible idea imaginable.

It wasn't.

JB: Your reference to Bertolt Brecht is fascinating in relation to one of the themes across your work, as I see it – namely the opening up of art's official spaces to scrutiny and to disruption. Is that too strong a connection to make?

LH: It's a very flattering connection to make. It's accurate, in part; that is exactly what I have spent decades trying to do. However, I have usually failed to get any admission from any of the arts organizations of the impact that my work has had on their policies, strategies or working practices. This could be because I am not interested enough in what institutions say, but am overly pedantic about what they do. I would tend to ask whether there is evidence that an organization changed its behaviour; if there have been improvements, who cares who made it happen?

JB: There is also a Brechtian dynamic to your installation work – the staged setting, disrupted and changed constantly.

LH: I love Brecht's work with a passion and would never have been interested in theatre at all but for his plays. I would go back to designing plays for theatre if I was invited to work on a Brecht: *Mother Courage and her Children*, the *Life of Galileo*, *The Threepenny Opera* or *The Good Person of Szechwan* would all tempt me back. I do try to inject into the installation work an atmosphere of unsettled fluidity, as if it has been placed but only until it is placed again. Some of the painted canvas series should be viewed in such a way that it might be possible for an audience to change the setting, move say the image/text double canvases in *Plan B* and choose a different way of looking at the work by swapping the texts around or hanging all eight canvases together like a cartoon strip.

JB: What is your process of work – do you keep notebooks, diaries, do you make preliminary sketches, etc?

LH: I couldn't make work without making quick and quite scruffy pencil or ink sketches all the time every day at some point or another on all sorts of scrappy pieces of Xerox paper or in sketchbooks, sometimes on good paper and sometimes in the front or back cover of whatever rubbish novel I am reading.

Most ideas need working out before hand and most finished pieces are nothing at all like the preliminary sketches.

JB: Colour plays a significant part in your work; in the nine paintings of *Venetian Maps*, for instance, there is a rich and sensuous use of colour.[23]

LH: The use of colour was part of the strategy I used to get an audience to approach the work from a distance in the space of a gallery, like the relationship between flowers and bees; it's a way of seducing, engaging and becoming one. I wanted them to be rich, expensive, glorious works that collections would buy because audiences loved them. Idiot.

JB: The way you use colour is extremely evocative; in *Naming the Money* and *Talking on Corners, Speaking in Tongues* (2007) you evoke Venetian painting in the volume of the figures and the rich exploration of colour, or is your interest in the contrast of flat colour planes with highly textured areas rooted in other sources?

LH: The influences in these works are mostly French painting, Matisse and Picasso, and, yes, Venetian painting: Carpaccio, Veronese, etc. I'd looked at this kind of painting for pleasure for years since the age of five or so in London and from my teenage years all over Britain in stately homes and museums and all across Europe on numerous summer driving holidays with my mother and step-father. It is the unexpectedness of the deep, rich, powerful colour combinations that interests me, the surprise and delight of one complicated colour against another thereby making another nameless colour, creating a sound almost rather than a colour. It's why I love the work of Bridget Riley because she unpacked the formula and the structure of why and how one is enraptured by the rustling, flickering leaves on a tree after rainfall or the hypnotic effect of the endless sight and sound of sea tides dappled by changing light.

I was very influenced by my mother's profession as a textile designer. In recent years I have tried to make a comprehensive study of African fabric from right across the continent, sometimes buying it but mostly looking at/buying expensive books, looking at shop windows and of course women in the streets of London. The woven Kentes of Ghana and the printed Kangas of Kenya and Tanzania have been the most influential in terms of colour and combinations of colour, but Fante flags, Nigerian indigo batiks, and beaded work from South Africa have been very important too.[24]

JB: African textiles – woven and printed – have a richness and intensity in their colour confrontations, rather as you say about Bridget Riley

LH: The richness and intensity at the heart of these fabrics comes from the lives and histories of many diverse sets of people, as John Picton says 'it's about people leading successful lives making and using art, about production and patronage, about constantly revised design agendas thereby maintaining a contemporary relevance. It is about an ability to thrive in competition with all manner of rivals in an Africa that is not all about civil war, corrupt politicians, starving people and infectious diseases. It is about a series of engagements of artists and patrons with materials often at first imported from Europe (but now manufactured in Africa), and India (and Indonesia) figure in the narrative also.'[25] The power of Bridget Riley for me is that her narratives are seemingly astonishingly clear, a bit like a large advertisement for chocolate or underwear or cigarettes, but at the same time completely obscure, secretive and rather sexy.

JB: You've written that 'colour is a vital element a wild bold and tumultuous brushing on of a wide palette', is it still?[26]

LH: Colour is still a vital element, it is still the language, but there is no wild, bold or tumultuous brushing now. I don't want to be read in the same way or as a sub-species of Albert Irwin or Howard Hodgkin. I have become a very quiet and cautious, meticulous, obsessive painter, using tiny brushes and making tiny patterns for hours at a time. There is no hurry now, no need to express a masculine energy or an extravagance of paint. It does not matter now how long a painting takes or how many times I have to over-paint a tiny triangle to get the colour to lift and sing.

Much of that is also to do with the paint I use, the colours I mix and then obviously the colours I put next to one another. At one point long ago I painted in a studio with deep blue walls, which helped lift the colour too. Now every time I look up from the work there is an intense mass of green to compete with. My studio looks out onto the garden and then out onto a park.

JB: How do you work? Do you spend time drawing?

LH: I'd like to spend more time drawing, there is still a great deal of room for improvement there, but when I've had time recently I have spent it screen printing. A disciplined programme of work spread over a few weeks simply drawing to invent more marks and ways of making those marks would help improve everything I do. I manage to concentrate on improving my drawing and work hard at it now and again but it's frustrating to engage with failure day after day; luckily I believe that success in the visual can't be achieved without an understanding of failure. The days of painting fast in order to fill a gap in a gallery programme schedule brought on by a fortuitous funding package or to prove that I could maintain a vast output and teach five days a week are over. While making the *Lancaster Dinner Service* I started to overpaint previous work and specially selected *Guardian* newspaper pages and so since 2005 a major project has been to over-paint large old works, mostly *Beach Houses* (1985) so far, but also badly sloppily executed paintings from other series that I would never show again; this has continued and has become very important. I also work on very small paper pieces, which are then sent to New York to sell at Peg Alston's gallery.

JB: So your practice of over-painting produces palimpsest surfaces in obliterating appropriated imagery?

LH: All of those things, but each definition depends on the surface being over-painted or patterned. I certainly wish to obliterate the bad paintings and the paintings that hold memories of bad times. It's still possible with these paintings to see the few square inches of life and dynamism that exists from the previous work, but the new patterning should take over. When I painted over the ceramics for *Swallow Hard: The Lancaster Dinner Service* it was to make 'fakes', to indulge in remaking great British cartoons and to make a political point about histories having been obliterated. When I paint over a selected page from the *Guardian* newspaper it's to highlight the crude juxtapositions the paper has made between an image of a black person and the text chosen to accompany it. The African patterning covers the irrelevant text and also serves to reclaim the portrait of the person. It clarifies the unhelpful often crudely amusing design of the page but attempts to restore the balance.

JB: Where does your interest in maps and mapping come from?

LH: This is a London thing: a young life spent looking at the A–Z constantly to find specialist shops, museums, gardens, galleries, friends' houses, new contacts, simply learning how to navigate and explore the city alone. I lived in several parts of London so directions had to be re-learned. It was part of my everyday; it meant that no matter how little money I had everything was possible, no need for tube or bus fares or to learn to drive. Maps were/are enabling, a structure and a formula that could be interpreted, improvised, re-drawn. People ask me for directions nearly every day of my life, even today, I don't carry a map but nearly always know my way around the place I am in. Another sad case of needing to be seen to belong probably. I learned early that no two maps are the same (I love that) that maps are a guide for you to learn to discard really. They don't give the flavour, the colour, the smell or the sound of a place but encourage you to explore safe in the knowledge that with their help and the ability to think/read upside down you can always escape or delve deeper. You are never alone with a map.

In the painting work around colonial histories they became the symbol of the ability of the conquering world to divide, destroy and own natural resources and indigenous peoples. The women in my paintings were always ripping them up. In some works I paint over the maps rendering them useless. Futile expression of an angry and frustrated creative mind.

JB: Maps carry a visible and invisible narrative in *Venetian Maps* (1997).

LH: *Venetian Maps* (1997) depicted in nine large 7′×5′ acrylic paintings on canvas and a series of texts (now lost), the lost lives of the black diaspora, the unwritten but intensely experienced narratives of the everyday, everything from the simple yet long-lasting miseries of lost toys to the unrecognized contribution to Western culture, the rescuers of dropped relics, the slave servants, the princes, the visiting curiosities, the drowned treasures. It was too rich a story on the one hand and yet too simplistically made to be a nine-paintings project made over nine weeks. This work really developed into many other series of paintings, drawings, films and installations made between 1999 and 2000, until now really.

JB: So maps can carry many different mappings within one image, all working at different levels and intensities, in *Between the Two My Heart is Balanced* (Acrylic on canvas, 1292 × 1600 × 55 mm) in Tate, for example.

LH: *Between the Two My Heart is Balanced* attempted to have several conversations at the same time during the period it was painted (1991) and exhibited (1992). It was an attempt to paint in the same painting two black women who are not sisters and who are not mother and daughter and who are not on display for the benefit of a white audience. I could not find any other examples of this and so it was worth the difficulty of doing it. It was an attempt to show that we all have subtly different strategies from each other; we appear to be doing the same thing but are not. The woman on the left in the painting is taking navigation charts from a pile that separates them; the two women then rip these up, discarding the fragments. The other woman is ripping up maps and engaging with the rower of the boat; the audience.

It was also part of a conversation that I have had with paintings in the Tate collection since my teenage experience of visiting Millbank. The Tissot paintings in the collection were attractive and seductive; the women were creamy and dressed in divine garments and their languorous, poised, confident impact remained with me for years. I longed for my painting and Tissot's *Portsmouth Harbour* to hang in the same gallery at the same time.[27]

Tate acquired *Between the Two* in 1994 using their VAT surplus two years after I painted it, but not before someone had pierced it with a screw driver in the eyes and mouths when it was exhibited at the South Bank.

When Tate placed it in *Picturing Blackness* its reading was as a trophy, an acquisition part of a display to indicate that they were not ignoring the issues we were raising, nothing more or less. I was happy to have my work in the British collection; it changed my life. When they displayed it as part of *Re-presenting British art 1500–2000* it was not part of the curator's original game plan, so is not in the catalogue but was included on the last-minute instructions of a curator at Tate Modern.[28]

JB: The possibility that it can now be displayed again with two other paintings from the *Revenge* series might enable different placings in Tate, don't you think?

LH: It would be wonderful to think that a young curator might take time to consider different placings as you say, but I have not had the opportunity of discussing any possibilities with anyone. It would be great to see *Ankledeep* (1992) alongside Tracy Emin's *My Bed* (1998) and then *Carpet* (1992) could sit near Albert Irvin's *St Germain* (1995) and Howard Hodgkin's *Dinner at Smith Square* (1975–79) and have a real conversation with Chris Ofili's *No Woman No Cry* (1998). Dear old *Between the Two My Heart is Balanced* (1991) would still be interesting near the Tissot painting *Portsmouth Harbour* and a really cool Bridget Riley like *Nataraja* (1993).

JB: Painting the sea and water have been a key area of work for you since the 1990s in *Revenge*, and principally in *Plan B* in which the water is engulfing and menacing.[29] Why this concern with the sea?

LH: The concern with the sea stems from many things, an acute awareness of and fixation on my own history as a small island person born in Zanzibar. The treat, as a small child, of being taken to my Lancashire grandmother's house in Blackpool twice a year for holidays from London was a huge event. I have never been able to swim properly and am very frightened of the sea and of drowning. I used to constantly look at new ways of painting it as if it had never been painted. The reading of narratives about/by people being taken forcibly from west-coast Africa to the coasts of America in trading ships to be later used as slaves made an impact during the early part of my painting career. My Comorian grandmother's history of being taken to Zanzibar having been bought from her parents by a Portuguese woman resonated somewhat. She must have travelled in a dhow in around 1900 from one of the Comorian islands to Zanzibar.

The fear of and obsession with the sea used to exactly mirror my life at the time of painting these works in which I could not navigate my way out of the dangerous places because they seemed safe. The strategy for escape seemed more frightening than the known danger.

JB: So if water is a sign of fear and danger, it is also highly symbolic in diasporic narratives – as conduit, as sign of death and of memory. In *Revenge* and the ritual figures of mirror, cloth and bowl, in *Mirror/Cloth/Bowl*, and in *Swallow Hard* there are many references to water in these senses aren't there?

LH: I love to look at water from the shore to try to fathom it then to visually work it out then paint it. I love the sound of it, the noise of it even the repetitive drone of it, but the reality and intense magnitude of oceans and the confusion of fast-moving rivers is quite beyond me. There is no desire in me to navigate water, to enter it or to pit myself against it by swimming or sailing in it. It's the best expression I can put across in paint of something very frightening, which epitomizes to me a world beyond here but before the abyss, the nothingness. The moment before dying.

JB: There is a close focus on water and the sea in *Plan B*, the work you made during your residency at Tate St Ives, 1999/2000.[30]

LH: Yes, I painted that series at a time in my life when I was frightened a lot of the time. I painted the work in order to escape from that danger, to face it, to tell everyone about it and to leave it behind. The texts talk about being in danger and then getting out from under it, I was wishing myself into freedom and peace. The work depicted many empty rooms: uneasy spaces seemingly beautiful and safe compared to the danger of the ocean beyond the windows, but in reality they were dreadful airless places in which it was impossible to breathe and from which it was very difficult to leave. There were references to the holding stations for captured Africans along the west coasts of eighteenth- and nineteenth-century Mali, Ghana and Nigeria and also to the bombed streets and squares of Second World War London, but the experiential power of the work, even now ten years after it was completed, lies in the very real danger at the centre of my life at the time.

JB: In *Plan B* there are six two-part canvases. One contains an image and the other writing – a discontinuous narrative. What is the role of the writing here: does it activate a reading of danger?

LH: The two-part canvases are not really discontinuous narratives. The texts depict the scene either before the image or after the image, the viewer decides. The images are either places of safety finally arrived at or places of danger recently left. The writing gives you another picture for free, an active moving exterior setting in which to imagine the drama/reality/memory/dream or whatever. The writing gives you an opportunity in about seventy-five words to get from extreme crisis to a quieter safer zone. It is your map you make the picture and you follow the instructions. It allows you/me to be brave.[31]

JB: Writing seems to be a significant activity for you; do you, like Louise Bourgeois, write all the time?

LH: I do write all the time but it takes many different forms and is not really very unusual or creative. I make 'to do' lists and shopping lists, I write instructions/notes for my students to refer to when we have had tutorials and each semester have to write feedback forms for them. I write in a painting/making diary every day, which is left in the studio. I write notes most days about ideas for making pictures or short films in another notebook which is kept in my bag and travels about with me. I write mobile phone texts to friends and students and e-mails to most people, postcards to friends, typed and hand-written thank-you letters.

I sometimes write papers for conferences but they are hardly academic texts, more like performance scripts or long rambling prose poems.[32]

JB: The doubling of writing and making images is also a component of Kara Walker's work.

LH: I think we are trying to do very different things for very different audiences. The work I have seen of hers both here and in the States must have a strong resonance for an audience directly descended from either slave or master, an audience still grappling with what that means and how to deal with that a hundred and fifty years on. It's a challenge for me and many of my black women friends and colleagues just to be in the room with the work, to be in the same space as such scenes of degradation, violence and sexual exploitation, but Kara Walker is very well collected both by private collectors and museums internationally.

When I use text it's often to give you two pictures for the price of one. They tend to be descriptive and image based, designed to summon another time or place, a similar painting or familiar narrative.

JB: You have worked as a painter on canvas, paper, on cut-outs and on china during a period when much artistic practice was mainly conceptual and post-conceptual. How do you see being a painter during this predominance?

LH: My work is very rarely discussed in the context of contemporary practice; no one is interested in talking about it for its aesthetic value. Plenty of young artists are looking at the work to see what they can learn perhaps, to see what to avoid possibly, to see how to improve sure, but no one is engaging critically around the work as contemporary practice, so there is no dialogue about this anywhere for me to respond to. I am not a painter in the strictest sense; I didn't train as a painter and am not obsessed by the stuff of it, though I do use paint and do paint things. I am a political strategist who uses a visual language to encourage conversation, argument, change.

JB: Is the reception of your work – in its written, critical form and in the way galleries want to present your work or invite you to show work – locked into some postcolonial concept of 'Africanness'?

LH: It would be so interesting to hear the curators themselves talk about why they show the work, what purpose it serves, what funding it allows, which audiences they hope it will attract. It does not qualify as African, of this you can be sure. I am never in African shows. I was born in East Africa but am not considered to be part of that world, the world of El Anatsui, Sokari Douglas Camp and Yinka Shonibare.

JB: Kobena Mercer[33] and Olu Oguibe suggested that critics who wish only to hear about the artist's African 'essence' have silenced the contemporary African artist.[34] Does this apply in the UK?

LH: I don't see or hear the critics in the UK wishing to hear about anything at all to do with African artists or for anything but another opportunity to write about and discuss the same very small group of indigenous English artists in the hope perhaps that they may be compared to a group of European and Euro/American artists. What silences artists is the realization that most galleries and museums in Britain are too afraid to show the Africans who live here, don't know the African artists who live in Europe or those who live in many of the fifty-two African countries across the continent. Where on earth are these artists supposed to show art work in this tiny country? How could they be exposed to critical review when there is so little appetite for real and intelligent debate around visual art, whoever is making it? So few art magazines, so little online debate, so few critics, so few galleries with the balls to promote an open and active dialogue about creativity debates, unless these take place around the private and privileged metropolitan dinner tables.

JB: Where is your work going now?

LH: My work has become a little more playful now, both in the making and in the look and the feel of the objects themselves. I'm not under heavy pressure from anyone to sell it at any price these days either. At the same time I will continue with the *Guardian* newspaper over-painting project, probably the completion of one hundred pages will make the point. I have shows lined up for the next couple of years, small shows designed, without shame, by museums to widen participation. Each of the two exhibitions, one in 2010 and one in 2011, represents a great opportunity for me to make a series works for audiences to play with. I'd like to tour a couple of shows of mine which are currently languishing in my large, dry, warm (too expensive) studio store. *The Lancaster Dinner Service* and the *Negative/Positive Guardians* both need to be seen by more people.

The work itself could change dramatically during the next five years. Having completed the *Jelly Moulds* monument project at sites across Liverpool; following that, the Manchester Dandy project for Manchester Museums at the Platt Hall (costume museum) site, the work will have to renew in the studio. Usually it takes a year of making every day without a deadline at my own speed to develop a new direction, or perhaps it would be more honest to say that I will be looking for a new way of talking about the same things. I will probably develop my skills further in the print room with a lot more traditional screen print combined with etch and digital. I should draw more seriously, but it's more likely that engaging in collaborative projects as a director on moving image work will continue too.

Acknowledgement

I would like to thank Lubaina Himid for giving so generously of her time and her willingness to offer stimulating and engaging discussion of her work and a variety of issues.

Notes

1 See www.lubainahimid.info for the full range of her work.

2 Mike Tooby was at this time curator at the Mappin Art Gallery in Sheffield, now Director of Learning and Programmes, National Museums of Wales. *Depicting History for Today*, a group show curated by Tooby, was at the Mappin and Leeds City Art Gallery, Rochdale Art Gallery, 1983. There has been some discussion of Lubaina Himid as a history painter, and the issue is developed in discussion of *Revenge* in J. Beckett and D. Cherry, 'Clues to Events', in M. Bal and I.E. Boer (eds), *The Point of Theory* (Amsterdam: Amsterdam University Press, 1994), pp. 51–5; Maud Sulter situated Lubaina Himid's work as history painting 'in its ability to take on board massive issues of history and translate them into a language which gives voice to the disenfranchised'. *Venetian Maps*, exhibition catalogue, Harris Museum and Art Gallery, Preston, 1997; and further in G. Pollock, 'Revenge, Lubaina Himid and the Making of New Narratives for New Histories', in G. Pollock, *Differencing the Canon: Feminist Desire and the Writing of Art's Histories* (London and New York: Routledge, 1999), pp. 168–98.

3 François-Dominique Toussaint L'Ouverture, leader of the Haitian revolution, led the enslaved Africans to victory over the Europeans and secured the independence

of Haiti in 1792. The fifteen watercolours in Lubaina Himid's *Toussaint L'Ouverture* series are now in the Arts Council Collection.

4 Drawing on a form familiar from French restaurant signs and seventeenth- and eighteenth-century life sized companion figures, Lubaina Himid has used the cut-out format since the early 1980s in her series of white men with erect penis', exhibited in *Pandora's Box* (1984). Writing of the cut-outs in *Naming the Money* Himid insists that they are not sculptures but 'portraits, history paintings, political treatises, stand-ins, adverts, effigies'. L. Himid, *Naming the Money: Hatton-Gallery, University of Newcastle upon Tyne, 17 January–13 March 2004* (Newcastle upon Tyne: University of Newcastle upon Tyne, 2004), p. 4.

5 *Cotton.com*, Cube Gallery, Manchester, 2002; *Naming the Money*, Hatton Gallery, Newcastle upon Tyne, *Swallow Hard: The Lancaster Dinner Service*, Judges Lodgings Museum, Lancaster 2007.

6 *Swallow Hard: The Lancaster Dinner Service* was, like other works by Himid located in gallery settings, designed to work with a museum collection/display; in our conversation she said that 'The truth is that the invitation usually comes from venues keen to fulfil their BME quotas. I oblige and attempt to present an unsettling uncomfortable juxtaposition to the objects or histories on display.' In the accompanying exhibition pamphlet she comments further that 'it was an intervention, a mapping and an excavation. It is a fragile monument to an invisible engine working for nothing, in an amazingly greedy machine.' Himid in *Swallow Hard: The Lancaster Dinner Service* (Preston: Lancashire Museums, 2007), p. 1. Lubaina Himid talks briefly about the installation on YouTube, 13 July 2007.

7 'Black and British: Are We Suffering from a Crisis of Identity?', *The Voice*, 1339A (22–28 September 2008).

8 F. Fanon, 'On National Culture', in *The Wretched of the Earth* (New York: Grove Press, 1968).

9 Paul Gilroy has argued that cultural historians 'should take the Atlantic as one single, complex unit of analysis in their discussions of the modern world and use it to produce an explicitly transnational and intercultural perspective.' *Black Atlantic, Modernity and the Double Consciousness* (London: Verso, 1993), p. 15. This argument is discussed in conjunction with Himid's *Revenge* in A. Rice, *Radical Narratives of the Black Atlantic* (London: Continuum Press, 2003), pp. 72ff.

10 *Cotton.Com*, 2002, was an explorative work, looking at the connections between Manchester's cotton workers and enslaved cotton-pickers in South Carolina in the eighteenth century. A hundred monochrome pattern-painted square canvases were displayed opposite a brass panel reading, 'He said I looked like a painting by Murillo as I carried water for the hoe gang just because I balanced the bucket on my head.' Discussed, and illustrated, in A. Rice, 'The Cotton that Connects, the Cloth that Binds, Manchester's Civil War, Abe's Statue, and Lubaina Himid's Transnational Polemic', *Atlantic Studies* 4/2 (October 2007), 285–303; drawn into analysis of history and memory and illustrated in M. Crinson, *Urban Memory, History and Amnesia in the Modern City* (London and New York: Routledge, 2005).

11 Stuart Hall raises two distinct approaches to the concept of diaspora and cultural identity in S. Hall, 'Cultural Identity and Diaspora', *Framework: The Journal of Cinema and Media* 36 (1989), reprinted in 38/9 (1992), 222–37; quotation, p. 222;

see also S. Hall, 'Black Diaspora Artists in Britain: Three Moments in Post-War History', *History Workshop Journal* 61 (2006), 1–24.

12 *New Robes for MaShulan: Lubaina Himid Work Past and Present*, Rochdale Art Gallery. The Gallery commissioned Lubaina Himid and Maud Sulter to produce new work and curate the exhibition. The show included *A Room for MaShulan* and Himid's *Mirror/Cloth/Bowl*, 1986.

13 Explored in Himid's *Tailor, Striker, Singer, Dandy*, water colours and drawings, Platt Hall, Manchester 2011 and *Negative Positives Guardian paperworks*, 2007–09, screen prints.

14 P. Keiller, *London* (BFI/FilmFour, 1994). Keiller's film is a portrait of London shot over twelve months in 1992, when John Major was elected prime minister, there were renewed IRA bombings, the 'Black Wednesday' monetary crisis. The city is traversed and viewed through the unseen 'guide' Robinson.

15 Iain Sinclair, discussing Keiller's *London* in *Lights Out for the Territory* (London: Granta Books, 1992), pp. 296ff.

16 Reconsidered in *Thin Black Line(s)*, Tate Britain 2011–12.

17 The intervention of spectators is important to the installation; see the YouTube film of spectators in the gallery interacting with the exhibit, walking through the cut figures and responding to the music. In our conversation (July 2009) Lubaina Himid said that she 'would like to make work especially for an online audience rather than try to just show work that's already made. *Naming the Money* online was very useful though because not many people (6,000) saw the original show at Hatton. … Susan Walsh and I work on small moving image/voiceover ideas all the time in which what is said is equal to and interweaves with the image played out and many of these are more suited to being shown in this way; sort of three-minute wonders or two-minute pop videos or moving collages.'

18 Himid re-created Horace Vernet's *Interieur d'un atelier*, 1824 (copper-plate engraving) which depicts activities inside a studio, replacing the all male figures of the Vernet engraving with large cut-out and painted figures of women artists and their representations of women. Transmission Gallery, Glasgow, 2–26 February 2004.

19 For installation photographs of *Ballad of The Wing*, see www.lubainahimid.info.

20 *Naming the Money* (Hatton Gallery, Newcastle, January–March 2004) was an installation of one hundred life-sized, collaged and painted, cut-out figures, representing memorials to black slaves sold to European royal courts, which elaborated on the multiple themes of naming, belonging, invisibility and survival, structured in groups of ten, invoking the ten distinctive trades they took up. Of the groupings of the cut-out figures Himid wrote 'they cluster together, they stand apart, they think, talk, remember'. Himid, *Naming the Money*, pp. 5–6. The installation emphasized the interplay between the pain of enslavement and displacement and the making and re-making of identity. Hall's argument that there is no eternally fixed past waiting for discovery, rather 'identities are the names we give to the different ways we are positioned by, and position ourselves within, the narratives of the past', might usefully be developed in conjunction with *Naming the Money*. Hall, 'Cultural Identity and Diaspora', p. 222.

21 L. Himid, *Naming the Money* (Newcastle Upon Tyne: Hatton-Gallery, University of Newcastle upon Tyne, 2004; DVD).

22 *The Jelly Mould Pavilions* project was designed to find solutions to the challenge of how to commemorate the contribution made by the people of the African diaspora to the history, culture and rich fabric of the city of Liverpool; Lubaina Himid was awarded the Northern Art Prize – People's Choice Award 2011 for the exhibit. Sudley House, Liverpool Museums Service, 2010.
23 *Venetian Maps* was a series of nine paintings, shown at the Harris Museum in Preston, 14 May–21 June 1997.
24 In 1992 Maud Sulter noted that the paintings in *Revenge* 'weave around the concept of fabric. The making of cloth, the creation of pattern, women's clothing and fabric; the existence of fabric as a form of Black women's creativity. Lubaina has chosen fabric to be the ground, the arena for the battle with imperialism.' M. Sulter, 'Without Tides, No Maps', in Lubaina Himid, *Revenge: A Masque in Five Tableaux* (Rochdale: Rochdale Art Gallery, 1992), p. 24.
25 J. Picton, *The Art of African Textiles: Technology, Tradition and Lurex* (London: Barbican Art Gallery and Lund Humphries, 1995), p. 12.
26 L. Himid, 'Colour is a vital element a wild bold and tumultuous brushing on of a wide palette.' *Revenge* (1992).
27 *Between the Two My Heart is Balanced* (1991), 1292 × 1600 × 55 mm, acrylic on canvas, with *Ankle Deep* and *Carpet* (both Tate) and other works are from *Revenge: A Masque in Five Acts. Between the Two* re-inhabits the title of a dry-point by the Victorian artist James Tissot, entitled *Entrée les deux mon coeur balance.* The subject of Tissot's print, as in his oil *Portsmouth Dockyard* (Tate), c.1877 is choice; a Highlander is seated in a boat between two women. In Himid's canvas the focus is on the women. The paired black women symbolically re-addressing history has been a recurrent theme in her work, for example, in the 1992 *Five* (private collection) from *Revenge*, where two women, seated either side of a table on which the Atlantic slave trade route is delineated, engage in discussion.
28 *Picturing Blackness in British Art*, title of Tate Britain displays, 1995.
29 In 1998 Himid was artist in residence at Tate St Ives. Her studio, based in the Lifeguard's hut (not in use in the winter months), offered direct views of the sea and shore; the sea, near and distant, stormy and calm, recurs in the large paintings of the subsequent exhibition *Plan B* (Tate St Ives), notably in the painting *Plan B*, acrylic on canvas, 1999 (Birmingham City Art Galleries).
30 *Plan B* is discussed in Jane Beckett, *Plan B*, exhibition catalogue (London: Tate, 1999–2000).
31 A variant account of the place of text in *Plan B*, given in response to Alan Rice, suggests 'what I am trying to do is give you two pictures in one … with Plan B, you get an interior image, and you get an exterior text, and the exterior text you had to invent yourself. It says, "we cross the rivers" but you had to bring your own experience – whether it was a movie of crossing rivers, or whether you'd actually done it – you had to bring that … Whether it was twenty-first century, or seventeenth century, you brought it, it didn't tell you that that's what it was. There are no names in those, there are no dates. So mostly with text, I'm trying to make another picture.' Alan Rice, *Commemorating Abolition: Interview with Lubaina Himid*, www.uclan.ac.uk, February 2007, pp. 7/14.
32 Lubaina Himid's written texts are being collected for a forthcoming publication.

33 K. Mercer, 'Black Art and the Burden of Representation', *Third Text* 10 (Spring 1990), 61–78; reprinted in Mercer, *Welcome to the Jungle: New Positions in Black Cultural Studies* (London: Routledge, 1994); and see Mercer, 'Iconography after Identity', in D.A.Bailey, I. Baucom and S. Boyce (eds), *Shades of Black: Assembling Black Arts in 1980s Britain* (Durham, NC and London: Duke University Press, 2005), pp. 49–58.

34 Oguibe curated *Seen/Unseen* (Bluecoat Gallery, Liverpool) showing five African artists: Lubaina Himid, Yinka Shonibare, Folake Shoga, Uzo Egonu, and his own work; see O. Oguibe, *Seen/Unseen*, exhibition catalogue (Liverpool: Bluecoat Gallery, 18 June–23 July 1994); U. Egonu, *Uzo Egonu: An African Artist in the West* (London: Kala Press, 1995); O. Oguibe, *The Culture Game* (Minnesota: University of Minnesota Press, 2004).

A burd's eye view: Paula Rego's *Abortion Series*[1] 10

Michele Waugh

Over a six-month period between 1998 and 1999 Paula Rego (b. 1935) produced a series of ten pastels, plus a triptych, inspired by a political event in Portugal. These pastels are entitled *Untitled I–X* and *Triptych*. Each is mounted on aluminium and sized 110 × 100 cm. There is also a series of ten etchings, eight produced in 1999 and a further two produced in 2000, depicting scenes that are similar to those of the pastels. *Untitled I–VI* are sized 19.6 × 29.2 cm, *Untitled VII*, 29.2 × 19.6 cm, *Untitled VIII*, 19.8 × 29.5 cm, *Untitled 2000*, 19.5 × 29.5 cm and *Untitled 2000*, 20 × 29.7 cm. They all portray solitary women who have undergone an abortion. In this chapter I am going to examine this work by Rego in order to tease out the ways in which corporeal feminism can be a useful tool to assess the production of women artists practising in the UK today. The chapter will include a tight, focused discussion of a limited case study highlighting areas of concern for women in terms of cultural and societal identity. I will also reveal whether or not feminism is a conscious intention on behalf of the artist. Lastly, I will assess the reception of the work in the media asking the following question: has the intention of the artist been understood?

Rego, born in Portugal, first came to the UK in the 1950s, and then divided her time between both countries for the following twenty years. Since the 1970s she has been working and living in the UK. For her the sense of her Portuguese roots has remained very important: 'I am Portuguese. I live in London, I like living in London, but I am Portuguese.'[2] Nevertheless she is an established artist who has made a home in the UK. She has also said that the part of her that is Portuguese is related to her childhood and that her appreciation of poetry, for example, as well as the discussion of her paintings is better conducted in English.

> In literature I get on better with the English … in English than I do in my own language. And to talk about pictures for instance, I find it immensely hard to talk about them in Portuguese, I cannot. So English is for the grown up more, the Portuguese is the child-like, which also comes into the grown up and is totally precious, because without that we cannot exist.[3]

I would suggest that a close examination of Rego's work is useful to understand some of the ways in which contemporary women artists are testing the limits of existing maps of globalization. I am looking at globalization in terms of social and political readings – that is, ones that examine emerging forms of authority that are offering new grounds for political action including a reconfiguration of social space, or new understandings of identity or society. Rego deals with a complex web of myth and legend in her work, one that has a somewhat sinister edge. Her work confronts societal norms in terms of the relationships and stories she depicts.[4] Rego consciously engages with the politics of life as experienced by women in the societies with which she is familiar: Portugal, the country of her birth, and the UK, where she lives and practises. She uses her creativity and zeal to reach a larger audience by using traditional artistic media – painting and etching – and this in turn enables her to communicate her political views. Regarding the *Abortion Series* Rego said,

> There is a feminist angle, because I am a feminist, indeed I am, very much so … I didn't want to show blood, gore or anything to sicken, because people wouldn't look at it then. And what you want to do is make people look, make pretty colours and make it agreeable, and in that way make people look at life.[5]

The series was created in direct response to her anger following the 'No' vote for the legalization of abortion in Portugal. The work was not commissioned by an outside source, but something she felt compelled to do. They were first shown in Portugal at Centro de Arte Moderna José de Azeredo Perdigão, Lisbon 18 May–29 August 1999. The exhibition attracted both controversy and record attendances.[6] Interestingly she chose to dress the women within this series in English school uniform. This immediately highlights a notion of interculturalism as opposed to multiculturalism, by which I mean that as an artist Rego has experienced differing cultural heritages, but is able to exchange knowledge(s)[7] without losing either her own individuality or a sense of place and time. The feared homogeneity of practice by artists working on the global stage is not here in evidence. The concrete example of the *Abortion Series* is ideally placed to illustrate a reading of inter- and multiculturalism and how interculturalism informs that series.

This also enables an analysis of what that relationship tells us about Rego's approach to women, feminism and globalization. The fact that these images are accessible via the internet and in a book, as well as in their original form as paintings and etchings, challenges the hegemony of globalization. The web is an important tool in globalizing the economy, but, on the other hand, it also disseminates information and creates relationships among those who would like to challenge globalism's dominance. Admittedly there are still vast swathes of the world where access to the internet is either non-existent or in its infancy; this is changing week by week so that even remote places are gaining greater access. For example, there was an article in the *Boston Globe* in January 2008 discussing how a slum dweller in New Delhi has opened his first 'smart card' bank account using a technology that is so advanced it is not yet available in the USA.[8] Third-world countries are able to leap-frog over interim technological scenarios and plug straight into emerging networks of communication and trade. By utilizing the very tools that seem to threaten the uniqueness of social and cultural identity Rego is able to carve out a very personal position for 'woman'. The fact that this position is able to be communicated globally does not dissipate its power.

The background to the creation of the works is that on 28 June 1998 a referendum was held on the issue of abortion in Portugal. In order to understand the production of these pastels it is important to understand some of the political situation that inspired them. The relationship between church and state in Portugal is complex and not an issue for full debate here.[9] Suffice it to say that the cumulative effect has resulted in a society where gender roles are clearly defined. Men are expected to be the authority figure within the family, to work and provide for their families, whilst women are expected to fulfil a role as mother and homemaker, producing numerous, unplanned children for the good of the state under the headship of not only their husbands, but also the head of state, in his self-proclaimed position of father of the nation. All this is finally subject to the headship of God. This was the restrictive and prescriptive condition for women. Under António de Oliveira Salazar (1889–1970), the prime minister and dictator of Portugal between 1932 and 1968, women were not allowed to work, or to have a passport or bank account without written permission from their husbands.[10] Under the 1940 Concordat with the Vatican women were instructed to emulate the Virgin Mary, both culturally and maternally. These attributes of femininity were laid down in governmental statutes essentially insisting upon women's submission to a domestic, obedient and chaste life. The language of the Vatican Concordat with Portugal is instructive

> Women's work outside the family sphere disintegrates home life, separates its different members, and makes them strangers to each other … Life in common disappears; the work of educating the children suffers and families become smaller. … We consider that it is the man who should labor [sic] and maintain the family and we say that the work of the married woman outside her home, and similarly that of the spinster who is a member of the family, should not be encouraged.[11]

Rego was not brought up as a practising Catholic, not at home anyway, or by her father who was a democrat and a republican diametrically opposed to both clerical authority and Salazar's regime. However, an all-pervasive Catholic society left its mark upon the psyche of the young Rego. This encompassing Catholicism was due to the reported apparition of Our Lady in Fatima in 1917.

According to records the apparition took place on the 13th day of each month over six consecutive months to three peasant children. The result was a zealous re-invigorated Catholicism in Portugal. The apparitions were ratified by the Vatican and were seen by the faithful as an answer to the godless Communism engulfing Russia. The apparition is said to have revealed three secrets: the first secret was a vision of hell; the second secret predicted the end of World War I and the start of World War II, if Russia should not commit itself to the sacred heart; and the third secret was a vision of the death of the Pope (the secrets were not published until 1942).[12] The renewed religious fervour that swept through Portugal ensured that all children had to learn catechism from kindergarten onwards. Rego has said, 'The worst nightmare I've ever had in my life was because I imagined that if you left the door half open the devil would come in and get you at night … So religion to me was scary. Catholicism is ridden with guilt.'[13]

Apart from the enormous influence upon Portuguese society by Catholicism it is also worth noting the political position of Portugal within Europe. During the 1960s, 'the most important explanation for a prolonged series of colonial wars and an obstinate resistance to decolonisation was the nature of Portugal's dictatorial regime at the time.'[14] Portugal as a Fascist dictatorship, on the Fascist Iberian Peninsula, against Russian Communism and increasingly requiring investment from democratic wealthy nations on the world stage took a strongly conservative view of the role of women. This long period of oppression still leaves a legacy today. From a report commissioned by the European Commission in 2003 *Asking Young People about Sexual and Reproductive Behaviors, Results from Belgium, Czech Republic, Estonia and Portugal*,[15] 71.6 per cent of the students questioned in Portugal said they were Catholic; 36.2 per cent of young people relied upon the advice of friends for matters relating to contraception and sexual health, 19.4 per cent of young women relied on their mothers and only 4.5 per cent of young men and women sought advice from a medical professional. The report also stated that whereas other European countries predominantly used the pill as a form of contraceptive, condoms were used in Portugal. As Rego says in an interview regarding the series in a catalogue accompanying the exhibition *Celestina's House* at the Abbot Hall Galley in Kendal, 'How could they go on like this? I know there is birth control now, but not enough.'[16]

Under Salazar abortion was illegal, resulting in imprisonment. The offence could only be decriminalized in cases where the life of the mother could be proven to be in grave danger, or if the foetus was severely malformed. The law had been changed in 1984 to allow abortion in three specific circumstances. The two circumstances already discussed were now legal; in the third circumstance abortion was allowed if the pregnancy resulted following a rape. An attempt to bring in abortion on demand in the first ten weeks of pregnancy was refused by parliament in 1997. However, under the auspices of a different law in the following year abortion was essentially decriminalized. Under

Portuguese law it is not possible to hold a referendum on a law that has already been passed by parliament, but in this case due to unprecedented pressure the government agreed to it. Only just over 31 per cent of the electorate turned out to vote, and the anti-abortion faction won by just 1 per cent. The law was returned to parliament to be debated at a future date; a debate that has yet to take place. Abortion remains a criminal offence.[17] So whilst membership of the European Union in 1986 has meant that access to more information with regards to sexual health and contraception is at least available, the traditional values of a Catholic country still have an enormous influence. Whilst this is the case, Rego's paintings tell a contemporary tale. For Rego, who has been concerned in her work for much of the last fifty years with the condition of women in life under dictatorship of one kind or another, this was another outrageous example of women not being allowed to make decisions regarding their own existence. Against the religious background of Portugal associations have been made with the solitary space occupied by the Virgin Mary in depictions of the Annunciation. In fact, Ruth Rosengarten argues, 'the collegial Virgin Mary and the schoolgirl sleeping after the secret termination of her pregnancy are two sides of the same coin: teenage maternity spurned or fatalistically embraced.'[18] In a patriarchal society to say no to pregnancy is to say no to progeny, no to inheritance. Rego has said, 'The reason women are feared. The final power is to destroy.'[19] Germaine Greer (b. 1939) has said:

> A woman's body is the battleground where she fights for liberation. It is through her body that oppression works, reifying her, sexualising her, victimising her, disabling her. Her physicality is a medium for others to work on; her job is to act as their viceroy, presenting her body for their ministrations, and applying to her body the treatments that have been ordained. If she fails to present herself, if she refuses to accept the treatments, she is behaving badly.[20]

So, within the context of the situation regarding abortion in Portugal, in order to be behaving well a woman should have a sexual relationship only within the confines of a church/state-ordained relationship, in other words marriage. She should have as many children as possible for the benefit of society. Attitudes are changing very slowly. In the meantime Rego is angered by the suffering caused to women. She has said that she had to make these works. She has drawn a link between what she describes as the 'triumphant' state of women taking control of their own lives in the *Abortion Series*, and the series of paintings entitled *Dog Woman*. She explained, 'In these pictures every woman's a dog woman, not downtrodden, but powerful. To be bestial is good. It's physical. Eating, snarling, all activities to do with sensation are positive. To picture a woman as a dog is utterly believable.'[21]

Rego's *Abortions Series* places the viewer in a somewhat uncomfortable position psychologically. She has said about her work in general, 'I have a story to tell which is a female story. I do believe there is such a thing.'[22] Rego's *Abortion Series* engages with these ideas in a way that reveals an intercorporeal understanding of her place in the world as a woman as well as an artist. Of course in order to be 'inter' anything there have to be two things for the 'inter' to be between. What I am suggesting is that the phrase intercorporeal is the space between two bodies: the physical body and the body of knowledge/ideas, in other words the mind. There is also an element of the intracorporeal, where the mind exists within the interstices of the individual body. The two terms take us from the general to the particular: intercorporeal applying to the overall idea of a meeting between mind and body, intracorporeal applying to the subjective experience of the individual. Rego's work applies on both levels; by speaking for one woman, she can also be said to be speaking for all women. Intercorporeal can also apply to a sense of combined belonging; in this case a multiple identity: artist, Portuguese, English, woman, mother, grandmother, friend, widow, and witness, political, private. French philosopher Paul Ricoeur (1913–2005), who has made significant contributions to debates in phenomenology and hermeneutics, said:

> When we discover that there are several cultures instead of just one and consequently at the time when we acknowledge the end of a sort of cultural monopoly, be it illusory or real, we are threatened with the destruction of our own discovery. Suddenly it becomes possible that there are just *others*, that we ourselves are an 'other' among others.[23]

Essentially an intercultural exchange, rather than a multicultural melting-pot, is what I am suggesting is in evidence in Rego's series. Although, as has already been discussed, Rego has affiliations with primarily two nations and the global world at large, her voice is distinctive. Luce Irigaray has also spoken on the issue of 'otherness', saying:

> The discovery of the other presupposes the meeting of two irreducible worlds which recognise each other without being able to know each other. This mode of being or doing is still foreign to the Western subject, whose tradition has taught him to respect what he recognises as true and to approach within a non-hierarchical relationship, his equals, those who share in the same world and in the same identity. While he may be overwhelmed by the problem of alterity, the strategy adopted by him will be to raise the other to the status of an equal and similar – a woman is as good as a man, a black is as good as a white – rather than to educate consciousness to perceive itself as limited, both on the level of sensibility and on the level of thinking … [What is needed is the ability to accept] 'You who will never be either me or mine', I 'recognise' you, even if and perhaps because 'I will never know you', because you escape from any form of 'appropriation' on my part.[24]

I am using 'otherness' as an expression of difference in race, gender or creed. Irigaray is basically saying that in order for women to be truly liberated within society they do not have to become men; they have to be women. Otherwise the result will be that society will remain a patriarchal one within which women are accepted, or tolerated, only if they operate according to the patriarchal rules. The earth-shattering truth is that the whole basis of society needs to change in order for there to be liberation. This is applicable to the way in which Rego practises her art because she concentrates on a narrative, or illustrative way of working. In fact, narration in work has been frowned upon for much of the twentieth century by a canon still largely operated by men. What is interesting in Rego's case is that she is rapidly becoming a fixture within that canon whilst following her own way of working. Her work reveals the life of women and her work is particularly indicative of the psychological realities of female experience. Germaine Greer, whose portrait by Rego hangs in the National Portrait Gallery, has said, 'It is not often given to women to recognise themselves in painting, still less to see their private world, their dreams, the insides of their heads, projected on such a scale and so immodestly, with such depth and colour.'[25]

If we look closely at *Untitled IV* we see a girl lying on a leather sofa dressed in school uniform and trainers (Figure 10.1). Her knees are drawn up, her eyes closed and her head presses into the pillow as if it is a tremendous weight. She clutches the pillow with her right hand, a quiet and lonely desperation permeates the work. Jane Pilcher has suggested that society is in a state of disorder and due to this 'insecurity, unpredictability and the search for meaning, there has been a rise in the importance of bodies as signifiers of status and as a means through which identity or subjectivity are expressed'.[26] This would certainly seem to apply to Rego's series of works on abortion. The law on abortion is in disorder, not only in Portugal; in the USA anti-abortion groups have taken radical and sometimes violent action focusing upon abortion clinics and the doctors who perform them. In March of 1993 Dr David Gunn was shot outside an abortion clinic in Pensacola, but less serious attacks have ranged from vandalism to bombings. This type of action has spread to Canada and Australia. In China since the early 1980s some 400 million abortions of mostly baby girls has led the government to review its single-child policy.[27] Half a million abortions of girl foetuses in India has led the government to offer to pay families to rear female children.[28] In Britain 'British women's right to choose is under covert attack':[29] Libby Brooks of the *Guardian* identifies instances of spurious links made between the incidents of breast cancer with post-abortion women as a method of scare-mongering. The law in Northern Ireland is as it was in the rest of the UK before 1967.[30] On 29 February 2008 a man was jailed for 'slipping' an abortion pill into his wife's sandwich in an attempt to end her pregnancy.[31] So Rego's works speak

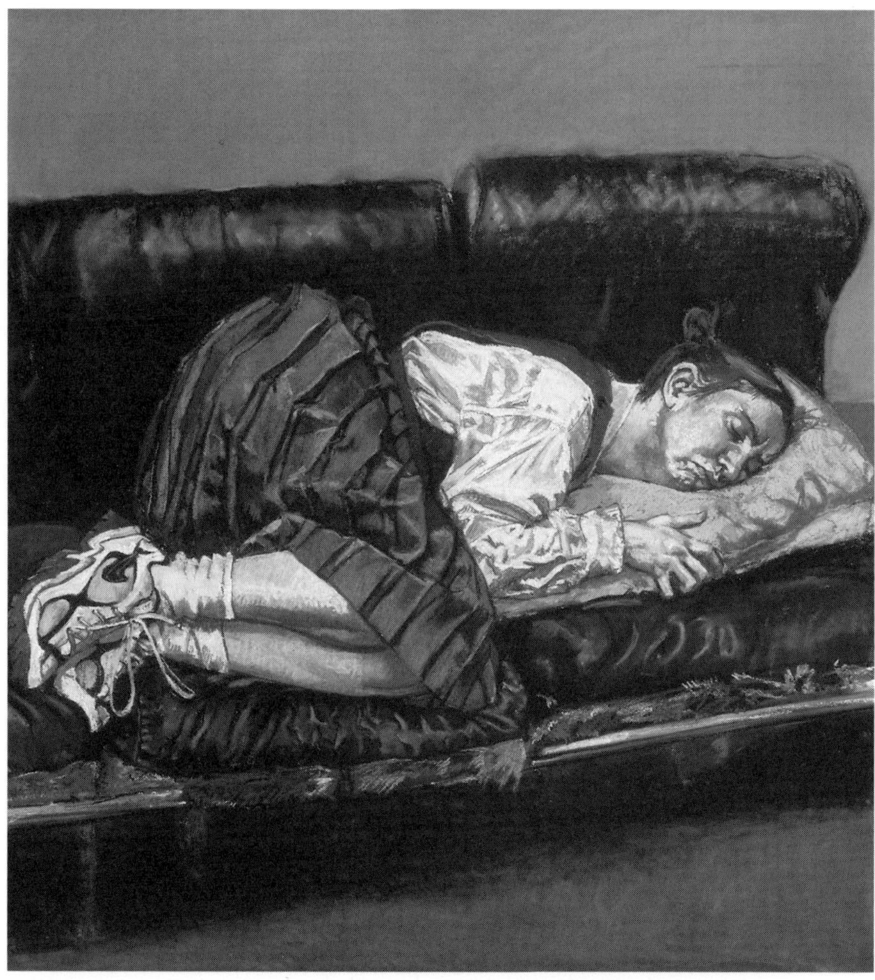

10.1 Paula Rego, *Untitled IV* (1998–99). Pastel on paper mounted on aluminium.

not only to the women of Portugal, but women worldwide. Art is a place where differences and similarities between people can become a forum of debate. On discussing this nature of art Marsha Meskimmon has said, 'In its embodied engagement with the world and in its potential to create new and changing cartographies, it can effectively initiate connections between diverse subjects without obliterating their specificity.'[32] Rego's paintings deal with a subject that has moved her, a subject inspired by political events in Portugal, but in doing so has raised the issue of women's rights to choose to a global stage.

The introspective nature of *Untitled IV* is not the case in the whole series. Some of the women stare out of the canvas directly at the viewer. The gaze is unflinching. The works include domestic items, not medical ones. Fiona Bradley has described the series thus, 'They are doing this, they are not having it done to them … Many of the women meet the viewer's gaze. Others are turned in on themselves, making it clear that what is happening is no one's business but their own.'[33] This portrayal of women in control has been described by Rego as her 'wishful thinking': 'My wishful thinking is that should be so. But it should be so, it should be so, the women should always be in control.'[34] The very domestic setting of these women pursuing an end to an unwanted pregnancy only compounds the sense of rage at the injustice of a situation where women cannot control their own bodies. That very domesticity also acts as a counterpoint to an idea of the global community. Each painting depicts a woman alone, facing an uncertain future. What she is doing has been deemed necessary by her, but the risks are enormous; the risk of being prosecuted as a criminal for herself, or anyone who assists her, the risk of death because of the lack of proper medical supervision. There is also the risk of public shame and humiliation. Last, but by no means least in a Catholic country, is the risk of public censure by the church. Rego's works do indeed deal with the subject of the whole woman. Although there is a display of women in relationship to their bodies, they are not sexualized in any way. The women are clothed. They are not displayed for our amusement or entertainment. These are thinking women. A body and a mind interconnected, they are intercorporeal. As Luce Irigaray says, 'Is not art a means of creating reality and not only of reproducing it?'[35]

Arguably, the works in this series are among Rego's most self-conciously feminist images, dealing as they do with the issue of abortion. The narrative is written onto the bodies of the women within the work. The stoicism of the figure wearing a yellow dress in *Triptych*, as she turns her head towards the viewer, is palpable. Not only is she bearing her experience stoically as the common modern usage of the phrase would suggest, she is also alluding to the original sense. The stoic sage was held to be immune from misfortune and it was believed that their own virtue was enough to lead to happiness. Stoic philosophy also stated that only stoics were free, whilst all others were enslaved. These women are liberating themselves to make a choice denied to them under the laws of state and church. In fact, *Triptych* really exists within a postmodern context because it is presenting two hitherto oppositional positions at the same time. In looking closely one can identify with woman as victim: victim of the state, victim of religion, victim of a patriarchal structure (Figure 10.2). One can also see evidence of woman as liberated, indeed liberating herself from the position of victim, a celebration of independence. Not since Gustave Courbet represented the countryside to the town in the mid-nineteenth century with his paintings *The Stone Breakers* and *Burial at Ornans*[36] has something been presented to the public that was so unexpected.

This series is presented in the form of 'history paintings'. The large-scale format and the use of time-honoured forms, such as the triptych, which also has an association with religious works of previous ages, all demonstrate a link with artistic tradition. The church is something that Paula Rego feels represses women in their pursuit of independence and liberation. In an era when there is an increasingly complacent attitude to feminism these works demonstrate that equality has yet to be achieved. Whilst this could be dismissed as occurring only in Portugal, perhaps an isolated situation, the previously mentioned newspaper reports demonstrate that this situation is much more global, as well as local. As Irigaray has said, 'The vocal message is made with the body itself and printed on the body of the other, which remains the place of its memories.'[37] The message that Rego reveals in the bodies of the women in *Abortion Series* reveals not only the memories of their own physical experience, but Rego's memories of her time in Portugal when poor women would ask for her help to take them to the 'wise woman' for a termination. The physical memories are also invoked for the female viewer, triggered not necessarily by a common experience of a termination, but by the physicality of being a woman. It is not a subject that has been tackled before; consequently, male viewers are exposed to an aspect of female experience with which they are unfamiliar. For those who would argue that human beings should be more neutral, less gendered, I agree with Irigaray when she says, 'the neutral individual is nothing but a cultural fiction'.[38] By representing a uniquely female situation affecting both body and mind the *Abortion* series of works demonstrates a feminist voice as well as an intercultural one. Rego says, 'I am interested in how an outer form or gesture or expression relates to an inner state.'[39] By making what she has referred to as 'pretty pictures' of what is an un-pretty subject she lures an audience to face unpalatable truths.

In *Untitled No. 1* a woman stares straight out of the painting at the viewer with an unflinching gaze (Figure 10.3). A tawdry plastic bowl peeks out from beneath the camp bed. A pretty china bowl lies beside her, in case she feels sick. The woman is sat upon a salmon pink coloured towel, her legs are drawn up and apart. She is clasping her legs so tightly underneath her thighs that her hands make deep indentations in her flesh. The simple blue shift that she is wearing is modestly pulled down to cover the space between her legs. She is also wearing a jaunty red and white scarf on her head, tied at the back. The colour of the flesh has a greenish-grey hue, suggesting sickness. The grim set of the mouth seems to display determination and resignation simultaneously; determination to pursue the course upon which she is decided and resignation to the circumstances of its procurement. The blue shift is a direct allusion to the colour predominantly associated with paintings of the Virgin Mary. Perhaps the headscarf could be seen as forming a halo around her head. The directness of the gaze represents a challenge to the viewer: judge me if you dare. Rego, as an outsider, has an individual way of perceiving the events taking place in Portugal. She is an outsider in terms of her life in self-imposed exile from the country of her birth. She is an outsider within British culture due to her birth elsewhere. And yet, this outsider is increasingly becoming part of the art establishment. *Triptych* was purchased with the help of the Art Fund[40] and is in the permanent collection of Abbott Hall Art Gallery in Kendal. Kendal was the site of the Women's Arts International Festival in 2007; the festival was such a success that it was repeated in 2009. Indeed, as an artist she seems to partake of the very sphere of participation in society that is advocated by Irigaray. 'Women make up half of human society. It is only just that they themselves should define the standards that suit them but not that

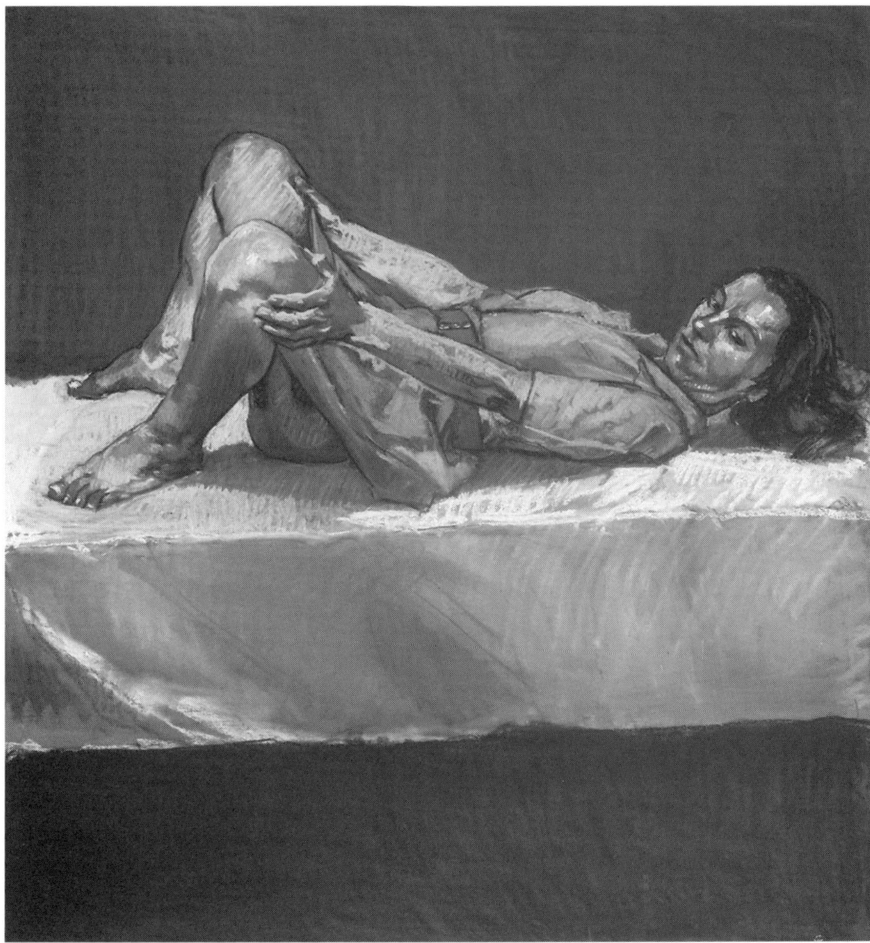

Paula Rego, *Triptych* (1998–99). Pastel on paper mounted on aluminium. 10.2

they should have to become men in their own right to participate in the public sphere.'[41] Rego highlights the situation of particular women in a particular situation in this series and by doing so creates a global ricochet.

Usually Rego does not produce a series of etchings following a successful series in pastel. Once she has completed a series she feels that the theme has been exhausted both artistically and intellectually. This is despite the fact that with incredible success on an international stage she could produce an endless quantity of repetitive images for an ever hungry market; whatever the subject matter. Following the success of the *Dog Woman* series, for example, she abandoned the attempt to produce etchings as the subject was no longer interesting to her; she wanted to move on to something new. The decision to produce a series of ten etchings[42] of the *Abortion Series* was therefore a political

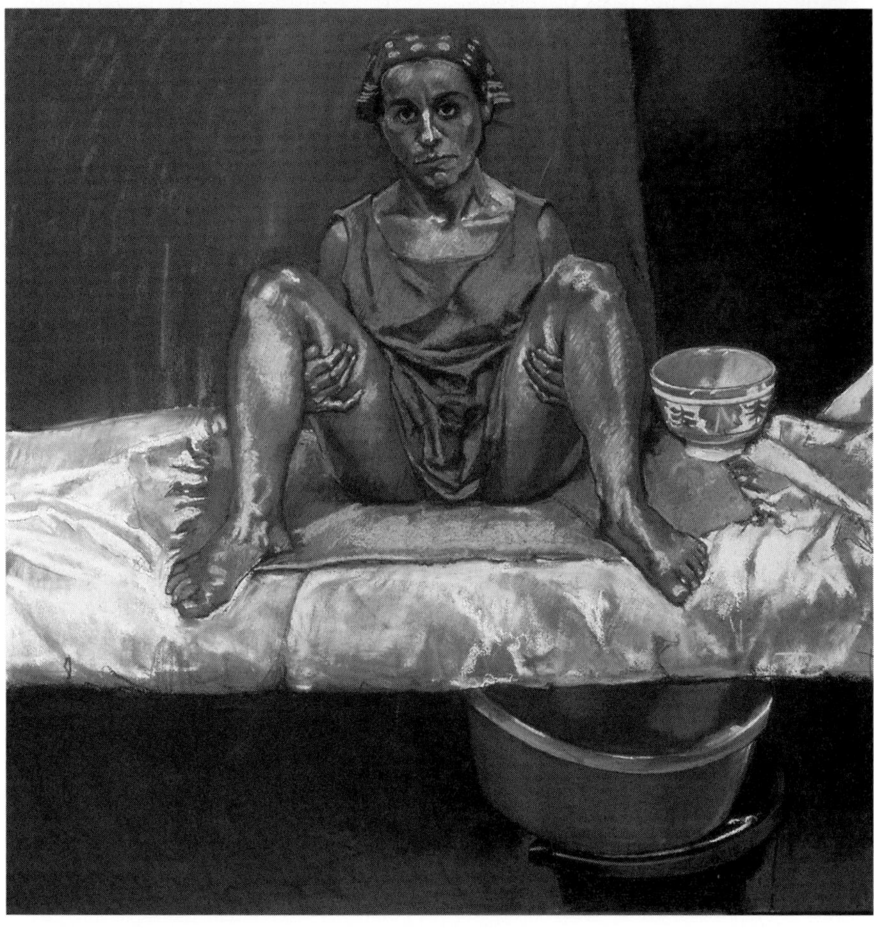

10.3 Paula Rego, *Untitled 1* (1998–99). Pastel on paper mounted on aluminium.

one. None of the etchings are identical to the pastels previously created. Each etching, although following the same theme with images revealing a woman alone, is taken as an individual art work (a selection of etchings is presented in Figures 10.4–6). Rego has donated a complete set of them to Tate. I agree with T.G. Rosenthal when he says that this is not merely art as polemic, 'But when great artistic vision merges with the passion of a great cause, whether it be anti-militarism or rage against the prohibitions against abortion and freedom of choice, remarkable art can be created.'[43] What is different about the etchings when compared with the pastels is the degree of suffering depicted. The bodies seem to writhe in anguish; they are painful to view.

Jean-François Lyotard (1924–98) wrote:

> it is therefore impossible to judge the existence or validity of narrative knowledge on the basis of scientific knowledge and vice-versa: the relevant criteria are different. All we can do is gaze in wonder at the diversity of discursive species, just as we do at the diversity of plant or animal species.[44]

I suggest that one reading of this could be to see Lyotard advocating a celebration of the uniqueness of a specific narrative; in this case, one woman's view of a story. Rego's engagement with the physical and mental aspects of her figures demonstrates an intercorporeal exchange. Although the depicted events are initially physical, the psychological effect upon the subjects, their obvious choice to go against societal norms, sets the work apart as a total experience

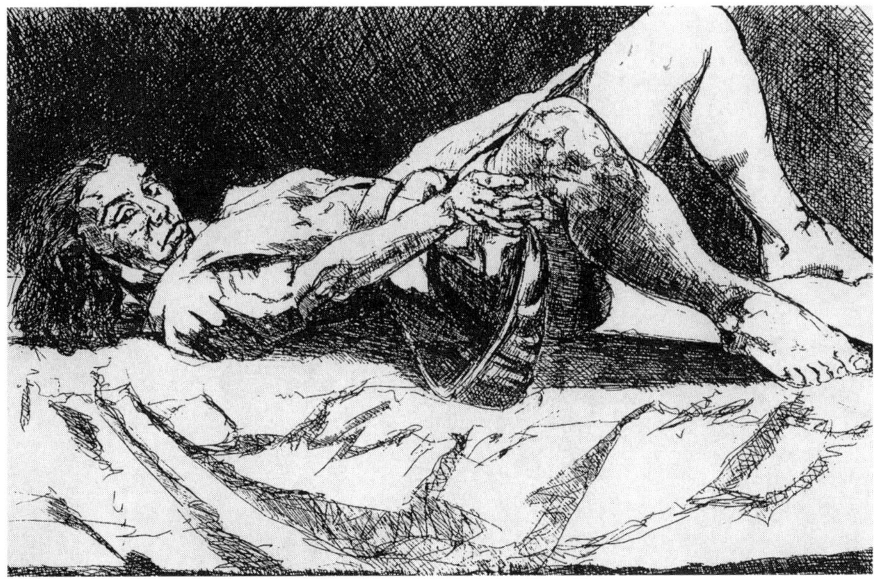

Paula Rego, *Untitled 2* (1999). Etching. **10.4**

involving body and mind; indeed, the body and mind not only of the subject, but also of the spectator. According to Deleuze, home, or notions of home, is not something that already exists. It is by virtue of the existence of external chaos that we draw a circle around ourselves in order to create a feeling of safety.[45] Rego has kicked over a rock to reveal the churning, wriggling chaos beneath. This is not an external chaos, but an internal one. Drawn closer by the pretty colours one is taken in to this private world, a world that is full of dilemma. Should one reach out to comfort, admonish or simply walk away? It is a sensation of trespassing into a private space. The prurient interest in other people's private lives displayed by the popularity of reality television programmes such as Big Brother is sideswiped. It is as if Rego is saying, you want to know about what goes on in private … here it is. Whilst the images do not display the blood and gore of the situation, the anguish, isolation and defiance are all flagrant. The series is thus signifying exactly the type of partnership between a political agenda and artistic practice that creates new and changing cartographies as suggested by Marsha Meskimmon. 'One critical forum for the articulation of such partnerships between differences is art. In its embodied engagement with the world'[46] Rego is not merely representing an event; she is exploring an aspect of cultural identity. Some of the identities would seem to be identifications as Portuguese, European, British and as a woman. Although I have hitherto laid down a case for the global significance of the work, due to political engagements with the theme of abortion worldwide,

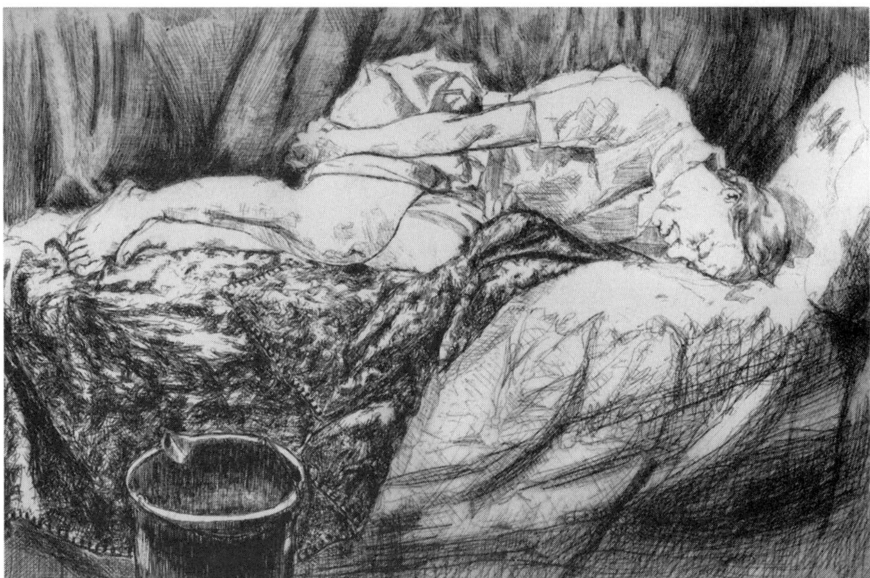

10.5 Paula Rego, *Untitled 4* (1999). Etching.

I do not believe that these works could have come from anyone else. They are a manifestation of one specific woman's view of a specific situation. As such, the *Abortion Series* is unique.

Rego is amazingly open about her life and is happy to answer questions when interviewed, but Suzie Mackenzie of the *Guardian* tells us not to expect a straightforward answer. It is not that Rego is being deliberately obtuse, but 'In Rego's work, as in the stories she tells about her life, there is no search for a rational explanation. What interests her is precisely whatever is distanced from our rational attention. Her gaze, and the gaze of the characters in her pictures, is entirely subjective.'[47] However it is during this interview that Rego reveals that she made the series with the specific intention of exhibiting it in Portugal. She also revealed that in the early days of her relationship with Victor Willing she had had an abortion herself. We're also told that whilst Rego loves saints, she hates Mother Teresa 'Because she never encouraged women to use contraception. She'd say, we have saved these little souls for God. Well, for a miserable life.'[48] Again and again articles have been written by people who have been moved by her work and who understand the message that Rego is communicating with this series of works. Greer writing in the *Guardian* said, 'No other artist has ever come close to capturing Rego's sense of the phantasmagoria that is female reality.'[49] Despite the fact that she constantly tells herself stories whilst in the process of creating her art, not all of Rego's work has a clear point to make. There can come a time during the produc-

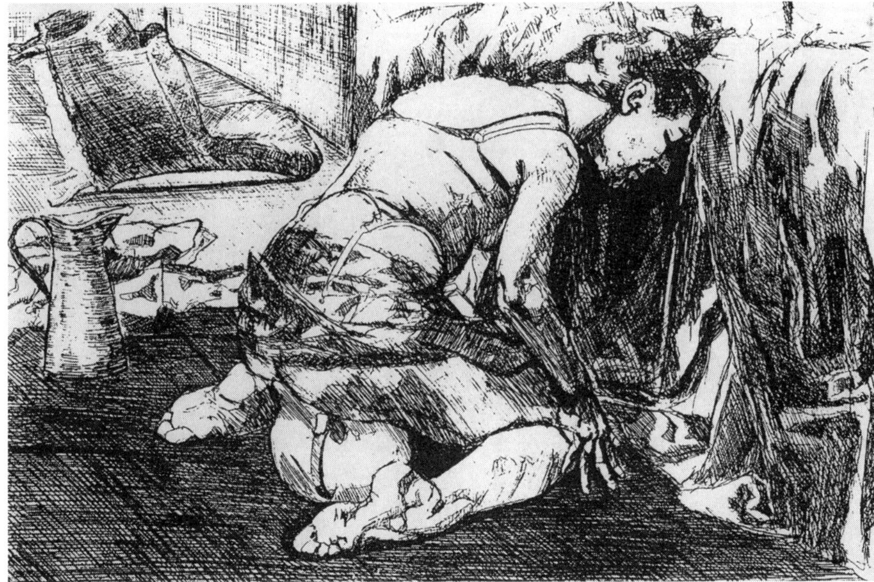

Paula Rego, *Untitled 5* (1999). Etching. 10.6

tion of a particular piece when the meaning becomes somewhat inscrutable. This has been referred to by some as ambivalence, but when asked about this Rego said:

> I know that it sounds odd but it's sometimes about both things, this thing and that thing which are opposites … Opposites can come together in a picture, and that is very interesting you see, you can have both resentment and affection – which happens in life you know – completely, resentment and affection, and these things come together in a picture I think – I think they do, they can do. So a picture can contain many different kinds of feelings and attitudes and stuff, and even the way that you behave, it contains all this, a picture can contain all these contradictions – that's why it's a picture. Because one's self is full of contradictions. I mean one is total … a bag of contradictions from morning till night, and therefore it would not be truthful if you just selected one side – well you couldn't if you go into a picture, you go full … you know, whole hog, you know, and there it is – phwar.[50]

By focusing discussion upon this limited case study, a discussion that highlights areas of concern for women in terms of cultural and societal identity, it has been revealed that feminism is a conscious intention on behalf of the artist. The *Abortion Series* demonstrates an intercorporeal and an intracorporeal engagement with the ideas of the female body and its unique experience. In assessing the reception of the work in the media it can be seen that the intention of the artist has definitely been understood. Corporeal feminism has also been a viable way of understanding Rego's practice, a practice dealing with the whole woman, a coalescence of mind, body and spirit. The series demonstrates that Rego's conscious compulsion to engage with the politics of life as experienced by women in the societies with which she is familiar provides her with the opportunity to use her creativity and zeal to reach a larger audience. Globalization and the movement of peoples is not something to threaten, but something to enrich the societies included. The standpoint of the artist, and their distinctive voice, allows them to reveal individual secrets and thereby challenge new ways of thinking about ourselves and our world.

Notes

1 The word 'burd' is Old English for maiden or young woman. There is a contrast between the idea of the type of decorous behaviour this word implies, particularly as some of the images depict young women in school uniform, and the visceral drama of abortion as depicted in the series. This chapter is therefore a burd's eye view.

2 Cited in M.M. Lisboa, *Paula Rego's Map of Memory: National and Sexual Politics* (Aldershot and Burlington, VA: Ashgate, 2003), p. 4.

3 Paula Rego, interview by John Tusa, broadcast BBC Radio 3, 2 June 2001.
4 '*Social norms* are customary rules of behaviour that coordinate our interactions with others. Once a particular way of doing things becomes established as a rule, it continues in force because we prefer to conform to the rule given the expectation that others are going to conform.' S.N. Durlauf and L.E. Blume (eds), *New Palgrave Dictionary of Economics*, second edition (London: Palgrave Macmillan, 2008).
5 T.G. Rosenthal, *Paula Rego: The Complete Graphic Work* (London: Thames & Hudson, 2003), pp. 146–8.
6 See J. McEwen, *Paula Rego*, 3rd edn (London and New York: Phaidon Press, 2006), p. 247.
7 There is not merely one form of knowledge, but several concurrent strands of knowledge.
8 J. Khan, 'Third World First', *The Boston Globe* (20 January 2008).
9 For a fuller explanation of the relationship between church and state see M.M. Lisboa, 'An Interesting Condition: The Abortion Pastels of Paula Rego', *Luso-Brazilian Review* 39/2 (Winter 2002), 220.
10 Ibid., pp. 128–31.
11 Cited by Marina Warner in *Alone of All Her Sex: The Myth and Cult of the Virgin Mary* (London: Picador, 1985), p. 337.
12 The controversial third secret was left in a sealed envelope to be opened in 1960, but the Vatican did not release the statement until 2000.
13 McEwen, *Paula Rego*, pp. 28–9.
14 A.C. Pinto, 'The Transition to Democracy and Portugal's Decolonisation', in S. Lloyd-Jones and A.C. Pinto (eds), *The Last Empire: Thirty Years of Portuguese Decolonization* (Bristol: Intellect Books, 2003), p. 17.
15 A copy of the report, *Asking Young People about Sexual and Reproductive Behaviours, Results from Belgium, Czech Republic, Estonia and Portugal*, can be seen at: http://ec.europa.eu/health/ph_projects/2003/action1/action1_2003_27_en.htm#3, accessed 18 April 2008.
16 Cited in Rosenthal, *Paula Rego*, p. 148.
17 For full details on the statistics and laws see M.M. Lisboa, 'An Interesting Condition: The Abortion Pastels of Paula Rego', *Luso-Brazilian Review* 39/2 (Winter 2002), 220–1.
18 R. Rosengarten, *Narrating the Family Romance: Love and Authority in the Work of Paula Rego (1987–2004)*, unpublished thesis (London: Courtauld Institute, May 2006), p. 226.
19 In M. Gee, 'Painter of Shocking and Painful Truths', *The Daily Telegraph* (15 February 1999), p. 19.
20 G. Greer, *The Whole Woman* (London: Doubleday, 1999), p. 106.
21 Cited on the Saatchi Gallery website, www.saatchi-gallery.co.uk/artists/paula_rego.htm, accessed 20 April 2008.
22 Cited in H. de Bertodano, 'Giving Fear a Woman's Face', *The Daily Telegraph* (30 May 1998).
23 P. Ricoeur, 'Civilization and National Cultures', in *History and Truth*, trans. C.A. Kelby (Evanston, IL: Northwestern University Press, 1965), p. 278, quoted in H.

Foster, *The Anti-Aesthetic: Essays on Postmodern Culture* (New York: The New Press, 1998), p. 66.

24 L. Irigaray, *Luce Irigaray: Key Writings* (London and New York: Continuum, 2004), p. 72.

25 Cited in M. Jaggi, 'Enduring Image', *The Guardian* (17 July 2004).

26 J. Pilcher, *Women in Contemporary Britain* (London and New York: Routledge, 1999), p. 92.

27 T. Branigan, 'Days of the One-child Rule Could be Numbered as Beijing Considers Change', *The Guardian* (29 February 2008).

28 R. Ramesh, 'India will Pay Families to Have Girls to End Foeticide', *The Guardian* (4 March 2008).

29 L. Brooks, 'British Women's Right to Choose Is under Covert Attack', *The Guardian* (17 October 2007).

30 J. O'Neill, BBC reporter, gives a full description of the high court ruling in June 2001 allowing a review of abortion law in Northern Ireland, http://news.bbc.co.uk/1/hi/northern_ireland/1386450.stm, accessed 28 September 2008. The 1861 Offences Against the Person Act makes all abortions illegal. The 1929 Infant Life (Preservation) Act was extended to Northern Ireland in 1945 and allows abortion to preserve a mother's life, as was the Bourne Judgement, 1938 – case law allowing abortion in circumstances of risk to mental or physical health. This issue remains unresolved and was in the news again in July 2008 as the United Nations Committee on the Elimination for Discrimination Against Women noted in its latest report that the 1967 Abortion Act does not extend to Northern Ireland. It also suggested this was having a detrimental impact on women's health.

31 N. Sears, 'Jail for Man who Slipped Abortion Drugs into Wife's Sandwiches in Bid to Kill his Unborn Baby', *The Daily Mail* (1 March 2008).

32 M. Meskimmon, 'Walking with Judy Watson: Painting, Politics and Intercorporeality', in R. Betterton (ed.), *Unframed: Practices & Politics of Women's Contemporary Painting* (London and New York: I.B. Tauris, 2004), p. 76.

33 Cited in McEwen, *Paula Rego*, p. 248.

34 P. Rego, interview by John Tusa, broadcast BBC Radio 3 (2 June 2001).

35 Irigaray, *Key Writings*, p. 97.

36 *Burial at Ornans* is in the collection of Musée d'Orsay in Paris; *The Stone Breakers* was destroyed during World War Two.

37 Irigaray, *Key Writings*, p. 102.

38 Ibid., p. 206.

39 Cited in R. Rosengarten, 'Home Truths: The Work of Paula Rego', in *Paula Rego* (London: Tate Gallery Publishing, 1995), p. 74.

40 The Art Fund is an independent charity that, in its own words, 'exists to save art for everyone to enjoy'.

41 Irigaray, *Key Writings*, p. 207.

42 It is important to note that only eight of the etchings finally made it into print, despite being proofed in the usual way; it would seem that ultimately these final two had nothing further to add to those already in production.

43 Rosenthal, *Paula Rego*, p. 149.

44 Cited in M.M. Lisboa, 'An Interesting Condition: The Abortion Pastels of Paula Rego', *Luso-Brazilian Review* 39/2 (Winter 2002), 216.
45 G. Deleuze and F. Guattari, 'Of the Refrain', in G. Deleuze and F. Guattari, *A Thousand Plateaus*, trans. B. Massumi (Minneapolis: University of Minnesota Press, 1987), pp. 342–86.
46 Meskimmon, 'Walking with Judy Watson', p. 76.
47 S. Mackenzie, 'Don't Flinch Don't Hide', *The Guardian* (30 November 2002).
48 Paula Rego cited in Mackenzie, 'Don't Flinch Don't Hide'.
49 G. Greer, 'Untamed by Age', *The Guardian* (20 November 2004).
50 Paula Rego, interview by John Tusa, broadcast BBC Radio 3 (2 June 2001).

11 Testing the limits

Oreet Ashery in conversation with Dorothy Rowe

Oreet Ashery (b. 1966 Jerusalem) is a London-based context-responsive visual artist who works in a variety of different media across a range of different genres including interactive live art events, video work, two-dimensional images, object-making, text and the internet. She is interested in the conceptual and process-based aspects of art practice in which research and everyday life are an integral part of the work. Her practice explores the complex interrelations between personal, cultural and identity politics at the nexus with the political realities of social experiences and artistic practices. She has an ongoing interest in the intersections between gender, race and ethnicity across Jewish, Arabian and Muslim identities. Her work tends to be complex and relational but at the same time often humorous and accessible to a wide variety of audiences and communities. She frequently performs herself as a fictional character including a rabbi, a black man, a farmer and an Arab man, amongst others (Figures 11.1 and 11.2). Her most consistently performed alter ego to date has been *Marcus Fisher*, an orthodox Jewish man who frequently inhabits non-orthodox spaces and engages in non-orthodox activities. Recent work has also focused on the historical, ethnic and gendered intersections between 'Oriental' Jewish identities and Islamic cultures. Most recently Ashery has been performing the character of Shabbtai Zevi, a seventeenth-century, Izmir-born, controversial and highly enigmatic Jewish False Messiah who converted to Islam. The descendants of his movement in Turkey today are called Dönmeh, meaning converters and traitors. The Dönmeh present a contentious issue in present-day Turkey, shrouded in mystery and conspiracy theory.

Ashery holds a BA in Fine Art from Sheffield Hallam University (1992) and an MA in Fine Art from Central St Martin's School of Art, London (2000). She was an AHRC-funded Fellow in the Creative and Performing Arts at Queen Mary University London (2007–10). She has had her work exhibited and performed across a wide range of international venues, including *Global Feminisms* (group exhibition, Brooklyn Museum, New York, 2007), *Bound* (solo performance, Tate Liverpool, 2007), *Right, Left* (solo performance,

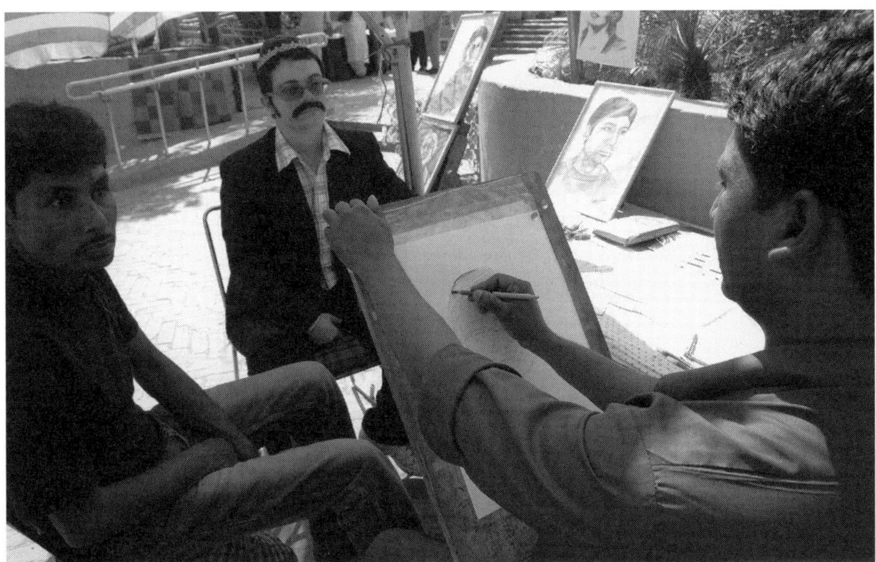

Oreet Ashery, *Portrait Sketch* (Jewish man) Dilli Haat, New Delhi, intervention, 11.1
drawings, photographs (2005). Ashery sat in front of the same portrait artist who drew her twice, once as a Jewish man and once as an Arab man. He did not know she was a woman, nor that she was the same person; there was a time gap between the two and he just drew what he saw.

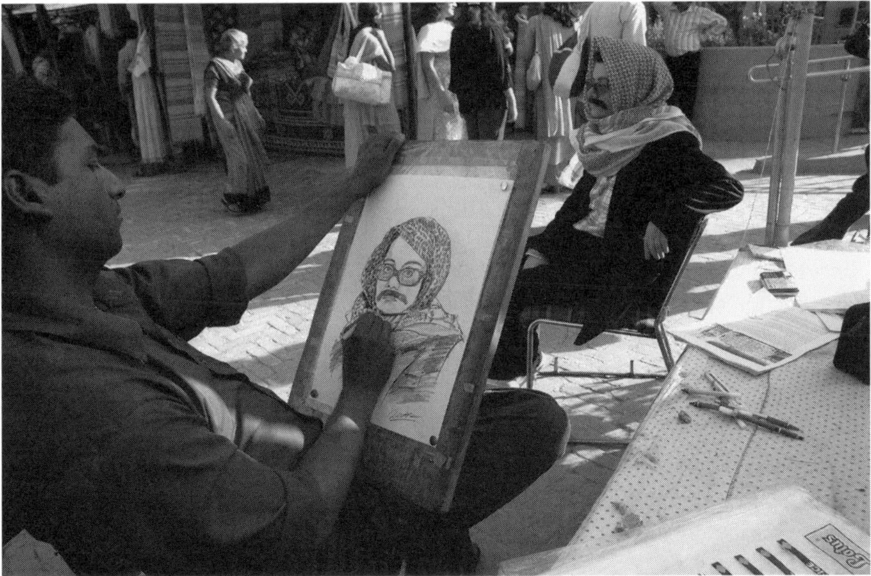

Oreet Ashery, *Portrait Sketch* (Arab man) Dilli Haat, New Delhi, intervention, 11.2
drawings, photographs (2005).

Freud Museum London, 2007), *Medium Religion* (ZKM, Karlsruhe, 2008), and *Staying* (an Artangel commission, 2009), amongst many others.

In 2007 the Live Art Development Agency London released a DVD of five short video works made by Ashery between 2000 and 2005 in their series *Unbound*. The first of these is *Marcus Fisher's Wake* (2000) a mock-documentary which ironically celebrates the life of her fictional alter ego in the context of his death. This is followed by the rather poignant 2002 film *Why Do You Think I Left?* in which, sixteen years later, Ashery returns to Israel from England to ask different generations of her family to respond to the question of why they think she decided to leave her home and her country at the age of nineteen. The variety of responses reveals as much about the family's own positions, biographies and self-constructions as contemporary Jewish subjects living with daily political and personal conflicts in Israel, as it does about their perceptions of Ashery's individual desire to leave. In *Dancing with Men* (2003), the third piece, she returns to Israel as Marcus in order to participate in the annual religious festival of strictly male-only dancing that commemorates the death of Rabbi Shimon Bar Yochai (70 CE), believed by many to be author of the *Zohar*. In 2009, the Live Art Development Agency published a book on Ashery's work with the title *Dancing with Men*, covering her interactive works. In *Oh Jerusalem* (2005), a 45-second single-screen video loop, Ashery performs herself Chaplinesque-style, as two male characters, an Arab and an orthodox Jew, both contemplating a drawing of Jerusalem and both bound up in an endless cycle of repetition. As the rhythm of the cycle accelerates, the men merge into one, suggesting a satirical probing of the protracted and unremitting histories of the Arab–Israeli conflict. The fifth and final work on the DVD is an engaging and moving travel diary, *Necessary Journey* (2005) in which she crosses a variety of both physical and ethnic borders within Israel researching pressure points where ethnic, racial, historical and gendered de-territorialization might be possible. She crosses the West Bank barrier to Ramallah in order to meet with Palestinian Arab architect Sameh Abboushi; she visits Jerusalem's Old City with her father in search of the place where his grandfather owned a shoe shop in the heart of the Muslim quarter, and finally she embarks on a research trip to Pequiln, an indigenous village in which Druze, Muslims, Christians and Jews continue to live alongside one another. *The Novel of Nonel and Vovel*, with the Palestinian artist Larissa Sansour, published by Charta in 2009, is a graphic novel that continues her work within the subject of anti-occupation remits.

The text below is an edited version of a conversation that took place in London in December 2007.

Dorothy Rowe: I've been interested in your work for a number of years now, really enjoying watching it develop. I think it explores a number of recurrent themes and ideas, particularly issues concerned with breaking taboos; explorations of subjectivity, identity and alterity; the limits of subjective identity formation and the various kinds of relationships that arise between feminism and globalization. It seems to me that an overriding characteristic of your practice is that you take great risks in your art: you take emotional risks, gender risks and risks with ethnicity and race. I was wondering whether you could talk some more about those risks?

Oreet Ashery: Yeah, risks … I'm aware of it occasionally from the outside, I'm aware that there is an element of risk-taking and I'm aware of the fact that the work has been described at times as risk-taking or cutting edge in that way. Although I guess from where I feel I come from, autobiographically and psychologically, it doesn't feel like a risk, it feels very much part of my sensibility, and how I live my life and how I operate in the world. So it's very normalized, my sense of gender fluidity and the whole idea of border crossing or ethnic questions. All of that has very much been there from a very early age when I actually objectively put myself at great risk as a child, wandering in places where I shouldn't have been, whether it's an orthodox neighbourhood in Jerusalem or an Arab village, but yet it all felt very natural as a kind of form of play and out of curiosity. And I guess my life work over many years has been to formalize it or articulate it in a way that other people can get something from it. So, I think the idea of risk, in terms of whether it's in queer thinking or whether it's simply a personality trait about what is perceived as risk and what to me is perhaps quite normalized, is what is of interest to me. And I guess where I really feel it is in the art world: where and how the work is accepted or taken, or why is it not commercial. All these questions, I think it is very much to do with that sense of, I really don't like calling it … it's not peripheral and its not outsider, it's not.

DR: Liminal?

OA: No, it's not. It's none of these but it's something else. So, with *Marcus Fisher* for example, now it's in the Brooklyn Museum's and ZKM's collections but it took a long time for that image to be accepted in the mainstream. Specifically, I think in political terms there is a lot of risk around attempting to collaborate with Palestinian artists; there is huge amount of risk in that. The risks to them are greater than mine; it's not equal and anybody that will tell you otherwise, they're lying. There's a lot more at stake for them than for me. But because of that there is a risk for me because at any moment our collaboration could fold and you've put a lot of effort into collaboration and then something like the second war in Lebanon could come or boycotting, which puts the whole project at risk.

DR: Is that when you are collaborating with Palestinian artists in Palestine or in the UK?

OA: Both.

DR: So there's risk in both arenas?

OA: I'm now embarking on a major collaboration with Larissa Sansour, a Palestinian artist who lives in Denmark [Figure 11.3]. We're doing a book together and it's also a comic book, and when we talk to each other we talk about the nature of the collaboration. It's very complicated and there's a lot of risk and I'm always on the edge with it, for many reasons. Politically, because I feel I'm not sure that Israelis and Palestinians should collaborate; I'm not sure that it really represents the political situation; it somehow betrays it and normalizes it and I don't feel comfortable with that. Also, the whole notion of collaborating, as long as it's a dialogue it's OK but I came to realize that working with Larissa that it's not just about that; it's not enough to just have a dialogue. She stressed that for her it is deconstructing a sense of history that is important, not just talking for the sake of talking. And on an emotional level I just feel that there is so much polarization and prejudice. Larissa's experiences of direct encounters with Israelis are generally not positive, as they are usually soldiers, or other border-control personnel, she has learnt to have little trust in them.

And so I just feel that whatever my personal character is, whether I am a determined person, or whatever it may be, it can all be interpreted as a kind of national characteristic, like an Israeli determination or Israeli aggression. So it was also in part emotional, the whole thing. She asked me 'what's the value of

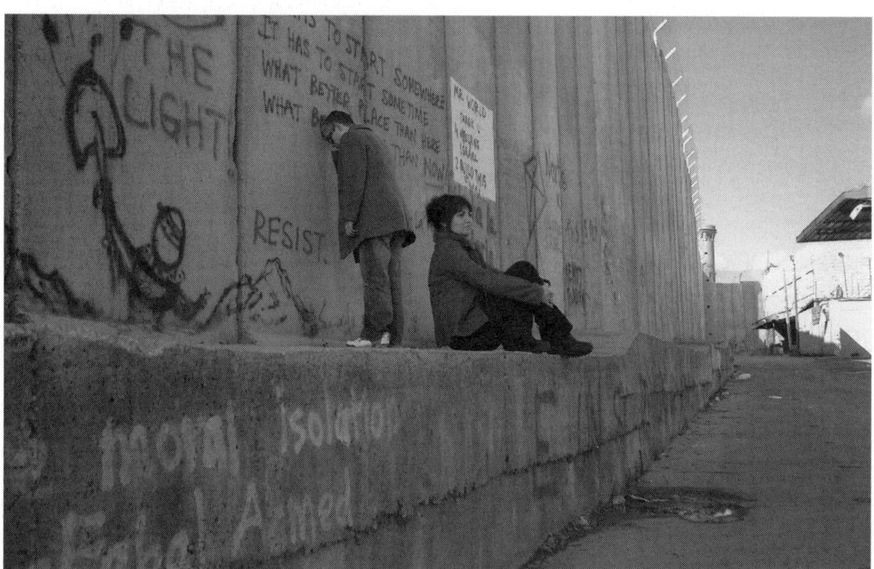

11.3 Oreet Ashery and Larissa Sansour, *The Wall Palestine* (*Peace Process*), from *The Novel of Nonel and Vovel* (2009).

it; why do you collaborate?' In my opinion, and I had to think about it really hard, the only real answer I could come up with was that simply the idea of having two perspectives put together creates a certain overview and a third perspective that would not otherwise emerge [Figures 11.4 and 11.5]. I could not make that book on my own and neither could she. So, it's really in terms of an artistic perspective I'm interested in it.

These answers were given to me by Ashery at the time of the interview. Since that time Ashery has had a look at the interview and explained that her views and feelings regarding the collaboration with Larissa Sansour, and following the recent attacks on Gaza, are constantly changing, and now that the book is published the impact is different yet again. But she decided to leave the interview as it was at the time, to reflect the discursive nature of the practice.

DR: It sounds as though she is asking you some very difficult questions in relation to the collaboration so I'm just wondering whose idea the collaboration was. Did it just emerge or did you approach her? Or did she come to you?

OA: I also had to ask her very difficult questions. We asked each other difficult questions. I think it was my idea and also what I'm saying in the text is that it will always be coming from the Israeli perspective. It's always Israeli people who have the motivation because of guilt and it's always also the Israelis

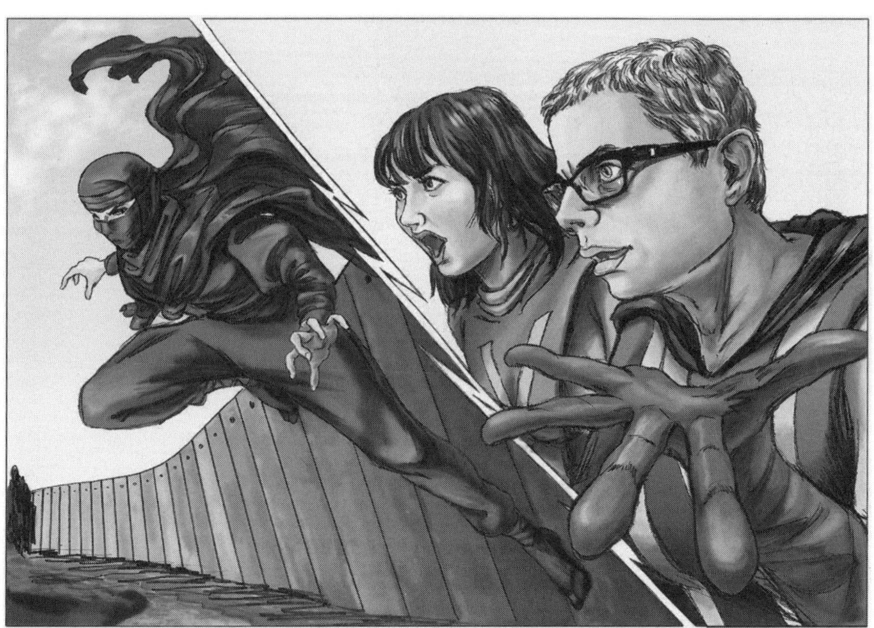

Oreet Ashery and Larissa Sansour, *Nonel and Vovel Save Palestine*, from *The Novel of Nonel and Vovel* (2009). **11.4**

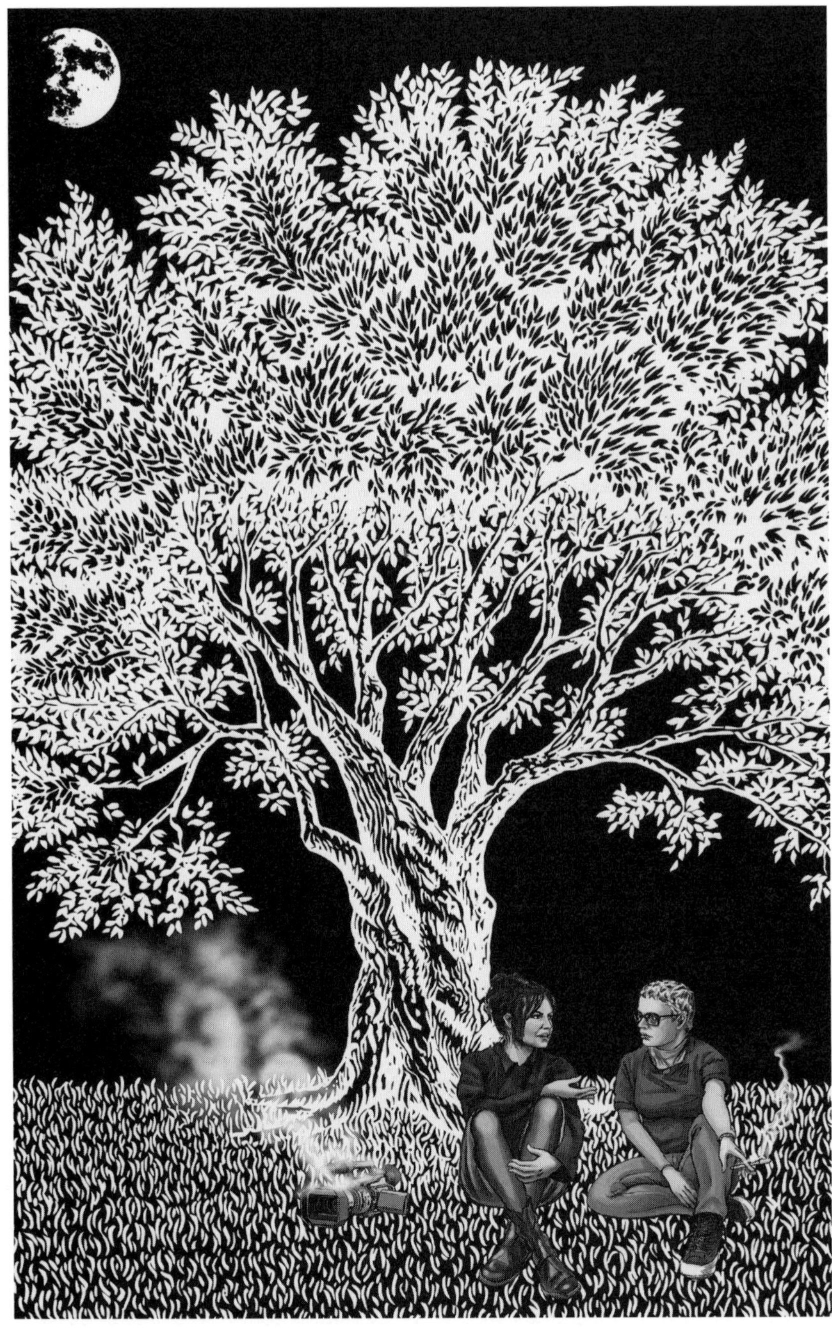

11.5 Oreet Ashery and Larissa Sansour, detail from *Nonel and Vovel's Inferno*, from *The Novel of Nonel and Vovel* (2009).

in Palestine or in Israel who have more of the networks. So they are in more of a position to do that. And also for a Palestinian there's a lot more to risk especially with the cultural boycott. So that's the one aspect at the moment that on a day-to-day basis I feel very on the edge about because I feel that sense of risk. I'm also sensing that nobody is going to be happy in the end, and so what is the value of collaboration in the face of what's happening politically? And you're right that emotionally there is always a lot of investment when I'm working with my family, and because my life and my work are so connected there are personal risks that are taken every day.

DR: Yes, I'm very interested in the idea that the micro-level of the everyday in which you work also has enormous resonances on a macro-level. And I think that's why it works as artwork for me, in that it enables a space for communication about difficult issues. And I think that that is a very brave manoeuvre; I find your work very enabling because of that. Do you feel brave?

OA: I think because I'm such a neurotic, because I have so many fears: I don't go on the tube, I'm a hypochondriac; I'm scared of crossing the road … anything …

DR: You had agoraphobia at one point and vertigo, I think … All of these things that come through your work ... they are very difficult psychological fears that you have and yet you create a unique public practice that is *incredibly* risky and brave. I think that is very interesting.

OA: And I see myself as a brave person because when I have to go on the tube it's so brave when I do it. I think it's really brave because I don't let it stop me. I fly; I do all these things. It's a lot to do with a sense of freedom. As soon as I feel constrained, like on a plane or in the tube, when my personal freedom is under threat, I just get very uncomfortable and so the physical world is a scary place for me. I work a lot with edges and fears and breaking through fears.

DR: And so does having an alter-ego in Marcus Fisher enable you to enter spaces that are risky? Does the alter ego combat some of those issues, or not, or is it just a way of working them through?

OA: No, I think having an alter ego or taking up a persona helps a great deal in channelling a lot of fears and a sense of restriction. Whatever it is someone feels restricted by, whether it's social taboos, whether it's family history, whether it's Christian guilt, whatever it is that somebody feels confined by, I think that any idea of persona helps and in a very, very simple way, like when people put on sunglasses, for example, they really feel much braver or different or better. It's not really the idea of masquerade that I'm interested in. I read somewhere about panic attacks, that it helps sometimes just to hold something, so it's more the idea of an accessory than a masquerade ...

DR: That's interesting because I think it relates to some of the experiences often articulated by Muslim women who choose to wear the hijab or the veil and the way that veiling can actually enable the freedom of subjectivity.

OA: Yes, not from the fact that you're hiding behind it, but the fact that you have some kind of agency … it's like having a T-shirt printed, you're kind of bigger than yourself; you're saying something about who you are.

DR: Coming back to your collaboration with Larissa, I was really interested when you were talking about the idea of Israeli guilt in relation toPalestine. I don't know whether you want to talk any more about that or not? But history tells me that it is a very difficult situation for an Israeli Jew to carry guilt. It is Europe that should carry guilt. It is Britain and it is Germany after World War Two that created the context for the political conditions that pertain in Israel and Palestine today, so this idea of a complex network of guilt that weaves through contemporary global histories is really quite problematic and I'm wondering whether any of us will ever get to excise that condition of culpability?

OA: It's a complex one. I mean with Israeli guilt I am talking about people like myself who oppose Israeli government policies. So it's that kind of guilt, a 'leftish' guilt, that I'm talking about, a political guilt, and it is heavy-duty guilt. I'm not getting into the idea of a personal responsibility. I don't think it's that. Of course it's not me it's the government. That aside, as it happens, I am born an Israeli …

DR: So, it's that collision of the political and the individual in the subjectivity of one person?

OA: As a citizen, I'm an occupier and it is a lot of guilt, and I mean my parents were occupied by the British so, in a way, I kind of always expect them to be reflexive about how they feel now as occupiers. I mean, they live in Jerusalem on land that is occupied. It depends on how far back you want to go but, to my opinion, it is occupied. That region has always been occupied. But, yes, there is guilt and then another question that Larissa asked me was about this new idea of anti-Zionism, and I read about Israeli academics – anti-Zionists – that want to form a new Israel. But that's where guilt goes wrong, you have it with Catholic guilt too, when you are only motivated by guilt that the outcome is actually ridiculous …

DR: It becomes separatism then?

OA: Yes. I mean they are proposing that Israel moves into lots of little colonies all over the world. How realistic is that? It's a kind of acting out something rather than addressing it directly …

DR: Again I suppose it's a way for them to come to terms with living as occupiers but it is a difficult issue and one which I don't think we are going to solve today …

OA: No …

DR: Turning to a more general issue, a lot of my thinking about your work stems from the pieces collated on the *Unbound* DVD that the Live Art Development Agency have recently released, which documents the five short films that you made between 2000 and 2005. I think that they reveal quite a lot about your practice, but it also seems to me that there is a shift now in what you're doing, a development in your thinking from something like *Necessary Journey* to the more recent collaboration with Larissa. Could you talk a little bit more about the five short films from *Unbound*?

OA: Yes, I think 2000 to 2005, the *Marcus Fisher* period, was very much a time of performance, where I was performing live all the time, literally travelling around with my bag and performing.

DR: That was a brave thing to do.

OA: I would never do it again. I was thinking about it a lot, in terms of other artists' careers and in terms of my own trajectory, and these five years could never happen again, because there was something so process-based about the work and so much about experimenting. It was so organic and there was really for me no difference between what I saw as a finished performance and what I saw as a scratch performance or what I saw as a test or an experiment … every opportunity was really just a chance to experiment, every performance was a scratch performance. Everything was about feedback, about a sense of exploration and really about process and I think there was a lot of, not exactly naivety, but a lack of self-consciousness in the work that I don't think I'll ever have again. It's like a rite of passage. You only have it one time, maybe like when you're a teenager and you have that sense that you don't care about consequences. It's a precious time for me because I was performing live a lot and because I took risks and because I don't really think that I cared at that time about how the work would be perceived. It was about getting it out and really developing the work through making it. Each performance would lead to the next one. The videos are all very much the result of that.

DR: Do you see them linked in any particular order?

OA: Yes I see them very much linked. I think *Marcus Fisher* works as the canon. It is very much about the idea of a mock documentary, about creating the life of a character, recycling everyday interventions and interactions and packaging a fictional self through a series of acts that nobody witnessed apart from people who were on the streets (Figure 11.6). There are a lot of multi-layered relationships between documenting and performance, and, again, it's a character that derived very organically from performance to performance. I think the parallel to that is, *Why Do You Think I Left?*, which is very much about a sense of absence from that environment, from where it all started in terms of Israel and my family. Then it's *Dancing with Men*, in which I return to Israel and Marcus is always in places where he is not supposed to be. So for the first time he is with people of his own, orthodox men.

DR: That risk again!

OA: Yeah that was really risky. It was really a very frightening situation. Then moving into *Necessary Journey* where I had to embody my ongoing

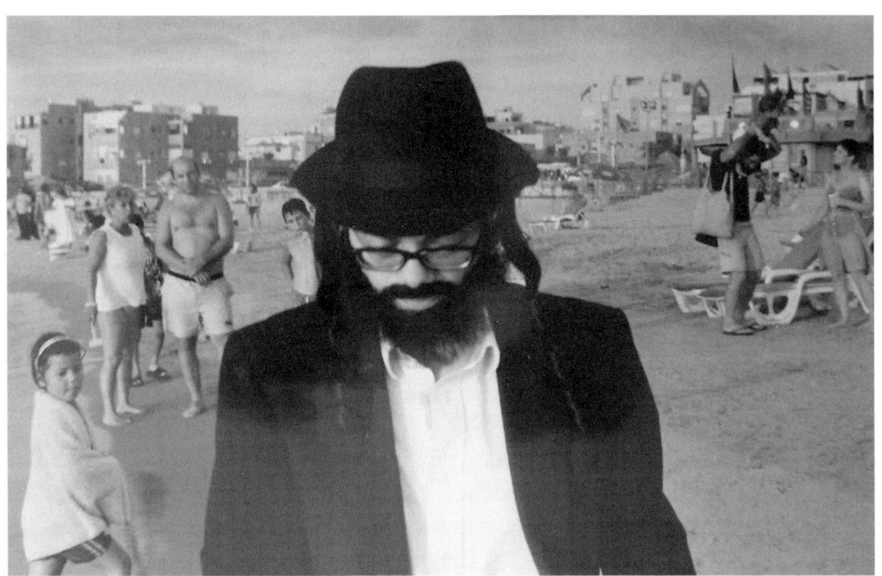

11.6 Oreet Ashery, *Marcus at the Sea-Side, Jerusalem* (2000), still from *Marcus Fisher's Wake*.

interest in the political situation in Israel and Palestine through a connection with Sameh, an architect in Ramallah whom I met. After years of hardly visiting Israel I had to go and see it for myself. And the last one, *Oh Jerusalem* from 2005, is where you see me perform as both an Arab and as a Jew

DR: Interchanging …

OA: Interchanging. This is also where the idea of *Marcus Fisher* starts to break down into the area that is currently my AHRC fellowship project, which is about Oriental Jews and where I'm starting to get more detached from it. The fellowship project is concerned with the idea of the Jewish connection with the Arab/Islamic world. When I did *Marcus Fisher* I used to go to clubs dressed up – it was my life, it was part of that kind of queer lifestyle – but now there's a lot more critical distance from my work; it doesn't necessarily reflect my everyday life in that way any more.

DR: So are you saying that maybe the performance of *Marcus Fisher* is over?

OA: Well I'm actually doing my first performance in a very long time in India in March 2008, where I will be a character but not Marcus; it will be another character which is to do with a Jewish Indian man so, I'm happy to return to that kind of work in that way …

DR: But adopting different alter egos exploring other versions so *Marcus Fisher's Wake* has come to pass perhaps?

OA: Yes.

DR: Part of the reason that we're having this discussion is because you participated in the conference 'Diasporic Futures: Women, the Arts and Globalization', which was held at the Victoria and Albert Museum, London, in July 2006 and from which this publication stems. What the conference organizers and editors realized in thinking about the conference, and then also the shape that the book was taking afterwards, was that the initial submission of abstracts and contributors predominantly revealed a set of interrelated concerns around the specific significance of the geographical location of the UK in relation to concepts of diaspora and globalization. Many of the contributing artists and the art historians who submitted abstracts ended up focusing on work by diasporic women artists who are based in the UK, who make their work from here but who were not necessarily born here or have specific ties, artists who have come from all over the world. In *Why Do You Think I Left?* Udi and Shoshy both give very moving analyses of this in answer to the question you put to them, 'why do you think I left?'. In particular, they pick up on the dialectical themes of dislocation and shelter, and they also make a really interesting point about geography. Shoshy says 'there's something in England that allows for anonymity … so it's easier', and Udi says 'it seems like England gives you a shelter from something'. I am wondering whether you agree with these statements and whether there is something specific or not about being located in the UK in relation to globalization. Do you think that geography does have that kind of impact on your work or not?

OA: I'm sure it does. I mean, I know that there was a big difference living in Sheffield as a BA student and then living in London in terms of the cultural diversity and general diversity that I experienced. Also I think generally if you're looking at an artistic community, I'm sure that it's a lot more international now in England than it ever was before and I do hear from people who live in Europe, whether it's from Holland or Denmark or France, that the immigration laws are really worrying in a way that here perhaps they might be becoming, but that at least here there is an opposition. Also, in terms of Islamophobia, as a minority I would like to think that Muslims have more of a voice here than they do in France or Denmark when faced with that form of racism. But apart from that the world is so global. I'm not sure how much of a difference it makes where you live in any way, shape or form. It is so embedded with technology and the internet, although England does have a kind of mythological reputation as a home for many immigrants who then become great cultural contributors. There is a sense of an English eccentricity where England accepts that it is a space in which to be different which I think is what my sister Shoshy was referring to, that sense of anonymity, particularly in London because of its size as a metropolis. There is a certain acceptance of individuality and open-mindedness that English people are famous for. So perhaps there is that.

DR: That's interesting because we are talking about the present whereas historically, in relation to the current impact of globalization and the post-colonial condition that gave rise to it, England has become a significant location because it was already 'networked' in to much of the rest of the world as a result of its colonial past far more extensively than America. During the modern era America guarded its borders and was very self-absorbed, whereas England because of its history of colonialism, already had networks to India, Africa, Australia, Europe and the Commonwealth. I think it is ironic such a problematic relationship between globalism and colonialism on its flip side enables the kind of creative counter-culture that we have been discussing through the number of international artists who are now coming here to work.

OA: Yeah, exactly, there is a lot of familiarity here with other cultures because of Empire, to a degree. It works both ways through assimilation and through racism and it's still apparent. So you do feel like an immigrant amongst immigrants, which is a very at-home feeling.

DR: I do a lot of research in Germany. And I know that when I go to Germany I don't feel as assimilated in Germany as I do when I'm in the UK because there seems to be much more segregation amongst the different ethnic groups and between the white Germans and the Turkish immigrant population in particular; although Berlin might be different I think?

OA: I have always just been in Berlin and I haven't spent any long periods in any of these countries but what I did find is that the people that I met for whatever reason through my travels or, let's say, to be very specific, in Berlin I met an Israeli Arab from Jaffa who also happened to be a lesbian; she came to my show. In her network of lesbians and playing basketball, there were Israeli lesbians, Turkish, Lebanese, Chinese and I think through subcultures there is already much more of a mixture than you might find in academic jobs where, although it's hard to generalize, but you really have to be German to get on unless you're already a big professor

DR: Although you've touched on it already, I wondered if we can go back and talk a bit about *Dancing With Men*. I think it's interesting because you have already alluded to the risk and the danger that you felt in that process, and I think that comes through in watching; I find it an extraordinarily visceral experience watching you as Marcus in that very testosterone-fuelled environment with all of those men dancing. And I think that one does wonder whether at any minute you will be 'discovered' as a woman and what the consequences of that might be for you. I was wondering whether it was difficult to film in that environment, or whether filming was something the participants were used to? I always felt that the medium that you were using, the film, as well as your role as interloper were the two things that created a double risk. I don't know whether you felt that too?

OA: Well, the filming itself wasn't dangerous because people do film, not the press, but people themselves bring cameras and video cameras, but focusing on me in the filming was extremely dangerous. I mean, the person who did it just happened to be the driver who drove me there. I just asked him to do it.

DR: Ah, I see, he didn't know you were in disguise?

OA: No, no he totally did. I had to get changed in the car! He totally knew that. But he's not a filmmaker, he's just somebody who was there and what I asked him was to film it as generally as possible because if people noticed he was filming me, this is when it would have become impossible.

DR: Attention would have been drawn to you …

OA: And really, really unrecommended. I think you can see that I'm there maybe for about 30 seconds. It was also very hard to focus on a single person through the masses. You have to be very near so technically it was nearly impossible to film. It was reviewed in *Flash Art* and referring to the filming the critic was asking why it was hand held but the idea of coming into that environment with tripod and lights would be ridiculous.

DR: I quite liked that hand-held amateur effect. For me, watching it and knowing what was going on, that was part of the danger, part of the immediacy of what you were doing; the fact that, with hand-held equipment, you could pull out at any minute if you had to do. I think that that worked. Also, do you think that this was a real historical moment in the making? Do you know of any other women who have ever done this?!

OA: Also that year there were two suicide bombers dressing up as Jews and that was my main fear. I was absolutely terrified and there was so much security around and police around that area. I was absolutely terrified in terms of the complications of that, the implications of that, more than the gender risks even. I was a security risk in that way and there were so many warnings about 'watch out for people in disguise'. That year it was literally only a few months before the ceremony that suicide bombers had dressed up as orthodox Jews and exploded a bus. That's why security was so high, in case somebody came in disguise, dressed up as orthodox. So that was mainly my fear. The woman thing was kind of another one, but the risk in dressing up that way was in the forefront of my mind.

DR: That's interesting because in the film you see some of the men that are not necessarily dancing but are just sort of hanging around and they're staring very, very directly into the camera looking quite suspicious or wary.

OA: Yes, people will take a picture of themselves with a friend but there wasn't a video camera constantly filming. People take snaps but to have a persistent person taking photos or filming all the time would have been very suspicious, that's why we had to wander around a lot as well, to keep moving. Also, and I don't know how it comes across in the film, but what I found most intriguing was the division between the Eastern European Jews who looked like Marcus who danced a very traditional European dance to Jewish music and the Ashkenazi Jews or if you like the Oriental Jews with the white robes. They use techno music and sampling and MCing and rave. I was absolutely amazed. I really didn't expect that the sense of division which exists in Israel so much would find its way into such strong musical divisions.

DR: Did your father know that you were going to do *Dancing with Men*?

OA: No, it was all a secret operation.

DR: OK. Thank you for speaking about *Unbound*, which is work that has now been archived in collaboration with the Live Art Development Agency, and so now you are involved in a collaboration with Palestinian artist Larissa and you also hold an AHRC Fellowship at Queen Mary, University of London. I wonder if you could say some more about the new work you are doing both with Larissa and for the fellowship? Perhaps we can start with your first visit to India since that came first chronologically.

OA: The trip to India was I felt very much about globalization. That was one of the strongest senses I got from the visit and what artists in India were talking about. In the *Lonely Planet* guide for example, it tells you to take any garment to a local tailor and he will replicate it for you within twenty-four hours so I took an Adidas tracksuit to see how they made it, but I asked for it to be made from sari material.

DR: It's beautiful material.

OA: And the way that they made it I think is amazing, the way they copied the Adidas symbol as hand embroidered.

DR: All that in twenty-five hours.

OA: Yes, and I think they were paid next to nothing, probably the equivalent of five pounds for the whole thing.

DR: But I really like that idea that you were taking traditional Asian materials, textiles and skills and then critiquing the idea of globalization as suggested by the consumerist principle of the *Lonely Planet*, which seems to endorse taking economic advantage of local skills and people. You offer a critique of capitalist consumption by making the Adidas suit from sari material. As well as this there were also other specific aspects to your visit to India as well, though …

OA: Well in India I found out about Sarmad. You see that little booklet there. I got that at his tomb. It's in Urdu. I had it verbally translated to me. And basically he was a Jewish traveller in the seventeenth century. He travelled to India and I'm very, very fascinated by the idea of Jewish travelling. Before Israel, Jews could go anywhere in the world. They could go to the Islamic world but now they can't go anywhere. So, it's that condition of Jewishness without a state that interests me

DR: The trope of 'the wandering Jew' perhaps, which was not without its historical problems of course.

OA: No, but nonetheless it also talks about a lot more of a natural connection between Judaism and the Islamic world that has been stopped through Israel. So, it's a kind of romantic notion but it's also sort of objectively, historically true. So Sarmad arrived in India. He was a poet, a philosopher, a theologian. He became a Sufi poet and a saint and he had loads of followers. He fell in love with a young Indian man, some say boy, some say man. They had obviously lots of versions of the story but in the original text, the Urdu text, it says they were living together, they were both in love with each other. He was called Abhai Chand and he taught him everything including Jewish texts. There was a lot of pressure on them to separate and they didn't, they just wanted to be with each other. I was amazed at how erotic the original Urdu text is. And in the end he was ordered by the last Moghul Mullah of the time to say there is only one God, Allah, but he refused to say it because he was a Sufi and he believed that each person has their own God. So he was beheaded in the mosque; opposite is his tomb and when I was in Delhi there were a lot of people visiting his tomb.

DR: So although he seems to have been a subversive character in a way, yet he's got a tomb near the mosque and he's remembered today.

OA: Oh yeah, he's very accepted. Interestingly enough I found out that some people claim he is an Armenian so he's either originally Armenian or of Jewish origin. There are similarities between Jews and Armenians and that kind of ideal of status and place and all that. So I don't think it really matters. Anyway, what matters to me is the terms of the pull I feel towards his story. When I was in Delhi I did a performance. I wrote eight letters from Sarmad to his sister in Palestine. In my story he was a woman who was travelling as a man, so the whole thing was about hiding his gender, being a traveller and how difficult it was to travel as a woman but slowly how he stopped getting his period and it stopped being an issue; it was just accepted and the pain he felt about leaving his Judaism behind and becoming Sufi, and there were lots of ups and downs in his life, and it was my re-adaptation in which I was lying in the centre and gave the audience, eight people, each a letter to read.

DR: Was the sister a fictional character?

OA: Yes, she was a fictional character. I created the sister.

DR: And did she write back?

OA: No, she never wrote back and he keeps saying it's been more than twenty years now and we have never met, thirty years now and we've never met. And the last letter is from the administrator telling her that he has been beheaded, that he is dead and that if she wants to visit his tomb she can, and telling her where it is and that he'd be happy to meet her and show her around. So it's quite sad.

DR: Did you leave the space open for the sister's replies deliberately? Is there a space open for the sister to reply at all at any point do you think?

OA: I think in some letters I mention things such as how I was sad to hear that her parents had died and that 'it must be hard for you'. So there was an implication that he had heard from her and about what was happening in Palestine. She's the little sister. He runs away in the middle of the night, leaving the sister behind to deal with everything but he just had to travel. Part of the AHRC fellowship is to make a big production of it. I want to work with students, a small group of students from the English, film and drama departments and really create a narrative for a film, possibly a performance but more likely a film – a bit Bollywood and a bit art film – about his story. But in the meantime I am going to Delhi. There is an international performance festival in Delhi in March and I'm doing a performance lecture about him. I'm combining it with modern-day Israeli tourism in India, which is a real phenomenon. If you read all the blogs and travel books to India they say you have to learn Hebrew if you go to India …

DR: You have to learn Hebrew if you go to India?

OA: Because there are so many Israeli travellers, so many falafel shops; they've taken over Varanasi. It's kind of the idea that a lot of young Israelis after their army service go to India. I wrote this script about these two Israelis who go to Varanasi. One of them has had a bad dream. He's having a nightmare about what they did in Gaza.

DR: It's a kind of a hippy trail is it?

OA: No, it's not hippy. It's very imperialist. It's very macho. Some of it is hippy. They travel in big groups. They take the army mentality with them into India. They're big travellers. Israelis love taking risks. They love partying. The trance music, Israeli trance music is doing really well; they're very good at parties but at the same time there is that sense of 'oh, there's another brown person who can serve us'. It's a racist culture, so that's what it's about as well, a sense of paranoia about being in India and getting something. That's the performance. It kind of brings Jewish travelling into the present as well.

DR: Is Sarmad well known in India?

OA: In India, no, he is not well known.

DR: How did you find out about him?

OA: It's a funny story. I went to some film festival, a Pakistani film festival. And I saw this guy there and I don't know why, I just went to him and asked him, do you know about any Indian Jews? He just looked at me. As it happens he was actually a guy from Raqs Media Collective, a group of three very successful international artists, and he said that he was a quarter Jewish and he knew a lot about Jewish Indian culture. He told me a lot about it. He told me that the Jews came across to Kachin in South India from Portugal in boats and were thought to be Muslims who just happened to celebrate Saturday instead of Friday, so they were called 'Saturday Muslims'. (Maybe that's what I should call the performance!) Then he told me about Sarmad so then I had to start following his trail and really discovering; it was a bit of detective work to find him in old Delhi but I found him.

DR: Is there an archive or publicly accessible information about him?

OA: One book, I've got the one book about him that's been published. It's called *Sarmad: The Jewish Saint*. Unfortunately there is another artist in India who copied my performance last year – everything, he wrote the letter, he copied it literally.

DR: So he'd been to your performance?

OA: He was one of the people who read the letters and he totally copied it and I'm very upset about it but when I challenged him he said 'oh it's different because I gave people rice, but it was identical. He took the idea of writing the fictional letters, the whole thing …

DR: What can you do about it?

OA: Nothing. I tried to stop him, I wrote to the festival and told him to stop it in Delhi but he didn't. I'm not happy about that.

DR: So when you came back from India, that's when we had the conference at the Victoria and Albert Museum and you brought the digital prints from 'The Village' series which you displayed for us at there.

OA: They're very much to do with ideas of globalization. They're very much affected by what I read in the newspapers. So there was a thing about an Indian bus falling down a mountain and there was a thing about a famous Bollywood actor holding his two fingers up. So they are taken from different things I read. The imagery was sort of images that I work on top of so they're really, really varied.

DR: I like the way you talk about this series on your website, about the medium you're using to talk about globalization. I think that's really interesting, the correlation that you talk about between the flat and digital image and the reach of globalization which smoothes everything out, a Starbucks in every city phenomenon.

OA: Exactly.

DR: I thought that was really interesting. This leads me in fact to the question of the choice of media in which you work. You have, as somebody else has put it, a very multivalent practice that you have made work for you. When you are thinking about your work and the ideas that will come in to your work, do you think first about the work and then about the media?

OA: Yes, that's why I call myself, a context-responsive artist because I respond to the context, whether it be where the work is going to be shown or with whom I am going to work. For example, I know that with Larissa, because she's not in England, it would have to be emails, and the book we are producing relates comfortably to that situation. We don't have so much need of physical contact. It's very much in response to that. It's really thinking about the context and then thinking about the kind of medium that serves that best.

But it's not easy in terms of archiving your work or in terms of documenting and disseminating it. It's very hard for people to get a sense of what I do, for me to relay back at people because the media are so different. It makes it very complex so in the end, different people know different fragments and very few people have a whole view of it. I can hardly hold the different strands of it together! But it's very much to do with context rather than medium.

DR: I think that is what makes it very interesting to me, that you're not defined by the fact that you're a painter so you're doing this or you're a photographer so you're doing this, but that ideas drive your work rather than the medium but you maintain the quality of the medium as well. I think that's quite a rare skill and ability that you have to do that.

OA: Yes, right now I just feel like a graphic designer now with the comic book. It's almost like learning new skills and there is this idea now that we are Renaissance people who can do everything well but we can't and it is hard to always feel that you have to master new skills. I think that the way to do it is to work with other people who are expert in that … or in the case of the comic book, to really look around and see what is there to see and what they are doing.

DR: And to see what kind of visual language will work?

OA: Yes, what visual language around comics is developing and how you want to reproduce it or subvert it. So just at the moment I am completely immersed as a graphic designer …

DR: If you had to choose, would you find it preferable to work in one medium over another? For example, if you were given a big grant to produce any work in any media for a specific space, would you privilege one media above another, or is that not how it works for you because your work is ideas driven rather than medium driven?

OA: It is driven but it's more to do with the ambition of the project. It stems from ambition, from the possibilities of scale. If I was given a lot of money to make work then I think my ideal ambitious work would be to make a big production of Sarmad and a proper film with a lot of people involved, using the model of collaborative filmmaking where a lot of people literally write a script together. There is a whole process for doing that which I would like to try to see if I can somehow use in terms of how people can make a story move.

DR: Will you try that with the AHRC Fellowship?

OA: Yes, that's what I will try. The second part of it is to work with students and other people towards the collaborative process of writing a script. I'd like to do a very big production of that; in terms of my ambition that would be my dream.

DR: That is very interesting. I once read an interview in the journal *n.paradoxa* with the artist Suzanne Lacy where she was doing collaborative work with a lot of community youth about their experiences of being policed.

One of the comments she made that I thought was really interesting concerned the idea of working collaboratively with other people whilst maintaining the control and the aesthetic of the piece as an artwork.

OA: I'm a terrible collaborator. I'm the last person who should collaborate. I am so single-minded and uncompromising in terms of ideas and aesthetics, yet I find myself over and over again collaborating. And I think it is really to do with my need for kind of other perspectives, other voices.

DR: And then negotiating those into a whole?

OA: Yes, but it is true that there is an issue of control that ultimately I have to maintain.

DR: Because ultimately your name is on this project and it's your work and so you need to ensure the overall aesthetic quality because otherwise political issues and ideas can overtake it as artwork if you don't?

OA: Yes, it is the aesthetics that I find impossible to compromise on really.

DR: I presume that is what distinguishes you as an artist rather than a politician or an activist or whatever else ultimately?

OA: Yes. You asked about the fellowship and so, apart from Sarmad, there are two more characters that I'm looking at which are absolutely fascinating. The idea is to make a video where the three characters are portrayed by me or maybe actors and then I have a psychological analysis of them that is both quite tongue-in-cheek and quite serious. I am reading a lot of theology, a lot about where they are coming from in terms of their religious beliefs, and I'm also very interested in the psychological makeup of the characters and the way I shall fictionalize them. In particular, one of them was officially a manic depressive and he had these messianic feelings only when he was manic. He travelled all over the globe actually and he had an assistant called 'Nathan from Gaza' who did his entire PR work for him!

DR: Which century was this?

OA: Seventeenth century.

DR: Are they all seventeenth-century characters?

OA: No, one of them is eleventh-century. He's known as an Arabic thinker although he was Jewish. I'm very interested in this. He was very influenced by Muslim thought. He wrote in Arabic. He was the doctor of the Egyptian Sultan of the time but, for example, what I read about him was (and it was something I suspected anyway), that in his writing he actually wrote the opposite of what he believed in, so there is this dialectical thinking at work. It's that sense of contradiction that he had, such that he's both a herbalist and a doctor, a scientist and a religious prophet. I feel that is why I am drawn to him. I'm drawn to these people for different reasons. So, that's the video. The comic book, which was supposed to be a tiny little project is becoming a mammoth eight-chapter book, so every page is illustrated. It's a major graphic work. I love it.

DR: Do you do it digitally? Do you send the graphics by email?

OA: It's partly hand, it's digital, it's a big graphic job. So, my research interest (which actually I've realized there's a big gap in the available literature for), is looking at the idea of visual artists and performance artists who use alter egos and fictional characters. There's absolutely no key text or writing about it that I found I could really refer to. I'm interested in the psychological side of it.

DR: Very interesting. Thank you. When I talk to you about Sarmad and the Jewish alter egos who are becoming your current project, it always reminds me of the poet Else Lasker-Schüler. She was a German Jewish poet in the early twentieth century. She performed herself as an Arabian prince. She called herself Prince Jussuf. I can send you some references.

OA: I'd love to have a reference, fantastic. I'm thinking to embody one female character as a Jewish character in an Oriental context. I was thinking of Scheherazade because of the Persian connection but I'd be really interested in finding out more about Prince Jussuf. I'd then be doing an alter ego of a woman who did an alter ego of an Arabian prince!

DR: I think what is very interesting about your work is the development from your earlier work (*Marcus Fisher* and *Say Cheese*, for example) to the current fellowship project. As I see it, holistically your work is very much a philosophical project driven in different ways by the idea of trying to deconstruct the rigid classifications and categories between Judaism and Muslim or Jewish and Arabic. It's about looking at other ways of interaction historically and in the present.

OA: Yes, exactly. I'm very interested in these issues but also from a feminist perspective. When the feminine has been extracted out of religion for so many centuries it is very interesting for me to read theological texts as a woman.

DR: Do you find it difficult?

OA: I find it difficult because they are very philosophical texts. I find myself taking it to a whole other world now when I'm really reading about religion literally and about belief systems very philosophically. As a woman you are totally excluded, especially in the Middle Ages, which is the period about which I am reading at the moment. There is a huge absence, a huge hiatus …

DR: Do you find the absence something that then enables you to want to create the missing voices or do you find it blanking you out? I find it a problem. I find it difficult to read texts like this that completely write women out. I find that my tolerance levels are really low and it is easy in the present for me to just dismiss them but to engage with them properly like you're doing is actually a much more difficult, challenging task.

OA: I think it is an element of a cop-out because my characters are male in the end. So in a way I'm not bringing the action of females into it, it's perhaps compromised for me in that respect.

DR: But then it comes back I think to the interview you had with Carrie

Moyer for the New York Foundation for the Arts, which is not a cop-out; it's only a cop-out if you believe in some kind of essential femininity.[1]

OA: Yes, it very much comes back to that. I can't quite get my head around. It's quite complex and I'm not a theory person to talk about that. I probably said this in the interview but there is a feminist reason for what I'm doing but whether I can fully articulate it I'm not sure, but there is a reason why it is still a feminist project.

DR: I see your work as a feminist project but not a feminist project in an essentialist way. It is very much a feminist project of the present. It's a kind of double-edged critique. It's a woman in drag playing a male persona in order to subvert masculine narratives. You're entering masculine narratives, you're entering masculine spaces, you're doing it in disguise but the joke on these narratives is that you're a woman so it parodies exclusive masculinities from within.

OA: And also the way I write them is very feminine. I know with the comic book that when I wrote the narrative for the actual comic strip part of it I showed it to a few men and interestingly enough their proposed contributions were always to do with some kind of a fight: 'so why won't these two characters beat them up?' It just would never occur to me, it's just not my style. So, although I've done a very generic comic strip story of two heroines, me and Larissa, who get caught in this big paranoid story where they get infected and the laboratory sends them to Palestine to save them but there's never a physical fight.

DR: Between the two?

OA: No. Between them and the lab, them and the evil forces.

DR: So there's never a speech bubble that says 'KAPOW!'

OA: Exactly. I just don't go there and that's where it speaks differently, in that way.

DR: OK, thank you very much. We've covered a lot of ground and it would be interesting to finish with a discussion of the processes that you go through when you decide with whom to exhibit or perform. I wonder if you might want to say a bit more about that?

OA: In terms of collaboration?

DR: Not just collaboration in terms of making work but also where you decide to exhibit, the spaces you select. For example, I read about one of your projects that you exhibited in a space in Jerusalem and it was whitewashed over. So again the issue of taboo comes up, you are breaking taboos but also your work is being made into a taboo as well.

OA: Yes, that was a wall with a drawing of a mushroom cloud that I did straight onto the wall, like an atomic bomb and it just got painted over, wiped out completely. In terms of the spaces where I show work, so far I have just worked with people who I feel understand my work, relate to it, where there's a dialogue, and that includes people I know and people whom I don't know, but if people ask to meet me, either to show my work or write about my work, or people approach me to assist me, I ask them if they know my work. If they don't know it, I don't generally meet with them. I want to know why they're approaching me and if they've got the wrong idea about the work, I'm not interested. If somebody says, 'oh because you're an installation artist' it's not interesting to exhibit with them if that's all they've picked up out of everything I do. Also, people who are late I don't work with and people who don't turn up I don't work with!

DR: At the beginning of our discussion you talked about the Brooklyn Museum and the fact that *Marcus Fisher* is finally in the Brooklyn Museum.

OA: Yeah but the Brooklyn Museum took the work to another show without asking me. It's now exhibiting in what's called *Global Feminisms Remix*.

DR: Do they own the work now, have they bought it?

OA: No but I think they should because they have used it again now without asking me and now it is in this show and a friend of mine just happened to be there and saw it and told me it was in another show. I didn't know that. I think as an artist you don't have a lot of control in the end over your work. It just circulates …

DR: I would imagine that would go against your grain because in that sense it becomes only a commodity and it seems to me that you're trying to work against commodification.

OA: I just think it is a natural response. *Say Cheese* was a very successful performance financially. I lived on it respectably but I did start to feel like a performing monkey. I had to be really drunk to do it in the end. I had to drink a half a big bottle of whisky to just get through it because I started to feel that the whole idea, which had started as an idea of very raw interaction, just became really commodified. I found it quite hard to continue with that. It is a big issue in terms of selling your work and I'm sure if I'd been in a position where there was a great deal of commercial demand for the work, I don't think it is possible to say no because I need to live. I think we all need the system whether we like it or not. What started for me in the early nineties as a way of working when I did my BA that was very much going against the YBAs and whole commercial art world is now mainstream. Sometimes, in ridiculous ways, political art is now mainstream. Artists who work in a commercial context in a very formal way, for example, suddenly the gallery feels that the press release has to be political: 'How does it work that light and shadow are connected to immigration?' At the end of the day everything is connected so it might be fine but for me a completely apolitical art world suddenly became ridiculously and tokenistically political. So in that way I do find myself in a really difficult position, much more than I was before when my practice was marginalized anyway in its interests.

DR: But as we discussed at the beginning, I think that your practice still maintains its critical edge because of the risks you take and the bravery involved in what you're doing. While that drives your practice, you maintain that edge. You have to think in a very particular way to take those risks as an artist, like going on the Arab bus for *Necessary Journey* for example.

OA: I have to do that again. I have to see Larissa in Beit Lahem (Bethlehem) in the next two weeks.

DR: But you almost didn't get out when you went there before …

OA: It's going to be the same issues. It's illegal. I have to go on an Arab bus. I have to go through Israeli checkpoints. I'm dreading it. It's happening again but I have to meet her there. And for her to come to Israel is a far, far greater risk so we have to do it that way. So I'm not looking forward to that.

DR: No but you do it anyway.

OA: I have to. I have to take photographs in the occupied territories. It's like a sequel to *Necessary Journey* so I have to go there. I'm not looking forward to doing something illegal again, having to face the soldiers and all that.

DR: I wish you luck. It's an illegal practice at the time but afterwards when you document it as part of your practice and then it goes public, then there's another risk. In a way, it's a double risk that you are taking. You've also just said this on film to me that what you're going to do is an illegal entry into Palestine.

OA: I've got a long way to go to be blacklisted by the Israeli service police. It's just simply that you are not allowed to cross as an Israeli citizen. I have got a British passport but it says on it my name and it says that I was born in Israel so it's obvious that I'm an Israeli.

DR: So it can be problematic in a sub-legal way, not exactly illegal but uncomfortable in terms of its possible consequences?

OA: Well either you are fined or you spend the night in a cell or they question you, especially if you stay overnight. It is illegal. Imagine yourself going to the supermarket and stealing something, if it's not something that you're inclined to do, it's not something you like to do. So, it's kind of like that and I hadn't realized before what it means to have to do something illegal. It's not a moral issue but it's just not very nice. And the fact also that from where my parents live to where Larissa lives is only twenty minutes on the bus and the fact that they're stopping us from meeting in that way is really disturbing.

DR: It would make me angry too ...

OA: Yes, very angry. Especially because the logistic behind this law is that they can't guarantee the safety of Israeli citizens in the occupied territory. So, providing that, it should be actually my choice if I want to take that risk but that's not what it's about. They just don't want that communication, they don't want that contact. It's kind of divide and rule. That's how it works so I am very unhappy with that.

DR: I'm not surprised. Also, I think that's why the *Unbound* video and DVD works so well because you have these public political risks that you're taking ideologically with the State by going on the *Necessary Journey* and you also have these private emotional risks that you are taking with *Why Do You Think I Left*? I think that's incredible and why I enjoy looking at the work so much.

OA: Oh great.

DR: So this is probably a good note to end on. Thank you very much Oreet.

Notes

1 In the interview between Ashery and Moyer timed to coincide with the inclusion of Ashery's *Marcus Fisher* in the 2007 Global Feminisms exhibition at the Brooklyn Museum of Art, New York. Moyer asked Ashery what she viewed as 'problematic' about feminism and Ashery's reply was extremely insightful and is worth reiterating here:

OA: … I perform myself – a woman, dressed up – and it is in this skin-deep illusion or almost banal cultural representation that I find the possibility for an expansive gendered space that is limitless in its variations. I use characters for social and political decoding and as a way of accessing different characters' consciousness. I think the reason I do not use female characters is a way to bypass the problematic associated with female representation.

CM: Can you talk more about what you view as 'problematic' about feminism?

OA: I consider feminism to be the backdrop to post-colonial studies, queer studies, identity politics, and everything else that is worthwhile. However, traditional feminism as we know it does not stick well with 'postmodernism' and notions of multiplicity due to its humanist, essentialist nature. It is less playful than queer or post-identity politics and aesthetics – and this is where the problems lie for those of us who like to play or like to feel like contemporary makers. References to retro 1970s/1980s feminism can be used in contemporary art as a strategy but it does not mean that we have managed to update it properly. In terms of art, feminism operates best as a referent for something we all cherish, something we all are in debt to, but at the same time something that we are unable to make contemporary for ourselves in terms of a declared art practice. It is something that never seems to emerge out of its historical premise. Contemporary feminism, I feel, works best in an art practice as a secret agent, an invisible agency that is there undeclared.

CM: I'm a little bit older than you are. One of the best things about Global Feminisms is how it demonstrates the continued relevance of feminism – both on an experiential level as well as a place to make art from/about. So I'm curious about your comment that the exhibition makes feminism 'sexy and relevant again'. To whom?

OA: In relation to my above answer, I feel that Global Feminisms has successfully managed to deal with the essentialist nature of the term 'feminism' and to bypass post-feminism at the same time by having a global focus, which is where I feel the relevance of feminism continues today …

The full text of this interview is available at www.nyfa.org/level3.asp?id=590&fid=6&sid=17.

Index

Note: 'n.' after a page reference indicates the number of a note on that page. Page numbers in *italic* refer exclusively to illustrations.